Clan, Caste, and Club

Clan, Caste, and Club

by

F. L. K. HSU

Chairman, Department of Anthropology
Northwestern University
Evanston, Illinois

VAN NOSTRAND · REINHOLD COMPANY

New York   Toronto   London   Melbourne

Van Nostrand Regional Offices: *New York, Chicago, San Francisco*

D. Van Nostrand Company, Ltd., *London*

D. Van Nostrand Company (Canada), Ltd., *Toronto*

D. Van Nostrand Australia Pty. Ltd., *Melbourne*

Published simultaneously in Canada by
D. Van Nostrand Company (Canada), Ltd.

PRINTED IN THE UNITED STATES OF AMERICA

TO MY WIFE

with love, gratitude, and respect

PREFACE

THE PRIMARY PURPOSE of this book is to explain the world as the Hindus see and approach it. For contrast I have compared the major manifestations of the Hindu view of the world with those of the Chinese view on the one hand and of the American view on the other.

My principal hypotheses are that the Hindu approach to the world is characterized by supernatural-centeredness or unilateral dependence in contrast to the American and Chinese approach which are characterized, respectively, by individual-centeredness or self-reliance and situation-centeredness or mutual dependence. Throughout the following pages there runs a basic assumption: that man's primary and most important relationship is with his fellow men and that, consequently, his relationships with other elements of his world are distinctly patterned after or visibly integrated with it. Hence, though family as an institution is not so overwhelming a key point in the culture of the United States and India as it has been in that of China, it cannot help being the basic transmitting and educating mechanism in all three. The family with its intensive and sometimes also extensive human relationships is the basic school of all cultures.

Starting with the family, our analysis moves into the secondary human grouping in each society. In China we find the all-important secondary human grouping is clan, as contrasted with the all important secondary grouping of caste in Hindu India and that of club (in its widest sense, meaning all free associations outside the kinship group for whatever purpose) in the United States.

Although my principal hypotheses regarding the Chinese and American worlds were developed in *Americans and Chinese: Two Ways of Life* (New York, 1953, and London, 1955), they are reexamined here in the light of many new facts as well as in terms of contrast with the case of Hindu India. In this three-way comparison, the problem of physical management of the materials makes it impractical to give all three worlds equal attention at all times. Consequently what I have done in this book is to treat the two Asian cases first. When that is largely accomplished from Chapters III to VIII, the American pattern of life is brought into focus in Chapter IX. All three worlds are compared and contrasted in some detail in the concluding

Chapter X. This somewhat unequal treatment, for all that the three cases are not presented at equal length, need not blur the resulting picture.

Studies in national character or in differing world views come under a special kind of criticism not vouchsafed to many other types of study: this in addition to criticism by professional standards. These special criticisms stem from the fact that everyone is, in a very real sense, an expert in his own culture, and they are made more pungent by the emotional involvement of most people in their own culture. Therefore, Americans, Chinese, and Indians who have read the manuscript of this book have often had intense personal reactions as well as professional ones. Their personal reactions are, to whatever extent I am capable of achieving this goal, made part of my data. Their professional reactions are, to whatever extent I have been able to profit by them, responsible for many changes that I have made in presentation.

These special criticisms, which often contain an undue degree of emotionalism, have come from Indians and Americans who have told me that I take a "rose-tinted," not to say nostalgic, view of traditional Chinese culture, and from Chinese and Americans who say that I am either pro-Hindu or anti-Hindu. Such criticisms are helpful, but they are helpful as data.

Studies in national character, perhaps more than any other in anthropology, make special demands on the reader: he must seek to understand his reaction to the data and the analysis at the same time he absorbs them. For precisely the same reason, such studies make special demands on authors. Obviously, neither author nor reader can be totally successful at all times. But awareness of this problem is the greatest asset in dealing with such studies.

It should be noted that, although most of the facts described about China pertain to the long period of that society before its recent change of regime, the analysis is vitally relevant to its present and future developments. There are only a few reports on conditions in Mainland China today, but some of their implications are not obscure and certain predictions, on the basis of what we know about the Chinese way of life, can already be made. These are given in the last chapter of the book. Since completion of this manuscript I have further explored the theories developed here not only in the light of our present knowledge about Communist China but also about Soviet Russia ("The Individual and His Society: China, U.S.S.R. and the U.S.A." in J. G. Tolpin [ed.], *The Other Half: The U.S.S.R. and China Today*, to be published in 1964).

The field work in India was made possible by a twenty-two-month leave from Northwestern University and grants from the Rockefeller Foundation, the Wenner-Gren Foundation, and Northwestern University's Graduate

Committee on Research. The Government of India's Department of Anthropology (now the Anthropological Survey of India), then under the directorship of Dr. N. Datta-Majumder, appointed me a Foreign Fellow. This position granted me some financial aid and many other privileges which greatly facilitated my work. The members of this department graciously treated me as a colleague and rendered me all possible assistance.

My indebtedness on the personal level is extensive. It is impossible to mention all by name. Among those who have helped me in India I must especially mention Miss Aileen Aderton, Dr. Anila Bannerjee, Mr. Arthur Bartlett, Mr. and Mrs. Aroon Basak, Mr. Bharadwaj, Mr. and Mrs. Narain Bhojwani, Mr. and Mrs. Kailash Chandra, Dr. C. Chandrasekaran, Group Captain and Mrs. H. N. Chatterjee, Professor Suniti Kumar Chatterjee, Mr. Nirad C. Chaudhuri, Mr. N. C. Choudhury, Mr. Philip Crosland, Mr. S. K. Dey, Dr. Douglas Ensminger, Miss Uma Guha, Mr. G. D. Gupta, Mr. P. N. Haksar, Sir Mirza Ishmail, Dr. Charles A. Johnson, Rajkumari Amrit Kaur, Dr. Saroj Khanna, Mr. M. Krishnan, Mr. and Mrs. H. K. S. Lindsay, Mr. Ajit K. Mathur, Mr. Moni Nag, The Honorable Nijalingappa, Mr. A. V. Pai, Mr. and Mrs. S. J. Poty, Mr. Jagdeesh Prasad, Professor P. H. Prabhu, Dr. Kodanda Rao, Lady Ramu Rau, Mr. Bhikram Singh, Mr. Indera Singh, Mr. Lakshmipat Singhania, Mr. C. T. Thomas, Mr. Veerabhadrya, and Mr. Christopher Van Hollen.

The Honorable Jawaharlal Nehru, despite the obviously many and severe demands on his time and energy, kindly allowed me to see him twice to discuss certain problems concerning national character. Though the pressing affairs of state finally precluded the possibility on his part of reading a draft version of the manuscript, I am deeply impressed by the depth of his understanding of man and grateful for his critical remarks which materially helped the progress of my work.

The manuscript went through many revisions. To this task my two office helpers, Mrs. Betty Reed and Mrs. Mayo Andelson, have contributed greatly. Professors Donald T. Campbell, McKim Marriott, and Milton Singer read it in its first embryonic form and helped much with their untiring and constructive criticisms. Others who have seen its later versions in part or in whole and commented upon them generously are Dr. Ishwar Dayal, Dr. Paul Fejos, Dr. Alfred Flarsheim, Mr. Robert C. Hunt, Professor David C. McClelland, Professor Raoul Naroll, Professor Phillip Rieff, Mr. Alfred Schenckman, Professor Richard Schwartz, and Dr. Surajit Sinha. Professor Paul J. Bohannan has had a special role in the evolution of the manuscript. He not only carefully read several different versions of it and gave to them unsparingly of his critical insights, but added much to the structural framework that is fundamental to my analysis.

My wife Vera accompanied me in the field in Southwestern China as well as in different parts of India. Though her field is biology, she perceives much that is in the human scene which has frequently added depth to my investigations. We have discussed together most of the manuscript in the course of its evolution and many of its pages bear witness to her valuable assistance.

Needless to say, I alone am responsible, in the final analysis, for the views expressed.

F.L.K.H.

Evanston, Illinois
July 1963

CONTENTS

	PREFACE	vii
I	THREE WORLDS	1
II	DATA AND METHODOLOGY	12
III	PATTERNS OF FAMILY AND PSYCHOLOGICAL ORIENTATION	27
IV	COHESION VERSUS DIVISION: CLAN IN CHINA AND INDIA	60

Appendix I

TERMS RELATED TO GOTRA — 80

Appendix II

TENSIONS IN CLAN: A CASE HISTORY — 82

V	COHESION VERSUS DIVISION: CASTE	93
VI	SOME THEORIES OF CASTE	123
VII	A THEORY OF THE HUMAN GROUP	138
VIII	THE PSYCHOLOGICAL BASIS OF CASTE IN INDIA	162
IX	COHESION AND DIVISION IN THE AMERICAN WAY OF LIFE	192
X	CULTURE PATTERNS AND HUMAN GROUPING	232

Annex — 263

A THEMATIC APPERCEPTION TEST STUDY OF CHINA, HINDU, AND AMERICAN COLLEGE STUDENTS

BIBLIOGRAPHY — 312

INDEX OF AUTHORS — 321

SUBJECT INDEX — 325

Chapter I

THREE WORLDS

MAX WEBER helped perpetuate a Western misconception that Hindus, as well as Egyptians and Arabs, are Orientals. Weber considered the civilization of India to be but one branch of the Oriental civilization, of which two other branches are the Chinese and the Japanese. He observed that China "played somewhat the role of France in the modern Occident," that "all cosmopolitan polish stems from China, to Tibet and Japan and to outlying Indian territories." On the other hand, he continues, "India has a significance comparable" to that of ancient Hellenism. Practically all major Asian ideas not dealing with practical interests originated in that land.*[1] Over the decades this misconception has persisted. Even F. S. C. Northrop groups India with China and Japan as representatives of "the East" in his *Meeting of East and West*.[2] But the Hindu way of life, whether we look at the family, political development, literature, art, religion, or caste, is as different from the Oriental as it is from the Occidental. One cultural core is found among the Chinese, Japanese and Koreans; quite another is found among the Hindus. To lump the two together as "Oriental" obscures more than it clarifies.

The present book outlines a hypothesis on the basic nature of the Hindu, Chinese, and American ways of life or worlds. The hypothesis states that the Hindu world is supernatural-centered, as contrasted with the Chinese situation-centered world on the one hand and the American individual-centered world on the other. These three worlds are deeply separated one from another, not only in their patterns of practical activities but also in their ideas.

The situation-centered world is characterized by ties which permanently unite closely related human beings in the family and clan. Within this basic human constellation the individual is conditioned to seek mutual dependence. That is to say, he is dependent upon other human beings as much as others are dependent upon him, and he is therefore fully aware of his obligation to make repayment, however much delayed, to his benefactors. The central

* Numbered references are listed at the end of the chapter.

1

core of Chinese ethics is filial piety, which defines the complex of duties, obligations, and attitudes on the part of children (sons) toward their fathers and mothers. Why do sons owe filial piety to their parents? Because of their "indebtedness" to the elders who brought them forth and who reared them to maturity. Since the kinship structure, no matter how widely extended, is built on expanded consanguine and affinal relationships represented in the parent-child triad, all members in it are either at the receiving or the giving end of a human network of mutual dependence.

The individual enmeshed in such a human network is likely to react to his world in a complacent and compartmentalized way; complacent because he has a secure and inalienable place in his human group, and compartmentalized because he is conditioned to perceive the external world in terms of what is within his group and what is outside it. For what is within his group and what is outside it have drastically different meanings for him. As he generalizes from this basic assumption, there are quite different truths for different situations throughout his life's experiences. Principles which are correct for one set of circumstances may not be appropriate for another at all, but the principles in each case are equally honorable.

The good situation-centered Chinese, in fact, tends to have multiple standards. The prisoner's standards are not his jailer's, and the man's are not the woman's. Because he enjoys within his primary kinship group a security, continuity, and permanency that he cannot find outside it, the situation-centered Chinese has a greater feeling of certainty about life than does an average individual in many other societies and therefore is more likely to be complacent. Since double or multiple standards of morality and conduct are normal, they present the individual with no inner conflict. The individual feels no resentment against conforming and no compunction about behaving differently under contrasting sets of circumstances. He may be taught charity as a personal virtue, to improve his fate and that of his ancestors and descendants, but he will have no necessary compulsion or desire to champion the cause of the oppressed as a whole or to overthrow the privileged position of all oppressors. The primary guide for his behavior is his place, the place of his primary group in the accepted scheme of things, and the knowledge of how to better that place; but he will have little sense of the justice or injustice of intergroup relations as a whole or any desire to change them. Consequently the Chinese society through history has tended to be remarkably static, for it lacked *internal* impetus to change.

The individual-centered world is characterized by temporary ties among closely related human beings. Having no permanent base in family and clan, the individual's basic orientation toward life and the environment is self-reliance. That is to say, he is conditioned to think for himself, to make his own decisions, and to carve out his future by his own hands and in his own potentialities. Emerson expressed the essence of this view eloquently. "The nonchalance of boys who are sure of a dinner, and would disdain as much as a lord to do or say aught to conciliate one, is the healthy attitude of human nature. . . . He cumbers himself never about consequences, about interests; he gives an independent, genuine verdict. You must court him; he does not court you." Again, "Whoso would be a man, must be a nonconformist. He who would gather immortal palms must not be hindered by the name of goodness, but must explore if it be goodness. Nothing is at last sacred but the integrity of your own mind."[3]

The individual brought up under this pattern will find being dependent intolerable, for it ruins his self-respect; but he will find having others dependent upon him no less problematic, for this position generates resentment on their part. Yet after struggling free of parental and other yokes, the individual finds that he is without anything or anyone positive to live for. He is, therefore, likely to be beset with the problem of the meaning of life. He tries to achieve this meaning by conquering the material universe, by militantly propagating his belief in his god or Utopia, or by exploiting or aggressively improving his fellow human beings in his own or other societies. Because he is not tied down by his primary groups, he finds the whole world his oyster; but because he has no permanent ties with his fellow human beings except those which he constructs with his own efforts, he is likely to view life and the environment in terms of unilineal absolutes. So that he may have something permanent to hold on to, the world is either absolutely good or absolutely evil, entirely romantic or entirely miserable, wholly for him or wholly against him. If the world is not all as he desires it, then it should be changed by his own hands. He tends to harbor universalism in a love or hatred hard to come by among his situation-centered Chinese brethren. At any given point of time the individual may be forced by circumstances to conform to a multiplicity of standards or organizational requirements, but because of the inner conflict such conformity generates, these very standards and requirements will be ammunition for individual rebellion and group reform or revolution. Consequently, throughout history the Western society, of which America is one of the latest versions, has tended to be remarkably dynamic, for it has great *internal* impetus for change.

The supernatural-centered world shares some of the peculiarities of both worlds just discussed. For example, in the supernatural-centered world ties among family and kin are more ephemeral than in the situation-centered world but less so than in the individual-centered world, while in other respects it is closer to the individual-centered world than to the situation-centered world. There is its emphasis upon absolute truth and the importance it attaches to priesthood, and these are not foreign to the individual-centered emphases. Again, the different dharmas for the different stations and occupations of individuals and castes among the Hindus is not dissimilar to the multiplicity of standards and principles of the Chinese.

The supernatural-centered world has, however, characteristics all its own. Both the Chinese and the Hindus attach great importance to status differences among human beings. The Chinese hold them to be changeable here and now and regard existence in this world as primary; the Hindus, in their basic philosophy, see no possibility of alteration except in future reincarnations, and they consider all temporal existence to be transitory and illusory. Again, like the Chinese, the Hindus may be opportunistic and entertain multiple standards of morality; but the Chinese regard these as part of the order of nature, while the Hindus' culture tends to lead them to regard the ups and downs of life as bubbles in a bottomless and shoreless ocean. The bubbles in the ocean will have their momentary places, but will not make any difference to the ocean in the final analysis.

The differences between the supernatural-centered world and the individual-centered world are equally striking. Like Westerners, Hindus have been lured by abstract truths; but in contrast to most of their Western brethren, the Hindus search for it through mysticism and not through science. On the other hand, while Westerners did and do put a high premium on priesthood, they have never long relied solely on it and many centuries ago emerged from its domination.

The supernatural-centered orientation enjoins the Hindu society to seek intimacy with the Ultimate Reality and/or Its manifestations and is commensurate with the idea, in interpersonal relations, of unilateral dependence. The difference between dependence and self-reliance is well known and needs no elaboration. The difference between mutual dependence and unilateral dependence is less obvious but not less important. Unilateral dependence is one-sided dependence. It means that the individual need feel no resentment against being a recipient, nor need he feel obligated to reciprocate what he has received. But if human relations must, in the final analysis, be based on balancing of obligations, however long delayed, how does the Hindu social system maintain and continue itself? The answer is that this nonreciprocal pattern of relationships has firm roots in the supernatural-centered orientation of life so eloquently expressed by S. Radhakrishnan:

> If the fundamental form of the Supreme is *nirguna*, qualityless and *acintya*, inconceivable, the world is an appearance which cannot be logically related to the Absolute. In the unalterable eternity of Brahman, all that moves and evolves is founded. By It they exist, they cannot be without It, though It causes nothing, does nothing, determines nothing. While the world is dependent on Brahman, the latter is not dependent on the world. This one-sided dependence and the logical inconceivability of the relation between the Ultimate Reality and the world are brought out of the word "Māyā."[4]

In this way givers and recipients need have no direct reference to each other, for the ultimate responsibility of their actions is found in dharma or sacred laws. If givers give because of dharma and recipients take also because of dharma, then human beings need not be indebted to each other at all.

The extent to which Hindus rely upon and are sensitive to the supernatural in all its manifestations is unknown in China and the West. The Chinese are probably too deeply enmeshed in their automatic network of human relationships to develop deep involvement with the supernatural. The Americans tend to be too interested in what they themselves can do to leave much room for the supernatural. Only among the Hindus, of the three peoples under our scrutiny, are we more likely to see the kind of psychic climate for complete acceptance of the power from above.

The basic guide for the Hindu's behavior is his relationship with the gods. His worldly ties with his family and others are often overshadowed, or at least strongly affected, by his ties with men of saintly propensities, namely, priests or holy men. This supernatural orientation dovetails well with diluted human bonds and fosters perpetual searches for nonworldly anchorages. However, searches for nonworldly anchorages lead to no visible destinations and provide no criteria for success except perhaps in the size of the following, which the true mystic will despise. Sects, cults, and schools of religious thought have been multifarious in Hindu society; but no sect, cult, or school has succeeded in subordinating all or even a portion of the others. Instead they all coexist on a more or less equal status. This state of affairs has caused many students to note the "tolerance" of Hinduism or its "capacity for absorption." What Hinduism has done is to claim all the divisive elements (and any and all extraneous elements which happen to come along) as part of itself by a continuous process of simple addition. The result is a situation rife with divisive tendencies, but with no genuine breaks. In other words, Hindu India is a society exhibiting a remarkable degree of internal dynamism that leads to *no* real change.

The dynamic growth or stagnation of a society depends to a large extent upon its ability or inability to generate new and more human groupings. The basic purpose of this book is to demonstrate how the development of human groupings is affected by the psychocultural orientations which guide the interpersonal relationships and give direction to the Chinese, Hindu, and American worlds. In this undertaking we shall not only take into consideration the detailed day-to-day reality seen in the life of humble folk but also relate it to the generalized traditions or ideals expounded and eulogized by the great and the wise.

Among human groupings the family is basic and ubiquitous in every society. It is everywhere the institution in which the individual begins to learn the way of life of the society into which he is born and with which he is identified for a number of years later. Yet though the family as the first human grouping is universally important, its importance to the individual varies enormously from society to society. For example the individual may be identified with the family of his nativity for life or till he reaches maturity; the family not only may be the individual's source of education but it also may arrange his marriage, be responsible for his conduct, and claim affiliation with his ghost after his death. On the basis of these and other criteria we can say that to the Chinese his first grouping is most important, to the Hindu it is considerably less important, while to the American it is least important.*

These differences are correlated with far-reaching consequences in the development of groupings beyond the family and within the all-embracing political boundary among each of the three peoples. Filling this vast middle region, the most important Chinese grouping is clan, the most important Hindu grouping is caste, and the most important American grouping is club. The importance of clan in Chinese civilization has been widely recognized in both scholarly and popular writing. It is no exaggeration to say that, to Western scholars, Chinese clan is as well known as Chinese family. In the major part of China, clan is organized to regulate the conduct of its members even to the extent of bearing a part of the government's responsibility for law and order. Similarly, the presence of caste in Hindu society has long been recognized in all literature on India. One cannot think of the Hindus and of their way of life without thinking at the same time of caste, and in actual fact caste tends to enter into every aspect of Hindu life.† The term club is used in its widest possible sense to denote any sort of free association consciously organized for any purpose whatever. Social fraternities, business syndicates, reformist groups or proselytizing societies and many other varieties of gatherings are, therefore, all examples of it.

The thesis of this book is that clan, caste, and club are important among Chinese, Hindus, and Americans because, much more than mere forms of human grouping, each of them represents the crucial and outstanding expression of a way of life. The Chinese, with his situation-centered world

---

* The observation that the first grouping is more important to the Chinese individual than to the Hindu individual is contrary to popular conception. In Western eyes, trained as well as untrained, the Hindu family system has been seen as bearing a basic resemblance to its counterpart in China. In fact, Western observers, while noting how the Hindu family system differs from their own, tend to regard it as identical with that of the Chinese. In the course of the following pages we shall demonstrate that the differences between the Hindu and Chinese family systems are no less than those between the American system and the two Asian systems.

† There is a good deal of writing on clan (*gotra*) or its equivalent in India. Recent field researchers have frequently dwelt on its importance in Indian villages. We shall see in Chapter IV that its role has in most instances been either misunderstood or grossly exaggerated.

and attitude favoring mutual dependence, tends to seek solutions to his life's problems in terms of the human beings of his first social group, the family. When and if he has to venture out of that first social group, he wishes continually to look for and build ties of a kinship nature in which his rewards and obligations are determined according to his place and rules of eventual reciprocity. Increase in population has simply led the Chinese to form cohesive clans which are mere extensions of families, for his psychocultural orientation assures him a relatively automatic framework for the satisfaction of his needs for relating to other human beings.

The Hindu, with his supernatural-centered world and attitude favoring unilateral dependence, tends to seek solutions to his life's problems by leaving himself in the hands of gods or persons who, compared with him, enjoy higher statuses or possess greater powers. But unilateral dependence upon the supernatural yields no concrete criteria for success or failure. It is likely to lead to more complex rituals to influence the gods and more distant pilgrimages to search for more efficacious gods. And unilateral dependence upon men of higher statuses or powers encourages unrealistic demands by the dependents and imposes unbearable burdens on those who are objects of others' dependence. It is likely to increase irresponsibility on the part of the former and desire to escape on the part of the latter. Both sets of circumstances are conducive to centrifugal tendencies among men, so that the individual's needs for relating to other human beings are not met automatically and easily. Caste is at once an expression of this centrifugality in the Hindu way of life (for as we shall see, divisiveness rather than cohesiveness is its outstanding characteristic) and provides a unilineal ladder of human groupings through which the individual, in his diffused world, can relate to his equals, but especially to his superiors and inferiors, with some clear demarcations of his obligations and rewards.

The American, with his individual-centered world and militant self-reliance, is conditioned to view his life's problems in terms of what he himself thinks and can do. The very definition of growing-up and manhood in his world means rejection of familial protection, and dependence is a totally undesirable state for all except married women and children. Like the Hindu he is faced with the problem of centrifugality among men. But unlike the Hindu, he must find his solution to it in mechanisms through which he can be assured of his independence as well as of the satisfaction of his needs for relating to his fellow human beings. Free associations or clubs fulfill the requirements of the American because they are organizations among equals on the whole voluntarily entered into and withdrawn from, and may be multiplied and expanded in any direction according to the wishes of the individuals concerned.

From this standpoint, as the following chapters will make clear, the three societies in our analysis exemplify what Bohannan, building on the Durk-heimian concepts of "social solidarity" and "collective conscience" ex-pounded in Durkheim's primary writings on social divisions of work,[5, 6] would designate as kinship solidarity, hierarchic solidarity and contractual solidarity.[7] "Solidarity" here denotes a characteristic mode of relationship among the roles making up a society. In this sense, kinship is not only the basic principle governing clans but also the backbone of mutual dependence; hierarchy is not only the basic principle regulating castes but also the out-standing attribute of unilateral dependence; while contract is not only the essential foundation of free associations or clubs but also the most important way in which self-reliant men can be bound one to another. Kinship, hier-archy, and contract are principles of social organization which have wider application to the interpersonal relationship in their respective societies than clan, caste, or club, as the case may be.

There is, however, another meaning in which the term solidarity is used. More than relationship, it denotes psychic or behavioral cohesion, or cen-tripetality among the members of a given social group or among different groups.* This primarily non-Durkheimian sense of the term is specifically employed by many social scientists, some of whom focus their attention on caste in India. In Chapter V we shall see how, in this sense, these students have exaggerated cohesion of caste in India. For psychically and behavior-ally clan, caste, and club differ greatly in cohesion or centripetality. But the two meanings of the term "solidarity" are functionally connected with each other. The dominant principles governing the relationship among the roles making up each society cannot but have significant bearings on the psychic and behavioral characteristics among the human beings who fill its roles. The distinctive purpose of our present analysis is to examine the characteristic patterns of behavior in Chinese, Hindu, and American primary and second-ary groupings and the psychic forces underlying them. It will make obvious not only that solidarity in terms of relationships is connected with solidarity in terms of behavioral and psychic cohesion, but also how the dominant principles in the former sphere influence the characteristic patterns in the latter. It will show, for example, not only that the Chinese clan is a grouping in which the members are related through kinship but that the Chinese clan does have greater cohesion over long periods of time than either caste or club because its members are encouraged to view the world of man in terms of those who are in the kinship group and those who are outside it, rather than in terms of supernaturals or truths or issues.

In treating the psychocultural orientations of large societies we must

---

* This is a meaning of the term which Durkheim seems to employ in his study on sui-cide but which has never been explicitly defined and differentiated from its other mean-ing by Durkheim himself or by later students of Durkheim.

constantly keep in mind one main precaution against oversimplification. When we characterize the Americans as self-reliant and the Hindus as unilaterally dependent we do not mean that examples of unilateral dependence are entirely absent in the former while those of self-reliance cannot be found in the latter. On the contrary, all three ideas, and probably some others unnamed in this study, prevail in one way or another among all three peoples. Apart from the obvious fact of variation among men in general, different ideas can underlie the history of one individual in each of these societies. For example, unilateral dependence characterizes the infant's relationship to his parents and guardians everywhere; mutual dependence is likely to mark the pattern of interaction between adult friends in any society; while most grown-ups who speak any language are likely to be more self-reliant than their juniors.

One basic reason for this similarity among human societies is that, to continue at all, every society has to fulfill certain basic functional prerequisites. Aberle, Cohen, Davis, Levy, and Sutton's list contains the following eight items:

A. "Provision for adequate relationship to the environment and for sexual recruitment"
B. "Role differentiation and role assignment"
C. "Communication"
D. "Shared cognitive orientations"
E. "A shared, articulated set of goals"
F. "The normative regulation of means"
G. "Socialization"
H. "The effective control of disruptive forms of behavior."[8]

Young and Mack's list is shorter but in substantial agreement with the above: "(1) reproduction, (2) socialization, (3) maintenance of a sense of purpose, (4) production and distribution of goods and services, and (5) preservation of order."[9] These functional prerequisites form the boundaries which limit the range of variations among societies. But what must be pointed out is that over and above their basic similarity, differences among societies can still be very great, and it is the latter that this book aims at elucidating.

The three worlds to be analyzed and demonstrated in the following pages must therefore be understood as principal psychocultural tendencies which encourage in each culture the elevation and domination of some ideas over other ideas, but not a total exclusion. In this way behavior patterns associated with the dominant ideas are taught to the young and honored, while those rooted in the other ideas are reduced, changed, disguised, and generally shown as undesirable. The relationship between the dominant ideas and the other ideas in each culture may be roughly represented as follows:

		AMERICAN	CHINESE	HINDU
DOMINANT IDEAS		Self-reliance	Mutual dependence	Unilateral dependence
OTHER IDEAS	A	Mutual dependence	Self-reliance	Mutual dependence
	B	Unilateral dependence	Unilateral dependence	Self-reliance

In the body of this book facts and theories bearing on the three worlds and how they express themselves in Chinese clan, Hindu caste, and American club will be analyzed in the following order. We shall begin with a comparison of the Chinese and Hindu patterns of family in Chapter III. The delicate combination and balance of forces give each family system direction which reintroduces and reinforces each way of life to every new generation. This will be followed, in Chapter IV, by an analysis of the characteristics of the clan in China and India, with a view to showing the centripetal nature of the Chinese clan as contrasted to the centrifugality of the Hindu clan; we shall show how these differences correspond to the differing characteristics of the two systems of family. Chapter V will examine the characteristics of Hindu caste and how they fit in with the characteristics of the Hindu clan. Chapter VI will deal with a number of theories on Hindu caste and the problem of their adequacy. Chapter VII will outline a theory of human group based on social needs, and Chapter VIII will show how differently the needs are met in the Chinese world and Hindu world, as well as how the differing modes of fulfillment of these needs may conceivably be linked with the Chinese way in clan and the Hindu way in caste. In Chapters IX and X, the dynamics of the Chinese and Hindu ways of life will be compared with that of the American way of life. But before we enter into all these facets of our task, we need to digress briefly into the subject of how our data are obtained and used. To this we now turn in Chapter II.*

NOTES FOR CHAPTER I

1. Max Weber, *The Religion of India* or *The Sociology of Hinduism and Buddhism*, translated by Hans H. Gerth and Don Martindale (Glencoe: Free Press, 1958), p. 329.
2. F. S. C. Northrop, *The Meeting of East and West* (New York: Macmillan, 1946).
3. Ralph Waldo Emerson, "Self-reliance" (1841), in Norman Foerster (ed.), *American Poetry and Prose* (Boston: Houghton Mifflin, 1934), Part I, p. 545.

* The general reader is advised to skip Chapter II and go on directly to Chapter III. Chapter II is specifically designed for students of social sciences who are interested in relating isolated community studies to large national cultures and other problems.

4. S. Radhakrishnan, "Introductory Essay," *The Bhagavadgita* (London: George Allen and Unwin, 1948), pp. 37–38.

5. Émile Durkheim, *De la division du travail social,* translated by George Simpson under the English title, *The Division of Labor in Society* (Glencoe: Free Press, 1947), pp. 70–132.

6. For an exposition of Durkheim's concept of collective conscience freed from its popular misconceptions see Paul J. Bohannan, "Conscience Collective and Culture," in Kurt Woolf (ed.), *Emil Durkheim (1860–1918)* (Columbus: Ohio State University Press, 1961), pp. 77–96.

7. Paul J. Bohannan, "Kinship and Social Organization," in preparation.

8. D. F. Aberle, A. K. Cohen, A. K. Davis, M. J. Levy, Jr., and F. X. Sutton, "The Functional Prerequisites of a Society," *Ethics,* LX, No. 2 (January 1950), 104–111.

9. Kimball Young and Raymond W. Mack, *Sociology and Social Life* (New York: American Book Company, 1959), p. 124.

Chapter II

DATA AND METHODOLOGY

THE CHINESE DATA used in this book are primarily derived from my own experiences and field work in that country up to and including 1944. Since then I have made a brief visit to Hong Kong in 1957 and another to Hong Kong and Taiwan in 1961 and have kept myself acquainted with more recent literature on life among the Chinese inside and outside China. The American data come from my own experiences since 1944 as a professor, resident, father with children in schools, public lecturer, traveler, participant in local affairs, and consultant in several psychiatric hospitals, as well as from written reports of scholarly and other researches. These facts were explained in some of my previous publications and should not detain us here.

The Indian data used in this study are part of the results of two years of library research between 1953 and 1955, and eighteen months of field work in India, from February 1956 to July 1957.[1] Since the object of this research was to arrive at, on a modest scale, an integrated picture of the Hindu view of life as it is manifested in diverse aspects of Indian society and culture, the field work was not localized in any village or community, though I have a much greater acquaintance with some small areas than with others. Among the relatively small areas with which I have some intensive acquaintance are Burdwan and Serampore, West Bengal; Moradabad and Marehra, Uttar Pradesh; as well as the cities and outskirts of Calcutta, Delhi, and Bangalore. In general, therefore, I am more familiar with the city-dwellers in the Bengali-speaking, Hindi-speaking, and Kanada-speaking parts of India than with other sections of the country, and the Hindu culture patterns described, insofar as they are based on firsthand material, pertain primarily to these areas.

My knowledge of Hindi and Sanskrit is minimal. At my most proficient I read very simple Hindi, and for about three months I attended a Hindi class with a group of Bengali public servants. This class is one of several in each city conducted by the Government of India for the benefit of government employees whose native tongue is not Hindi. I do not know Bengali and Kanada at all except for simple greetings and words and phrases used in pub-

12

lic places such as markets. All my field work was done through interpreters except for informants who happened to speak English—roughly two-thirds of them. My command of Hindi was totally inadequate for field work.

For the duration of my field work in India I was appointed Foreign Fellow in the Department of Anthropology, Government of India (now Anthropological Survey of India). This appointment not only gave me a modest stipend, and entitled me to join the Hindi classes for government employees mentioned above, but also provided me with invaluable contacts and entries into many facets of Indian society. I participated in the many activities of the Department and enjoyed the friendship of many of its members. I delivered to its members two series of lectures on psychological anthropology and entered into many private discussions on subjects of social or academic interest. Some of its members attended the same Hindi class with me.

The library sources drawn on for this research are of five varieties: (1) published material such as censuses and annual reports originating from governmental and other agencies; (2) scholarly works by Indians and non-Indians in the modern sociological and anthropological tradition; (3) literary and popular materials such as novels, stories, folk tales, and myths, told by peoples or published for Indian or foreign consumption in dailies, magazines, or elsewhere; and (4) sacred and traditional works such as the Vedas, the Upanishads, the Shastras, and their interpretations by Indians and non-Indians. In addition (5) certain historical facts are used. All of these materials were written in English or translated into English when published, or were rendered into English by one of my Indian interpreters.

While the present volume is the first of two books resulting from this research and therefore does not dwell on the whole range of subjects covered, the methodology followed in the entire undertaking requires a brief explanation here.

In the first place, it is neither strictly anthropological with participant-observation in one village, tribe, or a small geographical area, nor systematically sociological with heavy reliance on sampling procedures and quantitative collection and manipulation of data. Either or both approaches were used informally according to the convenience or suitability of the data to be collected. My rule is that cases collected at random or informally must reinforce the conclusions reached through intensive inquiries. Otherwise more work is done in both areas. I collected a total of ten life histories, five in Bengal and five in the Delhi area. With the aid of a few informants I intensively inquired into the customs and practices connected with life cycles in the Moradabad area of Uttar Pradesh and the Burdwan and Serampore areas of Bengal. I studied the parent-child relations among eighteen families in Calcutta, twelve in Bangalore, and eighteen in Delhi. In addition I examined specific areas of Hindu life such as suicide, mental illness, club activities, etc. Questionnaires were used among students at one college in each of the cities of Delhi, Calcutta, and Bangalore, where their use was feasible and deemed profitable; newspaper and magazine materials were relied on in all areas to provide many specific facts and opinions; police files and reports in several localities were consulted in connection with specific problems. The Annex by Dr. Blanche Watrous and myself contains parts of the results of TAT given to college students in India, Hong Kong, Taiwan, and the United States.

In the second place, the investigation is concentrated neither on the overall ideal nor on the localized reality of any particular time and place, but on the interaction between ideal and reality and on the significance of both in terms of the whole. The sacred books and most of the literary creations such as myths, folktales, dramas, novels, etc., probably express aspects of the ideal more than the reality. The contemporary facts garnered in different parts of the country, either by the sociological technique of topical inquiry or by the anthropological technique of community study, naturally approximate the reality more than the ideal. It has been my deliberate procedure to ignore the time differences between the literary, artistic, folkloristic and other written materials and the sociological facts observed by my colleagues and myself, and to concentrate on the relationship between the two.

Some students of folklore or history may be interested, for example, in what gods or goddesses worshiped today are survivals of which gods or goddesses in the ancient lores, or in the marriage of Draupadi to the five Pandava brothers reported in the epic Mahabharata, which is an instance of tribal polyandry prevailing at the time. Some students of caste are interested in tracing how the Gujara group, through a continuous process of spread and absorption, came to include diverse castes of different statuses (from Kshatriyas to near Untouchables) and in diverse localities (from Maharashtra to Delhi to Punjab), none of which may be aware of any or all of the others.[2] But the student of the science of culture must be primarily oriented toward the comparison of data, wherever they are found, in terms of the similarity or differences in underlying patterns or ideas. Dumont and Pocock, in their summary of and comment on Bouglé's and Hocart's theories on caste, to which we shall have occasion to turn later on, define the position succinctly: "Here texts are used not as historical evidence with which it is presumed that the present must accord but rather as offering certain systems of ideas with which the present may be compared."[3]

It is the relationship between the texts or historical data and the present events which is basic for the understanding of every society, unless we assume little or no integrative process in each social system. Before one succumbs to the feeling that the Hindu sacred books have little relationship with the life of the common people, he should reflect for a moment on the following well-known fact in Western society. The actual behavior of the nominally Christian peoples may not be very Christian; but there are few scholars or laymen who will insist that the Bible and other religious writings emanating from it have no relationship with the common people born in Christianity. Illiteracy on the part of the common people of India has been no bar to knowledge of the ancient heritage. The Vedas and other sacred literature are constantly recited and explained by traveling kathaks (story tellers) and holy men all over India, while the epics are dramatized and told in a thousand ways to all types of audiences. Of course, neither set of data is to be considered primary in the ultimate sense, but each influences the other.

Likewise, the Confucian precepts in China were certainly not all original creations of the sage himself. Some of the mores and customs he endorsed and propounded must have existed long before him in some parts of China, but after his teachings were widely known they, in turn, affected and reshaped the mores and customs of the Chinese as a whole. This process is essentially similar to what folklorists describe as "circular flow," which requires "time to simmer . . . to integrate . . . to rework."[4]

From the same methodological standpoint, sequences of facts and events, from historical to modern, are compared in an ahistorical but genetic frame of reference. The numerous characteristics which distinguish one biological organism from another are usually absent in early life. In fact the embryos of frogs and human beings in their earliest stages look remarkably similar. At birth the differences between a human being and a chimpanzee are also negligible. But the emergence of physical or behavioral characteristics which distinguish some biological organisms from others requires, in some instances, a few months and, in other instances, many scores of years. Hence a science of living things must be based on the characteristics of adults, although those of infants are also of interest. The characteristics which distinguish one society from another develop as a result of interaction among forces within the same society or as a result of mutual pressures between different societies. Sometimes these characteristics emerge quickly, but more often they do not do so till after a long time—not infrequently centuries. The French Revolution cannot be understood sociologically if we study only the facts pertaining to the reign of Louis XVI, for the simple reason that it was not only related to a wider European development which sprang from seeds sown in the reign of Louis XVI and earlier, but also to the Magna Carta, the Enlightenment philosophies, the Industrial Revolution, etc. In turn the forces underlying the French Revolution had a great deal to do with the American and even the Chinese Revolutions, the Meiji Restoration of Japan, and so on. It is therefore, methodologically sound to relate the French Revolution to the Magna Carta, even though the two events occurred nearly six centuries apart, and to relate the American Revolution to the Chinese and Japanese developments even though they occurred at different times and on different continents. It is for this reason that social scientists can speak of the repetitive social or cultural process; for processes which are repetitive through time are not the specific events and personalities but the patterns and ideas behind the events, or the roles and thought patterns molding or motivating the individuals.

The same methodological considerations govern my efforts to relate more or less contemporaneous facts from different geographical sections of India.

The above points, though they make up a research procedure drastically different from the modern anthropological emphasis on localized or community studies, are closely related to the notion, first expressly stated by Robert Redfield, of continuous interaction between a Great Tradition as abstracted and systematized by the specialist literati, mainly in urban centers, and the Little Traditions of little village communities.[5] The essential point of emphasis is not the detailed data in any one locality but the interrelatedness of different varieties of data to each other in terms of some central orientation which seems to represent the whole. The scientific universe is the whole of Hindu society instead of a single village. Therefore, while the bulk of the data in support of my hypothesis here on Hindu family, clan, and caste chiefly applies to those caste Hindus who are the relatively more active (in literary, religious, economic, political areas) elements of India society, and is not concerned with the Sudras and the Untouchables except where specifically noted, it must in the long run approximate the permanent aspects of the Hindu way of life through the processes of Sanskritization (Srinivas), and Parochialization and Universalization (Marriott). Sanskritization is the process whereby a low caste has adopted the customs, rites, and beliefs of the higher-caste Brahmans in order to rise to a higher position.[6] Parochialization supplements the process of Sanskritization. It refers to the fact that in its downward spread, the Great Tradition is obstructed or transformed by the indigenous Little Tradition. Universalization is the process whereby the materials of a Little Tradition are carried forward to form a relatively more articulate and refined indigenous civilization.[7]

Nevertheless certain possible objections to this approach must be examined at once. One of these is described by Singer thus:

> Some anthropologists advised me before I went to India not to spend much time preparing myself by studying the history of Indian civilization or reading the Indian epics and other texts. A field study, they said, has a strict obligation to record only those realities which the field worker himself can observe within a limited area and what is within the living memory of the people he interviews. Historical and literary research would only clutter the mind with

preoccupations, and if done at all, should be done after the field work is finished. Although I did not take this advice, the course of the study would seem to justify it: I was compelled to limit my attention to a particular group of people within a region restricted enough to be brought under a single conspectus of interrelations. I had to set aside generic conceptual categories about total civilizations in favor of concrete units of observation like cultural performances, and even the analysis of these cultural performances runs in terms of constituent factors like cultural media institutions, cultural specialists and cultural media which in part, at least, are amenable to the direct observation and interview of the field worker.[8]

I have had the same kind of advice as that reported by Singer and received it often in other connections. Although this notion seems to be basic to the thinking of many present-day field workers, it contains, in my view, several fallacies and I cannot, therefore, agree with Singer's justification of it. In the first place, no field worker can go to the field with an entirely open mind. His mind is cluttered with assumptions from his own cultural background and/or those from his scientific training. His scientific training is supposed to help reduce the biases of his particular cultural background which have "cluttered up" his mind and fill it with an outlook which is commensurate with the assumptions and methods of modern science. But however hard the field worker tries, the chances are that he is not likely to be entirely free from all the hidden assumptions from his own cultural background. How, then, can he be worse off as a field worker if he has some of his Western assumptions at least checked a little, before he goes to India, by some thinking about Indian history and texts?

In the second place, if the notion of "cluttering up the mind" were true, then scholars of India would no longer be able to study Hindu civilization, and their counterparts of the United States would similarly be disqualified from studying American life. This would just about write off the bulk of our published works on both societies. I doubt if the anthropologists who hold the "cluttering of the mind" notion are prepared to grant this. Fortunately they do not have to. The primary objective of the anthropologist is to ascertain the psychocultural commitment of the people he proposes to study. His anthropological training should enable him to perceive different ways of life, by acquiring as full a knowledge of each society and culture as possible, but, in his academic exercises, avoiding emotional commitment to any of them.

Finally, there is the possibility of cultural shock, which causes the newcomer to a strange culture to develop a neurotic and devastating reaction to it. There is less possibility of this among trained anthropologists than among others, but this is probably because anthropologists are better prepared. Preparation means not only knowing something about the diet and etiquette of the people to be studied, but also gaining as much familiarity as possible with their historical and literary background. To so limit the field worker that he can "record only those realities which the field worker himself can observe within a limited area and what is within the living memory of the people he interviews," especially in a society like India, is not only artificially to reduce local studies to no more than local significance (which, as we shall see later, is one of the causes of the confused state of our understanding of caste in India), but by limiting him to a myopic vision, seriously to endanger his very effectiveness.

Another objection that may be leveled at the method of approach in this book is the assumption that a study of such wide scope is bound to be more superficial than studies concentrating on single villages or communities—that it fails, for one thing, to take into consideration all internal variations within the same culture. This criticism principally comes from those for whom scientific anthropology has been equated with the concentration of the anthropologist upon some village community and his exact counting of heads. It is an interesting objection but not vital. To begin with, internal variation is to be assumed in any human group, however small, for the capacity to vary is one of the basic characteristics of man. In fact no two individuals are alike. But on the one hand, not all individual pecularities are relevant to his life as an active member of his society; and, on the other, unless we wish to equate the science of man with a science of individual differences we are obliged to deal with men in terms of larger or smaller collectivities which must, by definition, ignore some of the factors making for variation within each collectivity.

Of even greater importance here is the fact that anthropology is not the study of mere social and cultural life. It must ultimately unravel the ideas about such life which make it meaningful. The reason that Ruth Benedict gave us a masterly piece of work on the Japan she had never seen (though, had she seen it a few of her emphases might have been corrected) was that she never for a moment ceased dealing with the ideas in terms in which the Japanese see their lives and life.

Anthropology brings to social science *not* merely scientific rigor on a small scale, for that it shares with sociology or psychology. What it really brings is a scientific framework for studying the sweep of ideas that makes a people memorable, that enlightens our way of life (or any other) and that brings richness to human perception of the universe. To say that anthropology cannot study anything beyond the range permitted by a single field job is to confuse anthropology with one of its component fields—ethnography. Ethnography has its place.

Unless we want to reduce a civilization like that of Hindu India to no more than a collection of Little Traditions we must be interested in the broader ideas which are the essence of the Great Tradition and the backbone of each major way of life affecting hundreds of millions of people. But we go wherever we are likely to find such ideas in theory and as they are expressed in concrete acts: from the mouths of illiterate peasants or tribesmen in villages and backhills; from the testimony of merchant princes or Brahman priests in commercial centers and sacred places; from the great writings of ancient sages and modern pandits; and from the music, drama, and scenes in temple grounds no less than from ceremonials, pilgrimages, or public adorations to holy men. If the illiterate peasant can tell us the benefit of sila (stone object of worship) and the spiritual relationship between devadasis (temple ladies) and the gods, such information is important. But if the sophisticated intellectual can tell us that all sadhus (holy men) are fakes, or Hinduism is basically the same as Christianity, he is equally worth listening to. Ideas of a people can and must be studied on every social level. While genealogical tables and a knowledge of mother-in-law avoidance may be of help in our attempt to understand people's ideas, we should certainly not be tied to them. On the contrary, unless anthropologists can raise their sights and go beyond community studies, anthropology will never be fit for anything but the study of small and isolated societies. It is simply impossible to study a subject of broad scope without employing a method suited to it.

Indeed, the pitfall of trying to fathom a broad subject with myopic techniques can be illustrated by all too many examples. Thus, in Oscar Lewis' work on religion in a village of north India, the author begins by questioning Morris Opler's statement that:

> The fact that the highest goal of the Hindu is to eliminate earthly concerns, desires, and personal existence itself introduces a large element of asceticism, intellectualism, detachment, and withdrawal into Hindu religious philosophy. In no other country have so many men renounced the world, and in no other place is there so much fasting and mortification of the flesh. The world is considered transitory and an appearance. . . .[9]

Lewis presents "some quantitative data relating to the religious views of the people of Rampur," secured by a questionnaire filled in by twenty-five individuals, with no mention of the method of their selection. He modestly states that although his study "cannot be considered definitive, it does set forth a method of investigation which could be applied elsewhere for further research."[10] But what are the results? On the basis of such returns Lewis concludes, after a discussion of the differences between Brahmans and Jats, etc., that "the evidence from Rampur does not seem to support Opler's generalizations."[11]

That Lewis's conclusion may not even apply at the village level has been shown by Morris Opler in a subsequent article.[12] My relatively brief personal sojourns in villages in several scattered parts of the subcontinent and information from many villagers in cities also convince me that Lewis's conclusion on the subject is questionable. But there is no doubt that Lewis received answers to his questionnaires from twenty-five persons in Rampur; there is no doubt that his conclusion is based on the nature of the returns; and there is no doubt, too, that the facts gathered, such as they are, are exact. However, what would we think of a study of the place of Christianity in Medieval Europe or modern America based on one set of questionnaire returns from twenty-five individuals living in Belle-Île-en-Terre, Brittany, or Orchardville, Illinois? If such a study should reveal that the inhabitants of one of these localities knew little about the recorded doings of Jesus and his disciples, would our theologians, priests, mission board members, and even ordinary citizens who only occasionally see the inside of a church concede the unimportance of Christianity in Medieval Europe or contemporary America?

A somewhat different pitfall awaits relatively intensive community studies such as that by Bernard S. Cohn and others of the village of Senapur in Uttar Pradesh. Here we have rich details in a series of articles by Cohn, and by Opler and Singh,[13] of the castes, the law ways, the pasts, and the impact of Western forces and colonialism. Yet when some generalizations are called for on the interrelationship between modernization and the attachments to pasts, Cohn explains his inability to reconcile them in the following terms:

> In a changing social situation we expect to find a transitory attachment to the past, often in the *irrational* form of a nativistic movement. It is significant that the anthropological literature on this sort of attachment to a revitalization of the past has focused on the more spectacular messianic cults such as the Ghost Dance, cargo cults, and the Mau Mau. But we have not yet analysed the complex interaction of modernization and traditionalization, such as is found in the Arya Samaj, or the traditionalization of Chamar religious life as a result of literacy and urban experience. The apparent conflicting values, institutions, and behavior found in India seem to our minds *rationally incompatible. We cannot build their coexistence into our theories of change;* we can only describe them. Perhaps it is characteristic of members of modern societies to believe that consistency in social and intellectual life is a prerequisite to efficient functioning of either a social system or a theory. [Italics mine.][14]

The words "irrational" and "rationally compatible" are obvious expressions of Cohn's Western bias which, unless defined precisely, will befuddle any scientific analysis, for what looks rational to an American scholar may not look rational to his Hindu counterpart, though they may both possess college degrees in Western terms. But of more immediate concern here is Cohn's admitted inability or refusal to build any theory because of inconsistencies or incompatibilities in his data. The function of a theory or hypothesis is precisely to connect data which may be widely scattered, divergent, and incompatible. There would be no need for theory if all the data were uniformly consistent. The incompatibilities in the data may be more apparent than real. Or they may be more real than apparent. If they are the former, they should be reconciled; if they are the latter, they may possibly be linked. A single phenomenon may be correlated with many different factors just as one factor may be associated with different manifestations. The role of the scientist is to find the intermediary steps which link divergent phenomena, even complete opposites.

In the present instance the incompatibilities Cohn finds impossible to incorporate into one theory can easily be so encompassed if we examine them in a wider perspective and introduce the concepts of status-seeking and time lag. In a wider perspective the low-caste Chamars of Senapur move toward greater traditionalization as a result of modernizing forces such as literacy and urban experience because they, like their low-caste brethren elsewhere, wish to raise their status wherever and whenever they feel they can do something about it. The means they resort to in this status-raising effort is strongly determined by their model of high status. They will move toward greater traditionalization as a means (whether it is forbidding widow remarriage or creation of a fictitious Brahmanic past) as long as the modernizing forces have stimulated their aspirations but have not made any inroads on their model of high status. The Thakurs also wish to raise their status, or at least to maintain it. But being way above the Chamars on the caste hierarchy, economically better off and more powerful, the Thakurs have had more opportunity for contact with modernizing forces, and their model of high status has already been affected by some of the modernizing forces including those originating from Western missionaries and churches. Yet a group can no more completely abandon its past than can an individual. In seeking a modernized model of high status the Thakurs have to use the old as well as the new. As time rolls on and as modernizing forces expand their spheres of influence, the attainable model of high status for the low caste Chamars may well merge into some of the modernized features currently associated with the Thakur model. When that happens, we can expect the Chamars, too, to move toward status symbols which are mixtures of modernization and traditionalization.

These processes have been and are being repeated, with more or less intensity, in various societies in transition, but will be difficult to perceive until we raise our sights from the localized particulars.

Finally, it is a matter of common sense that intensity, even in the case of localized community studies, is a relative term. Understandably most anthropological field studies leave something to be desired in this regard. We do not have to speak of vast African societies like the Yoruba or Baganda, which number millions. Cora Dubois obtained life histories of eight somewhat misfit Alores and thirty-seven Rorschach protocols of others in a population of less than 600; John Honigmann registered among the Kaska Indians not more than six brief life histories and only twenty-eight Rorschach protocols among a population of one hundred and seventy-five; while Oscar Lewis' restudy of Tepoztlan, done with the help of a number of students and over a protracted period involving many visits, refers to Rorschach protocols on one hundred individuals and intensive data on seven families out of a village population of 4,000. Many anthropological field reports are far less explicit in quantitative terms, even though the need for quantitative evaluation was stressed by individual anthropologists long ago.[15] These facts are pointed out not to justify the present state of affairs but to underscore the lack of any clear criterion upon which a judgment of the intensity of anthropological field studies can be made. Lacking such a criterion, the one that we presently employ to evaluate the worth of a given field study is primarily qualitative: the fullness of the descriptive material, the extent of internal consistency, the training of the field worker, the conditions under which his field work was carried out, and in general, how his results compare with other results from a similar area. Some reports may provide more details than others but there is no reason to suppose that details as such are equivalent to intensity.

Today the science of anthropology appears to be at a major crossroad. After it had outgrown its earlier antiquarianism, the anthropology of yesterday continued to produce works which were very long on generalization and very short on methodology. In the process of the discipline's coming of age and under the critical pressure of sciences that consider themselves more advanced, many of us have tended to swing to the other extreme, hiding our ineptitude behind a smoke screen of scientific respectability and over-emphasizing localized details at the expense of wider perspective.* Thus we have today many tribal, village, and community studies but little to show in the way of an overall synthesis, by nation, by region, or in terms of mankind as a whole. The older concepts like culture area and the sketchy manner in which they deal with human behavior are now practically out of date except in small pockets of academic resistance. There has been nothing positive to fill the vacuum.

To this situation two reactions have so far emerged. One is exemplified by certain British anthropologists who seem to devote their entire creative energies to describing and analyzing one or two small tribes. These scholars have given us infinitely rich details and insights into the life of the small groups of humans they write about. But no matter what theoretical points

---

* Not realizing, of course, that some eminent scholars are beginning to concern themselves with deficiencies of overscientistic research in human affairs. For a brilliant exposition of the need in social sciences for emphasizing cogency of thesis rather than truth through formal methods, see Robert Bierstedt: "Sociology and Humane Learning," (Presidential address read at the annual meeting of the Eastern Sociological Society, April 1959), American Sociological Review, XXV (1960), 3–9.

they make, their central, and sometimes only, illustrations seem to be drawn from the one tribe or two tribes they have intimately studied. Some of them seem not only to avoid comparison between societies but seem consciously to believe that there should be no such comparison. It is perhaps not unfair to suggest that theirs is another form of ethnocentrism—not that of their mother cultures, but that of the societies they have studied.

The other approach to this situation is exemplified by those who constantly plead that we must wait for more localized or village studies before making any overall generalizations about any society, region, or people. They dwell on the complexity of each society, on the variations in details, and, in the case of India, seem to think that all generalizations about Hindu India are a long, long way off. These scholars have not reflected on two facts. First, there are about 500,000 villages in India. Even if we can expect fifty village studies a year, it would take ten centuries to complete 10% of Indian villages, by which time the earlier monographs would likely need some revision before they could be used for synthesis with the later products. The task is simply impossible. The second fact that these scholars need to reflect on is that, whether they like it or not, they and their colleagues, even if they have done only as much as one village study in India or China, will be called upon to teach courses on "Indian Culture," "Chinese Family," "Indian Political Institutions," "Chinese Village Life," etc., or from time to time, either for scientific or practical reasons, they will be forced to react to either culture or both cultures as a whole. Is it not a matter of scientific necessity for such scholars to become a little better prepared by looking into the connections between their own villages and the wider society as a whole?

What this book and its companion volume will attempt to demonstrate is a way of taking a broad view of India in comparison with China and the United States—societies so vast that it is impossible to encompass any one of them adequately by localized researches. The results of this research are not, as indicated earlier, intended to replace the localized findings but to complement them. But for the fruits of work by numerous other social scientists my present undertaking would obviously have been impossible. In this task I have also been materially helped by Redfield's conception, noted before, of a continuous interaction between a Great Tradition and Little Traditions, a conception which is well expressed by Singer in his preliminary report on his Madras study:

> But if such a unit [a village or a cluster of villages] is to disclose the cultural links with the past and with other regions, it cannot be regarded as an isolate but must be considered rather as one convenient point of entry to the total civilization. . . . Different field studies may of course choose different points of entry—in terms of size, character, location—but the interest in comparing their results will not be to count them as instances for statistical generalization

but rather to trace the actual lines of communication with one another and with the past. The general description of this organization in its most embracing spatial and temporal reach will then be a description of the culture pattern of the total civilization.[16]

Redfield's idea of continuous interactions between the Great and Little Traditions is a conceptual and methodological bridge between the localized studies and the total civilization. He and Singer have given impetus to a tide of anthropological works on India; but these works, while demonstrating the specific ways in which the Great and the Little Traditions interact, or how each is modified by the other, tell us little or nothing about the nature of the total Hindu civilization.

The aim of my procedure is to put in sharp relief the nature and characteristics of the total Hindu way of life by contrasting them with those of the Chinese on the one hand and with those of the Americans on the other. I firmly believe in the importance of the comparative approach, whether applied to single institutions or to whole societies and cultures. Lacking precise measurements in many respects the qualitative descriptions of facts often suffer from extreme ambiguity, thus rendering generalizations based on them of doubtful value. How permissive must be child-rearing practices of a people be to be designated as permissive? How oppressive must a political regime be to merit the adjective oppressive? The terms "individualistic," "freedom-loving," "superstitious," "autocratic," and many others have been applied to many peoples in many parts of the earth, but one will be extremely hard put to it to find any reliable criteria for any of them in most of these writings. One way to remedy the situation is through the comparative approach, so that instead of saying "A is oppressive," we can say "A is more oppressive than B but less oppressive than C." In this way, while still wanting in exactitude in the strictly quantitative sense, our statements at least gain in relative perspective.[17]

The other advantage of the comparative approach is that it will enable us to avoid generalizations based on data from a single example or society. The importance of this is so basic to science, so well propounded by scholars from Durkheim to MacIver,[18] that it is hard to see why so many scholars have continued to ignore it. The failings on the part of many social anthropologists who replace one sort of ethnocentrism by another have already been touched on. In the following chapters of this book there will be several occasions on which we shall analyze others who follow the same procedure, especially in the study of caste. As he proceeds from one chapter to the next, the reader will soon see for himself how the Hindu world will illuminate the Chinese world and American world as much as it is illuminated by them. In doing so I am aware of the fact that my task is open to a final methodological objection. This is that the data used in it are obviously selective—that is, arranged to suit my purposes. My answer to this objection is that no scientific study can use all data without discrimination. Even a descriptive monograph of a single village must perforce be restricted in its coverage. A complete coverage of all facts about all Hindu India or any other large society is an impossibility. The only practical criteria for judging the soundness of the selections are these: (1) Do the selected data make sense in terms of the thesis they are supposed to support? (2) Are there significant or obvious facts of comparable order which contradict them but which have been left out? The data selected in the following pages can probably pass the first criterion, in that they support the points made. But upon the second criterion rests the distinction between demonstrating a thesis and illustrating a thesis. In the present undertaking I am demonstrating my hypotheses concerning the three ways of life, not merely illustrating them. In the latter the adequacy of the work is measured by how well the thesis is supported by materials adduced, not by how much it is contradicted by other facts; in the former the adequacy of the work is measured not only by how well it is supported by data assembled but also by how well it can stand up against other data which contradict it.

However, when all this is said, it is necessary to point out that, while I claim a degree of adequacy for this book in demonstrating a way of looking at three large societies, each with its own view of the world, I must admit its inadequacy in terms of the cross-cultural testing of my hypotheses. From the latter angle the results contained in the following chapters are strictly preliminary and tentative, since they are only based on facts in three cultures. They obviously require more extensive validation in other areas of the world.[19]

NOTES FOR CHAPTER II

1. The field work was under the auspices of the Wenner-Gren Foundation for Anthropological Research, the Rockefeller Foundation, and the Government of India's Department of Anthropology.

2. Irawati Karve, *Hindu Society—an Interpretation* (Poona: Deccan College, 1961), pp. 62–65.

3. Louis Dumont and D. Pocock, *Contributions to Indian Sociology* (Paris and The Hague: Mouton and Company, April 1958, an irregular publication), No. 2, p. 49.

4. George M. Foster, "What Is Fold Culture?" *American Anthropologist*, LV (1953), 159–173.

5. Robert Redfield and Milton Singer, "The Cultural Role of Cities," *Economic Development and Cultural Change*, III (Chicago: University of Chicago Press), 53–73; and Robert Redfield, *Peasant Society and Culture* (Chicago: University of Chicago Press, 1955).

6. M. N. Srinivas, *Religion and Society Among the Coorgs of South India* (Oxford: Oxford University Press, 1952), p. 30. According to some authors the traditional Hindu society has not one (Brahman) but two (Brahman and Kshatriya) central models of popular cynosure. This question will be dealt with in Chapter V in connection with caste.

7. McKim Marriott, "Little Communities in an Indigenous Civilization," in McKim Marriott (ed.), *Village India*, Memoir No. 83 (Washington, D.C.: American Anthropological Association, June 1955), pp. 197–201.

8. Milton Singer, "The Cultural Pattern of Indian Civilization: A Preliminary Report of a Methodological Study," *Far Eastern Quarterly*, XV, No. 1 (November 1955), p. 34.

9. Oscar Lewis, *Village Life in Northern India* (Urbana: University of Illinois Press, 1958), p. 249.

10. *Ibid.*, p. 250.

11. *Ibid.*, p. 259.

12. Morris Edward Opler, "The Place of Religion in a North Indian Village," *Southwestern Journal of Anthropology*, XV, No. 3 (1959), 219–226.

13. Morris E. Opler and Rudra Datt Singh, "The Division of Labor in an Indian Village," in Carlton Coon, *A Reader in General Anthropology* (New York: Henry Holt, 1948), pp. 464–496; "Economic, Political and Social Change in a Village of North Central India," *Human Organization*, II (1952), 5–12; Morris E. Opler, "Factors of Tradition and Change in a Local Election in Rural India," in Richard L. Park and Irene Tinker (eds.), *Leadership and Political Institutions in India* (Princeton: Princeton University Press, 1959), pp. 137–150; Rudra Datt Singh, "The Unity of an Indian Village," *Journal of Asian Studies*, XVI (1956), 10–19; Bernard S. Cohn, "The Changing Status of a Depressed Caste," in McKim Marriott (ed.), *Village India* (Chicago: University of Chicago Press, 1955), pp. 53–77; and "Some Notes on Law and Social Change in North India," *Economic Development and Cultural Change*, IX (1959), pp. 79–93.

14. Bernard S. Cohn, "The Pasts of an Indian Village," *Comparative Studies in Society and History*, II, No. 3 (1961), 248–249.

15. Clyde Kluckhohn, "Theoretical Bases for an Empirical Method of Studying the Acquisition of Culture by Individuals," *Man*, XXXIX.

16. Milton Singer, *op. cit.*, p. 35.

17. Elsewhere I have elaborated this point. See Francis L. K. Hsu, "In Behalf of Comparative Civilizations Through Interdisciplinary Cooperation," in Ainslie T. Embree (ed.), *Approaches to Asian Civilization* (New York: Atherton Press, 1963).

18. R. M. MacIver, *Social Causation* (New York: Ginn, 1942), Chapter V.

19. This manuscript was in press before the appearance of Raoul Naroll's *Data Quality Control: A New Research Technique* (New York: The Free Press of Glencoe, 1962). Naroll's research instrument deals with diverse problems of comparability among ethnographical works and will undoubtedly give the comparative approach new impetus.

Chapter III

PATTERNS OF FAMILY AND PSYCHOLOGICAL ORIENTATION

FOR THE LAST COUPLE of decades, structural analysis has considerably advanced the study of social organization. It has been an invaluable instrument in anthropology both theoretically and ethnographically. There are, however, some facts of social organization which just cannot be revealed by a purely structural analysis.

I have introduced the concept of *content*, and have given a preliminary version of content analysis by applying it to four varieties of social organization. This has been done not to replace structural analysis, but to complement it.[1] In brief, content in social organization refers to the qualitative modes of interaction among individuals, while structure in social organization refers to the spatial and temporal web of duties and responsibilities which tie roles together. Thus, the political system of the United States is democratic, since it is based on a judiciary, a congress, and an executive branch whose officials are responsible to the people. The political organization of Saudi Arabia, on the other hand, is feudal; a lord gives the orders while the people worship or obey him. The differences between these two systems are structural.

The central political systems of most or all of the Latin American republics are structurally similar to that of the United States, but they are very different from that of the United States in the manner in which they operate. For example, the power of government in many Latin American republics can be seized by a military junta which then can either keep the power to itself or place its own strong man at the head of the government. This cannot occur in the United States, at least not as easily as it does in many Latin American republics. That is to say, the political systems of the Latin American republics are different from the United States system in spite of a broad similarity in structure. The difference is one of content. The political systems of the Latin American republics and of the United States are different not in their respective spatial or temporal webs which link officials with officials, and officials with the people, but in their respective ideas about and ways of handling interpersonal relations between officials, and between officials and the people.

SIMILARITIES BETWEEN THE CHINESE AND THE HINDU FAMILY SYSTEMS

From the structural point of view, there are many similarities between the Chinese family and the Hindu family. To begin with, the structural ideal for the majority of Chinese and Indians is the joint family system along the patriarchal line. The lower classes or the poor in both countries may seem indifferent to this ideal, for at any given point of time a majority of the people do not realize it in practice. But marriage is arranged by parents and is not based on Romantic Love. The normal practice in both societies is for the young man and his wife to begin their married life under the same roof with the husband's parents.

In South India, except for most of Kerala, and in Central India among the Rajputs and Maharashtrians, cross-cousin marriage is preferred, as in China. The preference for this kind of marriage is probably greater in India, especially in South India, than in many parts of China. Srinivas has observed that "intensification" is the operative principle in South India while "extension is the principle in the north." That is to say, in the south "preference for marriage with certain relatives tends to multiply the bonds one has with the same body or bodies of people," while in the north the preference is not only for village exogamy, but the latter is combined with hypergamy, so that the radius of the exogamous circle can extend to twenty miles, including many villages.[2]

Both China and India are known for patriarchal authority. The legally accepted pattern of inheritance in most of India (except Kerala, Bengal, and among the Rajputs of Rajasthan) and in China is the same—namely, equal division among the sons.[3] In both systems, seniority in kinship position and age normally determine the relationship among members of the family group, and inequality between the sexes is an expressed and accepted custom both in theory and practice. Widow remarriage is forbidden or frowned upon by the high castes in India and the higher classes in China.[4] Until recently polygyny was accepted both in India and China, especially if there were no heirs from a first marriage. In both societies, the individual is educated primarily for duties and obligations and not in the modern Western pattern of freedom and rights.

There are further similarities. The Chinese ancients said that a woman "follows" (is subordinated to) her father before marriage, her husband after marriage, and her son after her husband's death. The Hindu ancients said the same thing, except that the word "protects" is substituted for the word "follows." They concluded: "a woman is never fit to depend upon herself."[5] Yet in spite of this inequality between the sexes, there are mothers who wield great power over their adult sons in both systems. The Chinese feel this is due to the great physical debt the son owes his mother who carried him, gave birth to him, and nursed him. One Hindu sacred book said: "Teacher [is] 10 times more venerable than tutor (*upadhyaya*); father [is] 100 times more than teacher; mother [is] 1000 times more than father because she bears him in her womb and rears him up."[6]

DIFFERENCES BETWEEN THE CHINESE AND HINDU FAMILY SYSTEMS

The differences between the two systems are far more striking. If we examine the two systems closely, we shall find that their similarities are mostly in the realm of structure, while their differences are primarily matters of content, strongly reflecting the contrast between the Chinese situation-centered world and the Hindu supernatural-centered world.[7]

The traditions governing the purpose of life for a Chinese and a Hindu are dissimilar. "Of all the virtues, filial piety is the first." "Of the three offenses against filial piety, lacking descendants is the worst." These were expressions of the Confucian design which strongly influenced the Chinese individual for nearly two thousand years. The Hindu design is quite different. According to a Hindu law attributed to Manu, every man was born with three debts. The three debts were to the sages, to the gods, and to the ancestors. The debt to the sages was paid through learning, the first ashrama.[8] The debt to the gods was paid through sacrifices. The debt to the ancestors was paid by begetting sons who could perpetuate the giving of food to the dead.[9]

Furthermore, the passage already quoted above that "teacher is 10 times more venerable than tutor (upadhyaya)," which gives greater importance to parents than to the teacher and which is found with minor variation in several different sources, occupies only a very minor place among the Laws of Manu.[10] For this passage is immediately succeeded by fourteen passages and by many later passages, including the following, which extol the far greater importance of the teacher of Veda over all others;

> Let him consider that (he received) a (mere animal) existence, when his parents begat him through mutual affection, and when he was born from the womb (of his mother).
> But that birth which a teacher acquainted with the whole Veda, in accordance with the law, procures for him through the Savitri, is real, exempt from age and death.[11]

When the entire Laws of Manu are analyzed with a view to determining the relative importance of the parent-son relationship as compared with the guru-pupil relationship in the Hindu tradition, the following results obtain:

(1) laws concerning a father-genetic son relationship with no reference to teacher, 48 slokas (stanzas);

(2) laws concerning mother-genetic son relationship with no reference to teacher, 8 slokas;

(3) laws concerning parent-son relationship with no reference to teacher, 23 slokas;

(4) laws concerning teacher and pupil in conjunction with parents, 27 slokas; and

(5) laws concerning teacher and pupil with no reference to parents, 119 slokas;

(6) laws concerning father-nongenetic-son relationship, 24 slokas;

(7) laws concerning student with reference to all relatives of teacher, 9 slokas;

(8) laws concerning male's relationship with all other relatives besides parents or sons, 60 slokas; and

(9) laws concerning female's relationship with all other relatives besides parents or sons, 16 slokas.

It is clear that the laws concerned with parent-child relationships (79 slokas in all, the sum of Categories 1, 2, and 3) have far less prominence than those concerned with the guru-pupil relationship (119 slokas, all those in Category 5). When we add laws concerning teacher in conjunction with parents (Category 4) to the sum of slokas concerning parent-child relationship and to the sum of those concerning teacher-pupil relationship, we simply raise the comparative strength of the two relationships correspondingly to 106 and 146. When laws concerning a person's relationship with all other relatives, including nongenetic sons, are taken into consideration, the preeminence of the teacher-pupil relationship as contrasted to other relationships is somewhat toned down but still obvious (155 slokas, the sum of Categories 4, 5, and 7 versus 179 slokas, the sum of Categories 1, 2, 3, 6, 8, and 9). But a majority of the 179 slokas concerned with the relationship between a person and all his relatives consist of definitions of rules governing genetic sons versus nongenetic sons, the splitting of property in different ways, sons of wives of inferior castes versus those of wives of superior castes, etc. Furthermore, in Book XXI, Slokas 83 to 126, the study of Veda and serving the guru together with austerities, knowledge, subjugation of the organs, and abstention from doing injury, are the means by which a Hindu attains Supreme Bliss, while relationship with or serving parents has no comparable place either in this part of the Laws of Manu or anywhere else.[12] Thus while the Chinese tradition put first and foremost obligation to the parents, the Hindu tradition made this obligation neither the first nor the most important.

Let us see how these differing ethical ideals manifest themselves in practice. We shall begin with the wedding. The Chinese wedding is primarily secular in structure and content. The bride and groom perform a "Worship Before Heaven and Earth"; this expression, signifying marriage, is common throughout China. In many parts of the country the bride is also introduced to the ancestors in the family shrine. But the Heaven and Earth worship lasts not more than half an hour and the bride's ceremonial introduction to the ancestral spirits is continuous with and integral to her ceremonial introduction to the living relatives, lineal and lateral. The rest of a Chinese wedding has nothing to do with the gods except in the negative sense that gods and other spirits must not be offended. No priest has any part in the entire wedding.[13] The Hindu wedding, on the other hand, is laden with ritual. Hindu tradition has it that it is the gods who bestow the woman on her husband. With few exceptions, e.g., in the state of Maharashtra, there is a priest for the bride and another for the groom. The rituals, centering upon the starting and burning of the sacred fire, begin shortly after the first guests arrive and continue through the meeting of the bride with the groom. When the guests start to eat, the priests have done less than one-fifth of their work. They continue with their ritual duties. They may even quarrel with each other about the right way to perform a particular item. When the guests have eaten and retired for the night, the priests' work may be still only half done. It continues through the night and into the small hours of the morning. Of course, poorer and lower-caste families with limited financial resources may have the ritual shortened and simplified, but they will often do more than the minimum and certainly more than their resources allow. For many, if not most, families, a marriage results in indebtedness.

According to the ancient saints, the Hindu husband is the god of his wife (grihapati). He is her house lord. No Chinese counterpart of this concept exists at all. There are modern scholars who try to modify the force of this Hindu concept by pointing out that in the code of Manu, the wife's position is high. For example, she could, and in some instances must, make offerings to gods with her husband; and she was considered to be half of the self (husband).[14] But a perusal of the code of Manu indicates that such a sentiment appears as an occasional exception, not the rule. The fact is that the wife's position relative to that of her husband is much lower in the Hindu family than in the Chinese family whether by codified tradition or in actual life, for the simple reason that her activities have as their sole purpose his salvation, while his ritual works are only marginally of benefit to her. The early marriage of girls with mature men (in China, where early marriage occurs it is between young boys and older girls) is probably due, at least in part, to the husband's desire to assure for himself his wife's virginity. Both Chinese and Hindu males had the prerogative of taking more than one wife. But while the Chinese male (kings excepted) was under customary injunction to do so only if he had no heir, the Hindu male was not so restrained. (Concubinage was outlawed in China twenty years ago, and there is similar recent legal prohibition in India.[15]) Furthermore, however badly the husband behaves, he cannot be dethroned from his godship; there are even tales, in South as well as North India, of a devoted wife who, at her husband's command, carried him on her back to the house of his favorite courtesan. There is another episode attributed to the Tamil saint Tiruvalluvar (reputedly the author of the classic *Tirukural*), where the man publicly demonstrated to a friend how blindly obedient his wife was to him. The saint sent for his wife and ordered her, in front of the visitor, to sweep the floor of dirt. His good wife kept sweeping away even though there was not a speck of dirt on it. The question is not whether these stories were historically based; all stories intended to exemplify some principle or other will contain exaggerations, if not outright fabrications. But the fact is that China simply does not have stories in this vein. On the other hand, there are many Chinese stories, fantastic as well as realistic, exemplifying filial devotion and blind obedience of children to their parents.

WIDOWHOOD: CHINESE AND INDIAN CUSTOMS

The greatest differences between the Hindu and Chinese families have yet to be enumerated. There are three and they are interrelated. The first is in the customs as regards widowhood. Among the Chinese, a woman is no less a member of the family of her husband after her husband's death than when he is living. Widow remarriage is discouraged and a widow is enjoined in every way possible to remain with her deceased husband's family. If she has no son, efforts will be made to enable her to adopt one so that her husband's line may be continued. She is honored because she will remain faithful to the dead.

Many a Hindu widow tends gradually to drift out of her dead husband's home. In some instances she drifts back to her natal family, but in other instances she goes to live in a place of pilgrimage such as Brindaban. It can, of course, be demonstrated that some widowed mothers of advanced age are virtual rulers of their households of grown sons and their wives. Gitel Steed reports that the widows of Indrasingh's subcaste group in a Gujarat village had not only a lien on their husband's property but also power over younger persons in matters of discipline.[16] On the other hand, most Hindu widows practice austerity, according to the laws of Manu, by committing themselves to extreme vegetarianism, drab clothes, the observance of numerous fast days and other forms of self-abnegation; it is still not difficult to find widows today, young and old, with shaven heads, though the shaving of the head of a widow is an ancient high-caste usage that is less frequent today than in the past.* Constant devotion to the gods and a total separation from worldly affairs and pleasures are the ancient ideals of a Hindu widow. These usages prevail even among the Coorgs, whose widows remarry as a matter of course, and among whom there is said to be greater equality between the sexes than elsewhere.[17] In carrying out these austerity measures the widow is more likely to use her father's household as a base than the household of her deceased husband, for she no longer really has a place there, especially if her husband died young.

The Chinese and the Hindu share the belief that the widow in some mysterious way is the curse that caused her husband's death. But the difference is that while the Chinese husband's family will try to hold the widow and consolidate her place in it, the Hindu husband's family will make far less effort in that direction, though it will continue to oppose the widow's remarriage, especially if prohibition of widow remarriage enhances its caste status. For according to the laws of Manu, remarriage for widows is an act fitting only for cattle. And according to the same laws, only by austerity and self-sacrifice in her devotion to the gods will she contribute to her deceased husband's spiritual welfare and win a place for herself in the next world near that of the dead man.[18]

GURU AND SAMNYASI

The second of the three great differences between the Chinese and Hindu families concerns the presence in India of the institution of the *guru* and its absence in China. Among the Chinese family members, the problems of the family, individual or common, are supposed to be solved within the family. There is no question of seeking advice from outsiders in preference to some elder within the family or clan. In contrast, the custom of the guru is an old and still-prevalent practice in India. The guru may be roughly described as the personal preceptor who deals in matters usually spiritual, though sometimes today political or occupational as well, and to whom the disciple turns for supernatural (and sometimes worldly) guidance. There is a common notion in India, which has been embodied in a Bengali saying, that the father is a man's first guru. This, however, refers only to the fact that the father is the first teacher, for a guru is more than a mere teacher. He gives his disciple a *mantra*, a formula for his eternal protection, which is kept as a secret known only to donor and recipient. This is never done by the father for his son.

* Today widows with shaven heads are still numerous on temple grounds and among the audiences of scripture-telling sessions carried on by traveling pandits in the villages and the towns.

It is of course difficult to ascertain the proportion of the total population which actually uses this institution. In every part of the country which I visited I saw examples of this guru-disciple relationship; it operates differently among men and women of different castes and socio-economic and educational levels. The guru may be a half-nude holy man in some out-of-the-way shed, and his disciple a young wife from some high-caste family. Or the guru may be an English-speaking gentleman, able to handle a large audience as effectively as Billy Graham, and one of his disciples may be the head of a huge government factory. The shelters of the gurus vary as much as their qualifications and backgrounds. So do the material means and social positions of the disciples. Some gurus visit their disciples once in several years, others once every several months or even more frequently, and there are some disciples who spend all their time with their gurus. Usually the gurus are given the best the disciple-families can offer. They are served like gods, and are paid the utmost attention. The question as to what sort of individual becomes a guru and whether there are any insincere gurus is, of course, interesting, but it has no bearing on the present undertaking. The point is that members of a Hindu family often maintain such intimate extra-familial relationships, regardless of sex differences, age differences, and differences in social status between themselves and their gurus. These gurus counsel the disciples on anything that is important and puzzling to them. In a very genuine sense, they perform the outward role if not the actual function of the family counsellor and the psychoanalyst in America.

The institution of the guru is unthinkable to the ordinary Chinese. It simply has no Chinese counterpart. The teacher-disciple relationship has always been recognized in China but, except in the case of monks and priests, it has had no religious meaning and was designed only for the purpose of learning a specific skill or trade, and therefore it pertained to males only. But even then it neither approached the possible intimacy of the relationship between the Hindu guru and his disciple nor cut across the disciple's family relationship as it does in India.

Related to the guru-disciple custom is the fact that some Hindu men, like Hindu widows, tend to drift away from the family scene as they grow old. In contrast, the Chinese elders keep their family ties forever. According to Hindu theology, the individual's life is divided into four stages. The *brahmacharya*, a man's life before marriage, is a stage when he concentrates on learning and on controlling his instincts and impulses. The *grihastha* is a stage when life has matured and he is married. During this stage he begets children and carries out all sorts of obligations. The *vanaprastha* stage consists of a man's postmarital life when he must cultivate an attitude of detachment and reflection. In *samnyasa*, the last stage, he renounces his worldly goods and relations.[19] A majority of Hindus do not live according to this pattern, and this has probably always been the case; it is possible today to point to Hindus who, like the typical American executive, dread retirement from their active life.*

However, it is not hard to find examples of Hindu men and women in diverse stations of life oriented toward *samnyasa* when they get older. Despite gaps and uncertainty in the records King Bimbisara of the Saisunaga dynasty of South Bihar (522?–494 B.C.) and King Chandragupta Maurya (322–209 B.C.) were probably among those in high places who seem to have become *samnyasin*, in addition to Buddha, who was a prince from a small principality. Besides these I know of at least five other kings who were reported as having retired to ascetic life in old age.[21] Circulating among the people, in newspapers and magazines and by word of mouth, are many stories of this type. Three old grandmothers and one young man in Calcutta told me that they had heard of prominent but remote ancestors who renounced home and family. At least four informants in Delhi gave the same sort of account concerning their relatives. The attractive wife of a successful air force officer in the South told me, while we were en route with her husband to hear a prominent holy man, that she was contemplating eventually leaving home and following the latter after her children grew up.

I have no evidence that this last-mentioned lady was making actual preparations for taking the step she said she would take. It is possible that, since according to Hindu tradition it was the man who was supposed to follow such an ideal, this desire or gesture on the part of this modern educated lady was an expression of her emancipation. Nor can I be sure that all the informants who claimed that their relatives or kinsmen became *samnyasi* were totally accurate. I was unable to check their stories but the fact that some of them made this claim indicates that the *samnyasa* status is an honored one. Nonetheless, even though the fourth phase of life among many Hindus may not be strictly in accordance with the larger Hindu theology, the third phase of life is one in which a man's "main attention is turned toward God—slightly."[22] In the actual history of a Gujarat man, Indrasingh, Steed has shown how he turned from opium-drinking, one form

---

* Indeed, the "ideal four different phases of life" related to Gitel Steed by an influential elder in a Gujarat Hindu village, though similar to the four states given in the sacred books, differed from them especially with reference to the psychological condition of a man in the fourth and last phase of his life:

"During . . . old age all the senses are less strong. Teeth are lost from the mouth and discharges pass through the nose, because there isn't much control of the senses. . . . The ears hear less. . . .

"And the temperament again changes to anger—quite hot. An old man doesn't like anybody else's speaking. . . .

"He always has some disease, so the old man is full of disgust. He instructs people in the house and feels more disgust because no one listens. Old age is absolutely painful. Only a charitable soul can have peace during old age."[20]

of institutionalized retreat, to "goddess-worship which will change a man's past, present, and future," and that, "by other members of Kasandra society, Indrasingh's reactions were not regarded as socially deviant."[23]

On the other hand, in none of the Chinese communities with which I have had any acquaintance as a resident, visitor, or field worker during the course of over thirty years, have I heard any talk about an individual's leaving home in his old age, or found a single example of a respectable and successful citizen who renounced worldly goods and family connections toward the end of life. Taoist priests are as a rule men who take to their jobs as a matter of livelihood; they marry and grow old with their families like everyone else. Monks who forsake their families and become celibate and dwell in monasteries come either from families of low socio-economic status with too many mouths to feed or from the ranks of those who otherwise might have taken to soldiery, a haven in Chinese minds for the disreputable. In different parts of South China I did come across a few elderly widows who devoted some of their waking hours to reciting the scriptures or prayers—not by compulsion, but by preference—but in no case did they leave the worldly affairs of their families alone. Furthermore I know of no Chinese males, outside of the monasteries, who did what Indrasingh of Rajasthan did.

Throughout the lengthy Chinese history there have been some instances in which a successful official of one dynasty refused to serve another, but no such man ever renounced family or even career when he did not have to. The aide to the founder of the Han Dynasty (206 B.C. to 221 A.D.) left his post and disappeared into the forest as soon as the Emperor consolidated his empire. The man was not motivated by supernatural devotion but was merely exercising his remarkable foresight, for other important ministers were eliminated by the ungrateful emperor shortly afterwards because the latter feared possible rivalry for power on the part of his subordinates. Another scholar in the Tsin Dynasty (262–420 A.D.) left his post because he was disgusted with the bowing and scraping of the bureaucracy. He retired to his house and garden, where he wrote a poetic work which brought him great renown.

One may, of course, wonder whether all Hindus who enter *samnyasa* do so purely in quest of supernatural truths or connections, or if there is not often some ulterior motive. In fact, some students suggest that *samnyasa* is an escape from the rigorous oppression of the Hindu caste system. N. K. Bose says:

> The Sannyasin [sic] was put beyond the normal operation of social laws. He was no longer obliged to maintain the sacred fire, which is the householder's first duty. He is no longer under the compulsion of the State's laws, unless, of course, if he comes under the purview of criminal restrictions.

Thus, although Hindu society suppressed the individual under normal conditions, yet the restriction took on a more or less voluntary character, as he could escape from its rigours through the backdoor of the institution of Sannyasa. We may imagine that this safety valve was responsible, to a certain extent, for the stabilization of the Hindu order of society. Those who suffered from a feeling of oppression could escape and leave the organization itself to work as before. Higher castes could enter the Sannyasin's life without trouble. But, if a Vaishya or a Shudra wanted to renounce the world, he had to take special permission of the king. Later on in Indian history, when Vaishnavism and other reformatory sects became popular, the doors were opened wide to the Shudras as well as to women. And thus, in a way, this special arrangement for safeguarding the individual's freedom, acted like a compensation against the totalitarian character of the system of caste. Each helped to render the other more stable and permanent.[24]

Judging by what we know of the ways of mankind, I do not doubt that some Hindu *samnyasin* took on their holy profession for unholy reasons. Anyone who cares to do so can name some American "religious leaders" who entered the ministry for some compelling reason other than to serve God! Not infrequently American businessmen express the view that professors become teachers because they know they could not make it in the tough, competitive business world. There is undoubtedly some truth in these charges against ministers and professors; but it does not change the fact that many American ministers are religiously dedicated servants of God and many American professors are intellectually dedicated scholars. The fact which matters in the case of the Hindu *samnyasa* is that in a culture where gods, spirits, and the Universal Soul are very much part of the consciously inculcated values, far more Hindus than Chinese think of and resort to a religious "escape" from everyday life. Our evidence shows that the few Chinese who think about it and resort to it do so under compulsion. There certainly are no sane modern Chinese women who talk about going *samnyasa* as a gesture of their emancipation. Our evidence also shows that many Hindus who think about it and resort to it do not have to do so at all. The kings and princes who took this path are an effective proof of this.

TREATMENT OF THE DEAD

Funeral and Genealogy

The last great difference between the Chinese and Hindu families is to be found in their respective ways of treating the dead. The Chinese ancestor cult has had a much more elaborate development than the Hindu. In China, death does not sever the family relationship. The dead remain as members of the great family. Their bodies are kept in the house as long as it is financially possible to do so. Their graveyards are taken care of as though they were family compounds. They are welcomed home periodically each year to have reunions with the living and to be present on special occasions. The ancestral shrine, in elaborate or modest style, could be found in a majority of Chinese homes as late as 1949.

In contrast, the Hindu family's relationship with any of its members is almost completely severed at death. The fact that the body of the deceased is taken out of the house with all possible haste may be interpreted as a tropical necessity, but the practical need for the survivors and the house to undergo ritual cleansing from the pollution of death as soon as the dead is on the funeral pyre must be interpreted as partial evidence of the family's desire to part with the dead hastily and permanently. Even if one argues that this ritual is designed to cleanse away the death pollution but not to wash away the relative, one cannot fail to note the obvious similarity between this fear of the pollution of death and the higher castes' fear of pollution by contact with persons of lower castes. Conversely, even though the Chinese are afraid of the pollution of death by unrelated individuals, they are not sensitive to pollution by their own parents and kinsmen.

Among Hindus, genealogical records, though occasionally found in some families, are brief and sketchy. In Gujarat, princes, lesser chieftains, and other persons who wish to rise in caste or social position pay a great deal of attention to genealogy. For regular fees the Vahivancas record the genealogies of their clients up to a certain number of generations, and invent myths and tales to connect humbler lineages or families with more glorious branches, individuals, or heroes of the Mahabharata and Ramayana.[25] This custom of having genealogists serving a number of families is also found among the Balahis, an untouchable caste living in Rajput territories.[26] However, the differences are vast between this situation and the Chinese attitude toward genealogies. In the first place, this great attention to genealogy is confined to Gujarat, and it has no parallel in the rest of India. Most upper-caste families in Bengal (Brahman, Kayastha, Vaidya), and possibly some Brahmans elsewhere, may possess a sort of *kulapanjikas* (family records or commentaries) but they use the document sparingly. In contrast the Chinese interest in genealogy is universal. The poor are, of course, less capable of concretizing this interest than are the rich, but all members of a clan are included in the same kinship genealogical books financed by the rich. The rich are not afraid of kinship links with the poor.

In the second place, even in Gujarat, intensive interest in genealogy is confined to the princely and those with princely aspirations. Among the common people, there is little interest in genealogy, even though they may be aware of some of their illustrious ancestors and the famous events connected with their clan. In the third place, even among these highly placed elements of the population, the primary motivation for keeping the genealogical records is pride in a glorious ancestry (a European pastime, too, sometimes), which is a mechanism for claiming power or wealth or both, and, perhaps more importantly, for avoiding inappropriate marital alliances. But there is no feeling that this keeping of genealogical records is a provision for the ancestral spirits as a matter of filial duty.*

All of this is in sharp contrast to the Chinese interest in genealogy. The Chinese certainly desires a glorious ancestry and also does his best to make his ancestry glorious whenever possible. But throughout China the provision for and the veneration of the departed souls do not appear or vanish, increase or decrease, with the individual's desire to ascend the social scale or to worship some common deity unrelated to the question of his common ancestry. Besides, the Chinese consider genealogy an internal matter within the clan and would never entrust it to the hands of outsiders for recording and for safekeeping, as do the Hindus of Gujarat. The Chinese clan is integral, but the Indian clan can be fabricated.

Shrines and Graveyards

There are other profound differences between the Chinese and the Hindus in this connection. There are usually no tombs for the Hindu dead; there are no cremation grounds or graveyards which belong to particular families; and ancestral shrines are not a common feature in a majority of families. In all of India, there is but the scantiest reference to ancestor worship. And, where it does occur, ancestral spirits figure only slightly.†

* Examples indicating the lack of filial solicitude for ancestors combined nonetheless with a concern for genealogical records are many. Several of them can be briefly given here. (a) The Vahivancas will freely fabricate "names, events, and dates" to bolster up the claim to honorable statuses on the part of some families who can afford fat fees.[27] (b) The Rajputs were the principal clients of Vahivancas but as the "importance of the factual genealogy in the inheritance of property, office, and title" is reduced, they "pay less to the Vahivancas" though they still honor them as priests and for other reasons.[28] (c) The Kolis, because of their desire to claim Rajput lineage and Kshatriya casteship, resorted to the services of Vahivancas for fabricating genealogical links and as an external sign of the Rajput style of life.[29] The Patidars, though highly Sanskritized, patronized Vahivancas when they claimed to be Kshatriyas but have now lost interest in Vahivancas since they now claim to be Baniyas.[30] One additional fact is of interest here. "Though all the patrons of the Vahivancas are not exclusively mata worshippers, the worship of matas forms a significant part of the religious life of most patrons." There is thus a link between Vahivancas and their patrons in mata worship. The partial inverse proof of this is in the fact that Brahman and Baniya castes, which do not patronize Vahivancas, are not mata worshipers.[31]

† There are, of course, several important exceptions. The dead among some Vaishnavats, Coorgs, and certain untouchable castes such as the Balahis of Central India, and many holy men, are entombed. McKim Marriott, in a personal communication, tells that some sort of ancestral representation in family shrines is found in most families in Maharashtrian villages and in about 20% of the families in Uttar Pradesh villages. Among the matrilineal Nayars, each home traditionally contains a room devoted to lineage ghosts

All in all, whether among the Kallar or among the Nayar, in South India, worship of ancestors is neither systematic nor consistent nor important. One can only say that ancestor worship in the south, where reported, is little more than an incidental type of worship such as that seen among some wealthy Marwari widows in Rajasthan and elsewhere, who worship their deceased husbands and sons (each represented by two foot prints) in the family shrines dedicated to the Lord Ganesha and a host of other deities. In many Hindu homes all over India it is possible to find photographs of deceased close relatives hanging on the walls bedecked with garlands.

Whether or not the ghosts of these or other individuals will be "worshiped" in this manner depends strictly upon the feelings or preferences on the part of the living, for there is no definite rule about it. For example,

---

who are supposed to come and sit on the small, low stools on days when offerings are made.[32] Among the Coorgs the compound of each house includes a shrine, at some distance from the main building, devoted to the worship of ancestors. "During the periodical ancestor-propitiations, small figurines representing the ancestors are kept in the shrine and worshipped." In addition, one of the planks affixed to the top of the parapet wall in the veranda of the family home is called the "ancestors" plank and is regarded as sacred. "None may sleep in it."[33] Occasionally single ancestors who had reached special prominence in life would have tombs, crowned with figures of the Nandi Bull, just outside the ancestral shrine.[34]

Yet even these meager practices are not common to the rest of South India, e.g., the City of Madras and its environs, or within the old boundaries of Mysore. In the only scholarly and detailed study of the subcaste Pramalai Kallar of the southern districts in the state of Madras, there is but the scantiest reference to ancestor worship. There is no domestic worship, and ancestral representations occupy only a small fraction of their lineage pantheon. All their lineage temples contain 21 gods or a multiple of that number, such as 63. One example of a lineage pantheon is as follows [compressed by me]:

A. Vegetarian gods:
  1 box, and 12 named gods beginning with Siva, Ishwari, Avadi, and ending with Ganesha.
B. Carnivorous gods:
  1 box, 4 named gods including Virappattra, Tokkili, Sinna, etc.; 1 drum, 1 bull, 2 ancestors, and 1 lamp.[35]

It will be seen that the total is 21 and only 2 ancestors are included in the pantheon in addition. Furthermore, the carnivorous gods, including the ancestors, are all regarded as later accretions, not the originals, and while each box has a priest, the ancestors have none. The circumstances under which these ten carnivorous gods were added to the pantheon must be described as casual.[36] Once a year or sometimes more often the lineage assembles in the temple to celebrate a ritual at common expense, to which Kallars living outside either attend or contribute. Dumont comments on the part of the ancestors in this ritual:

"The ancestors have, or can have, a place in the ritual. A male ancestor is never the principal deity of a temple, there may or may not be one among the *accessory* deities [italics mine]; often it is a couple: an ancestor and his wife. In a temple where such is the case, there is even disagreement as to the identity of the ancestor who is represented as a warrior or a plinth, as often happens. In the same way, the ancestors are sometimes confused with the real deities, sometimes fully distinguished."[37]

There is no domestic shrine for ancestors or anyone else, and there is no private cemetery or cremation ground.

the Marwari widow's worship of her husband and son is not shared by her other sons or other males of the house.

By way of contrast the Chinese universally make representations of the ancestral souls in a shrine in their family homes and worship them regularly. The well-to-do will attempt to include in this worship as many lineal ancestors as they possibly know of. The poorer families will worship their ancestors at least up to the third ascending generation. This worship is the definite and regular duty of all the living, male and female, adult and child. In the matter of tombs and graveyards the contrast is even more spectacular. Throughout China, all persons who reached puberty before death are entombed. Any family or clan which is financially capable of doing so has a family or clan graveyard that is attended to as though it were the yard of a regular house. In fact, the Chinese differentiate between three types of graveyards. First, public graveyards where descendantless, unknown, or poor persons are buried by charity without regard to family or clan. These are dangerous places, to be assiduously avoided by everyone whenever possible. Second, family or clan graveyards not one's own. These are not dangerous but are not to be visited by members of other families or clans except for special reasons, such as by invitation. Third, the graveyards belonging to one's own family and clan. This is spoken of as a family's "other-worldly residence," in contrast to its living quarters, which is its "this-worldly residence."

The Hindus, for their part, maintain no such relationship with the cremation grounds or tombs of their own dead. There are only two kinds of Hindu interest in the cremation grounds. Some Hindus believe that they are the abodes of ghosts and sites for performing black magic. If possible, therefore, they are to be avoided by all except the magicians. This is perfectly consistent with the psychology of the Coorgs, the only group in India among whom the cremation or burial grounds of the dead have any particular connection with their families. Among the Coorgs, a part of the ancestral estate is used for burying or cremating the dead members of the *okka* (joint family). They differentiate between the part used for burial and its adjoining part used for cremation by two different terms. But these grounds are sacred "in an undesirable way: The term 'bad-sacred' has been used to denote such a ritual condition. (Bad-sacredness includes within itself both 'defilement and inauspiciousness.') *A visit to the burial-ground defiles a person and a bath is necessary to restore him to normal ritual status.*"[38] [Italics mine.]

The other kind of Hindu interest concerns the cremation grounds of national heroes such as Gandhi and Tagore, and of local characters such as women who have committed *sati*. These will become shrines of public worship but not, as they would be among the Chinese, the sole concern of the descendants of the dead person. In fact, I doubt if their descendants have either a special claim to them or interest in them. The latter type of interest also attaches to the individual tombs of Hindu holy men or Moslem holy men (*pirs*) scattered throughout the country. These are destinations of numerous Hindu (sometimes Moslem) pilgrims who pray for specific benefits.

Ritual Relationship with Ancestors

Finally, the Chinese and the Hindus differ in the extent to which each people maintains a continuous relationship with the dead. Regularly, at least twice a year, Chinese invite their ancestral spirits to return to their homes for a grand reunion at the mid-year and again at the end of the year. Once a year, in early spring, it is the custom for members of the Chinese family, old and young, male and female, to visit the family or clan graveyard with food and drink, and there to have a picnic with the dead. The food and drink are first offered to the dead in a ritual and then eaten by the living in the graveyard. On irregular occasions, when marriage or division of family property occurs, ancestral spirits will be notified or invoked as witnesses or judges in the lot drawing. When new corn or grains first come in season, most families will offer a little of them to the ancestral spirits before partaking of them themselves. These practices may vary somewhat from region to region, but this picture in its outline is, to the best of my knowledge, true of all Chinese (excluding Chinese Mohammedans).

Except among the Coorgs and the Nayars, there are few occasions on which the Hindu dead are welcomed back home among the living descendants. On the contrary, in most parts of the country rituals are performed which expressly compel the souls of the dead not to return. These rituals are directed not only against the return of malevolent spirits who might harbor jealousy and ill will toward the living but against all spirits of the dead. As the *Garuda Purana* puts it:

> Not yet tired of life, being cared for by his dependents, with his body deformed through old age, nearing death, in the house,
> He remains, like a house-dog, eating what is ungraciously placed before him, diseased, with failing digestion, eating little, moving little,
> Lying encircled by his sorrowing relatives; though being spoken to he does not answer, being caught in the noose of death.
> Wealth, sons, wife and family, body, kinsmen—all these are transitory. Therefore righteousness should be sought, so long as a man is alive he has a father and other relatives; but when they have known him to be dead, their affection soon fades away.
> He should constantly remember that the true kinsman of the self is the Self. If not to the living, much less will anyone give to the dead.

The relatives turn away with averted faces leaving the dead body on the
ground, like a lump of wood or earth, but righteousness goes with him.

Like creatures in a water tank, and like the motion of sticks in a river is one's
contact with mother, father, son, brother, kinsman, wife and others.

Whose are the sons, and the grandsons? Whose is the wife, or the wealth? In
the world of change nobody belongs to anybody. Therefore one should
make gifts himself.* [39]

In most parts of India there is a ritual worship of the ancestral spirits once
a year. This is *mahalaya*, occurring on the new moon day around the month
of October. Then the eldest son of the dead goes to the sea or to a river,
lake, or pond to offer water, food, and flowers to the ancestors. But this is
done only by the eldest living son, not by the other children; secondly, ancestors who benefit by this offering are limited to only a few recent dead
(others are not excluded but are not usually recalled by name); and thirdly,
the same offering is also made to other close relatives and even in some instances to friends. This picture is true of Bengal, Orissa, Uttar Pradesh,
Maharashtra, Madras, and Mysore, with some local variation in detail. In
Shamirpet of Hyderabad (now Andhra Pradesh) Dube reports that the
day of the water offering to ancestral spirits is called *petramasa* and occurs
on the last day of the dark half of the Hindu month corresponding to
August-September, and may be preceded by about two weeks of ritual
activity performed in memory of the ancestors if the family is well-to-do
and if there has been a recent death in the family.[40] In Uttar Pradesh and
Maharashtra, McKim Marriott reports that on this occasion a big feast takes
place in the house of the well-to-do, and that outside the house offerings
are made. Stephen Fuchs, among others, has observed of the untouchable
caste of Balahis of Central India, that an offering to the "deceased forebears
and relatives" is made during the *diwali* (Hindu Festival of Lights in which
the goddess Lakshmi is especially worshiped), which is celebrated among
them on the 14th of Kartik (October), two weeks after the Mahalaya.[41]

Deviations from this general picture are found among the Coorgs and
the matrilineal Nayars. Among the Coorgs, Srinivas reports, "during festi-
vals like harvest festival, and at marriage," and certain other fixed and
recurrent calendar days, food and drink are offered to the ancestors. There
are also other occasions "when the dishes cooked in the house are offered
to the ancestors before the members themselves partake of them."[42] Among
matrilineal Nayars of the Malabar Coast, dead legal guardians (*karanavan*)

---

* The *Garuda Purana*, which is the Hindu scripture used by the priests at funerals, had
1,274 slokas (entries) in the edition used here. It is interesting to note that of the sins
enumerated, sixteen slokas have to do with ill-treatment, disrespect and neglect of Brahmans but only five of parents and siblings, two of other relatives, and four of husbands
and wives.

or the eldest man of a joint ancestral household (*taravad*) (which E. Kathleen Gough termed lineage segment) of three or four to ten or more generations back are individually represented by low stools in shrines within the family courtyard and individually worshiped on the new moon day of two calendar months a year.[43] Gough rightly pointed out a certain similarity in significance between the Nayar cult of the dead and the Chinese ancestor cult: "The head of a family must care for his patrilineal descendants because it is part of his duty to the ancestors to provide happy and prosperous offspring."[44] However, even the Nayar cult is so much in the Hindu model that its basic differences from the Chinese far outweigh its similarities. The Nayars worship only their male ancestors who held the position of elder, while the Chinese worship all their ancestors, males who were born into the family and females who were married into it. The Nayars, especially the commoners, tend to worship only the ghosts of selected elders who are noted for some special achievement, while the Chinese treat even their humblest ancestors with the same ritual attention, albeit magnifying or even fabricating some of their achievements. Then, Nayar worship of selected ancestors often accompanies the worship of other deities associated with the kinship group such as Bhagavadi or Bhadrakali, while the Chinese worship of ancestors stands out by itself, and is never combined or shared with worship of other supernatural beings. The fact that the devout Hindu will perform water, food, and floral offerings daily to the sun or to one or another of the gods in or out of his home should confirm a fairly clear impression of the relative unimportance Hindus attach to their departed family members. It is perfectly true that the daily offering by Brahmans includes "ancestors" with the gods, but they are usually the *pravaras*, mythological progenitors; or gurus rather than actual ancestors.

In the final analysis, a Chinese will view his own ancestors as permanently distinct entities specifically related to him. The ancestral spirits may be meritorious so that they become officials in Heaven but they are still ancestors of the individual Chinese. The merits or demerits of the ancestors will be reflected in the prosperity or misery of their descendants, just as the conduct of the latter is deemed to have an effect on the welfare of the living and departed forebears. In India, certain literature indicates that in ancient times the Hindus entertained the notion that the sin of one individual would be visited upon his son or his grandson. But some statements conflicted with others, and the picture of the relationship between the living and the dead is neither convincing nor clear.[45] What impresses the student of Hindu society today is the fact that a Hindu, in contrast to a Chinese, considers his departed ancestors as having achieved the best fate when they have reached the ideal goal of all Hindus: a merging with the great Atma, the one undifferentiated Universal Soul.

Benevolence versus Malevolence

This leads us to the most fundamental difference between Indian and Chinese ancestor cults. The Indian ancestral ghosts may be benevolent to their descendants but they are also feared, even in Nayar and Coorg lands where the cult seems most in evidence. They are feared as sources of terrible punishments for offences ranging from inhospitality to guests and neglect of property, to failure to propitiate the ancestral ghosts. Among the Nayars, as reported by Gough:

> A Karanavan who amassed much property is most likely to resent extravagance on the part of his successors. Forebears who died prematurely are more punitive than those who died peacefully in old age. All ghosts, however, are somewhat capricious: a small offense may provoke stern retribution, and misdemeanors on the part of one adult may result in the sickness of another or of a child of the property group. In particular, a forebear who is injured or insulted by his juniors during life or after his death may wreak vengeance on the Taravad (lineage segment) even down to the seventh or eighth generation.[46]

It can be stated unequivocally that ancestral spirits, in every part of China, are believed to be only a source of benevolence, never a source of punishment to their own descendants. This is shown by the fact that when the Chinese is suffering from some misfortune, such as sickness or fire or flood or the lack of male progeny, he will suspect that the fault lies with any of a variety of deities or ghosts, but never with the spirits of an ancestor. The following episode from Hankow, which occurred in 1932, could be duplicated in any part of China.

> A Mr. T., instructor in mathematics in a missionary college in Hankow, died at the age of 25 of a stomach operation in a hospital. The illness was curable but the incompetence or the negligence on the part of the English missionary doctor made his case hopeless. He was survived by a widow, a daughter and two sons. One year after his death, his older son was struck by an eye condition which endangered the boy's vision. When medication failed to improve it, the widow consulted a female seer. The latter reported that the boy was struck by some supernatural wind, but he would recover from it, though with some damage to his vision, because his deceased father appealed to the deity to let his boy off and the deity had agreed to it. The seer offered, as proof of the authenticity of her connection with the other world, to describe to the widow the appearance of her deceased husband's spirit. Amongst other personal details she mentioned that the spirit was in chains. Hankow, as in the rest of China, believes that the soul of a person who dies prematurely or before his destined longevity expires turns into a grievous and embittered ghost who will vent his anger on innocent human beings. Hence such spirits have to be restrained with chains.

The most interesting feature of this episode, from the point of view of our present discussion, is the fact that the belief in the grievous state of mind of such a spirit has not affected people's belief in the benevolent relationship between the ancestors and their descendants. Such a grievous spirit will do harm to human beings unrelated to him but never to his own children. Consequently, when a Chinese wishes to propitiate the supernatural which might be the cause of any of his misfortunes, he will not include his ancestral spirits as objects of his propitiation. Only deities and ghosts who have no kinship relationship with him are so pacified. The most dramatic revelation of the Chinese attitude toward their ancestral spirits is seen in their efforts to deal with epidemics. The Chinese, when confronted with such disasters, believe in leaving no stone unturned. Yet, while every imaginable variety of gods and spirits and ghosts are appealed to and propitiated, the ancestral spirits do not figure in the rituals at all* [47] The Chinese simply do not believe that their own departed ancestors would be the voluntary cause of their troubles.

The psychological significance of these differences between the Indian and Chinese is far-reaching. It is obvious that the relatively few Hindus who consider their departed ancestors to be capricious, jealous, or in need of propitiation, have at best a precarious relationship with the dead, while the Chinese, who take their ancestors' benevolence and care for granted, enjoy a far greater degree of security and solidarity with them. The Hindus may experience as much parental love and indulgence as the Chinese, but for them death changes the parental and other ancestral images into alienated and hazy spirits who become actually dangerous. In the case of the Chinese, death does not alter or sever the permanent nature of the relationship at all.

Thus the difference between the supernatural-centeredness of the Hindu way of life and the situation-centeredness of the Chinese way of life is evident in the two family systems analyzed: in the philosophical basis of the family; in the marriage ceremony; in the husband-wife relationship; in the relationship of the widow with her deceased husband's family; in the institution of the guru; in the attitude toward old age; and in ancestor worship. Since the Chinese family is bound together by ties which even death

* As an example, in 1942, a cholera epidemic broke out in "West Town" (pseudoname) and numerous other areas of southwest China (known to the Western world then as "Free China"). Among the 8000 people of "West Town" the ravages of this epidemic lasted about a month and took a heavy toll. There was no doubt that the population was frightened and anxious to do its utmost to reduce and eliminate the danger. They used indigenous medicines and modern precautions at the same time. They distributed literature on morality. They abstained from a wide variety of foods including meat. With thousands of dollars from public contribution, they staged a series of nineteen public prayer meetings which lasted from one day and one night to six days and seven nights. These were complicated affairs involving a number of hired priests, musicians, pandals, processions, offerings, sacrifices, and so on. But their ancestral spirits were not appealed to on this occasion at all. The "West Town" pattern of relationship with ancestral spirits was typical of all China.

cannot sever, every interaction of the family is governed by a sense of the duties and obligations which each member feels towards the others. But the interactions within a Hindu family tend to be basically governed by supernatural or nonworldly considerations which give primary importance to gods other than those of the family's own ancestry. It is obvious that the Hindu pattern is affected by caste differences—between the Brahmans on the one hand, and the Kshatriyas and the rest on the other—just as the Chinese pattern is also affected by class differences—between the literati-officials on the one hand and the rest of the Chinese on the other. In the case of the Hindus, the Brahmans may give more visible evidence of their interest in the supernatural than do the members of other castes, but, as the facts show, even the other Hindus are much more affected by priests, sacred books, and pilgrimages than are the Chinese. Any Chinese man who spent most of his time worshiping goddesses in the way that Indrasingh of Gitel Steed's Gujarat village does would simply be regarded as extremely queer, if not plainly insane. Conversely, the Chinese literati-officials will be more ostentatiously dutiful to their ancestors and the big family ideal than will their brethren in lower stations of life, although the latter will lose no time in copying the former as soon as their financial situation improves. But both groups will have far less concern than the Hindus with priests, sacred books, and pilgrimages.

In content the Chinese family has greater cohesion and greater continuity than the Hindu family. The bonds of the Chinese family members are unbreakable, but the ties among the Hindu family members are much more tenuous and ephemeral, though stronger than among their western counterparts. To the Chinese his first and last duty is to his forebears and his descendants; while to the Hindu, his obligations to the gods and certain strangers (sages and holy men) take precedence over his obligations to all others. The supernatural-dominated events from marriages to sradhas do bring relatives together so that kinship bonds are renewed from time to time, but the central orientation of the society is unmistakable.

FROM STRUCTURE TO CONTENT

At the beginning of this chapter, I pointed out that the similarities between Chinese and Hindu kinship systems are primarily structural while their differences are primarily a matter of content. But structure and content, rather than merely complementing each other as separate entities, actually imply each other. In the kinship system of many a society one structural relationship is elevated above others. When this occurs it becomes demonstrable that other relationships are not only reduced in importance but greatly modified in their characteristics so that the total influences of the kinship system on the individuals reared in it are greatly determined by the inherent attributes of the dominant structural relationship. In other words, the inherent attributes of the elevated kinship relationship in each system, when magnified, are found to correlate with its kinship content.[48]

In spite of their general structural similarities, the central structural relationship which dominates the Chinese family is not that which dominates its Hindu counterpart. Among the Chinese the father-son relationship has the upper hand. Among the Hindus the mother-son relationship has the commanding importance. This difference in their dominant structural relationships is at the root of differences in their respective kinship contents, which express themselves in the total Chinese situation-centered way of life, characterized by mutual dependence among men, and the Hindu supernatural-centered way of life, characterized by the seeking of and dependence upon spiritual powers.

The importance of the father-son relationship in the Chinese family system is obvious in ideal and in practice, and needs no elaboration, but the prominence of the mother-son relationship in the Hindu situation occurs less by design and more by practice. In the Laws of Manu, as we have seen before, the father-son and mother-son relationships, next to the guru-pupil relationship, are treated unequally, except for an occasional sloka which elevates the mother's position far above that of the father and of the teacher. The real importance of the mother-son relationship over father-son relationship is a result—an unintended result—of the actual circumstances of life.

It is obvious that the Hindu culture, even more than the Chinese culture, is male-oriented. The males are the primary beneficiaries or sufferers in Hindu scriptures and ritual practices. Females seem primarily to have the role of accumulating spiritual merits for men, though they have no part in the major rituals of any worship. The ideal four stages (*ashramas*) of life which every individual should pass through—*brahmacharya* (studentship), *grihastha* (life of the married man), *vanaprastha* (life of the disinterested hermit, in which familial ties and social relations are renounced), and *samnyasa* (life of the ascetic)—do not apply to women.

Yet, despite the male-centered nature of Hindu culture the mother-son relationship attains far greater importance than other kinship relationships for the following reason. First, in the Hindu household adult males and females are much more segregated from each other than in the Chinese household. The higher the caste and the socio-economic status, the more the family tends to approximate complete segregation. Male children, before puberty or adolescence, tend therefore to be under the protective and guiding hands more of females, such as mothers and grandmothers and other females, than of fathers and grandfathers and other males. This seems not only to be the case of individuals like Indrasingh (reported by Gitel Steed)[49] who grew up in his mother's village because his father passed away when he was fifteen months old, but also in the case of numerous other men. G. Morris Carstairs reports the following picture in his Rajasthan village:

> Although it is particularly through his participation in the adult male world of caste and family discussion that a child receives the imprint of his community's values, the process has begun even before this, during his earliest years when he spent more time in the women's side of the household than in the men's. Brahmans commonly mentioned that it was their mother, or their grandmother, who first impressed upon them the need to bathe if they touched a low-caste person, until the response became second nature to them. It is women also who give a boy his early toilet training. . . . From his mother and his substitute mothers, a boy also learns how and what to eat, how to dress, what constitutes good manners and what is to be avoided as indecent or shameful.
>
> From his mother, grandmothers and aunts, a child learns the concrete details of religious observance at all the multitude of holy days in the calendar. . . . A part of the experience of every child in Deoli is to be taken by his mother to a bhopa when he is sick. . . .
>
> The child's sources of verbal instruction can now be viewed as a series of concentric circles, the innermost representing the women's world; then that of the extended family in which his father, if he himself is a younger son, may seem to play a minor part.[50]

A second element in the picture is already suggested by the concluding sentence in the last quotation: the relationship between Hindu fathers and their sons is less close than that between their Chinese counterparts. Elsewhere Carstairs more clearly states the lack of a close relationship between the Hindu father and his son.[51] Mrs. Gardner Murphy observes in her chapter on "Roots of Tolerance and Tensions in Indian Child Development" that Hindu children "are carried easily, first in cradled arms which do not grasp them possessively. . . . later they straddle a hip of a sister or a brother, father or mother, balancing comfortably. . . ."[52] My own observation is that a child may be carried in this way most frequently by a mother or sister, but less frequently by a young brother, and especially rarely by a father of high caste. Part of the reason, I think, is the Hindu male's strong aversion to pollution by the bodily functions of infants and children. But another part of the reason is that the Hindu fathers are also likely to be preoccupied with some aspect of the ritual activities, such as pilgrimage, designed to bring them closer to their deities or the Truth.

It is not alleged that all Hindus live strictly according to the injunctions of the ancient scriptures, any more than it can be said that all Americans live strictly according to the spirit of the Declaration of Independence and the Christian concept of turning the other cheek. But many Americans have undoubtedly been motivated by the high principles which form part of their heritage; just so, among Hindus, and not among Japanese, Chinese, or Germans, we find hundreds of thousands of devout human beings living in asceticism or penance, up in the Himalayas and other centers of pilgrimage. The great popularity of such a leader as Gandhi, with his supernatural-centered philosophy and ascetic practices, is unique to Hindu India. Therefore even though many Hindu fathers do not leave their homes to become hermits and ascetics as they grow old, most of them cannot but be affected in many ways by or attracted to their religious ideal and practices, especially away from home. Furthermore, my personal observation and Dr. Steed's show that it is not at all necessary for the Hindu to be aged to turn to seclusion and gods. Indrasingh, whom we have met in a previous paragraph, a man twenty-six years old with two wives but no children, turned from opium-smoking, one form of institutionalized retreat, to "goddess-worship which will change a man's present and future." Yet, "by other members of Kasandra society, Indrasingh's reactions were not regarded as socially deviant."[53]

Whatever the cause, the lack of a close relationship between the Hindu father and son is also evident from other sources. Dube's description of a Hyderabad village confirms Carstairs' findings except that it is more cursory.[54] In an informal inquiry among fifty-seven families* in Calcutta, West Bengal, Bangalore, Mysore State, and Delhi, I found at least one-fifth of the men with children who, at age forty, approximately, conducted themselves in a way more or less similar to Indrasingh, or left home now and then on long pilgrimages. Some, like an important educational official of Bangalore, made minor pilgrimages to places nearby before engaging in an extended pilgrimage to Badrinath in the Himalayas as a once-in-a-lifetime experience. Others had made several long pilgrimages to Nasik, Benares, Puri, and the like, while still in their mid-thirties. Five of my informants in these three groups reported distant uncles or grandfathers who had left home in "old age" to become *sannyasin*. It is not that Hindu women are less devout. But the worshiping activities of most wives and mothers tend to be at home or nearby where their children are usually on hand.

It remains for us to explain the link between, on the one hand, the importance of the father-son relationship and the Chinese situation-centered way of life characterized by mutual dependence, and on the other, the prominence of the mother-son relationship and the Hindu's supernatural-centered way of life characterized by reliance upon higher powers.

Two of the elementary attributes of the father-son relationship are continuity and inclusiveness. Each father-son relationship is a link in an endless chain of father-son relationships. For every father is a son and every son will, in the normal course of events, be a father. Enmeshed in a network of

* Including the forty-eight families mentioned in Chapter II, in which I studied the parent-child relationship in some detail.

continuous relationships, the individual is conditioned to orient himself first lineally and second collaterally within a well-defined group; he is naturally the product of his forebears before him as he is automatically the progenitor of his descendants yet to come. His position in that line is specific and inalienable. And his rewards and obligations as well as prestige and power are very much linked with his place, his situation in the closely knit and inalienable group. The continuity of the father-son relationship is as basic as its inclusiveness. The latter expresses itself vertically and horizontally. Vertically each father-son relationship is a necessary link in a chain connecting lineal descendants already born or yet to be born. Horizontally it is the model against which are measured attitudes, duties, and obligations toward all agnatic male kinsmen and their wives in the ascending or descending generations. In this web of kinship the individual has no freedom, for he is hedged in on all sides. But he also has little fear of being left out, for he can count on help from all sides, just as he is expected to give help.

The most important attribute of the father-son relationship is its *mutual* dependence. Superficially, the relationship seems to be one-sided; namely, sons owe much more to their fathers than their fathers to them. In reality the obligations are quite mutual. The son owes his father all sorts of services—unquestioned obedience, extreme respect, complete support in life as in death. But the father, on his part, owes the son marital arrangement, protection, and all his inheritance. The ideal son is sensitive to every whim on the part of his father. The father's every wish is his command. But the ideal father takes every precaution to see that his sons are well married, well educated, well connected, and well provided for. Death and torture are often endured willingly by sons and fathers in fulfilling some of these obligations. The mother, by virtue of her marriage to the father, her assumption of his clan membership, and the biological relationship with the son, is an integral part of this core relationship: whatever is due to the father is equally due to the mother, except that she is not expected to have the means to support her son. Starting from this basic father-son relationship, similar obligations extend both vertically and horizontally to the forebears of past generations and descendants yet unborn, as well as to collateral relatives of many degrees of nearness.

Like the father-son relationship, that between mother and son is inclusive, though not to the same extent. There is usually more than one son, and there is the perpetual desire on the part of the parents for more than one son. In Asia, high infant mortality is especially conducive to the usually conscious feeling that there is security in numbers. But, unlike the father-son relationship, the mother-son axis is discontinuous. No mother is a son and no son is a mother. A mother-son relationship is not, therefore, a link in a chain of a continuous mother-son line. The basic attribute which distinguishes the mother-son relationship from the father-son relationship, however, is its *unilateral* dependence (instead of *mutual* dependence).

An infant after birth is undifferentiated in its reaction to its surroundings, whether human, animal, or material. Watson, reporting the studies of Bridges, states that the emotional differentiations in the infant begin at about three weeks of age "when distress characterized by muscular tension, trembling, crying, and checked breathing can be distinguished from excitement" in general.[55] The mother-son relationship begins essentially with complete emotional and physical dependence of the son on the mother. As the infant grows in years he learns more and more to differentiate between persons, things, and ideas, as well as between different persons, different things, and different ideas. Paralleling these developments, there is another one. With differentiation of stimuli into categories, the infant finds that some categories are translatable, or more nearly so, into each other while others are absolutely immutable. For example, a toy cat and a toy dog are far more easily translatable into each other, from the point of view of the child, than a toy cat and an actual cat. For some time a toy dog and an actual dog may be the same to a child, but as he grows, he will perceive a greater separation between inanimate and animate things than between two animate or two inanimate things. Similarly as he gains in his power of perception there will be a point when he becomes aware of the differences between a toy cat and a toy dog, even though this pair will remain more translatable into each other than a toy cat and an actual cat. For some time baby sitters are likely to be translatable into each other. As the child becomes more used to one baby sitter than another, he may develop a preference for one over the other; thus some baby sitters are, for him, no longer translatable into others. But in the majority of cases, the younger the infant the more dependent he is upon his mother (since she is the answer to all his troubles and needs) and the more all categories of stimuli which come to him are translatable into each other (or mutable).

In the Chinese family, where the father-son relationship sets the tone, the son comes into close and continuous contact with his father and other adult males fairly soon; he early gains a good measure of the realities of life—that feelings, goods, and services have a way of circulating instead of going in any one direction and that their circulation is governed by rules depending upon gradation and their differentiation. In India, where the mother-son relationship is strong, and where the son keeps a close contact with the mother and other females until he is much older than is usual among the Chinese, the individual tends to be conditioned toward retaining more of the feeling for receiving than for giving (i.e., for greater desire for unilateral than mutual dependence), as well as toward retaining a thought pattern of greater mutability among categories of stimuli than the actualities of life would warrant. A high feeling for unilateral dependence and a high feeling for mutability among stimuli reinforce each other. The more the individual is conditioned to one-sided dependence, the more the object of dependence becomes an answer to all problems, the more all events and needs and rewards will be translatable into each other.

Unilateral dependence and a high degree of mental mutability of all phenomena are two of the most basic elements of any true supernatural orientation. The gods are overwhelmingly powerful, and humans, in order to receive protection and help, can only submit to them, or at best only invoke them by wile. The magic of the gods can change air into water, lead into gold, one into many, man into beast; in other words, the mutability of all into one or one into all.

It is impossible, of course, to determine whether the kinship content of supernatural-dependence or the structural elevation of the mother-son relationship came first. Elsewhere I observed that this is a spiral type of relationship; that given the cultural tradition of supernatural-dependence, the importance of the mother-son relationship generates the appropriate psychological characteristics in the individual for it, and the psychological characteristics, in turn, strengthen the tradition.[56] Ramakrishna, the greatest Hindu saint in modern times, asked: "Why does the God-lover find such pleasure in addressing the deity as Mother?" And he answered himself: "Because the child is more free with its mother, and consequently she is dearer to the child than anyone else."[57]

Sister Nivedita, one of Ramakrishna's European disciples (M. E. Noble) who remained a pillar of the Vedanta movement after the death of the master, related the following episode and sentiment:

> Shortly after her arrival in Calcutta, she heard a cry in a quiet lane. Following her ears, she traced it to a little Hindu girl who lay in her mother's arms dying. The end came soon, and for a while the mother wept inconsolably. After a while she fell back into Sister Nivedita's arms and turning to her said: "Oh, what shall I do? Where is my child now?" I have always regarded that as the moment when I found the key, says Sister Nivedita. Filled with a sudden pity, not so much for the bereaved woman as for those to whom the use of some particular language of the Infinite is a question of morality, I leaned forward. "Hush, mother," I said, "Your child is with the Great Mother. She is with Kali." And for a moment, with memory stilled, we were enfolded together, Eastern and Western, in the unfathomable depth of consolation of the World Heart.[58]

The complete dependence of the child upon the mother is a universal human fact. To the child, the mother is the magical source of all power, gratification, and punishment. This is the psychology that makes the widespread appeal of the creation story in Genesis of the Old Testament or other forms possible. In the Chinese system this mother-dependence is soon tempered by the authority of the father, father surrogates, and numerous male seniors, peers, and juniors, and later drastically curbed by the individual's integration into a network of specific human relationships, with specific duties, responsibilities, and privileges vis-à-vis forebears, including deceased ancestors, and descendants both born and unborn. The adult individual's place in the scheme of things is measured by concrete points of reference, and no longer submerged under the undifferentiated power of the mother. In Chapters IX and X we shall see how in the American society the culturally sanctioned demand for independence from parents, self-reliance in food and sex quest, and ability to make individual decisions and bear consequences makes it impossible for a majority of Americans psychologically to leave anything to God. It is only in a mother-son relationship which dominates a kinship system that a true desire for reliance upon the supernatural can be nurtured and made to flourish.

The contrast between the Chinese situation-centered orientation of mutual dependence and the Hindu supernatural-centered orientation of unilateral dependence is, therefore, not merely that the former implies greater reciprocity while the latter is more one-sided, but also that the dependence in the former is restricted to well-defined channels and limits while that in the latter is more all-embracing (since experiences are more mutable) and hence more diffused. The rule book in the Chinese system stipulates that every act of receiving means an obligation to return, and it means also that since human beings are parties to the exchange, there are concrete measures to determine the estimated equivalence or nonequivalence between values received and values repaid.

The rule book in the Hindu system, like rule books in all human societies, also must necessarily stipulate a degree of reciprocity, and "repayment of obligations" is in fact not a rare consideration in Hindu day-to-day patterns of thought. But when the individual's ultimate reliance is dependence upon the supernatural, there are no concrete measures for determining the estimated equivalence or nonequivalence between values received and values repaid. The worshiper-dependent can expect much more from the gods than he gives to the gods. With a high degree of feeling for mutability of all things, the worshiper-dependent can also demand simple boons to solve all problems, however difficult. Finally, when demands or supplication fail, the strongest step on the part of the worshiper-dependent is extreme passivity, fasting, abstention, and other forms of austerity, regardless of the reasonableness of the desired object or solution as measured by realistic human capabilities.

NOTES FOR CHAPTER III

1. Francis L. K. Hsu, "Structure, Function, Content and Process," *American Anthropologist*, LXI, No. 5, Part 1 (October 1959), 790–805.

2. M. N. Srinivas, "Introduction," in *India's Villages* (Development Department

of West Bengal Government, 1955), pp. 10–11. This is a reprint of articles originally published in different issues of *The Economic Weekly of Bombay* between October 1951 and May 1954.

3. About a quarter of the population on the Malabar Coast practice matrilineal inheritance. In Bengal, the property accumulated by the father's own efforts, as distinguished from property inherited from ancestors, was the father's alone to dispose of. Recent legislation (1956) has given Bengal the same law as the rest of India, except that the Malabar Coast remains outside the general pattern.

4. Among the poor and lowly in both societies, widows remarry as a matter of course. In some parts of North India, as among the Coorgs of the South, remarriage of widows and levirate are both common. For Coorgs, see M. N. Srinivas, *Religion and Society Among the Coorgs of South India* (Oxford: Oxford University Press, 1952), p. 48 ff. In China levirate sometimes takes place among the poor by convenience but not by custom.

5. *Mahabharata*, quoted by Haran Chandra Chakladar, "Social Life in Ancient India," in *The Cultural Heritage of India*, Sri Ramakrishna Centenary Memorial (Calcutta), Vol. III, p. 206.

6. *Brahmavaivarta, Ganapatikhanda*, Chap. XL, according to Vasishtha, quoted in *The Cultural Heritage of India, op. cit.*, p. 206.

7. The reader who is familiar with the American family but not with the Chinese family may have difficulty in grasping the Hindu-Chinese differences to be demonstrated in the following pages, especially since the evidence adduced is primarily qualitative. Such a reader may get the impression that the Hindu family pattern is quite similar to that of the Chinese when both of them are contrasted to that of the American, when in fact the purpose of this chapter is to show that differences between the Chinese and Hindu families are as basic as the differences between the Chinese and American families. This difficulty may be materially reduced by a reading of two chapters of the book, *Americans and Chinese: Two Ways of Life* (New York: Abelard-Schuman, 1953) (Chapters III and IV) referred to before.

8. *Ashramas* are the idealized four stages of life which every individual is supposed to go through from childhood to death. The first stage consists of learning, especially learning the *Vedas*.

9. Irawati Karve, *Kinship Organization in India* (Poona: Deccan College Monograph Series, 1953), p. 70.

10. *The Laws of Manu*, translated by G. Bühler (Ofxord: Clarendon Press, 1886), Book II, Sloka 145, pp. 56–57.

11. *Ibid.*, Book II, Slokas 147–148, p. 57. Also Book II, Slokas 225–233 (II 233 expresses the same sentiment as II 148).

12. *Ibid.*, The criteria which guided our analysis of the Laws are as follows (The analysis was primarily done by Vaughan Stapleton):

CRITERIA FOR ANALYSIS OF LAWS OF MANU

(1) Each count refers to a specific sloka except where a sloka is indubitably part of a preceding one. In the latter event the two or more slokas are counted as one. These are put in parentheses.

(2) Rituals performed for small children by the whole family are excluded from our total count except where father or mother performs a specific act.

(3) In Sraddhas (rites to the dead), only specific acts involving sons and/or heirs are counted. The slokas concerning *manes* are excluded because the latter

are defined in the Laws of Manu as sons of ancient sages who begot the gods (III 194–201).

(4) The chapter dealing with the king and his duties is excluded from our total count.

(5) In Book VIII, on repayment of debts after death, an heir is counted as a son, since this is noted first in slokas 159–160 of Book VIII.

(6) All paragraphs dealing with inheritance-father-mother-son relationships are to be included; naturally the teacher does not enter into this situation at all. Paragraphs dealing with nongenetic sons or heirs of any type are counted separately from those dealing with genetic sons or heirs. Genetic heirs are sons of the father who has begotten them. Nongenetic heirs include all heirs who are not genetic heirs.

(7) Laws pertaining to the determination of castes by birth in Book X are excluded.

(8) Laws concerning relationships between spouses are excluded except when they pertain to parent-child relationship.

(9) The following slokas are to be excluded for various reasons as separately stated:

(a) Sloka II 28 is not counted in Category 1 or Category 5. In this sloka the procreation of sons and the study of the Veda, as well as a number of other activities, are treated as fulfillment of the law with no implication of social or legal relationships.

(b) Sloka II 109 is excluded from our count because in it the "teacher's son" and "relative" simply designated persons, amongst others, who may be given instruction but imply no definite social relationships.

(c) Slokas III 184, 185, and several others are excluded because they refer to the duties of a householder toward many kinds of persons in general.

(d) Slokas IX 32–56 *passim* are excluded, since they merely discuss the problem of determining whether the male or female progenitor is the owner of the child.

The Categories and the exact slokas found in each of them are as follows (the Roman numerals refer to books and the Arabic numbers refer to slokas; thus, II 27 means Book II, Sloka 27):

CATEGORY 1—*Father-genetic son relationship without reference to teacher.* II 29, 30; III (136 and 137), 220, 221, 248; IV 173, 257; VI 95; VIII 159, 160, (161 and 162), 416; IX 9,[a] 105, 106, 107, 108, 112, 113, 114, 115, (116 and 117), 132,[b] 133, 134, 137, 138, 158, 159, 160, 161, 162, 163, 164, 165, 185, 191, 200, 214, 209, 210, 211, 213, 215, 216; XI 186.

a. Sloka IX 9 also bears on mother-son and husband-wife relationship, but it is included in Category 1 only because its central emphasis is on father-son relationships.

b. The following slokas are each counted twice: II 184 (Categories 7 and 8); III 119 and 148 (Categories 5 and 8); IV 180 (Categories 3 and 8); IX 132, 134, 162, 163, 164, and 165 (Categories 1 and 6); and XI 63 (Categories 5 and 8).

CATEGORY 2—*Mother-genetic son relationship without reference to teacher.*[a] II 50, 133; IX 3, 4, 140, 145, 175, 217.

a. Slokas III 262 and 263 are excluded from Category 2 because they are merely means for mothers to get good sons.

CATEGORY 3—*Parent-son relationship without reference to teacher.*[a] II (26 and 27), 227; IV 180; V 62, 91; VIII 389; IX (19 and 20), 104, (120 and 121),[b] (122 and

123), (122 and 124), 125, 126, 143, (149 and 150), (149 and 151), (152 and 153), 154, 155, 156, 157, 179, 190.

a. Sloka IV 239 is excluded from Category 3 because it disclaims the importance of all kinship relationships in the other world. Slokas IX 144, 147 and 178 are excluded from Category 3 because they merely specify nonkinship relationships. Sloka IX 220 is excluded from Category 3 because it merely summarizes what went before.

b. Slokas 120, 121, 122, 123, 124, 125 and 126 refer to both genetic and nongenetic sons.

CATEGORY 4—*Teacher-pupil relationship in conjunction with parents.* II 145, 225, 228, 229, 230, 231, 232, 233, 234, 235, 236, 237; III (147 and 157); IV 162, 164,[a] (179 and 190), 182, 251;[b] V 91; VIII 275, 299, 335; IX 187, 235, 237; XI 1, 60.

a. In this sloka son and pupil are classified together as contrasted to other individuals classified otherwise.

b. In this sloka the phrase "those whom he is bound to maintain" is interpreted to refer primarily to parents.

CATEGORY 5—*Teacher-pupil relationship without reference to parents.* I 103, 111; II 51, 69, 71, 72, 73, 108, 117, 140, 141, 142, 146, 149, 150, (151 and 152), 153, 159, 170, 171, (175 and 176), (175 and 177), (175 and 179), (175 and 180), (175 and 181), 182, 188, 191, 192, 193, 194, 195, 196, 197, 198, 199, 200, 201, 202, 203, 204, 205,[a] 206,[b] 208, 218, 241, 242, 243, 244, (245 and 246), 247; III 1, 4, 70, 95,[c] 119, (147 and 148), (149 and 156), (147 and 153); IV 101,[d] 102, 103, 104, 105, 106, 107, 108, 109, 110, 111, 112, 113, 114, 115, 116, 117, 118, 119, 120, 121, 123, 124, 125, 126, 127, 130, 153, 175, 252; V 43, 65, 80,[e] 81, 82; VIII 305, 317, 350; XI 35,[f] 49, 56, (54 and 63), 89, 104, (104 and 105), (104 and 106), (104 and 107), 118, 119, 120, 121, 122, 123, 124, 158, 159, 225, 252; XII 58, 83.

a. This sloka legislates respect to teacher's teacher.

b. This sloka legislates respect to teachers other than those of Vedas.

c. Cf. II 245, 246.

d. Slokas IV 101–127 prescribe the stringent rules pertaining to instruction and learning.

e. This sloka also refers to relatives of the teacher, but is not included in Category 8.

f. Laws referring to the violation of a guru's bed are counted under teacher-pupil relationships since such an act is interpreted as desecrating the status of the guru. Laws mentioning the guru's wife specifically (such as XI 55) are counted under the category of teacher's relatives.

CATEGORY 6—*Father-nongenetic son relationship.* IX 127, (130 and 131), 132, 134, 139, 162, 163, 164, 165, 141, 142, 146, 167, 168, 169, 170, 171, 173, 174, 177, 182, 190, 183.[a]

a. This is a case of mother-nongenetic son relationship.

CATEGORY 7—*Student with reference to all relatives of teacher.* II 184, 207, 209, 210, 211, 212, 216, 217; XI 55.

CATEGORY 8—*Male's relationship with all other relatives besides parents or sons.* I 115, 118; II 34, 130, 132, 133, 184; III 55, 56, 57, 58, 59, 119, 148, (147 and 154), (147 and 160), 171, 172, 173, 222, 264; IV 180, 183, 184, 185; V 58, [59, 60, 61, 67,] 70, [(74 and 75), (74 and 76), (74 and 77), (74 and 78), (74 and 79)];[a] VIII 166, 198; IX 57, 58, 59, 109, 110, 111, 118, 136, 187, 192, 193, 205, 207, 208, 212, 214; XI 59, (54 and 63), 61, 171, 172, 173.

a. Bracketed slokas refer to Sipanda relatives.

CATEGORY 9—*Female's relationships with all other relatives besides parents and children (but not marriage ties with husband).* III 27, 28, 29, 30, 35, 51, 52, 53, 54; V 148, 149, 150, 152; IX 194, 197, 198.

13. All facts used in this paper regarding the Chinese family are based on situ-

ations obtaining before the 1949 Communist Revolution, except where otherwise specified.

14. The Laws of Manu contain 87 slokas which bear on the husband-wife relationship. Of these, 48 slokas concern duties of a wife to her husband; 16 concern actions (in most cases not duties, but such provisions as what days of the month he may or may not approach her, what rites he has to perform after her death before he may remarry, etc.) on the part of a husband towards his wife; 2 slokas concern mutual obligations of the husband and wife toward each other; while the remaining 21 define other aspects of the husband-wife relationship such as the most auspicious nights for conjugal union which may determine the sex of the child conceived.

15. Ever since the Independence of India, government servants have been prohibited from having more than one wife.

16. Gitel P. Steed, "Personality Formation in a Hindu Village in Gujarat," in McKim Marriott (ed.), *Village India* (Memoir No. 83, Washington, D.C.: American Anthropological Association, June 1955), p. 130.

17. M. N. Srinivas, *Coorgs*, p. 48 ff.

18. In this connection we have no need to mention the custom of *sati*, the commitment of which will send her husband, his family, and the *sati* herself straight to heaven. This was absent in China; it is still practiced sporadically in India though rigidly forbidden by law.

19. For an excellent exposition of these stages of life see Pandharinath Prabhu, *Hindu Social Organization*, 3rd rev. ed. (Bombay: The Popular Book Depot, 1958), pp. 83–89 ff.

20. Gitel P. Steed, *op. cit.*, 123–124.

21. The other instances were (1) Narasimha, a Ganga ruler of Kalinga sometime at the end of the tenth century A.D., who became a Jain monk in later life; (2) the last Rashtrakuta ruler Indra, during the last half of the tenth century A.D., who became a Jain monk late in his life: (3) a ruler of Pala dynasty of Bengal named Vigrahapala, who abdicated the throne sometime before 854 A.D. and retired to ascetic life; (4) a Paramara king of Gujarat named Siyaka II, who adopted the life of an ascetic sometime after 972 A.D.; and (5) King Ballalasena of the Sena dynasty of Bengal, who retired to ascetic life with his wife sometime before 1178 A.D.

22. Gitel P. Steed, *op. cit.*, p. 123.

23. *Ibid.*, pp. 141–142 and p. 143.

24. Nirma Kumar Bose, "Caste in India," in *Man in India*, XXXI, Nos. 3 and 4 (1951), 115–116.

25. A. M. Shah and R. G. Shroff, in Milton Singer (ed.), *Traditional India: Structure and Change*, published as Bul. 71, No. 281 of the *Journal of American Folklore* (July–September 1958), 246–278.

26. Stephen Fuchs, *The Children of Hari: A Study of the Balahis in the Central Provinces* (New York: Frederick A. Praeger, 1951), 74–76.

27. Shah and Shroff, *op. cit.*, pp. 261–263.

28. *Ibid.*, p. 264.

29. *Ibid.*, pp. 266–267.

30. *Ibid.*, pp. 268–269.

31. *Ibid.*, pp. 269–270.

32. E. Kathleen Gough, "Cults of the Dead among the Nayars," in Milton Singer (ed.), *op. cit.*, (1958), p. 448.

33. M. N. Srinivas, *Coorgs*, p. 77.

34. *Ibid.*, p. 161.

35. Louis Dumont, *Une Sous-Caste de l'Inde du Sud* (Paris: Mouton et Cie, 1957), p. 169 and pp. 357–358.

36. *Ibid.*, p. 360.

37. *Ibid.*, p. 169.

38. M. N. Srinivas, *Coorgs*, p. 78.

39. *Garuda Purana*, Chapter 1, Slokas 21, 22, 24; Chapter 8, Slokas 97–99, 101, 105, 106, translated by Ernest Wood and S. V. Subrahminyam, with an introduction by Sri Chandra Vasu, "The Sacred Books of the Hindus Series," Major B. D. Basu, I.M.S., retired (ed.), published by Sudbindra Matha Vasu, from the Panini offices, Bhuvaneswari Asrama, Selahabad, 1911.

40. S. C. Dube, *Indian Village* (Ithaca: Cornell University Press, 1955), pp. 97, 103.

41. Stephen Fuchs, *op. cit.*, p. 327.

42. M. N. Srinivas, *Coorgs*, pp. 161–162.

43. Gough, *op. cit.*, p. 448.

44. *Ibid.*, p. 452.

45. See K. M. Kapadia, *Hindu Kinship* (Bombay: Popular Book Depot, 1947), pp. 240–244.

46. E. Kathleen Gough, *op. cit.*, p. 449. S. C. Dube's account of Shamirpet, Hyderabad, shows that ancestral spirits may be angry and cause sickness or misfortune and must be propitiated. (Dube, *op. cit.*, pp. 128–129.)

47. F. L. K. Hsu, *Religion, Science and Human Crises* (London: Routledge and Kegan Paul, 1952).

48. Francis L. K. Hsu, "Kinship and Ways of Life: An Exploration," in Francis L. K. Hsu (ed.), *Psychological Anthropology: Approaches to Culture and Personality* (Homewood: Dorsey Press, 1961), pp. 400–450.

49. Gitel P. Steed, *"Life History Documents, I (Indrasingh)"* (Hectographed) (New York: Columbia University Research in Contemporary India Project, 1950); and "Personality Formation in a Hindu Village in Gujarat," in McKim Marriott (ed.), *Village India* (Chicago: University of Chicago Press, 1955), pp. 102–144.

50. Morris G. Carstairs, *The Twice Born* (London: The Hogarth Press, 1957), pp. 148–149.

51. *Ibid.*, pp. 67–70.

52. Lois B. Murphy, "Roots of Tolerance and Tensions in Child Development," Chap. IV, in Gardner Murphy, *In the Minds of Men* (New York: Basic Books, 1953).

53. Gitel P. Steed, *op. cit.*, (1955), pp. 141–143.

54. S. C. Dube, *op. cit.*, pp. 148–150.

55. Robert I. Watson, *Psychology of the Child* (New York: John Wiley & Sons, 1959), pp. 199–201.

56. Francis L. K. Hsu, *op. cit.* (1961), p. 450.

57. F. Max Muller, *Ramakrishna, His Life and Sayings* (London: 1938).

58. Sister Nivedita (Miss M. E. Noble), *The Web of Indian Life* (London and Bombay: Longmans, Green, 1904), p. 17 ff.

Chapter IV

COHESION VERSUS DIVISION:
CLAN IN CHINA AND INDIA

COMPARED WITH THE FAMILY in the United States, the Hindu and Chinese families, as well as the families of Samoa and many other societies, have many common effects on the individual.[1] For the present their differentiating features must engage our attention. In the last chapter we saw how the Chinese family provides a basis for the situation-centered way of life with its emphasis on mutual dependence among men, while the Hindu family provides a basis for the supernatural-centered way of life with its desire for reliance upon higher powers.

The principal effect of the Chinese pattern on the individual is cohesiveness or a centripetal tendency among fellow men. Since the individual's first social group is the family, the centripetal outlook of the Chinese can be expected to lead him into a desire to remain within the family and, outside it, to keep within the boundaries of its immediate and direct extension —the clan—and not stray much farther beyond. The principal effect of the Hindu pattern on the individual is, however, divisiveness, or a centrifugal tendency among fellow men. Since the individual fails to find his firm anchorage in his first social group, the family, will the centrifugal outlook of the Hindus compel him to seek cohesion in its extension in the clan?

The analysis which follows will show that, while the situation-centered outlook did in fact lead the Chinese to consolidate themselves within their clans, the supernatural-centered orientation prevented the Hindus from any significant development of their clans. What we shall find is that the cohesive or centripetal tendencies of the Chinese family are clearly reflected in the Chinese way in clan, and the centrifugal or divisive tendencies of the Hindu family are clearly reflected in the Hindu way in clan. The Chinese clan has impressive strength and cohesion in contrast to the Hindu clan with its amorphousness and lack of cohesion.

Clan extends directly from the family along either the male or the female line. As the father-son based Chinese family increases in size through the

60

normal process of reproduction and marriage, the patrilineal clan is the larger grouping into which its centripetally inclined members will flow as a matter of course. But as the mother-son based Hindu family increases in size for the same reasons, its centrifugally conditioned members cannot be so confined. In the Chinese case the individual adheres to the same kinship principle whether he is seen as a member of a family or of a clan. But in the Hindu case the individual leaves the kinship principle in his extrafamiliar affiliations.

DEFINITIONS AND BASIC CHARACTERISTICS

Clan is incompatible with families organized on the conjugal principle. It is primarily an extension of the joint family with unilineal descent and is based on the consanguine principle.[2] Its usual characteristics include (1) a name, (2) exogamy, (3) unilineal, common ancestry, (4) the core sex,— men for patrilineal and women for matrilineal clan—and (5) use of kinship terms among all or most members to address or refer to each other. In many societies clan also has (6) certain forms of common property and (7) a degree of joint responsibility. A structure of this sort in which the common unilineal ancestry of the core sex is traceable genealogically is usually termed in most anthropological literature a lineage rather than a clan. But sinologists regularly employ the term *clan* for Chinese *tsu*. Furthermore, while this usage differs from that of many anthropologists, the Chinese group, *tsu*, seems to conform to George P. Murdock's "specifications" for clan. For the Chinese *tsu* exhibits, in addition to the seven characteristics already enumerated, the following traits: (8) patrilocal residence, (9) automatic membership upon marriage of the wife to her spouse's clan, (10) benefits for education and public welfare, (11) ritual worship of common ancestors, (12) clan ancestral halls, (13) clan graveyards, (14) legislation on rules of behavior, and (15) council of clan elders which pass judgments and settle disputes. In fact these traits not only conform to but also elaborate to an extraordinary degree Murdock's "major specifications" for clan, which are: (*a*) "it must be based explicitly on a unilinear rule of descent which unites its central core of members"; (*b*) "it must have residential unity"; and (*c*) "it must exhibit actual social integration."[3]

On the other hand what has usually been designated as clan in India— *gotra*—has only two nearly universal attributes as contrasted to the twelve attributes exhibited by the Chinese clan. The two attributes of the Hindu clan are a name and exogamy. The Hindu *gotra* is thus far short of Murdock's specifications for clan and is certainly not identical with lineage as the term is generally used among anthropologists.

Throughout China the common term for clan is *tsu*. There is besides another term, *tsung,* which is used when two or more clans bearing the same surname at first thought to be unrelated later turn out to be linked by a common ancestor. Such a linkage is called *lien-tsung.* But although the word *tsung* in this context seems to connote an aggregate larger than *tsu,* it in fact does not. For this larger entity will later also be referred to as *tsu* and there will no longer be any distinction between such a coordinated *tsu* and another *tsu* the members of which were known to be descendants of a common ancestor in the first place.

The Hindi and Sanskrit word *gotra* (sometimes *got*), usually translated as "clan,"[4] has the widest circulation in India. Except on the Malabar Coast, this term is used in every major region of India, among caste Hindus and even among untouchables such as the Balahis of Central India. There are, however, a number of other related terms which have been used in the past and/or are still used in various parts of the country today. The following list is not exhaustive but contains most of these terms: (1) *gotra* (*got*); (2) *vamsa* (*bansa*) (*vansham*); (3) *kula* (*kul*); (4) *gana* (*gaig*); (5) *pravaras;* (6) *sasan;* (7) *sapinda;* (8) *devaka;* (9) *bedagu;* (10) *bedaza;* (11) *bali;* (12) *keri;* (13) *kilai;* (14) *gatta;* (15) *gumpu;* (16) *veli;* (17) *intiperu;* (18) *vidu.*[5]

Even the meaning of *gotra* (sometimes *got* or *gotram*), which has usually been translated as "clan" or "lineage," and which of all the terms bearing on the subject enjoys the widest circulation in the country, is uncertain. The original Sanskritic meanings of the term were "assembly" or "enclosure" and "herd" or even a collection of cows, but it has been used in three contexts, as follows, to apply:

(*a*) To a group of persons who are alleged descendants of any one of the "seven *rishis*" (sages) and Agastya (the sage who brought the Vedic religion to the south).[6] * Between two members of such a group, marriage generally cannot take place.

(*b*) To all members of a local unit such as a village, or of an occupational group, among whom marriage is forbidden. This is the case among the higher castes of northern India. Such a group is designated by Mrs. I. Karve as a *gotra* even though the local people have no general term to describe it.[7]

(*c*) To the situation among the Rajputs today, where "all the clans have Gotras, i.e., names of the Rishis, attached to them. These Gotras do not seem to be of ancient origin, nor do they seem to have a function as regards

---

* Informants of my acquaintance in every part of the country are not sure of the original number of *rishis* involved. Some frankly say that they do not know its origin. Many speak about the "seven *rishis*," or "eight *rishis*," or "thirteen *rishis*." Some informants say members of a *gotra* are descendants of the disciples of one of the seven, eight, or thirteen *rishis*. As time went on, they say, and the population increased, more persons attained the position of *rishi* because of their achievements; this is why the number of *gotras* today is far greater than seven, eight, or thirteen.

Marriage."[8] In fact these *gotras* have no function whatever. The same is also true of the Kayasthas of Uttar Pradesh and elsewhere in the north, among whom the local or occupational groups are exogamous, but among whom *gotra* in the Brahminic sense (of being descendants of some *rishi*) has no function whatever.[9] *

The several branches of a Chinese clan of any size are designated individually as *fang*, meaning the subclan or house. *Tsu* and *fang* are the two terms used all over China to signify clan and subdivisions of a clan. Sometimes, coinciding with *fang*, but often not coinciding with it, is the group of agnates and their spouses who are described as being within the *wu fu* relationship (five mourning grades). Those who are within the *wu fu* relationship of an individual (designated here as ego) are: his lineal ancestors to his father's father's father's father and their spouses; his lineal descendants to son's son's son's son and their spouses; his brothers and their agnatic descendants to the third descending generation and their spouses; his father's brothers and their agnatic descendants to the second descending generation as well as their spouses; his father's father's brother and their agnatic descendants to the first descending generation as well as their spouses; his father's father's father's brothers and their agnatic descendants to ego's own generation as well as their spouses; and the sisters (but not their husbands and children) of all of the men included. Diagram I will make the relationships clearer. These are related men and women for whom ego has varying degrees of mourning obligations upon their death. The rule is that the closer the relationship as measured by patrilineal kinship linearity, the greater are ego's mourning obligations, which are expressed by lengths of mourning and other symbols. The husband's position in this scheme determines his wife's, but the husbands of the sisters of the men included have no mourning obligations here whatsoever.

Since this circle of *wu fu* is the same only for full brothers, it cannot correspond either with *fang* (subclan) or with *tsu* (clan). Its primary function is to specify the grades of mourning obligations, though occasionally it serves to mark the exogamous boundary for ego, if, according to relatively rare local conditions, marriage between a man and a woman bearing the same last (clan) name were allowed. But specification of the mourning grades is its chief function in all of China.

Within a very large clan, especially if it is spread over widely separated geographical areas, the scattered sections of the clan may be known as *tze* or branches. The same term *tze* may also be applied to the several formerly different clans subsequently linked together by a common ancestor. But more frequently the term *fang* is used in both these cases and is used in a

* The other terms related to *gotra* and their meanings are given in Appendix I to this chapter.

DIAGRAM I WU FU RELATIONSHIP

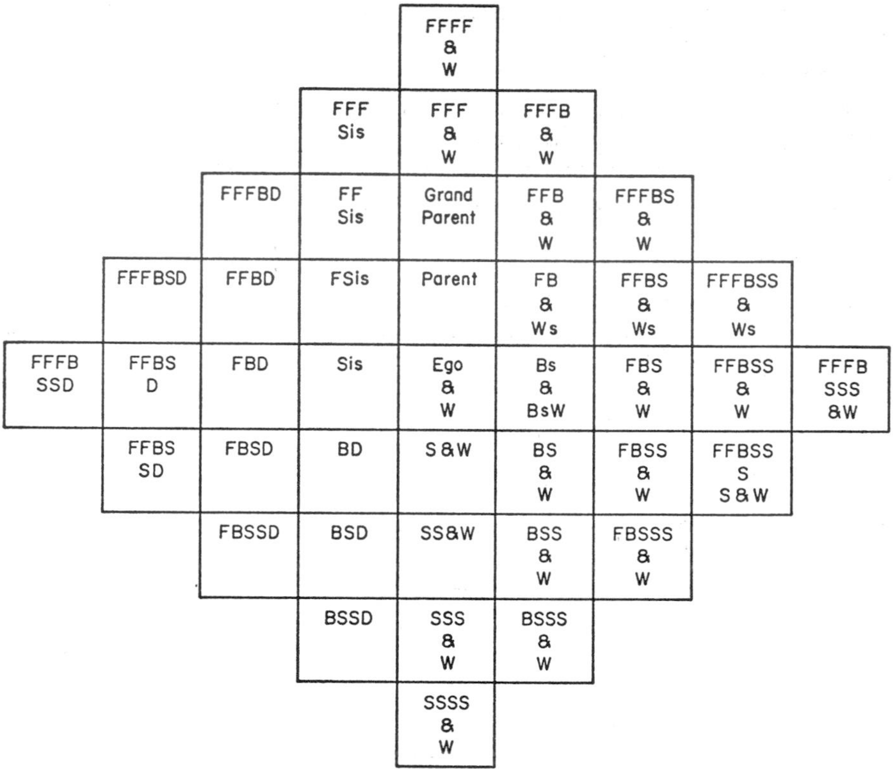

				FFFF & W				
			FFF Sis	FFF & W	FFFB & W			
		FFFBD	FF Sis	Grand Parent	FFB & W	FFFBS & W		
	FFFBSD	FFBD	FSis	Parent	FB & Ws	FFBS & Ws	FFFBSS & Ws	
FFFBSSD	FFBSD	FBD	Sis	Ego & W	Bs & BsW	FBS & W	FFBSS & W	FFFB SSS &W
	FFBSSD	FBSD	BD	S & W	BS & W	FBSS & W	FFBSS S S & W	
		FBSSD	BSD	SS & W	BSS & W	FBSSS & W		
			BSSD	SSS & W	BSSS & W			
				SSSS & W				

F   – Father   M – Mother
S   – Son   W – Wife
Sis – Sister   Ws – Wives
B   – Brother   D – Daughter
Bs – Brothers

purely figurative sense. In the same figurative way the word *chu* (pillar) is in some instances used to denote the subdivisions of *fang* (subclan). The image behind this metaphor is that since *fang* literally means "house," subdivisions of the "house" are "pillars."

THE IMPORTANCE OF CHINESE CLAN OVER ITS SUBDIVISIONS

Considering China as a whole, the use of the words *tze* and *chu* in this connection is the exception while the use of the terms *tsu* (clan), *fang* (subclan), and *wu fu* (five mourning grades) is the rule. In practice the Chinese tend to regard the *tsu* and any of its subdivisions (including *fang*) as being of far less significance than the distinction between one *tsu* and another. In fact *fang* has no definite boundary and the term refers to any large or small branch of a *tsu* at any particular point of time. At the time of the division of the family, three sons, each with their wives and unmarried children, may be referred to as three *fang*. On the other hand, a branch of a clan including several generations of departed ancestors and several generations of living may also be referred to as a *fang* with reference to the entire clan.

Some scholars err because they fail to appreciate the relative importance of the clan over its actual or potential subdivisions. Maurice Freedman's excellent analysis of the clan organization in southeastern China is one such example. His work raises many interesting questions but its basic weakness is its failure to see the woods for the trees. He sees all sorts of cleavages in the Chinese clan organization, but these alleged cleavages are often greatly exaggerated and sometimes they just are not supported by objective evidence. For example, he insists that there is a sharp differentiation between domestic worship of ancestors and common worship of ancestors in the common clan ancestral hall, and that this leads to "tensions" within the lineage (clan). His view is that the near ancestors worshiped at home are more closely tied to the living and therefore might simply be cared for as forebears, while the ancestors worshiped at clan halls are more remote and therefore less individualized as personalities in the minds of the descendants.[10] Arguing *a priori*, Freedman is undoubtedly on sound ground. An individual's relationship with his own parents and even grandparents will, in the normal course of events, be more intimate than that with, say, his great-great-grandparents, whom he is not likely even to have seen. The difficulty is that Freedman provides us only with what seems to be no more than a couple of additional *a priori* assertions to support his first assertion:

> The ancestors in such a case (domestic worship) had ceased to be foci for segments in a lineage, and had become beings whose relations with the living stood outside the hierarchy or agnatic units. It is obvious that a man who was worshipped separately in the several households formed by his patrilineal grandsons was the object of a devotion which did not directly relate to the maintenance of a kinship unity beyond the range of one family in a household.[11]

I find it not at all "obvious." Even when a clan has grown large enough to form many branches and small subgroups located in different areas, the ancestors often have to be honored in several ancestral temples in different places. It is not uncommon, on occasions of worship, for representatives of each subgroup to pay visits to all of these ancestral temples.[12] In other words, the worship of different ancestors in different ancestral halls does not seem to disrupt the kinship unity of the wider clan as a whole. Freedman himself is not unaware of the fact that there are many families in which the household shrine contains but one scroll or tablet which bears the general formula embracing "all the ancestors of a certain surname (clan)."[13]

In short, even though the *fang* and *tsu* distinction is found in all parts of China, everywhere their relationship is more characterized by unitary tendencies than divisive characteristics. Freedman himself briefly refers to a documentation by Dr. Hu of a clan in Kiangsi in which all men taking part in the main ancestral worship ritual had to be men of education or over sixty-five years of age. The head of the *tsu* or clan participated actively in the rites first only to the extent of carrying the tablets of the first ancestors, and then the next day taking the place of honor at a clan feast. The participation of the heads of *fang* or subclans was limited to carrying out tablets of the ancestors of each subclan and, during the following feasting, to cooking and supervising the serving of dishes.[14]

In a similar vein Freedman speaks of the "tensions between the principle by which families related within the agnatic Wu Fu were ritually encouraged to come together and the principle according to which they might legitimately conduct their own domestic rites as separate units."[15] Here again there is nothing but *a priori* reasoning. The facts, including some quoted by Freedman himself, show no sign of tension along this line whatsoever.

It is, of course, not alleged that Chinese clans are free from internal tensions. No human organization can be entirely free from internal tension, no matter how small it is, how carefully it is designed, or how smoothly it is run. The two-member organization composed of husband and wife is often productive of tensions of the most violent nature. But first, there is no evidence to show that tensions in the Chinese clan organization occur at points where Freedman suspects they would occur. And second, there is remarkably little intraclan tension; and when it does occur, it is not very explosive. Certainly I do not know of any clan in China which has been split, with subsequent moving away of some members of the clan to a new locality, because of an irreconcilable quarrel. Some Chinese clans have split and some of their components have moved away, but when this occurred it was invariably because of political upheaval, or more likely, because of poverty, famine, and the need for new space for livelihood. The following quotation from Fei, which Freedman uses elsewhere in a footnote, is typical:

> According to the accepted principle, all the patrilineal descendants and their wives that can be traced to a common ancestor within the five kinship grades consider themselves as belonging to a kinship group called *Tsu*. . . . But in practice this strict genealogical accounting is not important . . . if the principle were strictly observed, theoretically there would be a division of *Tsu* for each generation. But *Tsu* are seldom divided for this purpose. . . . The *Tsu* will not be sub-divided if there is no increase of members.[16]

Freedman's possible reply to these arguments is that he is employing, as do many structurists, the words "unity" and "tension" not in terms of individual behavior content or psychology, as I do here, but solely in terms of structure or role and that, therefore, "unity" and "tension" simply mean, respectively, compatibility and incompatibility. Unfortunately such a position is hard to defend except for those who maintain that theory has nothing to do with facts. Theories, however attractive and logical, help us little in understanding the facts unless the conclusions they bring us to can ultimately be related to the facts. But theories cannot be related to the facts unless the basic premises of such theories are rooted in the facts to begin with. The trouble with the purely structurist arguments is that their premises are not rooted in the facts and therefore their conclusions have no relation to the facts. The structurist would point to "tension" wherever he finds a possible *theoretical* cleavage in the social organization. But any supposed "tension," to be of scientific significance, must manifest itself in some psychological or overt behavior among some or most members of the social organization.* Consequently structurist arguments must be based on or at least related to the facts in content. Otherwise they will have no relevance to the situation at hand and cannot possibly help us understand it. If a theory predicts tension and no tension appears, it means either the theory is a poor theory or the theory has no bearing on the problem at hand. Many Western observers of Chinese religion first imagined that the Chinese divided themselves into followers of Confucianism, Buddhism, and Taoism, and then were baffled by the fact that a Chinese easily might be all three and more at the same time while not caring too much about any of them. The fault in this case is with the Western assumption of the desire on the part of believers for a religious schism which is common in Western culture but which is absent in Chinese culture. Any structurist theory based on the assumption that worship of different gods leads to schism will therefore only confuse our understanding of religion in China, not clarify it.

THE SUBSTANCE OF HINDU CLAN

From our analysis of Hindu terms bearing on clan, two points emerge. First, there is a great deal of uncertainty in the exact meanings of the terms in India, as a whole, though presumably the inhabitants of any one local area, using terms familiar to themselves, are not bothered by such uncertainty. Second, the basic substance, actual or supposed, common to most of this array of terms consists of no more than what is represented by

* In this we do not necessarily mean individual behavior but behavior of individuals in groups; nor do we necessarily mean tensions as feelings in the individuals although such tensions may be a result.

gotra: a name and some sort of exogamy. In fact some of them possess less content than *gotra*, since they are names only. Not only are the majority of Hindus hazy about most of these terms, but, as we noted above, they have a great deal of uncertainty even about the most widely used of these terms, *gotra*. Some Hindu groups attach greater significance to *gotra* than others. Some Rajputs may take pride in the *gotra*, as they would in some of their actual ancestors, even though their *gotras* do not have any connection with their ancestry in the genealogical sense. The *gotra* members of some sub-castes, such as the Balahis of Central India, worship a common deity, though he is not an ancestor.[17] As we noted before, the Rajputs show some interest in genealogy, and, with the Coorgs of South India, they may worship some famous remote ancestors. The Coorgs, in addition, maintain some graves for the dead. In the case of the Gaddis, *gotra* has some bearing on the inheritance of property. Newell reports:

> The field can be used to illustrate the Gaddi idea of property in land. In the first place each field belongs to a male member of a certain *gotra*. When he dies, it is inherited first by his son or grandson and then by his brothers by the same father. But in default of any sons or brothers it reverts back to his *gotra* among the members of whom the land is divided. In default of any *gotra* members being alive, it reverts to the *rajah*, whose property all land in the State really is.[18]

This is the only instance where the *gotra* has some economic function, and presumably consists of members who can trace themselves to a common ancestry. In the rest of India no one except some Brahman-Pandits in Madras[19]—and some Rajputs, with assistance from Vahivancas—can claim a genealogy which enables fellow members of a clan to be linked together by a remote common ancestor. The Rajput interest in genealogy is linked to a characteristic interest in land, pride of history, and conquest, in contrast to the Brahmans who have less interest in land.* Another possible explanation is that the Rajputs were of different origin from the Aryans, and therefore are still distinguished from the rest of the Hindus by differences in cultural tradition. There is a question whether Hindu India has one central point of cultural orientation, namely the Brahman, or whether the Brahmans and the Kshatriyas (to whom the Rajputs as a rule claim to belong) form dual foci of cultural orientation. This question will be dealt with later in connection with caste. But it can be stated at once that, in spite of the fact that the militarily ambitious Rajputs need the manpower of the clan for defense and offense, the clan among Rajput chieftains has no clear organization. In fact, the Rajput's interest in his ancestry is primarily concerned with how a glorious ancestry can buttress and raise his own claim to supremacy over other Rajputs, not with a desire to provide for the departed

* Personal communication from Drs. Bernard Cohn and McKim Marriott.

ones, and maintain a filial relationship with them, as in the case of the Chinese. Rajput interest in genealogy is essentially similar to that of those Irishmen or Americans who expend money and effort to prove their connection with royal forebears.

Aside from the exceptions noted, the attributes of the clan in India must be described by a series of negatives. The surname of every Chinese is the name of his clan; a vast majority of Hindus never use their *gotra* names at all for this purpose, even when they may have what may be described as a "surname." Many Hindus do not in fact know what their *gotra* names are and, when asked, have to check with their elders to find them out. Nowhere in Hindu India can there be found clan ancestral halls, common clan worship of ancestors, councils of clan elders (as distinct from council of village elders) capable of passing judgments or settling disputes, any notion of joint responsibility for crimes committed, or, apart from certain Rajputs, any notion of the sharing of honors. To enumerate other attributes which the Chinese clan possesses, but which the Hindu clan does not, would be sheer redundancy. If we note that the Chinese clan is of great significance in Chinese society, we cannot fail to note that the Hindu clan is but a minor phenomenon in Indian society. Its Hindu form can hardly be described as an organization, for there is neither any idea of a definite membership nor any interaction among such individuals as happen to have an identical *gotra.**

TENSION AND VARIATION IN CHINESE CLAN

We have already stressed that tensions can exist within Chinese clans. Rivalry between different branches of a clan, like rivalry between two or more brothers in a family, does exist and flare up often. The facts pertaining to a feud within the clan of Dr. Hu Shih, the famous Chinese philosopher and statesman, detailed in Appendix II to this chapter, tell us much about the nature and outcome of interclan tension which is well known elsewhere in China. Briefly, in 1865 the members of the clan wanted to erect a new ancestral hall, since the old one was destroyed during a civil war about fourteen years earlier. A committee of four was set up which was to assess the contributions by various members of the clan according to their prominence and ability to pay. By 1871 the main room for keeping the ancestral tablets was completed and many members of the clan wanted to leave the construction at that point, but one energetic member decided otherwise. Two factions in the clan developed and hot arguments between them ensued. During the succeeding years many debates and quarrels took place.

* Our observations find additional support in the work of T. N. Madan with reference to Kashmir Brahmans given in his article, "Is the Brahmanic *Gotra* a Grouping of Kin?" *Southwestern Journal of Anthropology* XVIII, No. 1 (Spring 1962), pp. 59–77.

Several times it looked as though further progress in the project would be impossible. Many members refused further contributions while other members supported the opposite view. The leaders of one faction even went so far as to order swords from a blacksmith with the apparent intention of going to battle to the death against members of the other faction. In the heat of the seesaw arguments, many other matters besides the question of monetary assessment entered into the picture. In the end the man leading the faction which stood for completion of the project according to traditional standards prevailed. The intraclan battle did not come off as feared.

This interesting case tells us that, though tensions exist, there is no real desire on the part of the parties in the conflict to break off. Even those who tried to withhold their shares of contribution in cash or labor to the common cause did so not with the intention of setting up any separate clan organizations. They did so out of stinginess, jealousy, chicanery or for other reasons, but when the chips were down the clan members fell in line and the unitary forces of the clan organization prevailed again. (For details of this case see Appendix II to this chapter.)

Conflicts of this kind are quite common, though the reasons for them obviously vary. Their solutions take different forms, though the courses they follow may be similar. Not all clans can build expensive clan ancestral halls as did the Hus; some clans have far less common property than others and are able to provide no benefits for education and welfare of poorer clan members; some clans have common graveyards which do not adequately meet their needs; some clans do not have councils of elders, and others have councils which are too weak to pass judgments and settle disputes, for the strength of the councils depends upon the ability and leadership of individual officers and some clans have such poor genealogical records that they neither are exact nor extend to many generations past. Unquestionably, however, clans do not remain in such conditions of their own volition, for as soon as a member of a clan becomes well-to-do, and especially if he achieves some prominence through the examination system, he tends to spare no effort in rebuilding his clan ancestral hall, widening the genealogical records, and generally improving or strengthening the organization and affairs of his clan. All this he does by following the ideal model set forth by his own ancestors according to the classics. In doing so he is not necessarily moved by altruism. On the one hand, he will derive great pride from being a member of a prosperous clan with its many external signs of affluence. On the other hand, he is discharging his duties toward his forebears according to his ability, exactly as he expects his descendants to discharge theirs in the years to come. The better example he sets himself to be, the greater is the likelihood that his descendants will follow in his footsteps. For in viewing life he is thinking of the future no less than of the past, but his concept of both is channeled into the narrow familial and clan path. He is unconditionally dependent upon it, just as it is also entirely dependent upon him.

Besides variation in the attributes of the clan according to social class, there is also variation in the strength and organization of the clan according to geography. Broadly speaking we may, for this purpose, divide China into three regions. In south and central China the clan is the strongest; in north and northeast China it is much weaker; in southwest China it tends to have more external trimmings than inner cohesion.[20] But regardless of these variations, the general and basic pattern of clan is the same all over China. In the north and southwest are to be found numerous clans with printed genealogical records no less voluminous than those of clans in the south and central regions. These works do not contain simple genealogical tables or trees of the clans concerned. They detail the history and achievements of the ancestors in such fields as literature, art, military exploits, and officialdom and extol such personal attributes as charity and virtue. Many of them also provide samples or complete works (such as poems and essays) of the ancestors. The shortest genealogical record I have seen was in two volumes, and the longest was forty volumes. No one knows exactly the total number of clans which have such genealogical records in China, but Columbia University's Far Eastern Library, which has the largest collection of such records in the United States, has nearly a thousand of them. They are not all from different clans. Since the records tend to be revised, enlarged, and brought up-to-date whenever a member attains prominence, many genealogical records exist in several different editions.

The north has perhaps fewer stately clan ancestral halls than do the other regions, and some sections of the southwest probably have a disproportionate number of them compared with the south and central regions; but such halls are not rare in any area. Even Generalissimo Chiang, after he assumed great prominence in China, built in his native place, Feng Hwa, Chekiang Province, an imposing edifice to honor his near and remote ancestors. On any fair day around the festival day called Tsing Ming during the third lunar month, one can see streams of men and women, young and old, with baskets of food and cooking utensils carried by themselves or by servants, moving toward their respective clan graveyards. They go on foot or by various conveyances to hold a cook-out reunion with the dead. Some clans may have several smaller graveyards belonging to several branches of the clan rather than one common graveyard for the entire clan. In such an instance it is usual for members of the one branch to visit and pay homage at the graveyards of the others, just as in the case, mentioned before, of a clan having several ancestral halls. The principle of joint responsibility in the clan is extended to joint sharing of honors: the punishment for serious crimes, such as treason, may visit members of the entire clan, but honors, especially great ones, achieved by any member of the clan also glorify all members of the clan, especially the lineal ancestors and descendants.

It is now pertinent to pause and review what has been said about clan in the two societies to determine the meaning of cohesion or its relative lack in a social group. The foregoing pages of this chapter have, I think, made it clear that the Chinese clans are associated with the following broad features:

(1) A definite organization with expressed rules of behavior which refer to the group as a distinct body; (2) authorized leadership with one individual as the recognized head or a group forming a council which exercises the leadership; (3) a leadership which commands the respect of the members and exercises control over their conduct; (4) exact and clear criteria for membership and records of its membership; (5) lack of fission due to internal tensions and cleavages; (6) pride in membership and *esprit de corps* among its members; (7) close social, economic or ritual relationship among its members. In contrast, it is also clear that the Hindu clan exhibits none of these characteristics. Pride in membership occurs among some small sections of the population, but even this is unimportant for India as a whole.

This summary of their respective characteristics leads us inevitably to the conclusion that, while the Chinese clan shows a high degree of cohesion, its Indian counterpart does not. Regardless of regional variation, the clan in China has a degree of *esprit de corps* and of positive entity, and is a significant organization for the regulation, consolidation, and continuation of the family and community life. Its power over the individual is commensurate with the security it provides for him. In the words of Hu:

> The security offered is twofold: religious, in that the *tsu* (clan) assures the individual that the rites in his honor will be continued indefinitely; and social-economic, by assuring each member of assistance in case of need, both from the group and from individual fellow members. The poor look to it for protection, while the wealthy and prominent expect from it a safeguard against the loss of social and economic position. The former are glad to depend on their group, and the latter find it useful for building up a following and for extending their influence. The larger, the more prosperous and cohesive the *tsu*, the more beneficial it proves to all its members.[21]

On the other hand the "clan" in India has no *esprit de corps*, no positive entity, and is not a significant organization for the regulation, consolidation, and continuation of the family and community life. It occupies no place of practical importance in Hindu society and culture.

COHESION OF CLAN AND CENTRALIZATION OF GOVERNMENT

The centripetal Chinese family is enclosed within a cohesive Chinese clan, while the centrifugal Hindu family is loosely connected with an amorphous

Hindu clan. Our hypothesis is that the centripetal characteristics bred in the Chinese family are more consistent with a cohesive clan, while the centrifugal attributes of the Hindu family are more commensurate with an amorphous clan.

Cohesiveness and divisiveness, with regard to the human group, are, of course, relative terms. We must now move to the outer boundary of the cohesiveness or the lack of it in the wider social organization. According to Lowie, "clans do not arise in the very earliest stage of society, but on somewhat higher levels play their part for long periods, ultimately disappearing under a strong centralized government."[22] If this observation is sound, then we should expect to find a tendency toward centralized government in India, where the clan is amorphous and practically nonexistent as an organization, and to find a tendency toward regional governments in China, where the clan is stronger and often highly organized. What we find, however, is exactly the reverse.

It is, of course, impossible to assess the histories of India and China in a small section of a book, but an attempt, for at least its suggestive value, is imperative.

India had only two nearly nationwide periods of centralized government before the advent of the Moguls and the British. These were the empires under Chandragupta (who died in 298 B.C.) and his grandson Asoka (who reigned from 273 to 232 B.C.) Both empires were short-lived, and disintegrated after the passing of their energetic founders. There were, of course, strong regional political entities in the long history of India: the Pandya, Chola, Pallava, Cberi, or Kerela dynasties in the south; the Sunga, Andhra or Satavahana, Vijayanagar, Gupta, Harsha, Palla, and Sena dynasties in the central and north, not to mention the numerous smaller Rajput and other kingdoms which existed before, at the same time, or after them. Many of them lasted several centuries. The Andhra or Satavahana dynasty is particularly notable. After the downfall of the Mauryan Empire, particularly after the death of Asoka, the Satavahana dynasty came into power in the Deccan. From about 230 B.C. this dynasty maintained its rule for four and a half centuries. At its highest glory, the Satavahana empire covered the whole of Deccan and parts of Northern India. We do not know what other kingdoms existed beyond the regions of Deccan farther to the south. Nilakanta Shastri thinks that the Satavahanas were the only rulers in the Deccan during these four and a half centuries.[23]

However, in the first place, none of these dynasties had control over even a major part of India. The Satavahana dynasty just mentioned was rivaled by the Maha-Meghavahana or Chedi dynasty in Kalinga and adjoining districts for nearly a hundred years from the second century B.C. In the second place the careers of all Indian dynasties, with the possible exception

of that Asoka, were not only coterminous with a number of other independent dynasties of varying sizes, but also marked by constant struggle
with them for existence. Even Asoka was never in control of the southern
kingdoms. The other rulers were constant aggressors and objects of aggression. This actual state of affairs was what prompted V. A. Smith, the English
civil servant and historian, to observe, in connection with his narration of
the period after Harsha's death:

> Harsha's death loosened the bonds which restrained the disruptive forces
> always ready to operate in India, and allowed them to produce their natural
> result, a medley of petty states, with every-varying boundaries, and engaged
> in internecine war. Such was India when first disclosed to European observa-
> tion in the fourth century B.C., and such it always has been, except during the
> comparatively brief periods in which a vigorous central government has com-
> pelled the mutually repellent molecules of the body politic to check their
> gyrations and submit to the grasp of a superior controlling force.[24]

Being an English official and writing in the days when the British were the
colonial masters of India, Smith naturally could be suspected of playing
up to his vested interest by his observation quoted here, but I see no serious
alternative to Smith's statement as far as the facts are concerned.

To gain a clearer picture of Indian political rule, Nirendra C. Choudhury
and I examined the Indian history from 600 B.C. to 800 A.D. and tabulated
the dynasties of the country in fifty-year periods, differentiating South from
North India. What we find can be put in the form of the following table.

DYNASTIES IN 1500 YEARS OF INDIAN HISTORY[25]

	PERIOD	NORTH	SOUTH
(1)	600–350 B.C.	34	None known
(2)	350–300	3	None known
(3)	300–250	1	4
(4)	250–200	1	5
(5)	200–100	Maurya ends, succeeded by Sunga	1
(6)	100 B.C.–300 A.D.	Andhra (in part)	2 to 4
(7)	300–350 A.D.	2	3
(8)	350–400	3	8
(9)	400–450	2	13
(10)	450–500	5	16
(11)	500–550	7	19
(12)	550–600	12	12
(13)	600–650	15	13
(14)	650–700	10	9
(15)	700–750	14	8
(16)	750–800	5	5

Each of the dynasties at any given time depended strictly upon a single vigorous ruler to maintain a hold on its empire. The Maurya Gupta empire depended on Asoka; the Sunga dynasty on Pushyamitra; the Dushan dynasty on Kanishka; the Imperial Gupta dynasty on Chandragupta I, Samudragupta, and Chandragupta II or Vikramaditya; Harsha's empire on Harsha; the Vijayanagar empire on Krishnadeva; and so on. In almost every instance the empire was established by a vigorous conqueror and disintegrated or was reduced to a subordinate position by some neighboring power or powers after his death, unless it was rescued by another vigorous conqueror who had to engage in unceasing internecine warfare to keep what he had. This pattern continued under Mogul rule except for perhaps twenty years during the reign of the Emperor Aurangzeb. During the British domination only an outside power with far superior organization and weapons was able to keep the multitude of warring elements in the Indian body politic in check, but not in unity, for over a hundred years.

On the other hand, the strength and long duration of the centralized governments in premodern China are facts so well known as to make any statement of them a mere repetition of the obvious. From 206 B.C. to 1912 A.D., China was ruled by nine major dynasties, each of them lasting eighty to several hundred years. Each was the undisputed master over not only entire China proper but also, as in the case of the Han, T'ang, Yuan, Ming and Ching dynasties, over a considerable amount of territory outside China. The dominions of Tsin and Sung dyasties were reduced to the southern half of China during the latter portion of each because of the pressure of Tartar invasions from the north. Other than these two times, China was without a central government for only three comparatively short periods during the last twenty-one centuries of its existence. These were (a) 221–262 A.D., the time of the famous Three Kingdoms; (b) 420–587 A.D., when South China was ruled by a succession of four dynasties and North China by a succession of three dynasties; and (c) 907–960 A.D. when North China was ruled by a succession of five dynasties and South China was a mélange of ten warring kingdoms.

The history of China contrasts with that of India, therefore, in several important ways. First, the periods of political disunity in China were far shorter than those of rule under one central government, while the reverse is true of India. Second, of the three periods of disunity in China, only the first and part of the third were characterized by simultaneous existence of more than two dynasties warring against each other. The first featured three contenders in all China while the third featured ten contenders in the South. Added together, these two periods of disunity came to a total of a little less than one hundred years. Furthermore, during the second and longest period of disunity, the South and the North each had one dynasty ruling at a time. The dynasties were short-lived and they succeeded, but did not coexist, with each other. In the third period of disunity, too, only one dynasty at a time ruled the North. No period of Indian history is marked by the supremacy of one dynasty over the entire country, not even the reign of Asoka.

Third, while the numberless warring factions which kept India in a constant state of turmoil were indigenous as well as foreign, practically all of the contenders for empire and all the struggling petty rulers who contributed to the periods of Chinese disunity were foreign. Only during the period of the Three Kingdoms (221–261 A.D.) were all contenders indigenous. Six of the seven successive dynasties which ruled China in the South and in the North during 420–589 A.D., three of the five successive dynasties in the North during 907–960 A.D., and both of the northern dynasties, when the Sung dynasty was confined to the South (1127–1280 A.D.), were Tartar in origin.

The last point of contrast between Chinese and Indian histories is most striking. It has been shown that the very existence of the Indian dynasties, foreign or native, and the control of their territories depended strictly upon the energy and intelligence of the individual rulers. The Chinese dynasties, though always started by powerful rulers, were not, for very considerable periods of time, dependent upon such rulers for their continuation. The distinguished career of the T'ang dynasty (618–907 A.D.) may be taken as a typical example. The dynasty was founded by Tai Tsung who expanded his empire to the greatest extent that China had ever known before the Mongols. He reigned only twenty-three years. Succeeding him was a long line of monarchs consisting not only of cruel and murderous individuals but outright incompetents who indulged in sex and drink, were dominated by eunuchs and concubines, or were lost in the search for an elixir of immortality. Their misrule was notorious. Sixty years after Tai Tsung's death one of his descendants reigned as Hsuan Tsung (713–757 A.D.). He was infatuated with a beautiful concubine snatched from the harem of one of his sons. The emperor appointed her brother prime minister. The country was so badly managed that the Tartars invaded the empire from the outside and one of the emperor's powerful ministers revolted from within. The emperor had to flee the capital and on the way was forced to order the execution of his favorite concubine. The rebels overran the capital and sacked it savagely. In spite of this, a loyal general was able to rally enough support to crush the rebels and invaders and restore the entire empire, the rule of which was then taken over by one of the useless emperor's sons, in whose favor the emperor was compelled to abdicate. Under similar adversity any one of the Indian dynasties would have either perished or been reduced to the position of a minor vassal. But after this debacle the T'ang dynasty was not succeeded by wise and energetic rulers. On the contrary the later monarchs were cruel,

stupid, and generally unfit to be rulers. Of the eighteen sovereigns of the
T'ang dynasty, three abdicated, ten were murdered or died from some sort
of elixir, and only eight died a natural death. Yet, it was not until one
and a half centuries after Hsuan Tsung abdicated (757 A.D.) that the domin-
ion of the T'ang dyasty came to an end.

For the student not thoroughly familiar with Chinese history three kinds
of misunderstandings often occur. The first is that Chinese dynastic governments were authoritarian. This is not so. In my view they were autocratic
or despotic, but not authoritarian. Authoritarianism is synonymous with dic-
tatorship and assumes a positive totalitarian control of the people. What the
Chinese dynastic governments desired and obtained was the passive acquiescence and obedience of the people.

Another misunderstanding is that Chinese dynastic governments were
too weak to exercise control over the entire nation because of the effects
of regional autonomy. It is easy to show that this notion is erroneous. Every
successful Chinese dynasty not only had to overcome initially the various
contenders for the throne but also to crush internal revolts and external
invasions, to undertake public works connected with irrigation and flood
control, and to select and appoint district governors and higher officials
who enjoyed enormous powers and prestige in every province. Furthermore,
during most of these dynastic rules, the governor of a distant province would
quietly commit suicide if he was ordered to do so by the emperor reigning
thousands of miles away.

The third kind of misunderstanding can easily obscure the essence of our
argument here. This misunderstanding is due to a confusion between state
and society. The Hindu *society* in terms of shared ideas, customs, groupings,
and tools may well have been more stable than the Chinese *society*, for the
social structure of Vedic India did not materially differ from that of pre-
British India, but the social structure of China at the time of Confucius
was very unlike that of eighteenth-century China. However, the Hindu
state in terms of territory, centralization of power, continuity of that
power, and general ability to provide peaceful government is a far cry from
the Chinese *state*, for it is obvious that most of the dynastic governments
of China were more centralized, more extensive, more stabilized, and hence
more continuous than any in India.

We should, therefore, expect India to show a greater clan-consciousness,
a fuller development of the clan as an institution, and a more extensive
existence of the clan organization in all parts of the country than is found
in China. Yet this is not the case, for as a whole the Indian clan is no more
than a name to be looked up before a marital alliance is contemplated. The
clan is amorphous in India, where the government was weak and lacked
centralization, while it was much more developed in China, where the politi-

cal situation was quite the reverse. Even among the Rajput princes and their imitators the interest in clan and genealogy is primarily for the purpose of hypergamy[26] in particular, and social exaltation in general, not, as in China, for the purpose of mutual benefit and solidarity between a specific group of departed ancestors (male and female, exalted and humble) and their true living descendants.

Superficially the facts presented here seem to contradict Lowie's observation on the inverse relationship between clan and strong centralized government. However, it is equally possible that the basic personal outlook of the individual fostered in the family is stronger than the power of governments. The Hindus do not have the strong feelings for family, kin, and ancestry that their Chinese brethren entertain. They have developed no clan organization comparable to that of the Chinese even though there was little in the way of political forces to suppress it. The Chinese maintained their clan in spite of such interfering political forces.[27]

NOTES FOR CHAPTER IV

1. The most important of these common effects is that the individual's process of growing up in Hindu and Chinese families lacks the sort of upheaval characteristic of the individual's development in the American family. The reason is that Hindu and Chinese children are initiated into the adult world without the sharp discontinuity commonly experienced by their American counterparts. For a description of the contrast between Chinese and American families in this regard, see F. L. K. Hsu, *Americans and Chinese: Two Ways of Life* (New York: Abelard-Schuman, 1953), pp. 334–340. For Samoa, see M. Mead, *Coming of Age in Samoa* (New York: Morrow, 1928). A Hindu educator said to Mrs. Gardner Murphy, when she and her husband were in India on a UNESCO research mission studying tension: "We live with our children; you bring yours up." See Lois Murphy, "Roots of Tolerance and Tensions in Indian Child Development," in Gardner Murphy, *In the Minds of Men* (New York: Basic Books, 1953), p. 51. Earlier another student on India made similar observations.—Quoted in David Mandelbaum, "The Family in India," *Southwestern Journal of Anthropology*, IV, No. 2 (Summer 1948), 123–139.

2. Ralph Linton, *The Study of Man* (New York: Appleton-Century, 1936), pp. 197–200.

3. George P. Murdock, *Social Structure* (New York: The Macmillan Co., 1949), pp. 68–69.

4. For example, David Mandelbaum, "Social Groupings," in H. L. Shapiro (ed.), *Man, Culture and Society* (New York: Oxford University Press, 1956), p. 295; I. Karve, *Kinship Organization in India* (Poona: Deccan College Monograph Series, 1953), p. 58, and many others.

5. This list is compiled from my own field research and from published sources as detailed in Appendix I to this chapter.

6. I. Karve, *op. cit.*, p. 59; and Pandharinath H. Prabhu, *Hindu Social Organization*, 3rd ed. (Bombay: Popular Book Depot, 1958), p. 155.

7. I. Karve, *op. cit.*, pp. 119–120; Oscar Lewis, *Village Life in Northern India* (Urbana: University of Illinois Press, 1958), pp. 160–162.

8. I. Karve, *op. cit.*, p. 141.

9. *Ibid.*, p. 119.

10. Maurice Freedman, *Lineage-Organization in Southeastern China* (London: The Athlone Press, 1958), p. 84.

11. *Ibid.*, p. 84.

12. See for example, Hsien Chin Hu, *The Common Descent Group in China and Its Functions* "Viking Fund Publication in Anthropology," No. 10 (New York: Wenner-Gren Foundation for Anthropological Research, 1948), p. 37 and pp. 122–124. This phenomenon is very common elsewhere.

13. Maurice Freedman, *op. cit.*, p. 84. In southern Fukien and among the Formosan-born Chinese "all" the ancestors of the clan are represented at the family shrine by what is known as the "Picture of Ten Thousand Longevities," that is, a large or small red scroll bearing the word for longevity (*shou*) in gold, written in a hundred different forms. This scroll is hung just behind the tablets representing individual ancestors up to the third or fifth ascending generation counting from the head of the household. In some instances one or two additional tablets representing recently deceased, who may be junior or senior to the head of the household, are also placed in the same shrine.

14. Hsien Chin Hu, *op. cit.*, p. 117. Freedman refers to this fact. Freedman, *op. cit.*, p. 80.

15. *Ibid.*, p. 84.

16. H. T. Fei, *Peasant Life in China: A Field Study of Country Life in the Yangtze Valley* (London: Routledge and Kegan Paul, 1939), p. 84. Quoted by Freedman, *op. cit.*, p. 42.

17. Stephen Fuchs, *Children of Hari* (New York: Frederick A. Praeger, 1951), pp. 238–245.

18. W. H. Newell, "Goshen, a Gaddi Village in the Himalayas," in *India's Villages* (West Bengal Development Department, 1955), pp. 52–53.

19. According to Milton Singer, Personal communication.

20. See F. L. K. Hsu, *Under the Ancestors' Shadow* (New York: Columbia University Press, 1948), pp. 122–130. A most brilliant structuralist-functionalist analysis as applied to the Chinese kinship organization, especially in Fukien and Kwangtung provinces, is to be found in Maurice Freedman, *op. cit.*

21. Hsien Chin Hu, *op. cit.*, p. 95.

22. R. H. Lowie, *An Introduction to Cultural Anthropology* (New York: Farrar and Rinehart, 1940), p. 256.

23. Nilakanta Shastri, *A History of South India* (Oxford: Oxford University Press, 1955), p. 95.

24. *The Early History of India*, 4th ed. (Oxford: Oxford University Press, 1957), p. 370.

25. This tabulation is based on the following books: R. C. Majumder, H. C. Raychudhuri, and K. Datta, *An Advanced History of India* (London: Macmillan, 1948); R. C. Majumder, III, *The History and Culture of the Indian People*, 5 vols. (London: George Allen and Unwin, 1957); and V. A. Smith, *Early History of India* (Oxford: Oxford University Press, 1957).

26. This fact will be discussed in Chapter V.

27. Probably the regional variation of the clan in China was correlated with the political factor. It should be logical to assume the strength of the centralized gov-

ernments to be greater near the national capital, but weaker farther away from it. The Chinese clan was strongest in the south, weaker in the north, and more formal than solid in the southwest. Practically all the capitals of the major Chinese dynasties were located in the north.

APPENDIX I—*Terms Related to Gotra and Their Meanings*

Vamsa. This term is defined in the classical sense as "a successive line of descent from father to son" (I. Karve, *Kinship Organization in India*, 1953, p. 50). In contemporary Rajput usage, the term is *bansa*. Karve translates this term as the "superclan" of the Rajputs. *Bansa* is not, however, exogamous. On the contrary, it tends to be endogamous, since the *gulas* (major clans) which compose the *bansas* intermarry with each other (*ibid.*, p. 140).

Kula. In the classical sense this term means "the whole of the patri-family residing at one place." According to Karve the difference between *vamsa* and *kula*, in ancient India, was that the former "was a linear arrangement" while the latter "referred to an 'aggregate'" (*ibid.*, p. 51). On the other hand, *kula* is the term used by the Rajputs today to designate a division of the *bansa:* the "major-clan" (*ibid.*, p. 140). Yet sometimes the terms *gotra* and *kula* were used interchangeably in various classics to denote "clan." The picture was further muddled by two facts: (*a*) "Descendants of one ancestor were in the habit of having many Kula by taking on the names of any of the famous ancestors they chose" (*ibid.*, p. 59), and (*b*) in referring to royal lines the word *kula* has been translated as dynasty [Nilakanta Shastri, *A History of South India* (Oxford: Oxford University Press, 1955), p. 87].

In a Deccan village in Hyderabad, Dube reports the use of the term *vansham* which he describes as a subclan, as distinguished from *gotram*. An individual in this village must marry outside one's own *gotram* and *vansham* [S. C. Dube, *Indian Village* (Ithaca: Cornell University Press, 1955), pp. 42–44]. Miss Gitel Steed in a personal communication told me of *kul* in Gujarati, which is also a division within the *gotra*. Members of a *kul* are forbidden to marry each other. McKim Marriott speaks of each local caste group of a village in Uttar Pradesh as comprising "one of several lineages—patrilineal and patrilocal kin groups," within which some economic cooperation is present, but he does not specify its name nor mention the question of exogamy [McKim Marriott, "Social Structure and Change in a U.P. Village," in *India's Villages* (West Bengal Development Department, 1955), p. 99].

Gana. This was described by Mrs. Karve, on the basis of the ancient texts, as a division of *gotra*, among members of which marriage could not take place. The term also has two other meanings: (1) a tribal republic among the ancient Aryans [A. L. Basham, *The Wonder That Was India* (London: Sidgwick and Jackson, 1954), p. 41]; (2) a demigod attendant of Siva (*ibid.*, p. 308). In contemporary Bengal the term *gain* is known to some informants as referring to a territorial unit of some kind, where the Kanauj Brahmans of Western Uttar Pradesh were invited to settle by King Adisura in the early centuries of the Christian era. These families were the Pancha Gaur Brahmans (Pancha means five; Gaur was the ancient capital of Bengal). Each family was given several villages for its support and each group of such villages made up a *gain*. Brahmans of the same *gain* could not intermarry. Strictly speaking even two Bengali Brahman families such as Ganguli and Mukhopanyay, which could and can as a rule intermarry, would be forbidden to do so if

COHESION VERSUS DIVISION: CLAN IN CHINA AND INDIA

they happened to be from the same *gain*. However, *gain* no longer has any function in marital arrangement or anything else. It is possible that the nameless exogamous territorial unit in north India, mentioned above, may be a survival of this.

Pravara. The term means "excellent ones" according to one authority (I. Karve, *Hindu Social Organization*, pp. 58–59), and "invocation" or "summons" according to another (P. Prabhu: *op. cit.*, p. 155). It is the name of one of the famous ancestors chosen arbitrarily by a Brahman when declaring his own *gotra* or when invoking Agni (fire god) to carry libations to the gods. A Brahman may have one, two, three, or five *pravaras* but not four. In general, according to the ancient rules a man and a woman who had one *pravara* in common could not marry, with certain exceptions (I. Karve, *Hindu Social Organization*, p. 60). When other castes like the Kshatriyas imitated the Brahmans they adopted the *pravaras* of the Brahmans as their own [K. M. Kapadia, *Hindu Kinship* (Bombay: Popular Book Depot, 1947), pp. 81–82]. The *pravaras* were therefore not their ancestors at all. The Rajputs mentioned before are a modern example of this. Today *pravara* has no marital function in any region of India. In Bengal *pravaras* may be recited when a Brahman priest performs certain rituals for a family during the Upanaya (sacred thread ceremony), Sandya (morning and evening prayers before the family shrine), Sradh (mortuary rite), and Mahalaya (annual water offering to ancestors). On such occasions the priest who officiates will be given a piece of paper on which are written the *pravaras* of the family for his recitation. Sometimes the priest keeps a list of ten *pravaras* of each of the families for which he regularly works. Some Bengalis tell me that they used to keep such a list in their families but that lately they had lost the papers on which the *pravaras* were written. In Madras and Mysore some middle-aged Brahmans could repeat some of the names which their family priests recited on ritual occasions but did not know if they were *pravaras*. In the same two southern states I did not meet a single individual of thirty years or younger, educated or otherwise, who had more than a vague idea as to what *pravara* was about. The average priest of mature age usually is very specific in his exposition of its classical meaning. Such a person usually also knows his own *pravara*.

Sasan. "A royal charter by which Brahmins were given land by the ancient and medieval kings in India." "The Brahmin families in one Sasan are prohibited from intermarrying even though they belong to different Gotras." According to Mrs. Karve this term is still used today in Punjab and the Delhi region to cover exogamy of a given locality (I. Karve, *Hindu Social Organization*, pp. 117–118).

Sapinda. The word *pinda* means an object formed by compressing or heaping articles together. Today when cooked rice is formed into a ball to be used as offering to ancestors, it is called a *pinda*. *Sapinda* means people who are descendants of a common forefather, but it also includes relatives to a certain degree on the mother's side. It is said that, according to the *sapinda* relationship, "a man should not marry a girl who is related to him through a common male ancestor up to the seventh generation in the father's line and up to the fifth generation in the mother's line" (*ibid.*, p. 55), but the precise number of generations involved has always varied in the codes and practice of different groups. However, the boundary of this relationship has never been clear. Various sages said it should include the seventh generation on both sides; ninth on the father's and fifth on the mother's; or third on the mother's and fifth on the father's, and so on (K. M. Kapadia, *op. cit.*, pp. 72–82). Today the *sapinda* relationship is not a factor in mate selection nor in grouping of relatives.

Devaka. A symbol connected with the Maharashtran *kulas* (clans); it may be a living thing or an artifact. *Devaka* is worshiped at the time of marriage, but has "no significance in ordinary life." No two people having the same *devaka* can marry. "Very few people seem to carry the name of Devaka as the family name. The Devaka is not known to many people . . ." but "elders . . . look into these matters at the time of the marriage" (I. Karve, *Hindu Social Organization*, p. 157). I have not come across this term in North India, Bengal, or South India.

A whole series of terms are used for an exogamous unit in different linguistic regions in South India) nos. 9 to 18 in the list on page 62). *Bedagu* or *bedaga* or *bali* is used among many Karnatak castes; *keri* among the Kotas of Nilgiri hills; *kilai* among the Kottai Vellal; *gatta* among the Koya; *gumpu* among the Kuruba; *veli* among the people of Travancore; *inti-peru* among Telugu speakers; and *vidu* among Tamil speakers [*ibid.*, p. 182, quoting Edgar Thurston: *Castes and Tribes of Southern India* (Madras: Government Press, 1909)]. Other variations are not enumerated here. The actual names of these units have meanings which vary from those of plants and animals to those of inanimate things and artifacts. These units have no other function except exogamy. The individuals belonging to each group cannot and do not care to trace themselves to a common ancestor.

In addition to the eighteen terms listed and discussed there are *sanobhi*, *jna*, *jnati*, *api*, *jami*, *sajata*, *bandhava*, terms used in ancient texts to refer to kin in general or to somewhat nearer relatives. The meaning or meanings of these terms are extremely vague (K. M. Kapadia, *op. cit.*, pp. 124–131). At any rate none of these terms has, to my knowledge, any circulation in the major regions of India. Oscar Lewis reports from his North India village the use of the term *kunba* as a "group or relatives who trace their relationship through the male line," but its boundary can vary from a father and son to all male descendants of a great-great-grandfather (Oscar Lewis, *op. cit.*, p. 22). At the other end of the scale, Lewis describes the *bisagama*, which consists of twenty villages and which forms "an exogamous as well as an administrative unit." But the *bisagama* leaves out branches of the *gotra* which moved away, and includes the incorporation of five villages of other *gotras* by adoption (*ibid*, p. 23), and is therefore not within the meaning of clan.

APPENDIX II—*Tensions in Clan and Its Resolution: A Case History*

The following extended narrative, taken from the autobiography of Hu Shan, father of Dr. Hu Shih, the famous Chinese philosopher and statesman, tells us much about the nature and outcome of intraclan tensions in China:

In 1865, when the author was 25 years old, the *tsu* debated the question of erecting a new ancestral hall, the old one having been destroyed during the T'ai-p'ing Uprising in 1851. Four delegates (szu-shih), including the author, were chosen and commissioned to plan and carry out the project. As the author had the best ideas, he was chosen to work out a scheme for obtaining money. His plan was to raise the funds in three ways:

1. By individual compulsory contributions, each man paying 200 cash per year, other persons 100 cash each.

2. By labor contributions, each strong man between the ages of 18 and 60 per-

forming the equivalent of two days of labor per year. Those who did not work had to pay 140 cash annually.

3. By contributions according to business enterprise, people who had capital invested in business paying one thousand to several ten-thousand cash annually according to their profits.

After the scheme was worked out, rites to the ancestors were performed to advise them of it, and then it was made public to the *tsu*, after which preparations for the work began.

During the next years the author was occupied mostly with his studies, and the other delegates were left in charge of the work concerning the ancestral hall. In 1867, on a visit to his father in Shanghai, he helped several *tsu* uncles and granduncles to urge members of the *tsu* in business there to report the amount of the annual contribution they proposed to make for the ancestral hall. They also asked each person who was an employee to give one month's salary annually. The author was able to contribute $500 in silver (Chinese currency) to take back to his village.

In 1871 the main room for keeping the ancestral tablets was completed. The members of the *tsu* wanted to leave it at that, but the author insisted that it should be finished like the old one that had been destroyed, with three sets of rooms: the front gate, the central hall, and the smaller rooms where the tablets were stored between rituals. He felt that as a plan had been formulated by which money could be obtained it was best to finish the construction. If it was discontinued the *tsu* would probably grow weary, and it would be difficult to resume work. So far few contributions had been paid and the work was sustained mainly by what the author and his two *tsu* uncles could collect in Shanghai. After the front gate and the right- and left-hand buildings were completed the work stopped. As the author was the only one insisting that it should go on, and as he was studying away from home, the other delegates asked him to return, for the *tsu* members were growing tired. He consulted his teacher and was advised that, according to the classics, his duty lay in completing the ancestral hall.

When he returned he first went to see a *tsu* granduncle by the name of T'i-ch'ing, in the nearby town of Hsiu-ning, because this man was the eldest and most influential in the *tsu*. Later, when he met with the *tsu* members they complained of the inadequacy of financial means. They would need at least several years to accumulate the 3000 strings of cash (one string equals 1000 cash) necessary for terminating the construction work. He insisted it should be carried out in one year, so as not to allow the enthusiasm to die down. But the problem could not be settled.

The next year there was a reshuffling of delegates. Some had died, some lived away from the home village or took no interest in the scheme. Knowing the difficulties of realizing the original plan, each one hesitated to accept the responsibility. The author knew that the crowd was hard to argue with, "they could be made to follow, but not to know." Hence, he stopped the discussions and spent the following months measuring the completed part of the ancestral hall in detail, and calculating the costs of the materials necessary to its completion, the costs of preparing the woodwork, of transportation and all other expenditures, down to the number of nails and tiles. He found that 3000 strings of cash would be amply sufficient, as he had told the *tsu*. He went over the account-books of contributions, determined the financial circumstances of each individual family, and estimated how much money could be asked from each one. But after two months, when he had worked out the whole scheme by which funds could be raised and used to the best advantage, he realized that he would have to devote himself completely to the task in order to bring it to completion. One of the other delegates looked up a calendar, and found the next year would be extremely propitious for dedicating the ancestral hall. He decided it must be in time for that date, even if he, the author, had to take the whole responsibility upon himself. The other man was skeptical. The next day the *tsu* was assembled and was told that next year the ancestral hall would have to be finished. They all agreed. The 15th of the 10th month was chosen for the day of inauguration. The fall and winter of this year the author spent in selecting timber for beams, traveling up and down the whole neighborhood in search of suitable wood. In this he was helped by a relative in the lumber business. All travelling expenses were borne by himself.

Early in 1873 the author moved into the building next to the ancestral hall to supervise the work and at the same time to keep an eye on the studies of his younger brother and nephew. On the 11th day of the 1st month he assembled the other delegates to discuss with them the first steps of the undertaking. He showed them his scheme for raising funds: individual contributions to be increased tenfold, labor contributions to be increased by the same amount, and contributions by business five-fold. All were appalled and said the *tsu* would be unable to bear this burden, it was better to reduce the dues. The author said it was too late if the work was to be terminated at all. They would have to face the fight, otherwise they could not win. Asked if they wanted to bear the blame for the failure they did not answer. The plans were then made public and able-bodied men drafted for transporting lumber from the mountains. Within the 2nd and 3rd months the wood was to be brought to the village. *Tsu* members, seeing that the lumber had been prepared and that the work was to begin at once, though grumbling about the exorbitant demands made on them for providing funds, were anxious to start so as to see the ancestral hall finished soon. The author was glad of this enthusiasm, for transportation costs would have been considerable. By using *tsu* members for the work he saved this money. Also he had purposely increased the individual and labor dues. While forgiving the transport workers their contributions he saved over a thousand strings. After the 120 men had given their work the rest would not be able to refuse the payment of contributions.

All the lumber had been cut to size and shape at the place of felling. The author visited each place, he estimated the weight of every piece, and numbered the lumber, entering all details into his book. Then he returned and sent two, four, six, eight or twelve men to each location, according to the size of the job. He gave each group a slip bearing the number of the piece of lumber they were to carry, so as to avoid conflict and confusion. After they returned, the details were entered in a book to avoid oversights. At this time there was no work to be done in the fields, so people had enough leisure for this extra work. Also, as the winter wheat had not yet sprouted, little damage was done when the roads were too narrow for the porters. Since all knew that the work had to be done soon in order to complete the ancestral hall, they all worked cheerfully. A few men came to ask for remuneration. The author explained to them that their individual and labor contributions were to be cancelled against this work. According to the rule of the ancestors, those whose individual contributions had not been paid could not install the tablets of their family dead in the ancestral hall. Now their personal ancestors were assured of a place therein. No one objected. The transportation of lumber was completed in the 3rd month.

When he had an opportunity to visit Hsiu-ning, he urged the relatives there to pay their shares and brought back some money. During the second part of the year various building materials arrived and funds became indispensable. Some *tsu* members were not doing well in business, and they could only double the original assessment. Others were well enough off to meet the new five-fold increase demanded and were eager to do it. There were many disputes among relatives and it was hard to arrange things to suit everybody. Worrying about ways to get relatives to pay, the author conceived the idea of adding two extra rooms at the end of the ancestral hall: one on the east side where the tablets of the virtuous men and women of the *tsu* would be installed, and where those who paid 500 strings of cash after their death would be associated in the sacrifices. In the room on the west side there were to be three shrines: one for the rites to those who had exerted themselves in the service of the ancestral hall, where the ancestors of those who paid 100 strings would be associated. The shrines to the right and left were to be reserved for the ancestors of those who paid 50 strings each, these tablets to be called "those keeping company in eating." All contributions from business members since 1866 were to be put to the credit of the contributors. All those who paid twice, three times or five times the original assessment during the coming year, were to be credited with twice the amount of their contributions, which were listed in an account called the "Emergency Public Contribution." If several brothers or nephews paid the business contribution without being able to pay in full, such contributions were to be added together and the tablet of one of their ancestors installed in one of the two end-rooms so as to be associated in the enjoyment of the sacrifices. (The others were entitled to have four generations of ancestors installed.) All these were to be honored with special rites at the spring and autumn equinoxes. This procedure was modelled on the systems of rewards for contributions to the national treasury.

When in the 7th month the author thought of taking the provincial examination, the work was in mid-course and the other delegates were afraid of taking over the responsibility. No one would take over the author's job in his absence. So he asked a *tsu* uncle whom he knew as reliable to come and supervise the work, first paying small amounts to the merchants who had to deliver goods, and enjoining them to bring their materials, but they all agreed not to expect any more money till his return.

After the examination the author went to Shanghai where his father had fallen sick. When his father seemed to be on the road to recovery, the author set out to collect contributions. Two of his *tsu* uncles, knowing his difficulties in completing the ancestral hall, urged all members in the city to contribute to the best of their ability. All knew that he was torn by worry about his father and worry about the ancestral hall, and they gave generously. In less than twenty days, he was able to obtain 1500 strings. He at once dispatched a letter to his home reassuring the *tsu*.

Just at this time his father died. The five sons were all in Shanghai at the time, and after placing the body in the coffin they accompanied it home.

On the journey the author fell ill of liver trouble which grew worse after his arrival at home. Yet all the delegates for the ancestral hall came daily to discuss business matters. The construction was under way, the beams had been put in place, but the work was not finished. Fortunately he had the money to satisfy the artisans. By December the work was completed. The costs were found to be just over 2930 strings and the *tsu* members saw that the author had been right in his original estimate of 3000 strings.

The ancestral hall now had a central hall, 60 feet wide and 30 feet high, with beams 12 feet in circumference. The stone pillars in front of this hall and out on the porch were from one foot to one and one-half foot square. The original store-rooms for the ancestral tablets were hardly the size of this new building. In all some 5000 strings of cash had been used for the structure.

However, the ancestral hall still needed inner decorations and furnishings which would cost another 3000 strings.

During 1874 the author was sick part of the time. Work on the walls and roof of the ancestral halls was completed.

In 1875 the author discussed with other scholars in the neighborhood the best arrangement of the tablets. (The account of these two years is extremely short, part of the manuscript having been destroyed by fire.)

Early in 1876 the author talked over the question of funds with his uncle. They went over the books in which the property of *tsu* members were listed and the registers of yearly income; they also examined the list of members for those who smoked opium. They found that the *tsu* spent more for opium alone than its income from rice, wheat, bamboo and tea, and was maintained entirely by remittances from members abroad. The author told his uncle that the work on the ancestral hall must be finished within this year, or the *tsu* would so deteriorate that it could never be done. The uncle asked how he was going to raise the money since all possible contributions had been collected. The author showed him from a list that a number had not yet paid. According to the rule of the ancestors, whoever had not paid the dues could not place the tablets of his recent ancestors in the hall. So the delinquents would have to pay. The uncle asked: what if some people refused contributions even though their ancestors were neglected. Moreover, payments would not come in till the ancestral hall was ready for opening, while the workmen had to be paid as soon as the work was done. The author said he believed that if the relatives abroad were notified to return for the first ritual in the new hall, the stubborn members would not dare to refuse when the neighboring *tsu* and their ancestral halls sent presents and the relatives-in-law began to arrive. Meanwhile, payment for the workers could be put off until the completion of the work. The uncle said: "If you can take the responsibility, do so, I don't dare to." The author had studied books on ritual and had decided to arrange the ancestral tablets on the right and left in alternate generations, beginning with the first ancestor. The uncle said it looked all right to him, but all the *tsu* in the neighborhood placed their first ancestor in the center; the members of the *tsu* might think this new arrangement too extraordinary. But the author wished to establish this new way. If there was too much objection, they could always return to the old system.

One day, speaking to a *tsu* uncle, the author mentioned the fact that only 300 strings were needed immediately for the completion of the hall on schedule. The uncle promised to lay out the sum. The date chosen for the inauguration was the 13th of the 10th month.

The *tsu* granduncle T'i-ch'ing was most influential. He was prosperous and had over twenty brothers (i.e. cousins) by the same grandfather. *Tsu*-members used to call him "hsien-sheng"—"sir." When he had been asked to undertake the building of the ancestral hall he had refused on the grounds of age and the distance of his residence from the village. He had known the difficulties involved, having witnessed the building of the former ancestral hall. He had suggested that the author, his uncle and another *tsu* uncle be appointed for the task. The delegates for the ancestral hall had consulted him whenever an important step was taken, to be sure of his support, and they had always been encouraged by this granduncle. This man's son, however, was not well disposed toward the author and had sometimes insinuated that the latter was trying to appropriate the dues for his own use. Now, in the 3rd month of 1876 this *tsu* uncle offered a suggestion, allegedly from his father, that at the inauguration of the ancestral hall all those who had not paid their dues in money or labor were to be forgiven, and their ancestor's tablets accepted regardless, just as the government at times forgives taxes to the destitute. Those who had not yet paid their contributions to the ancestral hall were most of them tricky men and hence rejoiced at these words. They went so far as to deride those who had paid their dues beforehand, priding themselves on having withheld the contributions for so long. The author would not listen to such a suggestion and maintained that the rule must not be broken. A group of the delinquent members went to visit the granduncle T'i-ch'ing and were met by his son in the near-by town. He rejoiced that his trick was working, and told the delegation that the author wanted to control the construction work ("run the show himself"), but that he and his near relatives would see to it that the *tsu* had its say, so that the ancestral hall would not be dominated by the author alone. He said there was no need to see his father, and so they did not consult the latter.

In the 6th month the author had to leave for another examination. Before his departure he had a conversation with an uncle, begging him to lay out $200 for the workmen. He himself would be going to Shanghai after the examination to collect business dues for the year. He explained that he would not return until the 9th month, close to the inauguration date. Therefore he knew that before he left the workmen would come to ask that their wages be paid at least in part. They would have to be satisfied, so as to assure the smooth continuation of the work. He expected, too, that the relatives from Hsiu-ning would stir up trouble when the time came. If Granduncle T'i-ch'ing would be present personally at the dedication, "on the basis of feeling and reason" there was the possibility of a peaceful settlement. If his sons came there was likely to be an acute conflict, but by that time the work would be finished. The author would have fulfilled his duty to his ancestors, and he could therefore justify himself in front of the *tsu*, which at the dedication would include relatives who had come from far away to take part. Now if the opposition wanted to take over the affairs of the ancestral hall, they would be welcome to do so, if they acknowledged the debts incurred. If they refused to, he, the author, would remain adamant and other members would have to compose the quarrel, and at least the enemies could not speak for those who refused to pay their dues. The *tsu* uncle with whom he was having this conversation agreed to lay out the $200. His own uncle, who was also present, expressed the opinion that Granduncle T'i-ch'ing would not appear on the occasion and he himself had always disliked to speak to T'i-ch'ing's sons. Hence, when they arrived he was determined to close his doors and begging his nephew's pardon, he would refuse to see them. (This uncle was one of the delegates for the ancestral hall.) His nephew, laughing, said it was all right.

They further discussed whether they should provide a theatrical performance for the opening of the ancestral hall, as had always been done. The author said it would be essential to provide it. He also said he would start the registration for the new genealogy on the very date of the hall's dedication. It was necessary to give the opening of the ancestral hall as much eclat as possible. The performance and the registration for the genealogy would satisfy the expectations of the members of the *tsu*, so it would not be difficult to register on the spot the ancestors whose tablets were being brought in, and to trace their relationship to the membership as given in previous genealogies. He planned to raise the dues for entering the tablets of the ancestors and for registration in the genealogical lists from 60 to 300 cash. This would give the opposition another argument for attack. However, they could not restrain the delegates for the ancestral hall from performing the rites for the first ancestor and various other ancestors, including those of the people who had paid their dues and contributed their labor as required. However, in the face of the delegates from neighboring ancestral halls and the relatives-in-law of all *tsu* members who would be present to enjoy the theatrical performances, the feeling for justice would not be lacking and *tsu* would not follow the opposition. They might feel ashamed to continue the dispute at all. Yet he deplored the weakness of their own following, which made a strong stand difficult. He foresaw that, when the individuals from Hsiu-ning came, the discontented would flock to them "like a boiling cauldron, like a river breaking its dam." However, he foresaw that other delegates, afraid of being implicated, would keep away. Not only would the very few who were determined to make a stand have to face a crowd, but they had many tasks before them: the purchase of equipment and of sacrificial animals to be used at the rites, the greeting of guests who came to congratulate them, the preparation of the offerings and the feast, the working out of the accounts of dues already paid and still outstanding, the receiving of dues that would come in, and the registration of the tablets of various ancestors, the supervision of the theatrical entertainment and of the workmen around the ancestral hall. Without a doubt many quarrels about inheritances would be taken to the ancestral hall for arbitration, and there would be accusations against persons for accepting inheritances without sending in the tablets of the persons they were heir to. He foresaw great difficulties in attending to all these different details. However, answering a question by one uncle, he said, since his cause was right and his goal a great one, he intended to stand up for his program with body and spirit. He knew that his opponents dared not fight before they had assembled; but during the first ten days of the 10th month, when the ancestral hall was about ready, the trouble-makers would gather their strength and start a quarrel. As they grew in strength, his party would grow weaker, and who knew where the troublemakers would stop. However, even though he, the author, failed, the ancestral hall would be completed, and in some way the rites would be performed and his efforts through ten long years would not be spent in vain. "Since I undertook this work as the member of a younger generation, if they accuse me of grabbing power, I have no way to argue for myself. How can I hold out to the end?" However, he was determined to hold out as long as possible, and not to show any weakness till the inevitable happened. If his party showed no determination at the point, their cause would be lost.

After the examination he, together with two *tsu* uncles, collected $1000 in Shanghai from business relatives, much to his joy. When he returned in the middle of the 9th month his son was sick and the bad news came that he himself had failed in the provincial examinations (as he had previously), but, disregarding everything, he plunged into the work relating to the ancestral hall.

The members who had not paid their individual and labor contributions came to ask whether their ancestors could be installed first and the dues paid later. The author refused. They argued that all *tsu* members agreed that it was all right; how could he alone object? He asked if they were prepared to take over the responsibility for the debts incurred. They evaded the question and still maintained that, the ancestral hall being the property of the whole *tsu*, its affairs had to be decided by the whole *tsu* and not by him alone. He asked whether it was reasonable for the *tsu* to champion those who were in arrears with contributions for many years, without thinking of some way of paying the debts? They had no answer.

Very soon, someone warned the author that some of his opponents had ordered swords from the blacksmith. He would not be moved. More reports came that eighty men in the village had equipped themselves with a sword each to fight him. He thought the situation over, then decided that if he showed fear, they would become all the stronger. So he ordered two coffins made, one for the future use of his mother, one for himself. When his mother heard of this, she reproved him severely. He explained the situation to her in detail. Privately he told his younger brother not to be afraid. Should he actually be killed, the brother was to place his body in the coffin, and to install the latter in the central hall of the ancestral hall. "To have built this ancestral hall by straining to the limit the resources of the *tsu* members, in order to house my coffin, will be a satisfaction to me though I die (literally, 'I shall have no regrets to die'), he said sarcastically. When the coffin was completed, the author asked the elders and the delegates for the ancestral hall to move into the offices of the ancestral hall to await him.

In the first days of the 10th month the *tsu* uncles from Hsiu-ning came, together with their brothers and cousins, some twenty men in all, but not the granduncle. They felt that the *tsu* members had acted too rashly, and came with kind words to beg the ancestral hall to have mercy on the poor in the *tsu* who were unable to pay their dues. In this way they tried to advance their own plan. The author laughed at them, saying that they did not have to beg at all. The members of the *tsu* had prepared eighty swords already, he himself had prepared his coffin and was just waiting for them (that is, the leaders of the opposition) to fight it out. "When I die, you gentlemen can take over." The uncles protested that there was no such intention, nobody had swords. The author turned to the crowd that followed them and, laughing, told the recalcitrants that their swords being ready, they might just as well go ahead. The uncles were afraid that some accident might happen and ordered the crowd to retire. Continuing their discussion with the author in private, they asked whether he suspected they had come to fight him to the finish. He said he did not have to suspect it. The *tsu* members had threatened him, but so far they had lacked a leader. Now the uncles had come. The ancestral hall was completed, and he, the author, felt he had done his duty to the ancestors. He believed he could not escape the catastrophe; he did not have to imagine the danger. This was the 7th, he reminded them, only five days before the date fixed for the installment of the ancestral tablets. If he did not die, he would be an obstacle to them. If they did not carry out their purpose quickly, they would not have time for the rest of the work. They still maintained that they were trying to negotiate peacefully with him. He asked what was there to negotiate. *It was the rule of the ancestors that when dues had not been paid by an individual, his ancestral tablets could not go up into the ancestral hall.* That was not his ordinance. 2000 more strings of cash were needed to pay for the work and the equipment of the ancestral hall. He had planned to pay this with the contributions which some people had owed for many years, and with the fees for entering the ancestral tablets and for registration in the genealogy. If only the uncles would take the responsibility for paying this sum out of their pockets, the ancestral hall would be free of debt and the members of the *tsu* would be most grateful to them. They said they were unable to take the responsibility upon themselves. The author answered: "During the last few years, I have borne the responsibility for the ancestral hall alone. You uncles may have heard of the innumerable difficulties connected with it. And yet, this small matter (which I lay before you) you cannot take upon yourselves? If you will not take it upon yourselves, I still have to bear it, and I certainly shall not shirk it. Yet you come trying to change the rule of the ancestors and to mislead the *tsu*, so as to cause difficulties for me and bring disaster on the affairs of the ancestral hall. For what purpose is that?" They explained that they wanted to talk it over with the elders and the other delegates for the ancestral hall. The author told them that the others were too frightened to appear. He alone did not fear death and awaited his "punishment" at the ancestral hall. They might try to ask the delegates to come, he was unable to persuade them.

The next day the uncles had persuaded the other delegates and elders to gather together. They did not raise their voices again for those who refused to pay their dues, and only alleged that the *tsu* did not like the arrangement of the tablets, by which the first ancestor would be placed on one side. Since the day before the author had insisted the "rule of the ancestors" be observed, they now used the same argument, charging that he was arbitrarily changing the original arrangement. The author said, when the plan for the new arrangement was devised, he had consulted their father, Granduncle T'i-ch'ing, and, showing him the diagrams, had obtained his consent. Before the ancestral hall was completed he had once more gone with the other delegates to ask his advice. One son of the granduncle now present knew of the plan, and at the time had not expressed disapproval. The individual in question now said that he never had approved of it. The author asked where in the classics he found the system which the *tsu* demanded, by which the first ancestor would be placed in the center, and the other ancestors on the right and left according to sex (this being the arrangement common in this neighborhood). He challenged the uncle to find the passage in the classics to prove his point. The uncle said though the classics did not prescribe it, the ancestors had practiced it for many years. He, the author, had no right to change it arbitrarily. The author asked him whether he could be considered arbitrary, since he had formulated the plan only after consultation with the other delegates, and then had personally consulted his opponent's father about the plan. The uncle said that even his father could not change the institution at will. The author countered that if his opponent dared openly in the ancestral hall to blame his own father for changing the system, he, the author, would also have to accept personally the same blame. However, in the matter of ancestral rites, *li* (ceremonial) was involved. If an act is in accordance with *li*, a change is right and a neglect of this change is wrong, for *li* is directly related to *i* (duty). The question was whether the change was in accordance with *li* or not. The uncles still maintained that the system used by the ancestors could not be changed, or the members of the *tsu* would not follow him. The author then pointed out that the last time when the building of the ancestral hall had been completed, the tablets of ancestors in mythical times had been abolished. How could that change have been effected by their predecessors, if the system of the ancestors was always to be maintained in its entirety? The uncles had no more argument and the crowd gradually dispersed.

The situation grew more tense. The other delegates kept away and left the author alone to confront the opposition. His mother was much concerned about his health and safety, and sent his brother to call him home. But he could not leave, although he felt extremely weary. Meanwhile the opposition did not insist on refusing the dues, but concentrated their demands on the point that the old arrangement of the ancestral tablets be retained. His own uncle now sent advice that the author should give in on this point and stop the dispute. Some other *tsu* uncles also asked him to give in on the most important points. On the 9th the neighboring ancestral halls began sending congratulatory gifts. Members of the *tsu* who had paid their dues came to ask for tablets on which to inscribe the names of their ancestors and to ask for registration in the genealogy. But there was only the author to take care of all the work involved. On the 10th his mother came personally to the ancestral hall to reprimand him severely. So he finally agreed that the tablets of the ancestors be arranged in the old way. On the 11th the conversion was effected by placing the tablet of the first ancestor in the center, but his idea that each individual bring four generations of ancestors to the ancestral hall was retained.

On the 12th all preparations for the rites were completed, offerings made ready, rites explained by the author, etc. On the 13th the tablets of the first ancestor and several other ancestors up to the time this branch of the Ming-chin Hu had moved into the village, were installed. Representatives of the ancestral halls of neighboring *tsu* came to present their congratulations and relatives-in-law of all *tsu* members arrived for the same purpose. The recalcitrant members of the *tsu* now came forward to pay all their dues, because they could not bear not to see their ancestors installed with the rest. The author and the other delegates were kept very busy. The income from the dues, plus the money collected in Shanghai, was ample to pay for everything. However, there being few helpers, some workers had to be hired to perform different kinds of work. The theatrical performance for the entertainment of the guests lasted six days. Much as the author deplored the expense, it had to be held for the prestige of the *tsu*.

After everything was over, the debts incurred and all expenses of the rites and entertainment were paid, the ancestral hall was still left with 300 strings of cash. The only job left incomplete was the list for the genealogy.

The building of the ancestral hall had cost a total of 13,300 strings of cash from 1866–1876 and was paid entirely out of contributions of members. The finances of the *tsu* had been drained and the forces of the author strained to the limit.

At the winter solstice the author asked for the privilege of performing the rites for the first ancestor himself in spite of his status as a member of a younger generation (he was 36 years old at this time). The other delegates granted that he had a right to lead the ritual at the first winter solstice after the completion of the ancestral hall. After the ritual there was a gathering of all members over 60 years of age, and of those who had achieved a rank through examinations, 160 persons in all, and they went through the ceremony of drinking together. At this banquet the author explained that he had taken the responsibility for building the ancestral hall because his uncle had always wished to see it done, and because he had been entrusted with it by the older members of the *tsu*. He recounted his difficulties which almost led to the loss of his life. He gave thanks to the spirits of the ancestors and the presence in the *tsu* of a great number of people who, knowing *i* (duty), had contributed to the limit of their ability, so that the construction finally could be completed. He formally handed over the keys of the ancestral hall, the account-books and drawings related to the building and announced his determination to retire from office. The crowd wanted him to stay, as there were various matters that still had to be wound up. They praised his endurance and tenacity which had brought the construction work to a successful finish. His fellow-delegates expressed the wish to retire with him, since according to regulations the *szu-shih* should be changed once every five years. Now they had been in office for 12 years and a number of them had retired during this time. When the first part of the ancestral hall had been completed they had wanted to give up their office, but the author had prevailed upon them to stay until the work was terminated. Now the work was done, there was still plenty of money left, after all the equipment had been provided for adequately. All that was left to do now was to prepare the offerings at the right season and carry out the ritual to the ancestors. They, the elders of the *tsu*, could perform these duties very well.

Three days later he reassembled them, and asked who had been chosen as his successor, but the answer was that there was no one to take over. Then the author and the other delegates put on their ceremonial robes and caps and advised the ancestors of their decision. They sealed the books and locked the cupboard and store-rooms. The keys were left at the home of the head of the *tsu* and everyone went home.

Someone asked him: what if by the next spring equinox the *tsu* still had not chosen a person to succeed him. His answer was: "I performed my duty according to the best of my ability, because my ancestors' souls had no place to which they could attach themselves. Now they have such a place. Should it happen that by the next spring equinox the members of the *tsu* do not perform the rites, I shall personally prepare food and wine to offer to the ancestors, thus still attempting to perform my duty to the best of my ability. If I did not retire, the *tsu* would suspect I had the intention of keeping my office permanently by any means, and I would have no way of clearing myself. There is *i* that has to be performed, and there are times when action is appropriate. Formerly I was asked by the *tsu* to retire and I would not do so; now I am asked to remain in office and I will not do so; this is because I act according to the exigency of time and *i*.*

* Hsien Chin Hu, 1948: pp. 169–180. In undertaking the summary-translation of this document (entitled in Chinese *Tun-fu Nien-pu* or "Autobiography of Tun-fu"—Tun-fu being probably the ceremonial name of the author Hu Shan), Miss Hu explains her effort with the following note: "The MS. has been preserved by Dr. Hu Shih, the son of the author. Part of it was mutilated by a fire, but the story is clear nevertheless. However, because of the many incomplete sentences it was deemed wiser not to make a direct translation, but the expressions used by the author have been retained and nothing added to their meaning."

Chapter V

COHESION VERSUS DIVISION: CASTE

IF THE HINDUS have a relatively centrifugal family structure and but a nominal clan system, what are the groupings within which the Hindus find their greatest cohesion? The answer is, superficially at least, *caste*, which at once takes us to the phenomenon for which India has been best known for centuries.

Caste is as well known in India as it is unknown in China. In ancient China slavery existed and, during the last ten centuries, people who practiced certain occupations (such as musicians, prostitutes, and actors) were barred from taking the Imperial Examination, which by and large was the chief avenue for individual advancements. But this prohibition applied only to the third descending generation from the individual so occupied, and his great-grandsons would be free to enter into the competition. In China there simply has never been any question of a permanent caste group or organization, in theory or practice. Yet caste has been a basic principle of the Hindu society since ancient times and remains an important social force today. Is it possible that, though the amorphous and unimportant nature of the Hindu clan seems to reinforce the centrifugal outlook of the Hindu family, the strength and cohesiveness of the Hindu caste show the Hindu orientation to be not so centrifugal after all?

The question may be put somewhat differently. The centrifugal orientation is the cardinal point of our hypothesis concerning the Hindu way of life. The characteristics of the Hindu clan lend support to that orientation. But if the Hindu caste system is characterized by strength and cohesiveness, as it is commonly known to be, will its existence not be a direct refutation of our hypothesis on the Hindu way of life? For both clan and caste are circles of social relationships which are larger than the family but inclusive of it. In functional terms, either of them can fulfill the need for ties beyond the immediate family. Unless we assume that the orientation developed

93

in the family is unrelated to the individual's orientation toward his fellow human beings in the wider circles, we must expect to find a similar orientation governing his relationships in both the former and the latter. Conversely, if we find that the individual's orientation in the larger group is opposed to or significantly different from his orientation in the smaller, primary group, do we not have legitimate reason to suspect that there is something wrong with our understanding of the smaller, primary group in the first place?

At the outset it should be observed that the Hindu caste does have (and has had throughout history) strength and cohesiveness at different times and in many places. Superficially this fact would seem to refute, at least in part, our hypothesis on the Hindu way of life. The reality is far different. As our argument unfolds gradually, we shall see that part of it is based on the fact that cohesiveness is often more apparent than real. But of even greater importance is the fact, as we shall see in Chapter VIII, that because of the very centrifugal tendencies and diffuseness of the Hindu supernatural-centered orientation, there is a strong psychocultural necessity for strict arrangements.

THE CHARACTERISTICS OF HINDU CASTE

This is not a treatise on caste and therefore I shall not attempt to present a complete list of caste in any community, nor make a scale of ranking castes, nor discuss the economic bases of the castes, nor show the regional differences in castes, though some of these points will enter into the discussion when they are found to be relevant to our arguments. What I shall do is, first, outline the general features of caste and, then, ascertain the relationship between the essence of these caste features and the Hindu psychocultural orientation.

Historically the Indian term associated with caste is *varna*. According to this scheme, there are four varnas well known to the rest of the world, namely, the Brahmans (priests), the Kshatriyas (warriors), the Vaishyas (businessmen), and the Sudras (artisan-laborers). Outside these four are the outcastes or untouchables known as Parayer in Tamil, Chandalas in the law books, and sometimes the Panchamas or the "fifth."

In the early Vedic times the term varna, which means color, was applied only to the fair Aryan people to distinguish them from the dark Dasa people or peoples. It did not then refer to caste as it did later. The history of how the term varna came to be associated with the fourfold scheme need not detain us here.[1] This association has long been firmly established in the minds of educated Indians as well as many other Indians, and in the minds of most students of Indian society and culture. Theoretically all four varnas existed in all parts of India, but in fact south of the Vindyas Mountains "there are no genuine Kshatryas and Vaishyas."[2] According to the ancient law books, each varna is endogamous, and its members could share water and food together.[3] In reality the restrictive lines are far narrower. First of all, caste is tied to locality, so that Bengali Brahmans and Telugu Brahmans will not intermarry. They may on some occasions share food, but it is doubtful whether they would exchange visits in their homes. Secondly, Brahmans of each region are subdivided into a number of groups. For example, Bengali Brahmans are divided into Kulin, Shrotrya, and Bhonga Brahmans. Kulins are the purest, Shrotryas lower, and Bhongas the lowest. The latter were Kulin Brahmans who allowed their daughters to be married to persons belonging to the next lower caste. This is not all. The Barendras (or Varendras) are Bengali Brahmans from north of the Ganges river while the Rarhis are from south of it. Then, descendants of Bengali Brahmans who took alms at *sradhs* (a ritual sacrifice to the dead performed a certain number of days after the funeral) are Agradanis, and are therefore separated from others whose forebears did not take alms at *sradhs*. The distinctions made here are by no means exhaustive, but these examples will serve our present purpose. Each of these subdivisions of the Brahman caste in Bengal is endogamous and, strictly speaking, will also restrict sharing of water and food to it own members.

In addition to these and other Brahman subdivisions, there are numerous groups and subgroups in different regions of the subcontinent. All of these are called *jatis* in Hindi, most other Indo-Aryan languages, and Telugu. The term *jati* has been translated into English as "subcaste" or "caste." This indefinite equivalence is assumed by Indians as well as Westerners. When one Hindu meets another he may ask, "What is your jati?" The reply will be "Brahman" or "Kayastha" or "Reddy" as the case may be. If the speakers use English, the word for *jati* may be either "caste" or "subcaste." In Bengal, if the inquirer wishes to know the subdivision to which the other person belongs he will again ask, "What Brahman are you, Rarhi or Barendra?" etc.* In Uttar Pradesh he will ask, "What Brahman are you, Chhatri, Upadhaya, Tiwari?" etc. But often these subcastes or castes cannot be grouped under one of the classical varnas such as Brahman, Kshatriya, etc. For example, Srinivas lists for the state of Mysore, before the 1956 reorganization, a total of twenty-three main Kanada (language) castes and sixteen non-Kanada castes. He adds that these again contained numerous "subdivisions."[4] On the other hand, the higher castes as a whole are grouped

_____

* Today many college students in Bengal tend to answer the caste query, if made in English, by saying "Hindu" or "Moslem," but will have no hesitation in following the pattern here described if the Indian word *jati* is used instead of the English word *caste* by the questioner.

together as Ashrafin in Bihar, Bhadralok in Bengal, and Pandhar-pese in Maharashtra.[5]

This state of affairs has prompted students of Hindu society and culture to stress the importance of separating the term varna from the terms caste and subcaste, reserving the former as a mere conceptual scheme for Hindu society as a whole, and the latter for a description of the real situation.[6] But this by no means settles anything. A rigorous distinction between varna and jati is desirable, but, according to Ghurye, is not always practical. For the word jati "is sometimes indiscriminately used for 'Varna' " as well.[7] The fact is that while the varna scheme does not correspond to the local reality, it does provide a framework which conditions all Indian thinking about and reaction to caste. When the mobility of a caste is in question it is "frequently stated in Varna terms rather than in terms of the local caste situation."[8] The other problem is that the terminological differentiation between caste and subcaste is only found in English, not in any Indian language. A Bengali Brahman is known to the outsiders as a Bengali or Brahman, but to a Bengali Brahman he is better known either as Rarhi or Barendra or Kulin, etc. Similarly, in Maharashtra, a Saraswat Brahman is known to the outsiders as a Saraswat, but to a Saraswat he is better known either as a Shenvi or as a Sashlikar or Pedaekar. Ghurye observes that "though it is the caste that is recognized by the society at large, it is the subcaste that is regarded by the particular caste and individual."[9]

We shall return later to the fact that the term subcaste is not known by any Indian term. For the moment it is necessary to point out that, from the evidence avaliable, it appears that varna, caste, and subcaste have their own separate importance and reality in contemporary Hindu thinking on caste, and that when Srinivas says, "it is absolutely necessary for the sociologist to free himself from the hold of the Varna model if he wishes to understand the caste system,"[10] he is probably guilty of an underemphasis of the older concept.

We must, however, further explore the specific relationships between varna on the one hand and caste and subcaste on the other. The formal four-varna scheme laid down by the ancients was indubitably hierarchical. When the varna scheme developed into the caste and subcaste situation later, the hierarchy idea remained. In reality, however, no effort in ranking castes or subcastes in any part of India has been successful. Efforts along this line have been so unsuccessful that David Mandelbaum has been prompted to ask why they are ranked at all.[11] Mandelbaum's query is not a sign that he is throwing up his hands simply because of the difficulty involved. His view probably agrees with my own observation: namely, that the multitudes of castes in India are not rankable, and that any ranking is never lasting and is subject to dispute at all times by most Hindus who are ranked anywhere on the middle or lower levels.[12]

The lack of permanency of ranking is shown by the fact that, when the 1921 census of Mysore was compared with that of 1931, at least six castes had taken over new names. In addition to these six, the Bedas (hunters) had even taken on the name "Valmiki Brahmanas" which will greatly confuse future rankers of castes by its similarity to Brahmans (priestly caste).[13]

This process is so well known that Srinivas remarks, in connection with the Amma Coorgs who some one hundred years ago formed a splinter group and separated themselves from the main body of Coorgs: "Amma Coorgs exemplify a tendency which has always been present in the caste system: a small group of people break off from a larger whole of which they are a part, Sanskritize their customs and ritual, and achieve a higher status than their parent-body in the course of a few decades."[14] As to the dispute over caste ranking, the public furor following the 1931 census is a good example. The last census of India (1951) therefore gave the list but made no effort to rank the castes. But the disputes go on. Illustrations of such disputes abound. Many Kayasthas of Bengal say they were Kshatriyas who took up the pen instead of the sword and became scribes in the Mogul period and government clerks during British overlordship. Others (among them some learned Kayasthas themselves) say that the Kayasthas were originally Untouchables but as they rose in power under the dominant Moguls or British, they raised their caste position to just below that of the Brahmans. In the Telugu-speaking Andhra state, the numerically large and politically and economically important Reddy (farmer) caste presents a similar situation. Its members claim to be a subcaste of Vaishyas (business caste) or a caste apart, while others say that they were originally Sudras but have risen so that their position today corresponds to that of Vaishyas.

The extent to which the dispute over caste ranking can go is beautifully illustrated by the fight started by Yogis, a "clean" caste of weavers of the Namahsudras, agriculturists, and boat-plyers, in Bengal not so long ago. From 1901 onwards the Yogis organized themselves to uphold their claim of a higher caste status than that which was assigned to them by the census. They published booklets and articles in a journal specially founded by the organization to validate their claim. During the census of 1921 only the priestly section of the Yogis claimed to be Brahmans. During the 1931 census the entire caste claimed the status of Brahmanhood. The entire caste donned the thread by resolution in the latter year. The Namahsudras did similar things and as they advanced their claims to Brahmanhood, they discouraged widow remarriage, which previously had been a long-standing custom with them.[15]

We are not here concerned with the true history of the castes in question.

What we wish to highlight is the lack of agreement and the disputes which constantly arise over caste ranking, a situation which is obvious and ever-present. The ephemeral nature of most ranking, and the perpetual lack of agreement over which caste is higher than which, would seem to warrant the conclusion that probably the only caste which can be clearly distinguished from and placed above the rest, by custom and by consensus, is the Brahman caste, and the only castes or subcastes which can be equally clearly distinguished from and placed below the rest are various sorts of Untouchables. But the subdivisions (additions and accretions to) within the Brahman caste which claim superiority over each other cloud the picture here as elsewhere. In the last analysis, no caste or subcaste is so sure of its position as to be above rank dispute. The following episode well illustrates the psychology which underlies such disputes:

> Some years ago it happened at Harsud that members of the higher castes decided to abolish untouchability. They arranged an intercaste dinner, and a *Brahman*, a *Bania*, a *Balahi* and a *Mehtar* were invited to eat together. The dinner took place in public and the pioneers of caste-abolition were applauded by many lookers-on. When the dinner was over, the diners were received by their caste community without objection or censure. Only the *Balahis* (an untouchable caste) objected and outcasted the representative of their community because he had eaten with a *Mehtar* (an untouchable caste lower in rank than the *Balahis*). The *Mehtars* answered this slight against their caste by outcasting their representative because he had eaten with a *Balahi!* When the *Brahmans* and *Banias* heard of this, they could do nothing else but outcast the man who had eaten with a *Balahi* and a *Mehtar*.[16]

These and other facts force us then to view the Hindu caste system as almost as much a horizontal arrangement as a vertical one, with numerous groups everywhere trying to fortify themselves behind self-imposed walls of subcaste, each seeking to insulate itself (ritually and socially though not economically) from the others and usually to claim superiority over them. This process is going on all the time.[17]

FEATURES COMMON TO HINDU CASTE AND HINDU CLAN

These two features in the Hindu caste situation, namely, the efforts to fissure and to insulate behind socially and ritually closed walls, and the claims of superiority on the part of one caste group over another, are so persistent and deep-seated that they seem to color the Hindu idea of clan. In a previous connection we noted the fact that in contrast to other Hindus the Rajputs, especially those who have chiefly aspirations, seemed to pay more attention to their own genealogies. We have already seen how this interest is essentially rooted in their pride in a glorious ancestry, and their desire to use it as a means of claiming power or wealth or both. Their interest in ancestry has little to do with a sense of filial duty toward the ancestral spirits. We can now see how that Rajput attitude toward clan is founded particularly on the desire to avoid inappropriate marital alliances, and therefore is much more in tune with the endogamous spirit of the Hindu caste than with the exogamous Chinese clan. The Rajputs have clans which are so arranged as to form (1) endogamous circles so that only certain clans can intermarry with each other while others cannot do so; and (2) hypergamous alignments so that the clans which receive women from certain other clans can only receive and not reciprocate.

Exactly the same marital arrangements involving clans are found among the northern Maharashtrans, and the Kayasthas of Uttar Pradesh. In the south, generally speaking Brahman marriages are not only restricted to the endogamous circles of clans, but often the possibilities for marriage are practically narrowed down to two families which have a different *gotra*, but belong to the endogamous circle of clans.[18] In Mysore there are the Asta Gramas (Eight Villages). The Brahmans from these Asta Gramas are Asta Gramis. Only Asta Gramis with different *gotra* names can intermarry. This rule has tended to hold even when an Asta Grami has moved away from the villages of his origin. The Asta Gramis have no other occasion on which they need to cooperate.

The contrast between such South Indian marital customs and those of the Uttar Pradesh and Punjab, where there is village exogamy (or exogamy within a territory about four to twelve miles in radius), caused Srinivas to comment that "intensification is the operative principle in south India while extension is the principle in the north."[19] This difference is, however, more apparent than real. Srinivas is impressed by the difference because he fails to weigh the local difference against the all-India similarity. This is another example of how concentration on local details tends to obscure rather than clarify our understanding of the larger picture. In the first place the Mysore and Maharashtran pattern of marital alliance among several clans prevailed in Bengal not so long ago. Today many Bengalis can describe an arrangement called *phulmel* (*phul*, flower; *mel*, similarity) among the Brahmans. There were different kinds of *mels*. The membership of each *mel* consisted of families of several *gotras* which alone can intermarry. In other words, *phulmel* is a sort of endogamous circle of intermarrying clans. In the second place even in today's north India, whether we consider Bengal or Uttar Pradesh, village exogamy or exogamy of a larger territorial unit is never on an open field basis but is invariably limited to a certain circle of villages or territorial units. That is to say, the families which by custom look for marital alliances outside their village or particular territorial unit will never do so with the idea of alliances with families in just *any* village but invariably with families to be found in certain villages of the same subcaste and, in all likelihood, within an established endogamous group of villages.

If the above facts are found in a social context where marital alliances are freely contracted and where caste is nonexistent, Srinivas might be justified in interpreting them as he has. But where caste is all-pervading, Srinivas' interpretation would seem to be quite wide of the mark. For the facts we have just examined are perfectly in tune with the same basic characteristics of caste, namely, the frequent formation of groups each of which aims at social and ritual insulation and each of which claims superiority over others. Both aims culminate in endogamy or hypergamy.

Thus the Hindu clans, especially among Rajputs, where clans seem to have more substance than among other Hindus, are drastically different from Chinese clans in spite of their superficial similarities. The Chinese clans are strictly exogamous with no question of alliances of endogamous circles or hypergamous lines.* In one historical period or another some Chinese clans might be more powerful than others. This was especially likely to occur in parts of south China, where clan feuds were common up to a decade or so ago and where smaller clans might form alliances to deal with their more powerful common foes. But the relationship between these opposing groups was purely a matter of physical protection and survival, and not of superiority in ritual status or descent from glorious ancestry. It was a relationship based on practical considerations similar to those sought after by weak nations which have to form alliances, temporary or lasting, for defense against powerful neighbors.[20] The greatness or weakness of the ancestry of a man or woman's clan was no bar to marital connection. In fact, the peasant son of the humblest clan would be the object of marital offers from some of the wealthiest and most powerful families of the land (sometimes including that of the ruling emperor) as soon as he passed one of the higher imperial examinations. And as soon as the peasant son of the humblest clan rose in wealth and power he was supposed to initiate fresh "research" to compile into book form the genealogy of his clan or revise and enlarge it if such a book was already in existence. The "achievements" of some of his ancestors were often exaggerated and embellished, but the resulting volume included (not excluded) the humblest members of his clan: the men who were born in it and women who married into it. A Chinese is proud of the glory and honor and wealth which are associated with his clan. But the prosperity and continuity of the clan is an expression of the merits of its ancestors, and the gratitude its members feel toward their forebears, and a symbol of the solidarity between all the living and all the dead of the clan,

* Between the years 420 A.D. and 589 A.D., when China was divided and ruled by a series of unstable and mostly foreign dynasties, certain clans in the south did form some endogamous circles; but this practice was not widespread at the time, nor were the circles hypergamous, and the custom was nonexistent before this period and never recurred after it.

from the most highly placed to the least significant. Thus, for the Chinese, the clan is not, as for his Rajput brethren, an instrument for the glorification of one individual or a basis for ritual and social insulation, or for endogamy or hypergamy.

THE QUESTION OF CASTE SOLIDARITY*

One more aspect of the Hindu caste remains to be investigated. The Hindu caste system is horizontal but primarily and predominantly it is vertical, for everywhere it contains numerous groups trying to fortify themselves behind self-imposed walls of subcaste, to insulate themselves (ritually and socially though not economically) from the others, and often to claim superiority over them. Granting all this, we must still examine the question of the solidarity among the members of each contending subgroup. There is no question but that in numerous parts of India, today and probably even more so long ago, caste groups do have some solidarity at any given point of time. While councils of clan elders capable of passing judgments on and settling disputes among its members are not reported anywhere in India, caste councils and associations which can impose fines, expulsion, etc., are common in all parts of the country. In view of this fact, the question must be asked: How far are such caste councils and associations expressive of a centripetal rather than a centrifugal outlook?

Our answer, made after a careful analysis, is that such caste councils and associations present much evidence which supports our hypothesis. In the first place, there is no specific Indian distinction between caste councils and panchayats or village councils.[21] That is to say, if a village happens to be inhabited only by members of the same caste, then the panchayat of that village is also a caste council. On the other hand, if the village is inhabited by members of different castes, then the panchayat is a village council and not a caste organization at all.

> The decisions of the village councils that have come down to us from the Maratha country, bear the signatures of almost all the village-servants, including the untouchable Mahar and Mang. An entry in the Private Diary of Anandaranga Pillay of the middle of the eighteen [sic] century refers to a case of temple-desecration "in which people of all castes—from the Brahman to the Pariah—took part." Dr. Matthai quotes a description of a meeting of a village Panchayat in which both the Brahmins and the Sudras took part. . . .[22]

* The term *solidarity* is used here to denote *behavioral cohesion or unity*, as the latter terms are employed elsewhere in this book and by most other authors whose works are discussed in this section. The relationship between the psychic and behavioral sense of this term and the sense in which Durkheim used it (or the structural sense) have been dealt with in Chapter I and in the last chapter when we discussed Maurice Freedman's analysis of the Chinese kinship system. It will be touched on again in this chapter in connection with our review of Dumont's contribution on caste.

Thus, while members of a one-caste village live in that village, their social and ritual affairs will be governed by the village panchayat which is also the caste panchayat; but if some of them move out of the territory, this relationship is broken off. When a village is inhabited by many castes but the village panchayat remains one, the panchayat is not an expression of caste cohesion.

In the second place, every caste is divided into numerous endogamous subcastes. In such a situation Ghurye observes, "each subcaste manages its own affairs quite independently of the others, and in the case of the lower castes each has its own separate panchayat or standing committee, by which all social questions are decided."[23] * The divisive psychology underlying the phenomenon of subcastes becomes evident in an examination of the bases of distinction which underlie the names of the subcastes. These bases are: (1) territorial or jurisdictional separateness; (2) mixed origin; (3) occupational distinction; (4) some peculiarity in the technique of one and the same occupation; (5) sectarian differences; (6) dissimilarity of customs including food habits; and (7) adventitious circumstances, suggesting certain nicknames.[24] In other words, almost any imaginable reason could be the provocation or basis for the formation of a new subcaste.

In spite of the brittle nature of subcaste grouping, field workers persistently speak of the solidarity of the subcaste, usually making no particular distinction between caste and subcaste when referring to groups which not only exist within a village but which have connections between villages. Srinivas, in speaking of the Coorgs, states that "caste has a tendency to stress horizontal ties. It unites members of the same caste living in different villages and distinguishes them from other castes in the same village."[25] However, he gives scarcely any facts to show the specific nature of this unity beyond some sort of endogamy. Certainly the village assembly or assemblies which enforce caste rules by imposing fines or excommunication are not identifiably caste assemblies, except when a majority of the inhabitants of a village or a group of villages happen to belong to one caste or subcaste.[26]

To be sure, Srinivas warns against the pitfalls of overemphasis on horizontal solidarity at the expense of vertical solidarity.

> The view that the solidarity of caste is so great that it nullifies the unity of the village community in those villages in which live more than one caste, is so plausible that it has misled not a few. But a moment's reflection will expose its falsity. It is true that caste is an institution of prodigious strength, and that it is pervasive. It undertakes numerous activities, and occasionally, the members of a sub-caste living in neighboring villages meet together to consider a matter of common concern to the caste. But all this does not make a caste self-suffi-

* Ghurye's qualifying remark "in the case of the lower castes" seems unnecessary, for subcaste panchayats are also common among the higher castes.

cient. The castes living in a village or other local area are interdependent economically and otherwise. Ideally, each caste enjoys a monopoly of an occupation, and this monopoly both unites as well as divides the people enjoying the monopoly. While the members resent other castes taking over this occupation (this is not true of agriculture though) and secrets of the occupation are closely guarded among the members, rivalry between the members for the customs of the other castes does, in fact, exist and it divides them. The fact that the members of a caste in a village are, at any rate in South India, linked by ties of kinship does not lessen the rivalry. . . . The strong rivalries which exist between the members of a non-agricultural or servicing caste often force them to seek friends outside their own caste. . . . The ties cutting across the lines of caste are as important as the ties of caste. . . .[27]

If the question is not one of caste or subcaste solidarity which totally eclipses village solidarity, surely the question must be, how much evidence *is* there for caste or subcaste solidarity? The answer is that evidence for caste or subcaste solidarity tends to be outweighed by evidence indicating lack of such solidarity. Of the fourteen village studies which make up the volume *India's Villages* (published by the Development Department, Government of West Bengal) from which the passage quoted is taken, only nine contain some meager information about the caste or subcaste panchayat within the village or about some sort of caste or subcaste unity within the village or among a number of different villages,* while the other five give no indication at all of, or are far less explicit about, caste or subcaste organization or unity.† Srinivas has formulated, in connection with his study of the Coorgs, some explicit statements on the theme of horizontal solidarity of caste or subcaste, as opposed to village or territorial solidarity. "Each of these subcastes has a distinctive tradition with strong ties with the same subcaste in villages nearby. Each caste again has a solidarity cutting across the village."[28] But even in the village of Rampura, which provides the basis for these statements, the evidence for "strong ties" among members of the subcastes in the same village or "with the subcastes in villages nearby" is thin.

The following facts may be regarded as indicative of a degree of solidarity: (1) each caste's (subcaste's) annual worship of its tools; (2) the occasional fights between subcastes; (3) the existence of caste courts which can impose fines and excommunication on offenders; and (4) the reported (but not definitely verified) occurrences in some villages which have been described in *India's Villages*: "Stones have been planted to mark the bound-

---

* The nine are: (1) Rampura, Mysore; (2) Fatepura, Rajasthan; (3) Kerala villages; (4) Goshen, in the Himalayas; (5) Bhil villages, Western Udaipur; (6) Kumbapettai, Tanjore; (7) Kishan Garhi, United Province (*sic*); (8) Dewara, Deccan; (9) West Bengal village.

† The five are: (10) Kula, in the Himalayas; (11) Bisipara, Oriya; (12) Hattarahalli, Mysore; (13) Nilgiri Hills; (14) Punjab villages.

ary of a caste" and "a man who finds himself on the wrong side of the
boundary might be beaten."[29]

Contrasted with these indications of solidarity are several indications of
the lack of caste or subcaste solidarity: (1) the known grouping or re-
grouping of castes or subcastes into larger entities such as Desba versus
Nadu, or "with one-colorness" versus others, or right-hand versus left-hand
divisions, the boundaries of which are "not very easy to discover"; (2) evidence which indicates that some lower subcastes apparently have no caste
courts to enforce their intracaste rules; (3) the lack of an exact line of distinction in authority between certain caste heads (such as that of the Okkaliga) and the village head; (4) the fact that courts of a higher caste are often
asked to pass judgment on cases of lower castes; and (5) the existence of
factions within and without castes and subcastes.[30]

Furthermore, as to the possibility of caste or subcaste solidarity among
different villages, there is mostly evidence to the contrary. For example:

> There are caste-courts for the Potters at Keragodu and Ashtagrama. These
> courts are called *gadi* which literally means frontier or boundary. Each caste
> has several caste courts and they are said to constitute a hierarchy. But the
> hierarchy does not seem to be clear. For instance, there is a keen rivalry be-
> tween Keragodu *gadi* and Mysore *gadi*. The Mysore people claim precedence
> over Keragodu on the ground that they represent the *gadi* of the capital of
> Mysore State. To this the Keragodu people reply that this *gadi* came into
> existence during the time of Hyder Ali, father of Tipu Sultan; and even then
> Keragodu had precedence over Ashtagrama, the then capital of Mysore State
> —that is to say, Keragodu has always enjoyed precedence over the capital.
>
> Two years ago, representatives of the Potter caste in Mysore started claim-
> ing precedence over Keragodu representatives in villages such as Kere, Pura,
> and Kadlagela. In none of the places did they have any success. But in Taga-
> dur *gadi* they were successful in pressing their claim.
>
> Again, Kere *gadi* claims to include under it Keragodu *gadi*, but the latter
> considers itself to be a separate *gadi* and not merely part of Kere. It is said
> that formerly Potters had 48 *gadis*, and at a wedding in a Potter's house, 48
> betels had to be kept aside, irrespective of the fact that only a few of the 48
> representatives were present.
>
> The ritual of betel distribution at a wedding reflects the village organiza-
> tion, and also reveals the existence of a hierarchy of caste-courts. Sometimes,
> the hierarchy is not clear, and one of the reasons for this may be the fact that
> a caste-court which is supreme in one area tries to assert its authority in a dif-
> ferent area. This would reveal that the process of unification had not been
> carried sufficiently far.[31]

Srinivas' interpretation in the last paragraph just quoted is completely
baseless, and his last sentence is highly misleading, in the light both of the
facts presented by himself and of all the facts presented so far in this collection of village studies. Neither in Rampura nor elsewhere is there a

tendency to unification in caste and subcaste groupings, hierarchies, prerogatives, or attributes. On the contrary, Srinivas' own facts show that there is perpetual disagreement as to who or what is higher and who or what is lower and who has jurisdiction over what. Furthermore, if we refer to the criteria indicating a social group's solidarity, which were given in Chapter IV (page 72), we shall see at once that the condition of the castes or subcastes in Mysore, as described by Srinivas, fails really to measure up to any except perhaps the first. The Mysore castes or subcastes have organizations with specific caste laws governing behavior, but each caste seems to have a multiplicity of courts claiming conflicting jurisdiction over the same body. Furthermore, each possesses no individual or group of individuals enjoying the undisputed leadership; each engages in constant disputes, both internal and with other castes or subcastes, over questions of ranking; each suffers from frequent fission within itself, and keeps no exact records of membership. From my own observations in Mysore City and in two villages near Bangalore, I can also state that the caste or subcaste in Mysore, in common with its counterpart in Bengal and elsewhere, may, initially, have some clear criteria for its membership, but when fission occurs, new or additional criteria are so freely introduced as to defy complete description. Close social, economic, or ritual relationships may be maintained among the members of a caste or subcaste while it is still one, but after fission the ties, especially the social and ritual ones, are necessarily severed. Pride in membership of a caste or subcaste is similarly affected by the constant separatist tendencies.

A close examination of the other eight studies in this volume, *India's Villages*, in which the question of caste or subcaste solidarity is touched upon, does not change the picture outlined here. Of the eight, five mention caste panchayats or caste elders who have or had the power, in large or small measure, to settle disputes or enforce caste regulations (Fatepura, Goshen, Bhil, Kisan Garhi, and West Bengal villages), while the other three indicate some horizontal solidarity or allegiance among members of the same caste or subcaste in villages nearby (Kerala villages, Kumbapettai, and Dewara). Characteristically, if the majority of a village belongs to one caste, the caste council and village council are not distinguishable.

In the discussion of the Gaddi village of Goshen we read:

> Caste is the means by which inter-village and intra-village marriage is regulated. Caste is that system which limits those who are one's kinsmen and to whom one can marry one's son or daughter. The caste is a large community, the relations between members of whom can be strengthened by marriage so as to forward economic, religious or friendship ties. It is marked by the members being able to sit around the same fire, smoke with the same pipe-stem and eat the same food. *Formerly members of this community could be expelled by a village council for infringing caste rules. . . .*[32] [Italics mine.]

The ethnographer does not state when is "formerly," nor does he indicate whether such a reference to former times represents a truly historical statement or whether it is merely an expression of wishful thinking about things which never were real.

The remaining four studies treat this subject even more briefly. In a Rajasthan village Carstairs mentions "unrelated informal Panchayatis" some of which presumably were subcaste or caste based.[33] He points out, in a later publication on the same village, that, in former years, "the conferences of all male members of each caste were most important. It was here that joint decisions were taken, and these meetings had the power to out-caste offenders against their accepted customs—a very potent sanction."[34] But none of these panchayats had a recognized headman, the size of their memberships had no regularity, and at their most formal, they were merely conferences of the extended family.[35] In the Bhil, West Bengal, and Uttar Pradesh studies there is only the merest mention of the caste or subcaste panchayat which formerly settled disputes or passed judgments.[36]

Considering the importance of caste as an institution in India, and the fact that each author goes to some length in describing other aspects of the social organization, the paucity of descriptive material bearing on caste or subcaste solidarity might reasonably be considered as indicative of the lack of such solidarity, just as the brevity of the accounts on the structures and activities of caste or subcaste councils might be indicative of their insignificance. Furthermore, when something specific is said about caste or subcaste solidarity, it becomes apparent that such solidarity is absent as shown, for example, by the following passage from Marriott's account of Kisan Garhi:

> The tenants and wealthier artisans of eight other castes in the village are trying to consolidate their economic gains by securing a ritually higher position in the caste hierarchy; they are helped in their efforts by older caste rank-raising movements outside the village. But most castes and clans cannot even agree to rise together, for they are as divided as the Brahmans by internal rivalries which represent intrusions of the economic situation with its recent changes.[37]

From what we have seen of the divisiveness of caste and subcastes, Marriott's description fits the picture well. It is, however, not entirely clear why Marriott feels that this divisiveness represents "intrusions of the economic situation with its recent changes." It is true that the caste rank-raising movements on a broad regional or national level are of relatively modern origin. The well-known and modern Untouchable Uplifting Movement led by Dr. Ambedkar is one obvious example of it. But the analysis made by Oscar Lewis (whose study we shall return to shortly) of intracaste factions in Rampur, a village near Delhi, shows that the phenomenon of factions within caste and subcaste is not exclusively economic in nature and that it is over one hundred years old.[38] If the facts presented so far in this monograph are at all accurate, it should be clear that there is every reason to suppose caste and subcaste divisiveness to be much older, perhaps as old as the institution of caste itself, although there are, of course, those who have fancies about a golden age when strife and disaffection were unknown.

Turning now to the three remaining studies in the volume in question, we find that each of them, as in the study of Rampura by Srinivas, dwells on the subject of caste solidarity within the village, but in addition also refers to caste solidarity among adjacent villages. But the evidence for such solidarity, too, is either meager or unconvincing. In the case of the Tanjore village of Kumbapettai the "unity of the individual caste group," according to Gough, was "usually, until recently, the unity of a single street. The members of a caste within one village are first united by similarity of occupation, of rights in the land, of income, and of ritual beliefs and practices." The Brahmans in this village still have "common lands" and "common money." Except for the Brahmans, each caste street elects two "headmen who are responsible for maintaining law and order in the street."[39] In spite of these signs of unity, Gough emphasizes the fact that "as in all Indian villages . . . a unity of the whole village overrides the separateness of each caste."[40] And no wonder. For the facts are that, "as long as the system remained stable . . . in spite of the covert antagonism between people of different castes . . . *open quarrels demanding united action on the part of the group could take place and between groups of the same order* [caste] for example between branches of the same joint-family, joint-families of the same caste-group, between all non-Brahmans or all Adi Dravides of adjacent villages."[41] [Italics mine.] In other words, caste disunity seems to be at least as obvious as caste unity, as far as observable behavior is concerned.

The extent to which each Indian village develops a unity of its own is dealt with briefly in the following section of this chapter. Suffice it to say that such unity can nowhere be taken for granted, as Gough seems to do. For example, in one of her own publications Gough speaks of the "horizontal unity" of each endogamous subcaste which "counter-balanced" the vertical unity of the village. This "horizontal unity" could extend in former times to from fifteen to thirty villages.[42] Since there is no indication as to what this wider subcaste relationship meant other than in the question of endogamy, a statement like this is not an indication of any high degree of actual village unity at all.

In the Dewara study of Dube we have a picture of three kinds of panchayats governing respectively the village, the *guda* (or a division of the village) and the caste. The panchayats of the first two groupings have each a recognized "headman." "Intracaste disputes" and "intercaste" disputes of a "simple nature" are judged by the headmen of the caste and *guda* respectively, after consultation with members of the panchayats; but more serious matters are referred to the village panchayat, which nominally consists of the headmen of all the *gudas* and caste and other "persons of influence." Dube describes the relative importance of the caste and *guda* thus:

> Each *Guda* has an identity, and also some bonds which give it a feeling of solidarity. . . . In inter-*Guda* quarrels people are expected to side with their neighbors living in the same *Guda*.
> But more effective and important than the *Guda*, is the unit of caste. Members of the same caste living in the village have close interaction. . . .[43]

But the author fails to show how the caste is "more effective and important" than the *guda*. And, in fact, the last quotation is immediately followed by the observation that "most of the castes can be further divided into endogamous subcastes," and the "prohibition of intermarriage between the different subgroups . . . forces each to seek a horizontal solidarity with its own subgroup living in neighboring villages," although subcastes "share a common caste-name and occupation with the other subgroups, have a common mythology, and inter-dine with the other sections of their caste more or less on a basis of equality."[44] From statements like these we may justifiably believe that caste is not really more effective and important than *guda;* and that the so-called "horizontal solidarity" of the subcaste in different villages again consists of little more than marital alliances of individual families.

Miller's study on North Kerala more plainly confirms the impression that caste is not more effective or important than territorial groupings. He tells us that each village usually contained between 15 to 25 interdependent castes, each of which was united by kinship bonds based on hypergamy, and "each had its own internal administration under its more prominent elders" which was usually "conterminous with the village." In the lowest castes of serfs this internal administration "was often inadequate since there were and there remain cleavages between local factions owing allegiance to different landholders." "Within the village there was a constant tendency for disputes unsettled inside the caste to be referred upwards to a caste higher in the scale." From these facts Miller concludes that "the main structural cleavages were between territorial units—villages, chiefdoms, and kingdoms—not between castes," because the castes in each of these territorial units were often related in a sort of "vertically arranged system of rights and obligations."[45] Among caste members of adjacent villages Miller speaks of horizontal unity based on common culture. However, only the Nayars and the Nambudiri Brahmans, which comprise a little more than a quarter of the population of North Kerala, had any sort of caste organization beyond the *nad* or chiefdom, while the rest of the castes rarely had any organization which extended even as far as the *nad*. There is no information regarding the structure and function of such organizations.[46]

Thus we can obtain little satisfactory evidence for intravillage or intervillage caste or subcaste solidarity in the studies reviewed. When field workers say such solidarity exists, their statements are usually accompanied by a scarcity of descriptive material which can substantiate them.

THREE CASE STUDIES

The lack of substantiating material for caste or subcaste solidarity in these studies reviewed is, as we noted before, more likely to indicate the lack of such solidarity, and not to be merely due to brevity of coverage. An examination of more detailed works on local communities upholds this conclusion. For in works of the latter type there is an equal dearth of facts showing intravillage or intervillage caste solidarity. Dube's book on Shamirpet in Hyderabad provides us with the following facts: (1) each of the individual castes has a headman or headmen who sit with other persons on the village panchayat; (2) the caste headman links his caste fellows with the rest of the village as well as represents his caste fellows in the intervillage organization of his caste; and (3) he is supposed to "keep his people under control . . ." to prevent them from straying from the "traditional ways of life." But this is all we have from Dube on intervillage caste solidarity. He found that even within the village, caste headmen have so little statutory authority over their caste fellows that some of them are "only nominal members of the Panchayat and that at its meetings others speak on behalf of the caste." At the time of Dube's study the views of all the caste headmen of his village except one commanded no respect among their caste fellows, and the men who had force of personality, but who were not headmen, were the true powers of control and direction.[47]

In Lewis's above-mentioned study of Rampur, near Delhi, the lack of caste or subcaste solidarity comes to us with fuller details. First, the village panchayat is dominated by one caste, namely the Jats; while Lewis fails to distinguish between the village and caste panchayats when describing their functions.[48] Second, since village exogamy is the rule, casts or subcastes of different villages are maritally allied.[49] But just how caste fellows in different villages show their solidarity, aside from the marital alliance, is nowhere clear. Third, in place of caste solidarity, and in spite of Lewis's statement that "the caste system divides the village and weakens the sense of village solidarity"[50] we find that intracaste factions (*dhar*) are most common and that a study of this phenomenon "takes us to the very heart of village life."[51] In a village of 1,095 inhabitants there are, according to Lewis, twelve factions distributed by caste as follows: six among the 78 Jat families; one among the

15 Brahman families; two among the 21 Camar families; two among the 10 Bhangi families; and one among the 7 Kumhar families."[52] Dhillon finds a similar phenomenon of intracaste factions in a village in South India.[53] While both Dhillon and Lewis emphasize that factions are not only based on hostility towards other groups but are held together primarily by cooperative economic, social, and ceremonial relations, these phenomena are but two sides of the same coin. Factions cut across both kinship and territorial boundaries, and most of the factional groups are plagued by a situation in which a very large number of men all claim to be spokesmen or leaders.[54] This inevitably reminds us of the multiplicity of contenders for leadership in the castes and subcastes, which we discussed under the Question of Caste Solidarity, above. Such unsolved contentions are probably some of the bases for the formation of new factions or new subcastes.

The two studies just reviewed concern villages in which castes of higher ranks predominate. We should now examine a study which concerns a group of much lower order. The subcaste Pramalai Kallar in the southern districts of the state of Madras, as presented by Louis Dumont,[55] is a group which from 1918 to 1947 was administered under the Criminal Tribes and Castes Act instituted by the British in 1911 to combat the lawless activities which many members of this group carried on as a matter of livelihood. They have since largely reformed and are mostly engaged in agriculture and other ordinary pursuits. In caste ranking, according to Dumont, they are in the middle, as far below the high vegetarian castes as they are above the Untouchables. The author tells us in detail about the chiefs, the caste hierarchy, the territorial units, the caste assembly and tribunal, and the methods of justice, etc. It is interesting to note that, while the Pramalai Kallar possesses a little more organization than castes we have already discussed, its organization is more formal than effective. Unlike other groups, the Pramalai Kallars have a chief (*tevar*), but this term for chief is extended to all the men of the group.[56] The prerogatives of the chiefship, other than precedence in legal assemblies, are purely honorary. Furthermore, today even these prerogatives are nonexistent and two men claim the title in some fashion. The holder of the official insignia is poor and inconsequential, and the other claimant, though representing the junior branch, is younger and richer and tries to represent his group in public affairs.[57] It seems that the chiefship was awarded by the King of Madurai several hundred years ago, but there is nothing else within the caste which would justify the pre-eminence of one lineage over others. Dumont concludes his discussion of chiefship thus: "We can also see that the modern decadence of the chiefship is very natural; if authority is based on an outside sanction, it is only normal that it cannot be maintained without formal recognition by the government."[58]

This lack of a true leadership or authority covering the entire caste is, as we have already seen, typical of Hindu castes. Just as typical of the Hindu castes is the fact that the Pramalai Kallars were not only detached years ago from the Ambalakkarar Kallars, a group to which they now feel inferior, but are also divided among themselves into territorial units of two or more unequal kinds.*

Dumont concludes that "the hierarchy, the gradation of status and rank, seems to be the true expression of the unity of the group."[62] This conclusion has no connection with his own facts unless Dumont is using the term *unity* here to denote Durkheimian *solidarity*. In that sense it means no more than a structural tie or relationship: different subcastes among the Pramalai Kallars are tied to each other exactly as the Negroes and whites in the Southern United States are tied to each other. For the "superior" whites want to keep the "inferior" Negroes in their place exactly as the "clean" Hindus may resort to force to keep the "unclean" Hindus in their place. Subtract either one from the Hindu hierarchy or the American hierarchy and the hierarchical relationship ceases to exist, for the other will have no point of reference for its "cleanness" or "superiority." But then Dumont's use of the term *unity* has little in common with what we have so far tried to elucidate: solidarity as psychic or behavioral cohesion. On the other hand, if Dumont does claim the psychic and behavioral aspects, his term *unity* must be subjected to the same test against observable facts as we did of Freedman's term *tension* in an earlier connection. When this is done we find Dumont's use of the term *unity* to describe caste behavior among Pramalai Kallars without any justification. For the different sections of the Pramalai Kallar subcaste do not have cohesion with each other and Dumont himself observes later in his

---

* According to one formula the Pramalai Kallar country consists of a hierarchy of "4 Tevar, 3 gods, 8 provinces and 24 secondary villages" while according to another the list is "4 Tevar, 8 provinces, 24 secondary villages, 7 'tattu', 8 'Kamuli' and 5 (?) 'internal divisions.' "[59] Whichever formula we take, the caste is obviously heterogeneous, each group including chief, gods, lineages, and territorial units. The number of "Tevars" involved is an uncertainty; the relative superiority of at least the first of "8 provinces" is confused; and the different list of "24 secondary villages," which are inferior in status to the "8 provinces," greatly differ from each other because the actual number of such units does not matter to the Kallars; what matters to them here is the number 24, just as the number 21 in important deities, and the number 108 in other connections. In reality there are other Kallars living in villages with other castes or forming villages of their own, but 24 is the number which the Kallar choose to designate. As to the "8 tattu" and "8 Kamuli," the ethnographer is able neither to understand the meanings of these terms nor to describe them as entities.[60]

The above unequal groupings, though miscellaneous and unclear, do seem to form, as a whole, one major division of the Pramalai Kallars because they at least intermarry. The "internal divisions," on the other hand, are impure Pramalai Kallars with whom other members of the subcaste will not intermarry. Here again the number of such groups is uncertain. The only informant on the subject told Dumont there are five such groups but Dumont himself finds two more. The impure or degraded Kallars were probably descendants of irregular unions.[61]

book that "the hierarchy of caste corresponds to the battle for supremacy, with emphasis on competition and rivalry even inside the caste," and that bloody actions resulting from these and other conflicts "are open and developed manifestations of a general characteristic of South India."[63]

Dumont's account of the Kallar assembly and tribunal in action adds little evidence in favor of Pramalai Kallar solidarity as a subcaste. The "Royal Assembly" which existed once upon a time is no longer a reality. At present the "Communal Assembly," whether of the whole district inhabited by Pramalai Kallars or of a single village, deals with matters of general interest such as celebration of a festival, offenses against the temples or caste, and so on, while the panchayat in the strict sense of "tribunal" deals with litigation, conflicts, and other breaches of law. The arrangements are highly fluid. The affairs of general interest may be dealt with either by a full "Communal Assembly," which includes heads of all households, or by a few individuals called, in a loose manner, a panchayat. On the other side, the "tribunal" may be composed of a few experts, in which event it is designated as a panchayat, or it may include the whole male population of the village or district. The recruiting of members of the tribunal panchayat is always done on the spot. Even at the village level there is not one village chief but several lineage chiefs and other expert jurists who take charge of the assembly. Authority is plural. "It would seem that the one among the old specialists who is the most interested in the affair or who sees a solution takes charge."[64] There is no majority vote. Unanimous decision is the rule. Each tribunal is independent, having no hierarchical or other relationships with others. The decision of one tribunal may be appealed against itself by the same defendant, or appealed in another tribunal at another locality, as many times as he can afford it. The forces which make the Kallar obey an authority so fluid in nature are several: (1) the customary formality between the assembly or panchayat and the litigants or defendants; (2) the fact that the authority of the panchayat practically originates from the parties to a dispute; (3) the banning of one who refuses to abide by the decisions of the tribunal; (4) the possibility of appeal to different tribunals; and (5) the moderation of the judgments.[65]

In the matter of government and justice the Pramalai Kallars seems to lie between those groups of mankind in which law and order are purely a matter of private, individual action and those other groups in which law and order are entirely in the hands of trained specialists. But this sketch says nothing about the solidarity of Pramalai Kallar as a subcaste for the simple reason that these assemblies and tribunals do not govern the subcaste as such but are fundamentally village-wide or local in nature. Even if we agree with Dumont that caste, territory, and kinship relationship cross each other in the Kallar conception of their human groupings,[66] caste is at best only one of three principles involved. The fact that no comparable assemblies and tribunals on an exclusively caste basis are found where many castes live in the same village or locality should be an effective caution against our thinking of caste as an integrating factor. And the lack of concern of Pramalai Kallars who live together for their caste fellows who are scattered elsewhere is another fact bearing on the same point. In other words, it is very doubtful whether the Pramalai Kallers would have developed any assemblies or tribunals for themselves as a subcaste if they lived in multicaste localities. And lest we think of these assemblies and tribunals as simply village or local phenomena, there is sufficient evidence that they can be more or less duplicated in many other areas of India. Even as village or local bodies, the panchayats or assemblies of the Pramalai Kallars do not escape the centrifugal characteristics of the caste system, for they are as unrelated to each other as possible—this in spite of the fact that an external political authority in Madurai had in the past encouraged the Pramalai Kallars to form a greater unity under a chiefship.[67]

Thus, wherever we look we find little consistent evidence to show caste or subcaste solidarity in the psychic and behavioral sense. On the contrary, there is much evidence to indicate its lack. The argument for caste or subcaste solidarity is not improved by Leach's suggestion that "caste as distinct from either social class or caste grade manifests itself in the external relations between caste groupings," and that "these external relations stem from the fact that every caste, not merely the upper élite, has its special 'privileges'." Leach is of the opinion that the sometimes "violent political revolt" by the low castes "against the formal strictures of the caste system" is due to the fact that "these people are the victims of extreme economic insecurity"; they rebel "not because they are low castes but because present conditions have turned them into an unemployed working-class."[68] According to this thesis the different sections of a caste or subcaste would tend to cohere simply as a matter of economic expediency, if nothing else, regardless of their position in the caste hierarchy, and, therefore, intra- and intercaste contention is a relatively recent phenomenon, due to the breakdown of the caste system. But we have seen in some of the foregoing pages that intra- and intercaste fission and strife are not modern phenomena. Bernard Cohn's work in Senapur, a village in North India, shows how the myths concerning the origins of some of the low castes have always revealed their dissatisfaction by explaining the loss of their previous high status through trickery, accident, or other external causes.[69] The importance of the external relations between caste groupings has been exaggerated. The fact that "a caste does not exist by itself" and "can only be recognized in contrast to other castes with which its members are closely involved in a network of economic, political, and ritual relationships"[70] is no more significant than the fact that a group comprising all men does not exist by itself except in contrast to that group comprising all women, "with which its members are closely involved. . . ." Exactly the same observation can be applied to higher and lower classes, employers and employees, greater and lesser talents, or different races. The external relations among some castes and subcastes may be somewhat more formalized and perhaps more binding in a sense than those among some of the other groupings named above, but that feature alone does not make caste so qualitatively different from the rest.*

More important, however, is the fact that numerous caste divisions have nothing to do with economic privileges or any other privilege—not even the privilege of claiming some sort of superiority—except the privilege of division. Speaking of Rampura, Srinivas makes the following point to show intra- or intercaste solidarity which illustrates our point well: "There is another type of solidarity besides those of kinship, caste, and village. The various subcastes in a village are grouped into two divisions, viz., Nadu and Desha. It is not very easy to discover which subcastes belong to the Nadu division and which to the Desha."[71] It is not clear on what basis Srinivas speaks of solidarity here. Our immediate question to such a statement is, if there is a solidarity, for economic or any reason whatever, in each of these two divisions, then why is it so difficult to find out which subcastes belong to which? Had these divisions carried on antisocial rituals and activities, then some secrecy might be necessary, and this would naturally make them difficult to identify. But they are not antisocial divisions and caste members are under no compulsion to be secretive about the identity of their castes and subcastes. The only logical conclusion we can draw from Srinivas' evidence is that these divisions have no real solidarity at all, and they are merely more expression of the same divisive tendency among Hindu castes which can be seen in the constant fission into new groups and the constant claims of superiority which each group makes against the others.

A final piece of evidence indicating the lack of intracaste or subcaste solidarity, for economic or other reasons, is to be seen in the many caste- or subcaste-raising movements under modern impact. Miller in his Kerala study mentions the development in recent years of internal organization of castes over wider regions (perhaps Kerala-wide) which are designed to reform internal custom along the line of all Indian Hinduism and perhaps to obtain political representation.[72] We have already noted the fact that rank-raising

---

* Some students may insist that caste is much more a closed system than that which operates in class or employer-employee relationships. But in view of the fact that the Hindu caste system has always incorporated new caste groups with ease, the evidence for such a contention is not impressive.

movements of most castes in Marriott's Uttar Pradesh village are hampered by internal division.[73] But a fuller account of this point is recently given by N. K. Bose in an article on "Some Aspects of Caste in Bengal."[74] Quoting an earlier study by Priti Mitra to show that there have been some changes in the internal affairs of caste besides widespread shifts in occupation, he states:

> After an analysis of census figures, Mitra proceeded to investigate some of the caste organizations separately. It appears that from about the beginning of the present century, when castes and their ranks began to be recorded in census returns, many organizations along modern lines have also been established in India to take charge of a few of the interests associated with caste. . . .
> . . . in the case of West Bengal . . . associations were formed at or near the [1901 census] by castes like the Yogi, Sadgop, Ganhabanik, Subarnabanik, Namahsudra, Kayastha, Vaidya or Brahman. These organizations appear to possess very few functions in the ordinary life of their members. *But when there is some question of rank involved, popular enthusiasm can be raised high,* and even made to serve some purposes of internal social reform. *In the case of castes enjoying a high rank, like the Brahman, Vaidya or Kayastha, the specific organizations do not ever seem to have reached any high point of activity.* [Italics mine.][75]

In other words, the primary motive behind such efforts at wider organization is the claim or attempted claim to superiority in rank made on the part of some caste or subcaste over others. And if this motive cannot be fulfilled by organizational activities, then it may find expression in hiring genealogists and certainly in fissiparous development of new subcastes, which are generally made by instituting customs such as forbidding widow remarriage. The anxiety of groups high on the caste hierarchy to keep and maintain their privileges, economic and other, is understandable and plain to see. This sort of attitude is perfectly comparable to that of the union members in modern industrial societies who want to find every means to control their economic preserves. In every human society groups which enjoy some economic advantages will always be loath to give them up, whether or not a caste system relates them to the rest of the society, if in their views their social disability does not greatly outweigh their economic advantages. When, on the other hand, they see their social consideration as outweighing their economic advantages, the anxiety on the part of groups low on the Hindu caste hierarchy for social esteem at the expense of economic position is equally easy to discover. In such a situation caste groups will not hesitate to refuse new and more productive ways of making a living if the more productive ways are considered socially more disadvantageous than the older ways, nor even hesitate to give up existing economic advantages to gain a point or so on the social ladder. The former condition is one of the chief obstacles to India's economic development,[76] while the latter is found when, from time to time, low castes attempt to free themselves from some of their so-called economic "privileges."[77]

THE QUESTION OF VILLAGE UNITY

The main conclusion of this chapter is that centrifugal tendencies dominate the Hindu caste much more than centripetal tendencies. We have seen also that even the Hindu clan, wherever it is found to lead more than a nominal existence, exhibits the same characteristics as the Hindu caste. But before we proceed any further we must examine whether the centrifugal tendencies, though obvious in caste and clan, are not overshadowed by centripetal tendencies in another grouping: the village.

For some years a few students of Indian society, including Srinivas, have tried to emphasize the unity of the Indian village at least as a rival to the solidarity of the Hindu caste. Srinivas in the Introduction to the collection of studies entitled *Indian Villages*, says:

> The unity of the village is a point made by many of the contributors to this series. A body of people living in a restricted area, at some distance from other similar groups, with extremely poor roads between them, the majority of the people being engaged in agricultural activity, all closely depend upon each other economically and otherwise, and having a vast body of common experience, must have some sense of unity. . . .
>
> The view that the solidarity of the caste is so great that it nullifies the unity of the village community in those villages in which live more than one caste, is so plausible that it misled not a few. But a moment's reflection will expose its falsity. It is true that caste is an institution of prodigious strength, and that it is pervasive. . . . But all this does not make a caste self-sufficient. The castes living in a village or other local area are interdependent economically and otherwise. . . .
>
> The strong rivalries which exist between the members of a nonagricultural or servicing caste often force them to seek friends outside their own caste. . . .
>
> The autonomy of a caste court is only part of the story—there is a tendency to refer disputes upward locally to the elders of the dominant caste as quite a few contributors have noticed.
>
> The ties cutting across the lives of caste are as important as the ties of caste.[78]

What Srinivas says about caste here merely reinforces our conclusion that it is divisive. But what Srinivas describes as evidence for village solidarity is misleading, because it is not placed in its proper perspective. A village community anywhere in the world will be spurred to intravillage cooperation during emergencies. We have already noted how the Chinese village will act in this fashion when confronted by epidemics, natural disasters, or governmental encroachment. Srinivas' evidence supporting the unity of the Indian village runs precisely in this vein. Thus about Rampura, the Mysore village which Srinivas reports on, he says:

> The village is a unity in several senses of the term. It is, firstly, a physical unity. If the monsoon fails, it fails for everyone. Formerly when there was an attack of cholera or plague or small-pox, the entire village acted as one, and moved away to a different place. They all joined together to propitiate the deities presiding over these diseases. The disease was ritually driven out of the village—the village boundary has a certain ritual significance.
>
> The ritual unity of the village is important. During the early part of the summer of 1948 there was a long drought. . . . The villagers felt that they were being punished by God. Some attributed the drought to the fact that the priest of the Basava temple . . . was living with two women to whom he was not married. . . .
>
> There was a striking demonstration of village unity during my stay. The government suddenly passed an order that fishing rights in tanks all over the state would be sold by auction. When Rampura people learnt of it, their spontaneous reaction was "What right has the government to auction fishing rights in *our* tank?" The government was, according to them, encroaching on something that belonged to them. . . . On the day fixed for auction, the villagers saw to it that nobody in the village or from any of the neighboring villagers was there to bid. The visiting government official had to return without an auction.[79]

Two additional facts are that the Rampura people consider themselves better in one way or another than people of other villages, and that sometimes fights occur between opposing groups originating from two villages.[80]

What Srinivas has failed to appreciate is that what he says about unity in his Indian village is not only equally applicable to Chinese villages but probably to villages in all Old World countries as well. In fact it can be applied to most any group of people living in a common local area, including Southern plantation owners in the United States and their one-time slaves. The inhabitants of one village, like the slave-owners and their labor force on a plantation, or shipmates in an ocean liner, will unite and cooperate in the event of sheer physical necessity, but they are hardly bound together by other ties. As proof for this contention it is only necessary to observe how overwhelmingly any multicaste and even single-caste Indian village is divided in spite of the many things (enumerated by Srinivas) which they have in common.

Although we can say that the characteristics of the Indian village are common to its counterparts in China and most of the world, we certainly cannot say the same about the Indian caste system. There the factors which bind men together or divide them are wholly of a different sort, a sort that is peculiar to the Hindu society. These factors will divide or unite men regardless of territory. The principle of caste is so important that even supernatural beings in many parts of India, especially the South, are separated by clean and unclean categories. These are considerations which make the Hindu world different from other worlds. It is these considerations in connection with Hindu caste that must engage our attention in the next couple of chapters.

NOTES FOR CHAPTER V

1. For a thorough treatment of this subject see G. S. Ghurye, *Caste and Class in India,* 2nd ed. (Bombay: The Popular Book Depot, 1959), pp. 44–118.

2. M. N. Srinivas, "Varna and Caste," in S. Radhakrishnan *et al.* (eds.), *Essays in Philosophy* (Barada, India: The University of Barada, 1954), presented in honor of A. R. Wadia. Republished in the University of Chicago's *Introduction to the Civilization of India* (Chicago: Syllabus Division, University of Chicago Press, 1957), p. 272.

3. Pandharinath Prabhu, *Hindu Social Organization* (Bombay: The Popular Book Depot, 1958), p. 154.

4. M. N. Srinivas, *Marriage and Family in Mysore* (Bombay: New Book Co., 1942), pp. 203–204.

5. G. S. Ghurye, *op. cit.,* p. 20.

6. M. N. Srinivas, *op. cit.,* (1954).

7. G. S. Ghurye, *op. cit.,* p. 57.

8. M. N. Srinivas, *op. cit.* (1954), p. 275.

9. G. S. Ghurye, *op. cit.,* p. 20.

10. M. N. Srinivas, *op. cit.* (1954), p. 272.

11. Mentioned by McKim Marriott in his paper entitled, "A Technique for the Study of Caste Ranking in South Asia," read at the American Anthropological Association meetings of 1957, in Chicago.

12. If we take a village, or a small group of villages, it is possible to identify a somewhat less disputed ranking of the castes of the local area. But even under such circumstances the ranking picture is never a certainty. Dube, for example, gives a table of relative superiority of the different castes in Shamirpet but says of the Panch Bramha group: "In the local caste hierarchy they should be placed below the Sale-Gaondla group" (which in the table is ranked directly below the Kapu-Kummari-Golla group). In addition the relative positions of the different castes in the middle regions of the caste spectrum are cloudy, as elsewhere—S. C. Dube, *Indian Village* (Ithaca: Cornell University Press, 1955), pp. 35–42. Mandelbaum says of the Kota of South India, in comparison with Rampura of Mysore and other villages: "In the Nilgiris also the ranking of villagers in day-to-day relationship will vary by situation and according to the specific combinations of evaluative factors. It would be, in a sense, false to set up a rigid rank order of castes in many villages of modern India. For some ritual purposes, such a listing may prevail. But individuals and even groups may be given one rank order in a particular context and a different ranking in another context"—David G. Mandelbaum, "The World and the World View of the Kota," in McKim Marriott (ed.), *Village India,* p. 241. Srinivas observes: "One of the most striking features of the caste system as it actually exists is the lack of clarity in the hierarchy especially in the middle regions. . . . It is necessary to stress here that the many small castes in any local area do not occupy clear and permanent positions in the system. Nebulousness as to

position is of the essence of the system in operation as distinct from the system in conception"—M. N. Srinivas, *op. cit.* (1957), p. 273.

13. M. N. Srinivas, *op. cit.* (1954), pp. 11–12.

14. M. N. Srinivas, *Religion and Society Among the Coorgs of South India* (Oxford: Oxford University Press, 1952), p. 35.

15. N. K. Bose, "Some Aspects of Caste in Bengal," in *Traditional India: Structure and Change,* guest-edited by Milton Singer, *Journal of American Folklore,* LXXI, No. 281 (1958), 405–406.

16. Stephen Fuchs, *The Children of Hari* (New York: Frederick A. Praegar, 1951), pp. 59–61.

17. H. N. C. Stevenson, in his brilliant article on "Status Evaluation in the Hindu Caste System," *Journal of the Royal Anthropological Institute,* LXXXIV, Pts. 1 and 2 (1954), pp. 45–65, concludes: "There is no fixed hierarchy of 'castes' and 'sub-castes.' Group status—both secular and ritual—is variable and relative in time, space and interaction. Relativity and fission are the characteristics which make possible the status mobility of endogamous groups" (p. 63). David F. Pocock in "Differences in East Africa: A Study of Caste and Religion in Modern Indian Society," *Southwestern Journal of Anthropology,* XIII, No. 4 (Winter 1957), pp. 289–300, makes the interesting point that Hindus in East Africa have developed a situation in which castes are "deprived of their religious context" and "reduced to cognizance of each other in terms of difference" (p. 289). In view of the analysis presented here it would seem that what Pocock has found in East Africa is probably nothing but the most basic feature of castes in India itself. This point will be dealt with later.

18. I. Karve, *Kinship Organization in India* (Poona: Deccan College Monograph Series, 1953), pp. 140–141; 156–159; 119–122; 183–186.

19. M. N. Srinivas, Introduction, in *India's Villages* (West Bengal Development Department, 1955), p. 11.

20. Maurice Freedman has made an excellent analysis of the situation in his *Lineage Organization in Southeastern China* (London: The Athlone Press, 1958), Chap. XIII, pp. 96–113.

21. G. S. Ghurye, *op. cit.,* p. 21. This is the case wherever specific local data are examined. Kathleen Gough, in her analysis of caste in the Tanjore village referred to elsewhere in this chapter, states that the panchayat of the Brahman lineages in the past was "also concerned with the administration of justice among the Brahmans and within the village as a whole"—Kathleen Gough: "Caste in a Tanjore Village," in E. R. Leach (ed.), *Aspects of Caste in South India, Ceylon and North-West Pakistan,* Cambridge Papers in Social Anthropology No. 2 (Cambridge: Cambridge University Press, 1960), p. 36. Adrian C. Mayer, describing the social system of Malabar, speaks of "a council of caste elders" which judge "each case," but admits at once that "there was no application of caste law above the village level, though there were often wider meetings to decide points of law"—Adrian C. Mayer, *Land and Society in Malabar* (Oxford: Oxford University Press, 1952), pp. 30–31. F. G. Bailey reports that in his highland Orissa village, "only the Herdsmen caste have a regular council meeting every two or three years to regulate conduct and hear disputes," and that he has "never heard of the Brahmans, Washermen, Sweepers, Barbers, or Templemen holding a full council"—F. G. Bailey, *Caste and the Economic Frontier* (Manchester: Manchester University Press, 1957), p. 103.

22. *Ibid.,* p. 25.

23. *Ibid.,* p. 21.

24. *Ibid.*, p. 35.

25. M. N. Srinivas, *Coorgs*, p. 43.

26. *Ibid.*, pp. 56–60 and 63–64.

27. *India's Villages*, pp. 6–7.

28. *Ibid.*, p. 24 and p. 28.

29. *Ibid.*, pp. 27–29.

30. *Ibid.*, pp. 27–30.

31. *Ibid.*, pp. 29–30.

32. *Ibid.*, pp. 54–55.

33. *Ibid.*, p. 37.

34. G. Morris Carstairs, *The Twice Born* (London: The Hogarth Press, 1957), p. 155. In the article he calls the village Fatepura, while in his book he calls it Deoli; but the descriptions of the location of the "two" villages in both publications make it apparent that these are but two pseudo-names given to the same village.

35. *India's Villages*, p. 37, and G. Morris Carstairs, *op. cit.*, p. 146.

36. *Ibid.*, p. 68; p. 103 and p. 174.

37. *Ibid.*, p. 103.

38. Oscar Lewis, *Village Life in Northern India* (Urbana: University of Illinois Press, 1958), pp. 113–154.

39. *India's Villages*, pp. 85–90.

40. *Ibid.*, p. 88.

41. *Ibid.*, p. 90.

42. E. Kathleen Gough, "The Social Structure of a Tanjore Village," in McKim Marriott *op. cit.*, p. 49.

43. *India's Villages*, pp. 185–187.

44. *Ibid.*, p. 186.

45. *Ibid.*, pp. 42–43.

46. *Ibid.*, pp. 49–50.

47. S. C. Dube, *op. cit.*, pp. 47–48.

48. Oscar Lewis, *op. cit.*, pp. 27–29.

49. *Ibid.*, pp. 160–162.

50. *Ibid.*, p. 314.

51. *Ibid.*, pp. 113–114.

52. *Ibid.*, p. 114.

53. Harwant Singh Dhillon, *Leadership and Groups in a South Indian Village* (New Delhi: Planning Commission, Program and Evaluation Organization, Government of India, 1955). Published in the name of the Planning Commission and not of the investigator and presumptive author, Dhillon.

54. Oscar Lewis, *op. cit.*, p. 125.

55. Louis Dumont, *Une sous-caste de l'Inde du Sud* (Paris: Mouton et Cie, 1957).

56. *Ibid.*, p. 186.

57. *Ibid.*, pp. 137–38.

58. *Ibid.*, p. 141.

59. *Ibid.*, p. 142.

60. *Ibid.*, pp. 142–149.

61. *Ibid.*, pp. 149–150.

62. *Ibid.*, p. 150.

63. *Ibid.*, pp. 286–287.

64. *Ibid.*, p. 294.

65. *Ibid.*, pp. 295–296.

66. *Ibid.*, p. 49.

67. A picture of caste organization similar to that of the Pramalai Kallars is found among the untouchable Balabis caste of Madhya Pradesh, as reported by Stephen Fuchs, *op. cit.* The Balabis live in even more complete physical segregation than the Kallars. But more description of the same is unnecessary.

68. E. R. Leach, Introduction, in E. R. Leach (ed.), *op. cit.*, pp. 6 and 7.

69. Bernard S. Cohn, "The Pasts of an Indian Village," *Comparative Studies in Society and History* (The Hague: Mouton & Co., 1961), Vol. III, No. 3, pp. 241–249.

70. Leach, *op. cit.*, p. 5.

71. *India's Villages*, p. 27.

72. *Ibid.*, p. 48 and p. 50.

73. *Ibid.*, p. 103.

74. Milton Singer (ed.), *op. cit.* (1958), pp. 397–412.

75. *Ibid.*, p. 405.

76. Mrs. Kusum Nair gives the following illuminating example. "Thus, in certain districts of Assam the local peasants have been living alongside immigrant settlers from Mymensingh, now East Pakistan, for three or four decades under identical conditions, often in the same village. They are all tenants or small land owners. The Bengali immigrants, however, are not only more hard working than the native Assamese, but they have varied and supplemented their work and income from the single-crop paddy fields of the area by cultivating vegetables. This has brought the immigrants prosperity, and the Assamese see it, but still they refuse to turn their hands to vegetable growing and continue to eke out a bare subsistence from their single crop of paddy, which gives them work for only three months in the year.

"Neither the example of their immediate neighbours over the decades nor the persuasions of the official extension agencies (parts of the area have been covered by the Community Development Programme since 1953) have succeeded in convincing the local Assamese to diversify their crops and so improve their earnings. 'For one thing, we have no experience—it depends on habit,' they explain. 'Mymensingh people have it, we do not. Secondly, it requires labour. Thirdly, the Mymensingh farmer will grow his vegetables and take them to the market in a basket on his head. That we cannot do. It is below our dignity. If we do not take it ourselves we shall have to hire a servant to do so; that would be expensive and the servant might cheat' "—Example from Mrs. Nair's book, *Blossoms in the Dust* (London: Duckworth, 1961), p. 138, quoted by the author in "Survey of India," *The Times*, London, January 26, 1962, p. viii.

77. "About fifteen years ago tension arose between the Thakurs and Nonias to elevate themselves in social status. Acting on the decision of their regional caste assembly, the Nonia men of Senapur suddenly appeared wearing the sacred thread and asserted that they were Kshathriya of the exalted Chauhan clan. If such a claim had been accepted, they would have outranked the Raghubanshi Thakurs and might have declined to carry out some of the more burdensome tasks which had been considered their lot. The Senapur Thakurs reacted to this social and economic threat, and one or two instances of physical violence resulted . . ."—Morris Opler and Rudra Datt Singh, "The Division of Labor in an Indian Village," in

Carleton S. Coon, *A Reader in General Anthropology* (New York: Henry Holt, 1948), p. 476. Similar expressions of resistance on the part of lower castes to forms of labor traditionally theirs are found in many parts of India.

78. *India's Villages*, pp. 5–7.
79. *Ibid.*, pp. 22–23.
80. *Ibid.*, pp. 23–24.

Chapter VI

SOME THEORIES OF CASTE

IN THE FOREGOING CHAPTERS we have seen how the contrasting patterns of family life in China and India foster, on the one hand, a cohesive psychological orientation among the Chinese closely related to their situation-centered way of life and, on the other, a divisive psychological orientation among the Hindus closely related to their supernatural-centered way of life. We have seen, too, how these contrasting psychological orientations find expression, respectively, in the cohesive features of the Chinese clan and in the divisive characteristics of the Hindu caste. We have seen that the Chinese clan tends to be well organized and to exhibit a considerable internal cohesion, while the Hindu caste is marked by a perpetual tendency toward fission and consequently by a lack of internal cohesion.

The Chinese clan is inclusive by design; the Hindu caste is exclusive in purpose. Two additional facts support this contrast. The centripetal outlook of the Chinese not only motivated them toward their cohesive clan pattern but led them to consolidate their clan affiliations, and this in spite of the natural increase in population and generations, and of forced migrations because of famine or war. For the last ten centuries the Chinese have had their *Hundred Family Names*,[1] a book widely circulated in villages and cities, which contains actually somewhat more than 400 surnames (clan names). I have never known a Chinese whose surname was not included in this list. But the number of surnames known among the ancient Chinese was about ten times as large as this list, while the number of surnames actually prevalent among Chinese today is not more than one quarter of it.[2] To be sure, two families bearing the same surname are sometimes known to belong to unrelated clans. On the other hand, there are many families bearing the same surnames and residing in widely separate localities, which are claimed as branches in the genealogical records of the same big clans. The centripetal orientation of the Chinese as expressed in their cohesive clan pattern is unmistakable.

The centrifugal outlook of the Hindu as expressed in their divisive caste pattern is equally unmistakable. Although it is not known how many castes existed in ancient India, it is clearly recognized that the Hindu castes and subcastes must have greatly subdivided and multiplied; this is true even in the same geographical area and even though there has been no migration. Multiplication of castes often occurred within periods of time too short for population pressure to be felt. J. H. Hutton thinks there are some 3,000 "castes" in India, but another authority, G. S. Ghurye, thinks that "in each linguistic area there were about two hundred groups called castes with distinct names . . . which were divided into about two thousand smaller units—fixing the limits of marriage and effective social life and making for specific cultural tradition."[3] There are fourteen major languages in India, including Urdu, which is spoken by Moslems among whom castes nevertheless exist. According to Ghurye's estimate we should find the amazing total of over 26,000 subcastes. If we take the round figure 370,000,000 as that of the total Indian population in 1951, we get an average size per subcaste of about 14,000 persons. Judging by the actual data from villages, the size of the average subcaste unit may be far smaller than this, while the total number of castes or subcastes in all India must be larger than the figure suggested above.

The cohesive-inclusive nature of the Chinese clan accords closely with the centripetal personal outlook fostered in the Chinese family. That the divisive-exclusive nature of the Hindu caste accords equally well with the centrifugal outlook of the Hindus is the reason, as we have seen, why clan, that group which is an extension of the family, remains either rudimentary or castelike in India.

The logical corollary of cohesion-inclusion is division-exclusion, however, and vice versa. When we speak of the Chinese clan as being cohesive-inclusive, do we not also have to presume its divisiveness and exclusiveness in regard to the wider Chinese society? Similarly, when we speak of the Hindu caste or subcaste as tending to be divisive and exclusive, do we not have to grant it a degree of cohesiveness and inclusiveness within each splintering group however small? In the previous chapter we have seen that castes and subcastes undergo constant fissions and have no tendency toward all-caste or subcaste solidarity on a wider nonlocal basis. But when we find one caste or subcaste opposing the rank-raising efforts of another, or one section of a caste or subcaste deciding to leave the main body to form a new subgrouping, can we then deny that in both cases there is a sort of cohesion at work?[4]

THE COHESIVE-DIVISIVE BALANCE

As already pointed out, a degree of internal cohesiveness and solidarity within a caste or subcaste at a specific period of time and in a particular area is indeed to be assumed even though the field descriptions on this subject are not, so far, as convincing as one might expect. At the outset it is necessary to realize that human groupings, whether they are characterized by inclusiveness and cohesiveness or by exclusiveness and divisiveness, are dynamic and never static. No matter what societies we speak of, the smallest nonliterate ones or the giant industrialized ones, their human components are constantly dying, being born, being adopted, being married, being killed, or otherwise just leaving or arriving. Their interpersonal ties are never idle: there is change and realignment all around at all times. Over and above the universally inevitable, however, some human groupings are far more changeful or dynamic than others.

It is not our thesis that Hindu caste groups have no internal cohesion at any time whatsoever. In fact some castes are known to act like labor unions at times and force specific concessions from landlords.[5] But our argument is based on the fact that in spite of such temporary successes the caste-groups are in constant processes of internal fission so that the internal cohesiveness of each caste-group can be maintained only for short periods of time. It is obvious that, other things being equal, groupings which undergo internal divisions have less internal cohesion than others which do not do so, or undergo them far less. The point is, the Hindu, while living in some caste at all times, is always trying to get away from it. Buddhism, Jainism, and numerous other protestant movements in India have been a perennial expression of this desire. Fissiparous tendencies within local caste-groups and caste-ranking disputes among different castes are other expressions of it. These features contrast sharply with those of the Chinese clan. Historically there have been in China no clan-reform or clan-abolition movements; most Chinese clans simply grew till famine or war or limitation of territory forced migrations elsewhere of parts of their membership. Even migration to faraway lands did not sever the individual's clan affiliation. Some clansmen will go to great expense to trace their kinship connection.

The contrasting dynamics of Chinese clan and Hindu caste are diagramatically illustrated on page 126.

Another point of difference between Chinese clan and Indian caste is to be found in intergroup relations. As pointed out above, animosity and sometimes open fights between clans occur in the extreme south and central China. But in the rest of China such interclan hostility is extremely rare. In fact, even in south and central China the acts of aggression are usually rooted in concrete reasons such as disputes over water rights between two localities each inhabited by members of one clan. In the normal course of events there are neither interclan disputes over clan ranking nor interclan claims of superiority. If and when the members of one clan feel superior to another, this superiority is understood and rarely if ever expressed, least of all by

CHINESE CLAN   HINDU CASTE

———————▶ Present line of actual or desired integration or splintering
- - - - -▶ Past line of integration
•••••••••▶ Line of opposition

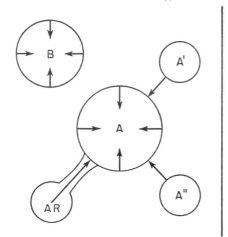

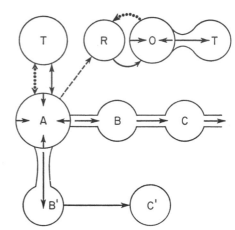

A is a main clan. Arrows indicate direction of cohesion. A′ and A″ are branches of the Clan A which separated from it some time ago, but the kinship connection with A will be traced through genealogy and reintegrated ritually and socially with an enlarged A. AR is in the actual process of reintegration with A. B is another main clan which may or may not be in a position of rivalry or antagonism with A.

A is a main caste-group and T and O are other such groups. In opposition to T members of A have solidarity among themselves. But splinters like B and B′ occur often. The B and B′ will become new caste-groups which will sever and deny all connection with A. Later C and C′ will become new caste-groups and will sever and deny all connection with B and B′. R is also a splinter caste-group from A (which previously attained its autonomy) but instead of maintaining its independence, it seeks to integrate with O, which happens to be recognized as higher in rank than A. But O will attempt to reject R. O will have its own splintering groups (such as T).

members themselves. There are specific Chinese rules of custom against open expressions of superiority. Such expressions are regarded as boastfulness even if they are founded in fact.

On the other hand, intergroup conflicts as well as disputes over ranking and superiority, which often result in violence, are so obviously part of the Hindu caste system that they need no elaboration. These disputes are not of modern origin. Long before Western impact, the panchayat at the village level, and the ruling Kshatriya in the wider administration area, have from time immemorial served as instruments of punishment for infractions of caste rules and statuses, especially when the infractions threatened the Brahman superiority.

The Chinese-Hindu contrast here is evident. The Chinese clan is far more internally cohesive and inclusive than externally divisive and exclusive. The Hindu caste, on the other hand, is far more externally divisive and exclusive than internally cohesive and inclusive. Each type of human grouping is a set of dynamic relationships. In the Chinese case the centripetal-centrifugal forces are balanced in favor of the former while in the Hindu case, in favor of the latter. The net result is that the Chinese individual grows up to look for a relatively straightforward set of relationships: his family first and beyond that, his clan, to whatever extent the latter may expand. He may personally have to leave these for periods of time, because of famine, profession, war, and other external circumstances. But he is encouraged to return to them, for it is with human beings within these groups, which include the remote dead ancestors and the yet future unborn, that he has his permanent ties. He owes everything to them. He makes *their* existence possible. The common web of mutual dependence knits him and his kinsmen (including those married into these groups) together forever.

The Hindu individual grows up into a more complicated picture. His family is a grouping through which he must pass but from which he must emerge to enter something higher. His clan affiliation is at most nominal but usually nonexistent. His caste is one grouping into which he is born and within which he must make and spend his entire life. But caste is nevertheless not a grouping that he can take for granted. If he is a member of a high caste, he has to guard against pollution by wrong food, wrong touch and association, and wrong marriage. If he is a member of a low caste, he must watch his step lest he be subject to punishment for polluting those of higher castes; otherwise he would sink still lower. Whether he is of high caste or low, the grouping to which he belongs may and usually does divide so that, without any action on his part, some of those with whom he once was affiliated no longer admit him as one of their own. If he is ambitious, he has to pursue this fleeing caste affiliation continuously, apart from whatever else he does for a living, for personal excellence, or for personal satisfaction. But even if he is not ambitious he has to watch his caste affiliation as a matter of sheer self-defense and self-preservation.

In the Chinese case there are no contradictions. The centripetal patterns of the family and that of the clan fit each other. In the Hindu context, however, there is a contradiction. The centrifugal pattern of the family coincides with the divisive tendencies of the caste. But what makes the Hindu continue to seek cohesion in caste affiliation while Hindu caste boundaries are so changeable?

To understand this contradiction we must reappraise some theories of caste.

SOME THEORIES OF THE HINDU CASTE SYSTEM

There have been many descriptions and studies of caste in India but there is a dearth of overall theory to explain caste. Dumont and Pocock have outlined the situation succinctly:

> The books of Professor Ghurye and Professor Hutton appear comprehensive and both are based upon more modern material [than the older works of the nineteenth century] as well as the author's own knowledge. Nevertheless it is our experience that apart from much valuable information about what happens and can happen in Hindu society, the student emerges from a reading of these works still without having gained a clear idea of the caste system. Particularly from Professor Hutton's book he derives an impression of immense complexity and inconsistency in Hindu life which appears to defy any kind of systematic understanding. It is not surprising, if, in reaction, he turns for enlightenment to this or that particular field study and feels that he will only begin to understand Hindu society when a large enough number of such studies has been made. But even here he must be disappointed for each author posits caste at the outset and then goes on to speak of his particular, local experience. In this way the caste system itself becomes a kind of unexamined assumption from which all the bewildering diversity flows. Professor Hutton's conclusion to his work is symptomatic (Hutton, 1946, pp. 164–5). He lists fifteen of the more obvious factors . . . probably contributing to the emergence and development of the caste system. We then read of "Primitive ideas of totemism, taboo, *mana*, and soul stuff," of beliefs in magic and in reincarnation, of undefined economic factors, of conquest, culture clash, color prejudice and the policy of priests. A blend, that is to say, of outmoded evolutionism, hypothetical history and imputed motive.[6]

With these words Dumont and Pocock justify their drawing the attention of modern social scientists to the theory of C. Bouglé, first published fifty-one years ago,[7] and to their own "Commented Summary" of this theory. In doing this Dumont and Pocock have performed a brilliant service. Bouglé's was a major pioneering theory on caste based on a remarkably modern methodology and outlook. It postulates three elements, namely, hereditary specialization, hierarchy, and repulsion. While the first two elements are integral parts of Bouglé's theory, the third seems to be the core and certainly provides his theory with its distinctive character. Hereditary specialization refers to the fact that the son of a blacksmith will be a blacksmith just as the son of a warrior will be a warrior, and that "professions become the obligatory monopolies of families, to perform them is not merely a right but a duty imposed by birth upon the children." Hier-

archy refers to "unequally divided right . . ."—to the fact that such prerogatives as dress, ornaments, wealth, and tax which are the birthright of one
are denied to another, and that "personal 'status' for life is determined by
the rank of the group to which one belongs."[8]

These features of caste have been pointed out by other scholars before
and after Bouglé, but the third element is exclusively his. Repulsion refers
to the fact that the "different groups of which the society is composed,
repel each other rather than attract, that each retires within itself, isolates
itself, makes every effort to prevent its members from contracting alliances
or even from entering into relations with neighboring groups." "It seems to
us that it is, as it were, designed to atomize the societies into which it penetrates; it divides them not merely into superimposed levels but into a multitude of opposed fragments; it brings each of their elementary groups face to
face, separated by a mutual repulsion."[9] But what makes the castes repel
each other and, at the same time, makes them, in spite of their mutual repulsion, unanimously admit the superiority of the Brahman? Here Bouglé
appears to be confused but Dumont and Pocock, examining Bouglé's pages
closely, suggest that the "organizing principle" of his elements is the "syn-
thetic opposition of the pure and the impure."[10]

After discussing Bouglé, Dumont and Pocock turn to the theory of
A. M. Hocart;[11] they feel it is complementary to Bouglé's theory. With
Bouglé, Hocart agrees that the caste system is founded on religious conceptions and on the opposition of the pure and the impure. But while Bouglé
thinks of caste in terms of a Hindu society divided into the classical four
varnas and Untouchables, Hocart notes the multitudinous *jatis* into which
the Hindu society is everywhere actually divided but which do not always
fit into the varna scheme. Instead of taking the *jati* scheme as a degenerated
varna scheme, or considering the varna scheme to be a pure fabrication of
the priests and thus to bear no resemblance to Hindu reality, Hocart considers the two to be interdependent, the former being the indigenous model
and the latter the social actuality. The problem of how this interdependence
works itself out in Hindu society is not tackled by Hocart to the satisfaction of Dumont and Pocock, but after adjusting his views with reference to
Dumezil, Srinivas, Stevenson, and Varma,[12] the two commentators point
out Hocart's real contribution. This is the discovery that the ritual purity
of the Brahman and the political and economic power of the Kshatriya are
mutually indispensable and therefore complementary to each other. The
power of the Kshatriya must be interpreted broadly here, so that it includes
not only the strength of the big chiefs or kings, but also that of other lower
castes which can afford to deploy the Brahman and members of other
castes ritually and/or economically. Thus, while the Brahman's superiority
in ritual purity maintains the religion, the Kshatriya or government or caste

which dominates a given local area maintains the social organization in which the Brahman's ritual purity is inherent.[13]

It is easy to see how the central theme of Bouglé's theory, namely repulsion, is out of line with reality. For instead of repelling each other the higher and lower castes or *jatis* need each other and cooperate with each other in well-defined ways within different local communities. Repulsion is out of the question here, whether we take it in the manner of the physicist or in the "emotive sense as describing attitudes which prevail between castes."[14] Furthermore, even in matters where exclusion is in force, it is primarily the higher castes which will exclude the lower ones, not, in the long run, the other way around. It is of course possible to find many local instances in which a lower caste seems to maintain its exclusiveness against a higher caste. We noted some of these examples in Chapter V. But such instances can easily be attributed to a well-known psychological mechanism of defense against one's own inferiority or weakness. Not only is there the nearly universal desire on the part of the lower castes to imitate the higher castes, but there is no question but that the higher castes will shun the lower far more often than the lower castes will shun the higher. Taking Hindu India as a whole, it is the members of lower castes who give their daughters to members of the higher castes in hypergamous marriages or alliances, and it is men and women of the lower castes who accept food and water from those of higher castes. In Bengal, I have collected many reported examples of wives of Brahmans throwing out all their utensils when a Sudra has entered their kitchens, but never a Sudra wife doing the same after the visit of a Brahman. Of course, wealth or the lack of it may interfere with the strictness with which individual caste members observe the caste rules and may affect the interpersonal conduct between individuals possessing unequal caste statuses, as Pocock's work in Gujarat clearly demonstrates.[15] The general picture of relationship between castes of unequal statuses presented above nevertheless remains correct.

Acknowledging Bouglé's error in the employment of the term "repulsion," Dumont and Pocock try to reduce its consequences by suggesting that what Bouglé really means is not repulsion but "opposition." Given the facts already reviewed, "opposition," if it is intended to mean mutual oppositions between castes, suffers from the same basic defect as does the term "repulsion." It is the castes with higher statuses which are "opposed" to the encroachment of those with lower ranks, and not vice versa.

The theory of Hocart, after being adjusted by Dumont and Pocock, takes us a little farther along the same line. It shows that there is not one dichotomy or opposition but many receding or expanding circles of it, depending on one's place in the caste hierarchy. The endogamous circles of

Rajput clans noted in Chapter V and the hypergamous circles of Six Villages and of Twenty-six Villages among the Charottar Patidars analysed by Pocock both exemplify this principle. The Six Villages, being at the top of the status ladder, consider the Twenty-six Villages and all others as lower than they. But the Twenty-six Villages, being lower than the Six Villages but higher than the Paridar Villages situated at the Border of Charottar, range themselves on the side of the Six Villages and consider all the others as lower.[16] Hocart's theory also shows that there is not one caste model for emulation but two or even more. With some modification, this again is substantiated by modern field research. While the ritual model of any given locality tends to remain in the hands of the Brahmans of that locality, the secular prestige tends to be provided by the dominant caste which possesses wealth, whether Brahman or non-Brahman.

But both Bouglé's and Hocart's theories, like that of Dumont and Pocock, suffer from their common emphasis on ritual purity versus impurity as the foundation of the Hindu caste system. Bouglé would regard the Brahman as the utmost model of ritual purity. Hocart would place in this role the Brahman, the Kshatriya, and the Vaishya in a series of receding or expanding dichotomies. Stevenson tries to separate the secular from the ritual, but neither he nor Dumont and Pocock consider this distinction of fundamental importance to our understanding of the Hindu caste system. In fact, Dumont and Pocock are quite categorical in their insistence that "there is one hierarchy and there can, therefore, be only one kind of status."[17]

If there is only one kind of status, namely, ritual status, and if the Brahman and/or the Kshatriya hold the highest or absolute status, why then do the Brahmans or Kshatriyas subdivide among themselves? The usual "explanation" for the Brahman subdivisions is that the lower-grade Brahmans are descendants of caste miscegenation, or that they had in some ways been subject to ritual pollution by lower castes. But there is no historical evidence that all the different grades of Brahmans originated in this manner. In particular, the mutual exclusiveness of the Brahmans of different areas (such as those of Bengal versus those of Madras) fails to show that it is caused by either miscegenation or pollution.

There is also the fact that the criteria for ritual purity and impurity vary enormously from region to region. Brahmans in Coorg and other parts of southern India are vegetarians, but their counterparts in Bengal are meat-eaters. The inhabitants of one village in the great Ganges Valley of Uttar Pradesh consider eating hen's eggs impure, while those of another see in it no such impurity. Marriage practices vary widely, just as rules governing who takes water from whom. In western and southern India all the three upper caste members are supposed to wear the sacred thread but in Bengal and eastern Uttar Pradesh only the Brahmans do so, though the Kayasthas also claim to be Kshatriyas.*

Even in a local area where the rules of purity are well defined, they do not always work out according to definition. In the Mysore village of Rampura, to which we referred, Srinivas reports that vegetarianism is generally regarded as purer than meat-eating, while abstinence is higher than toddy-drinking. He even presents a ranked ordering of meats and an approximate ordering of occupations from pure to impure. Yet in the same village, the vegetarian Trader caste, which should stand highest in rank because of its diet and work, ranks beneath the meat-eating Peasant and Shepherd castes. Widow remarriage, wherever it is practiced, is a sure sign of low caste status. Pocock finds that, while this practice is denied categorically by all Charottar Patidars, regardless of economic standing, it is certainly practiced at the lower economic levels, possibly practiced at the middle economic levels, and completely forbidden only at the highest economic levels. Pocock describes this state of affairs as "graduality."[18]

The plain fact confronting the ethnographer today is that he cannot construct any overall yet consistent picture of caste ranking on the basis of pure versus impure attributes. There seem to be almost as many criteria as there are local communities.

Finally, and this is the most important point of all, if caste is held to be peculiar to India, as Dumont and Pocock would seem to believe, we are at once confronted by the fact that the idea of ritual purity versus impurity is not. The universal occurrence of the latter distinction is such a well-known item in anthropology that any elaboration on it is sheer redundancy. On the other hand, if caste is held to be common in a number of societies, as Hocart would seem to believe, the burden remains with those who take purity versus impurity to be the governing principle of caste to demonstrate the forces which give the Hindu caste system its distinguishing characteristics. The difficulties posed here may be put differently in the form of two questions: if the idea of ritual purity versus impurity is an operative principle in many societies, why is it that caste does not develop in these other societies? For example, while the idea of ritual purity versus impurity has been an important principle governing the daily and national life of the Chinese for many centuries, the Chinese did not develop a caste system. On the other hand, if both caste and the idea of ritual purity versus impurity are present in many societies, what makes the Hindu caste system so strikingly different from caste in these other societies? For example, the Japanese society has for untold centuries had a sort of caste system differentiating the Etas, whose occupations include scavenging and other lowly forms of ac-

---

* There are no Vaishyas in Bengal. The few Kshatriyas in Bengal do put on the sacred thread.

tivities, from the rest of the population. What is it that made the Hindu caste system spread so that its spirit has entered into nearly every relationship in the entire population, while the spirit of the Japanese caste system has failed to affect even the unequal relationship between the Samurai and the peasants, or the aristocracy and the Samurai?

We have no alternative but to admit that since the idea of ritual purity versus impurity is present in all three societies, the explanation for the absence of caste in China, its limited existence in Japan, and its widespread tenacity in India must be sought elsewhere. Under the circumstances, to explain the Hindu caste system by the idea of ritual purity versus impurity is merely to take the part for the whole—a procedure to which Dumont and Pocock particularly take exception.[19]

THE INTERACTIONAL THEORY

To remedy the lack of definite overall criteria for establishing purity in dealing with the problem of status evaluation, McKim Marriott proposes an interactional theory, as contrasted to the attributional theory, to deal with the problem of status evaluation. The attributional theory, as we have seen, is based on the specific meanings or values assigned to symbols of status— clothes, foods, ornaments, or whatever they may be. Its basic defect is that the status values of the attributes vary from region to region. The interactional theory, which is based on the premise that "castes are ranked according to the structure of interaction among them," is supposed to be free from this defect.[20]

According to Marriott, villagers base their opinions of caste rank primarily and explicitly on ritual interactions of two principal kinds: The ritualized giving and receiving of food, and the giving and receiving of ritual services. As between these two kinds of interaction, food transfers are the most decisive for establishing rank. He goes on to give a fivefold classification of foods according to the usage prevalent in Kishan Garhi of Uttar Pradesh. From high to low in order of honor and purity they are

> (a) no food; (b) raw foodstuffs—the food of gifts; (c) superior cooked food (pakki)—the food of feasts; (d) inferior cooked food (kachchi)—daily bread, the food of wage payment; and (e) garbage or leavings from plates. . . . Foods of all five categories are dealt with by villagers of all castes; they do not constitute attributional differences of diet. . . .
>
> Givings and receivings of foods of these five types in interaction with persons of other castes create for each caste a lengthy index of relative caste standings. For example, Brahmans give garbage to the lowest castes and accept no food in return; they give inferior cooked food to all low and some high castes, while receiving in return either no food, raw foodstuffs, or superior cooked food in ascending order according to the caste of the giver. They need

give foods of the two highest categories to no other caste, and accept foods of the two lowest categories from no other caste. Brahmans thus stand clearly at the top of the local caste order of interaction in food. Lower castes follow along behind, giving more honorific foods to the castes above them in return for less honorific ones, while not being able to give the lower, pollution-bearing foods to as many castes below themselves. Such patterns of food transfer define five ranked blocs of castes very clearly, and five subdivisions of these blocs. Often viewed by attributional theorists as merely negative "restrictions" of "taboos" against caste interaction (Blunt 1931: 87–94; Hutton 1946: 62–67), these food patterns appear in Kishan Garhi as positive relational devices. Indeed, the circulation of food constitutes the life's blood of caste rank.[21]

At the outset it should be noted that neither the interactional theory nor the attributional theory aims at more than a descriptive and consistent criterion for caste ranking. But although the interactional theory might be regarded as an improvement over the older theory because it goes beyond specific meanings or values of specific attributes, its usefulness is limited by several difficulties. In the first place, the rank-order of the five categories of food in Kishan Garhi is not universally applicable. In the second place, if the circulation of foods is the "life's blood of caste rank" in Kishan Garhi of Uttar Pradesh, it certainly is not so in Bengal or in Mysore, where the giving and receiving of ritual services are at least equally if not more important. In the third place, the graded and hierarchical values of food transfers enumerated by Marriott, such as "the Brahmans give garbage to the lowest castes and accept no food in return," and so on, are in fact attributional values in disguise. For instead of assigning rank values to specific foods he merely assigns rank values to specific food transfers. If the same rank values of food transfers prevail in all India, the attributional theory will remain valid. If the same rank values of food transfers do not prevail in all India, then the difficulties of the attributional theory will not be overcome by the merits of the interactional theory. In the fourth place, if the interactional theorist should say that the focus of the theory does not lie in the specific rank values of specific food transfers but in the interaction which determines rank in each local community, he will find that his theory is reduced to such generality that it no longer has any scientific value for caste ranking or for anything else. It is similar to an observation made by Dumont and Pocock in their commented summary of Bouglé's and Hocart's works on caste: "The consistency of India lies at the level not of culture but of relations."[22] Since there can be no society without interactions or relations, it is obvious that interactions or relations as such are bound to be a consistent component of not only the Hindu caste system but also all forms of social organization everywhere. Mechanisms which are so basic to all societies obviously cannot account for the characteristics which are peculiar to any one of them. Societies differ primarily because of the particular ways different peoples look at and react to worlds of men, spirits, and things. Therefore, if the Hindus possess characteristics which are at all consistent throughout India and which enable us to distinguish the Indian society from other societies, the roots of these characteristics must be sought in factors other than those which Hindus and other peoples possess in common.

The interactional theory, even if it can produce the results which it sets out to produce, will do no more than enable us to understand the factors underlying caste ranking. What we must do is not only explain how the rules governing Hindu caste system as a form of social organization differ from those in other forms of social organization such as, for the moment, the Chinese clan (and later, the American club or association) but also understand the fundamental forces that sustain the Hindu caste system as contrasted with other fundamental forces that propel the Chinese clan system so as to make rules governing the two types of organization different from each other. In other words, we must search for factors underlying the Hindu caste system which should be applicable to it regardless of time.

In thinking of our knowledge of the fundamental forces which sustain the Hindu caste system, we are no wiser after examining the most recent theories than before. We have learned something more about the actual factors governing caste-ranking practices in several specific areas. We have learned a little more about the concrete manners in which the castes are juxtaposed. Finally, we have become aware of the interdependence of the Brahman with his ritual purity and the Kshatriya with his political and economic power. But all of these are, in the final analysis, but operational designs of the caste system. As such they are certainly far more complex than the operational designs of the clan system and greatly different from them. What we need to know, however, is not merely how the caste system operates specifically in given localities and as a whole (though this is important), but how characteristics of the caste system fit in with other aspects of Hindu social life in general. At the present juncture we are confronted with the centrifugal characteristics of the Hindu family, and in a later publication,* we shall show that these are the same characteristics in other aspects of Hindu society and culture. On the one hand, it is axiomatic that science must aim at explaining more and more facts with fewer and fewer theories. On the other hand, it is equally axiomatic that the way of life of any society, especially one which has lasted for many centuries, must in the long run be based on some fundamental features of unity. If the Hindu family is characterized by centrifugality rooted in their supernatural orientation in which all are One and One is all, what makes the Hindus so caste-minded, so vehement about caste details, and so long in remaining behind the particular

* Francis L. K. Hsu, *People of Gods*, in preparation.

walls of particular castes in spite of the many protestant movements against casteism?

To understand this riddle of contradiction we must momentarily digress to scrutinize the nature of man in terms of needs, social group, and culture.

NOTES FOR CHAPTER VI

1. This book is dated approximately from Five Dynasties (906–959 A.D.) or the northern Sung Dynasty (960–1127 A.D.).

2. A famous Sung Dynasty scholar, Cheng Chiao (1106–1160 A.D.), compiled from ancient texts a total of 1,745 surnames up to his day.—Yeh-Yu Yuan: *Chung Kuo Ku Tai Hsing Shih Chih Tu Yien Chiu* or *A Study of the System of Surnames in Ancient China* (Shanghai: Commercial Press, 1936), p. 18. Of this total, 295 were foreign or two-syllabled surnames. Herbert A. Giles, in his *A Chinese-English Dictionary* (2 vols., 2nd ed. Shanghai: Kelly and Walsh, 1912), pp. 1–8, gives 2,174 surnames. Chi Li, in his *The Formation of the Chinese People* (Cambridge, Mass.: Harvard University Press, 1928), p. 127, enumerates 3,736 surnames up to 1644 A.D. according to a Ch'ing source and cites a Ming source giving a total of 4,657 surnames. On the other hand, S. D. Gamble in his *Ting Hsien, a North China Rural Community* (New York: International Secretariat, Institute of Pacific Relations, 1954), pp. 53–54, counted only 110 surnames among 10,445 families in 62 villages up to 1937. Maurice Freedman in his *Lineage Organization in Southeastern Asia* (London: The Athlone Press, 1958), p. 4, reports having counted 70 Chinese surnames in Singapore in 1949. In 1949 also, the author worked among the Chinese in Honolulu, Hawaii, and found a total of 55 surnames. Combining the Chinese surnames found in Hawaii and those found in mainland United States, Canada, Mexico, and Cuba according to a book entitled *The Chinese in North America*, by Ling Lew (Los Angeles: East-West Culture Publishing Association, 1949), the author obtained a total of 90 surnames. The centripetal tendency of Chinese clans is well put by Hsien-Chin Hu: "A family that has established itself far from the old home may develop into a new *tsu* (clan). However, the social standing of the group improves with the increase of far-away members. Thus, the common descent group in China differs from clans in other societies in that it has no marked tendency to multiply itself continually"—Hsien-Chin Hu, *The Common Descent Group in China and Its Functions*, Viking Fund Publications in Anthropology, No. 10 (New York: Wenner-Gren Foundation for Anthropological Research, 1948), p. 14.

3. J. H. Hutton, *Caste in India* (London: Oxford University Press, 1951), p. 2, and G. S. Ghurye, *Caste and Class in India* (Bombay: The Popular Book Depot, 1959), p. 28.

4. David F. Pocock expresses the same thought in his paper, "Inclusion and Exclusion: A Process in the Caste System of Gujerat," *Southwestern Journal of Anthropology*, XIII, No. 1 (1957), p. 28.

5. Morris Opler and Rudra Datt Singh, "The Division of Labor in an Indian Village," in Carlton S. Coon, *A Reader in General Anthropology* (New York: Henry Holt, 1948), pp. 452–463.

6. L. Dumont and D. Pocock, *Contributions to Indian Sociology* (Paris and the Hague: Mouton & Co.), pp. 31–32.

7. C. Bouglé, *Essais sur le régime des castes* (Paris: Travaux de l'Année Sociologique, 1908; 2nd ed., 1927).

8. Translation by L. Dumont and D. Pocock in Dumont and Pocock, *op. cit.*, pp. 8–9.

9. *Ibid.*, p. 9.

10. *Ibid.*, p. 43.

11. A. M. Hocart, *Caste, a Comparative Study* (London: Methuen, 1950).

12. G. Dumezil, *Mitra-Varuna* (Paris: Payot, 1948); M. N. Srinivas, *Religion and Society Among the Coorgs of South India* (Oxford: Oxford University Press, 1952); H. N. C. Stevenson, "Status Evaluation in the Hindu Caste System," *Journal of the Royal Anthropological Institute*, LXXXIV, Parts 1 and 2 (1954); and Varma, *Studies in Hindu Political Thought and Its Metaphysical Foundations* (Benares: 1954).

13. Dumont and Pocock, *op. cit.*, pp. 45–58.

14. *Ibid.*, p. 42.

15. D. F. Pocock, *op. cit.*, pp. 25–31.

16. *Ibid.*

17. H. N. C. Stevenson, *op. cit.*, pp. 45–46, and Dumont and Pocock, *op. cit.*, p. 54.

18. D. F. Pocock, *op. cit.*, p. 27.

19. Dumont and Pocock, *op. cit.*, p. 49.

20. McKim Marriott, "Interactional and Attributional Theories of Caste Ranking," *Man in India*, XXXIX, No. 2 (April–June 1959), pp. 92–107. This and the following description of the interactional theory are both based on this article.

21. *Ibid.*, pp. 97–98. References in the quotation are to E. A. H. Blunt, *The Caste System of Northern India* (London: Humphrey Milford, Oxford University Press, 1931), and J. H. Hutton, *Caste in India* (London: Oxford University Press, 1951).

22. Dumont and Pocock, *op. cit.*, p. 56.

Chapter VII

A THEORY OF THE HUMAN GROUP

CASTE AND CLAN are different ways in which human beings group themselves. If they do so by one way but not another, and if a particular way of grouping has lasted for many generations and centuries, without significant changes and even resisting them, we have to assume that the human beings concerned must find certain satisfactions or fulfillments which they have not found in other modes of grouping. This is not to say that Hindus and Chinese, as human beings, cannot find other modes of satisfactory groupings besides their respective ways in caste and clan; the fact that all social organizations can be changed, some drastically through revolutions and others more slowly by evolutionary processes, is an objective proof that this is not the case. Nor would it be scientifically sound to view the man-group relationship as a one-way traffic in which the individual requires satisfactions from the groups he belongs to while the groups passively provide them. It is conceivable but not researchable, and in any case beside the point, that the first human beings formed their first groups to satisfy some needs. But as the groups continue while individuals are born into them and drop out of them by death or other processes, the initiates invariably enter into situations where they will be shaped and stimulated by the accumulated ways of the group. Between the individual and his group, represented to him in the form of tradition and sets of social relations, there is a continuous, mutual interaction.

GEORGE HOMANS' THEORY

In order to understand the position of the Chinese in his clan and of the Hindu in his caste we must, therefore, begin by ascertaining what we know about the nature of the human group.[1] In this task we shall resort initially to the work of George Homans, who has given us what seems to me a most comprehensive analysis of the subject. It will be recalled that his hypothesis is constructed with three elements: the environment in which the human group functions, the external system of the human group, and the internal system of the human group.[2] There is complete interrelatedness and mutual interaction among the three basic elements.

According to Homans, the environment consists of three main aspects: physical, technical, and social, "all of which are interrelated and any one of which may be more important than the others for any particular group."[3] The first aspect refers to such things as soil, temperature, rainfall, and mineral wealth. The second refers to such things as tools and skills. The third refers to the human beings outside the group but whose purposes, aims, ideas, and ideals control, direct, or otherwise influence the group. The internal system and the external system each consist of three elements of group behavior: sentiment, activity, and interaction. There is complete mutual dependence among these three elements in a circular fashion. The external system according to Homans, "is the state of these elements and of their interrelations, so far as it constitutes a solution—not necessarily the only possible solution—of the problem: How shall the group survive in its environment? We call it external because it is conditioned by the environment; we call it a system because in it the elements of behavior are mutually dependent."[4] The internal system is "the elaboration of group behavior that simultaneously arises out of the external system and reacts upon it." Homans calls the system internal "because it is not directly conditioned by the environment" and he speaks of it "as an elaboration because it includes forms of behavior not included under the heading of the external system." Commenting further on the two systems Homans observes that "we shall be not far wrong if . . . we think of the external system as group behavior that enables the group to survive in its environment and think of the internal system as group behavior that is an expression of the sentiments towards one another developed by the members of the group in the course of their life together."[5]

With the aid of this neat framework, Homans arrives at a number of generalizations on a variety of behavior in an array of human groups from the families in Tikopia and Trobriand Islands to the Bank Wiring Observation Room in a Chicago factory, the Norton Street Gang of Hilltown in New England, and the Electrical Equipment Company. For example, in the Tikopia system he notes that "the strength of sentiments of friendliness and freedom from restraint between two men varies directly with the frequency of interaction between the two and inversely with the frequency with which one originates interaction for the other."[6] Homans' analysis of the decline of Hilltown in New England is interesting. He analyzes the decline in the reduction of interaction among members of the group, the relaxation of sex norms, the absence of punishment for misconduct, and how these features are related to the relationship between the internal system and the changing social environment.[7]

SENTIMENTS OR SELF-INTEREST

Homans' analytical framework suffers from several defects. It will profit us greatly to examine these at some length. The first thing that bothers us is the lack of precision in Homans' understanding of "sentiments." He separates sentiments into two groups. On the one hand, there are sentiments which individuals bring into the external system and which originate from other groups in the larger society, such as the desire for wages to support a family in Boston or the biological drives of hunger and sex in Tikopia.[8] On the other hand there are sentiments which individuals generate among themselves as a result of interaction in the internal system, and which include a wide range of items from affection, sadness, intimate sympathy, and respect, to complicated psychological states such as antagonism against or liking for individuals and approval or disapproval of their actions.[9]

In defining sentiment, Homans relies on Raymond Firth:

> The use of the term sentiment in this book implies not a psychological reality but a cultural reality, it describes a type of behavior which can be observed, not a state of mind which must be inferred. Inflections in the voice, the look of the eyes and carriage of the head, intimate little movements of the hands and arms, reactions to complex situations affecting the welfare of parents or child, utterances, describing the imagined state of internal organs— such are the phenomena which are classed together under the head of sentiment, the qualifying terms of "affection," "sadness," etc., being given on the basis of distinctions recognized by the natives themselves and embodied in their terminology. Such distinctions, broadly speaking, correspond to those distinguished in our own society.[10]

Both Homans and Firth are much concerned with the question of observability of sentiments but neither seems to realize that, without indicating the specific relationships among the complex and heterogeneous sentiments, even a complete list of these cannot be of any use except as hunches. Homans does not even give such a list. Instead he stops at a few examples and seems to justify his decision by implying that on such matters the sociologists (and by implication the anthropologists) should not reveal their hopeless inadequacy by competing with the psychologists.[11] Besides, when he tries to relate the sentiments (which he calls motives at other times) in the internal system with those in the external system, he seems to engage in circular argument.

> The sentiments we have been talking about are part of what is often called individual self-interest. . . . If we examine the motives we usually call individual self-interest, we shall find that they are, for the most part, neither individual nor selfish but that they are the product of the group life and serve the ends of a whole group not just an individual. What we really mean by the celebrated phrase is that these motives are generated in a different group from

the one we are concerned with at the moment. Thus from the point of view of the Bank Wiring Observation Room, the desire of a man to earn wages was individual self-interest, but from the point of view of his family it was altruism. Motives of self-interest in this sense are the ones that come into the external system. Sentiments, on the other hand, that are generated within the group we are concerned with at the moment include some of the ones we call disinterested. Friendships between wiremen is an example.[12]

If by the statement that individual self-interest is the "product of the group life and serves the ends of a whole group not just an individual" Homans means to express the fact that no human being can be completely unrelated to and separated from other human beings, he is undoubtedly right. It no longer is a matter of argument that the unit of the human mode of existence is the group of which the individual forms a part, and not the individual alone. Therefore it goes without saying that every human act must "serve the ends" of some "group not just an individual." On the other hand, when Homans describes a man's desire for wages as acts of altruism with reference to his family, he is on extremely shaky ground. It is simply contrary to all common sense to say that men support their families because of altruism. If altruism were the only or even the main reason which propels man to support their families, we should find very few families ever supported. Furthermore, while we have whole economic systems built and operated on the express assumption of individual self-interest, we have yet to find a non-Utopian society and culture founded and continued on altruism. This is the case with all human groups—the "primitive" societies, the nonindustrialized but huge agricultural societies, and the industrialized societies.[13] What differentiates the Tikopian system from its American counterpart is that individual self-interest is a function of a wider circle of human beings in the former than in the latter. In the communistic system the individual is enjoined to express his self-interest in connection with a still wider circle of human beings. What Homans fails to see is that human beings, insofar as they absolutely need other human beings to lead their own human existence, cannot but express their own self-interest through their connection with some group. He further confuses rather than clarifies his presentation of sentiments by his failure to distinguish what he calls altruism and what he later terms disinterestedness in connection with friendship among the Bank Wiring Room workers, and by his seeming lack of concern for a definite relationship between his sentiments in the internal system with those of the external system.

THE NEGLECT OF CULTURE

The second defect in Homans' analysis is that he takes little or no notice of the role of culture in it. Homans is not unaware of culture. But where he deals with the concept he seems artificially to restrict it to norms or "statements of what ought to be and only this."[14] Therefore, insofar as Homans makes use of culture at all in his scheme of things, he is only making use of a portion of it, namely, that of value. In fact, since he proposes to deal only with what students of values would regard as *conceived* values in the ways of life of the peoples concerned but not their *operative* and *object* values, his path is even narrower than theirs.[15] A scrutiny of Homans' actual analysis, however, shows that he fails to make use of even this part of culture. For example, in stating the first basic element of his framework, environment, he lists only physical, technical, and social components—not ideological and supernatural. He does speak of two things which, we might suspect, hinge on the ideological, namely "norms," and "assumptions" or "values."[16] But on closer inspection his "norms" and "assumptions" appear rather trivial though not irrelevant. By "norms" he refers to such things as the proper output of a day's work of a wireman as conceived by the workers themselves in the Bank Wiring Observation Room; and by "assumptions" or "values" he refers to such things as criteria for job prestige in a factory. What he has not noted are far more embracing ideological elements which set the motivating norms for entire societies, such as communism, capitalism, Confucianism, or militarism, as well as those we have seen in this book so far, namely, the situation-centered orientation of the Chinese and the supernatural-centered orientation of the Hindus.

At another point Homans also speaks of religion together with the technical and social elements. But after unjustifiably criticizing Lloyd Warner for speaking of the technical, social, and religious systems "as if they all had something in common,"[17] Homans comes up with a most unwarranted notion of what constitutes religion:

> [The religious system] includes ritual and ceremonies, but it also includes myths, beliefs, and "absolute logics": and in this latter group our norms belong. They are part of Warner's religious system, but only a part. For example, cosmology—a people's scientific or pseudo-scientific view of the physical world—is an element of religion, but is something other than a norm.[18]

Quite apart from the fact that cosmology may be so severely tied to orthodoxy that it forms part of the social norm (as exemplified by the troubles Galileo had under Popes Paul V and Urban VIII), a people's scientific view of the universe is often not an intrinsic part of their cosmology and therefore not an element of religion. Priests and theologians may manipulate some scientifically derived knowledge to win converts to their doctrines, but except for such people as the adherents to the so-called Humanist Religion, they never will accept any scientific evidence which proves their doctrines to be untenable. Science and religion may both attempt to explain the universe and man's place in it, but the former argues from the known to the unknown, while the latter argues from the unknown to the known. One can never be an intrinsic part of the other.

After this digression into religion, however, Homans returns to his main trend of thought and seems to have no further use for religion. He apparently does not recognize that supernatural elements express themselves into forms of belief such as monotheism, polytheism, pantheism, or ancestor worship. Each of these represents an important variety of human conception. Each may be an important factor in the environment of a human group and make a material difference in its external or internal systems. As we have already demonstrated in the foregoing chapters, the greater cohesion the Chinese feel toward their departed ancestors as contrasted to the weaker link that the Hindus maintain with their departed ancestors is one of the cardinal forces affecting the psychocultural orientations of the two peoples.

Elsewhere I hope to demonstrate a positive correlation between strong ancestor worship and centralized government in the non-Western, nonmodern world.[19] But even at this point we can question the validity of Homans' statement, when he compares the Norton Street Gang and the society of Tikopia, that "the variations from group to group in the relationship between superior and subordinate are quantitative; in some groups the tie is hardly different from the tie between equals; in others, very different indeed."[20] There is every reason to suspect that the difference in the nature of leadership between Tikopia and the Norton Street Gang in the United States is not quantitative. The superiors in Tikopia are future ancestors who will continually exert their presence and authority after they die, because their subordinates will ritually worship them and consider themselves permanently tied to them. The superiors in the Norton Street Gang are but temporary leaders who can exercise their authority only if they fulfill the expectations of their subordinates. There is a permanency of tenure enjoyed by the Tikopian leaders which tends to overshadow their other immediate qualities and which is not enjoyed by the leaders in the Norton Street Gang. In view of this, one may safely predict that, while the Norton Street Gang leaders and leaders in other American groups may be dropped easily by their followers, the Tikopian superiors are far less subject to the whims of their subordinates.

We have abundant evidence in support of our view of the fate of the Norton Street Gang leaders and American leaders in general. Firth has given no corresponding data for us to say positively whether Tikopian superiors are often subject to rebellion and unseating by their subordinates. We do have a great deal of evidence from Chinese society, however, which suggests a leader-follower relationship that is also qualitatively different from that in the United States. At any rate it is logical to compare large societies with each other. What we find throughout the last two thousand years of Chinese history is a relationship between superiors and subordinates which is more negative than positive, in contradiction to that found in Europe and America, where it is more positive than negative. It will be too much of a digression to elaborate this difference here,[21] but suffice it to say that it is certainly a qualitative one; and as a result, the Chinese superiors, in comparison with their American counterparts, not only in the role of officials and generals but also parents, teachers, and jail wardens, have had far fewer occasions to be objects of rebellion and unseating by their subordinates.

CULTURE AND SOCIAL DECLINE

How Homans' inadequate attention to culture diminishes the value of his framework can be demonstrated in another area. His analysis of the decline of Hilltown is enlightening. The town's political activities have decreased sharply in importance as measured by attendance at meetings and other criteria. The town's people are far more indifferent to dishonesty in their officers than before. Some churches have disappeared and others lead a miserable existence. The social life is impoverished. The general standard of sexual morality has become much lower than before, as indicated by the fact that middle- and upper-class young women who are pregnant before marriage do not even attempt to hide it as they would have previously. Homans shows how all these are related to the changes in the environment, to changes ranging from soil depletion to improvement in transportation and to the psychological stimulation toward and demand for a higher standard of living, originating from general economic changes in the twentieth-century American society as a whole. These changes have brought about a decline in the "number and strength of the sentiments that led members of the group to collaborate with other members," which has in turn led to a decrease in "the number of activities that members of the group carried on together" and in "the frequency of interaction" between them.[22] In the internal system the corresponding changes are equally noticeable. The frequency of interaction here has decreased too, which has in turn led to "a decrease in the strength of interpersonal sentiments." Consequently social norms are less common and clear and social class distinctions blurred. The net result is the breakdown of the means of social control in Hilltown.[23]

So far so good. But why were Hilltown people so stimulated as to move out of Hilltown and never wish to return? Homans provides us with a faint clue, but only a faint clue: "The Yankees seemed to believe, not that wealth came next to godliness, but that the two were identical," that "the norms instilled in Yankees positively encouraged them to pursue the characteristic goals of American civilization in the nineteenth and twentieth centuries."[24]

Homans is describing a culture pattern here; for surely he must realize that "the norms instilled in Yankees," etc., are not the same as those instilled in the Chinese or the Tikopia. But having acknowledged the culture pattern which distinguishes the Yankee Hilltowners, he proceeds to make the following statement in his Summary chapter where he comments on the cohesion of the small group:

> At the level of the tribe, the village, the small group, at the level, that is, of a social unit . . . each of whose members can have some firsthand knowledge of each of the others, human society, for many millenia longer than written history, has been able to cohere. To be sure, the cohesion has been achieved at a price. *Intelligent men have always found small-town life dull, and the internal solidarity of the group has implied a distrust and hatred of outsiders.*[25] [Italics mine.]

Two features in this statement are definitely cultural and not universal as Homans would seem to presume. "Internal solidarity of the group" may imply "a distrust" of strangers everywhere, but it is not always accompanied by "hatred of outsiders." An exact measurement of this is hard to obtain, but the degree of tolerance of intergroup marriage is a reasonably good indication of it. Interracial and interfaith marriage is not only socially frowned upon in the West, it is often prevented by mob violence and forbidden by law. This attitude is not only absent in many nonliterate societies but was not shared by modern Japan even before World War II, when she was among the most powerful nations on earth.

The other culturally determined feature is mistaken by Homans for a universal feature when he states that "intelligent men have always found small-town life dull." This was presumably one reason why Hilltowners left Hilltown. But traditional China is an outstanding example where "intelligent men" did not seem to find "small-town life" dull. In fact, they did not even seem to find village life dull. Certainly they exhibited no tendency to flee from it as did their Western brethren. It is a well-known feature of Chinese society for the last twenty centuries that men who had achieved great prominence in the outside world as a rule cherished the desire to return to and settle down in their native villages or towns, however humble. These men would do several things. First, as soon as they had made the grade, and actively engaged in their busy life outside, they would make a visit to "shine" their native communities and to honor their parents, their kinsmen, and their ancestors. They might make many such visits during their illustrious careers. Second, when they were ready to retire, they would not choose anywhere else except their native communities where their departed ancestors were buried and where their own tombs might already have been constructed. Third, the prominent returnees would, if they could financially manage it, attempt in every way to enlarge and rebuild their own ancestral homes and clan temples as well as to improve their native communities. Thus we can readily see that where Yankees found good reasons to depart from their Hilltowns, the traditional Chinese would choose to return to their humble places of origin.

Homans' law linking frequency of interaction with friendship can be observed at work in the traditional Chinese situation. One may say that the Chinese notables preferred to return to their native places where their opportunities of interaction with fellow human beings were greatest and where, therefore, they would find their best friends and be most at ease in their presence. But Homans' law describing the relationship between superior and subordinate applies to the traditional Chinese situation only in part. The prominent Chinese returnees would indeed initiate more interaction for others not as prominent as they, and the more they initiated such interactions, the stronger would be the other villagers' sentiment of respect and affection for them. They must show their exalted status by carrying on activities expected of them by members of the local communities. They must stage big weddings for their children and grand funerals and birthday celebrations for their elders; they must donate generously to local causes such as prayer meetings to ward off cholera epidemics; they must live up to the joint-family ideal and welcome all relatives and pseudo-relatives who want to come. However, in contrast to Homans' "law," as long as the interactions such exalted persons initiated were not physically or economically harmful to the rest, there would be no such hostility toward them as Homans' American subjects would have. Being situation-centered in orientation, the traditional Chinese were conditioned to seek mutual dependence. They would be only too pleased if individuals of superior status to them cared enough to initiate interactions with them. They would gladly bask in the prominent men's glory, and they would not resent being dependent. The Americans Homans has observed are, as I have explained elsewhere,[26] and shall treat again in Chapters IX and X, individual-centered and conditioned to seek self-reliance. They always cherish some hostility for authority figures even when they are in the active process of showing them respect. This is why Western leadership is, as we noted before, so much more precarious than its counterparts in other societies, and why being a leader in America is such a difficult art. This fact can only remain buried unless we take into serious consideration the culturally induced psychological differences between different peoples under investigation.

The most basic weakness in Homans' analysis lies in his failure to realize that, had the Yankees been reared in the traditional Chinese culture, Hilltown would not have declined the way it did. The Chinese type of ideological and supernatural components of the environment would also have propelled the Yankees to go out in search of wealth and prominence, but they would have streamed back to Hilltown after "making the grade." Hilltown's social organizations, churches, schools, club houses, and family homes would have been *improved* with passage of time. The activities and interactions in both the external and internal systems of Hilltown as a human group would have been more frequent than before and the prominent Hilltown returnees would have initiated more interactions with their fellow Hilltowners, to the latter's delight. Hilltown Yankees would then still have been expressing the same needs in their relationships with their fellow human beings, except that the direction and way in which they would have tried to fulfill these same needs would have been Chinese instead of Puritan.[27] By giving little importance to the role of culture, Homans literally remains in the same error which Chapple and Coon fell into some years ago of trying to explain all or a major part of human behavior by the rate and intensity of human interactions.[28] What we wish to point out is that the rate and intensity of interaction among human individuals constitute only one variable. They are one common ground on which all human beings or even all human beings and all mammals stand.

It is interesting that the superior in Tikopia and the superior in New England both initiate interactions with their respective inferiors more frequently than their inferiors do with them. It is also interesting that as the solidarity among members of any social group declines, the rate of interaction decreases. But these and other similar observations cannot explain how the Tikopia are different from the Americans or how the Americans are different from the Hindus. Determination of the latter type of difference is even more crucial than that of similarities to any theory of the human group. It is to ascertain these differences that the present volume is undertaken. It is our thesis that understanding such differences is the very heart of any theory of human group. It is, furthermore, our thesis that differences in culture pattern are central to an understanding of these differences. In spite of many universals, human beings do not simply react to their environment—human, physical, or supernatural—in any uniform way. It is differing ways of responding to the same environment which make humans human. Any culture-bound scheme or any scheme which fails to take cultural differences into serious consideration is wide of the mark and is therefore doomed.

THE UNIMPORTANCE OF THE PHYSICAL ENVIRONMENT

Once this is admitted, it becomes clear that another one of the defects of Homans' theory is the undue importance given to the physical element which he discusses as the "environment." The central focus of any theory of the human group is not the physical part of the environment (or the ecological factor as some students of society would have it), although that is not totally without significance,[29] but the human part of the environment, which consists of the relationships among men as these relationships are shaped and reshaped by the accumulated culture (techniques, ideologies, supernatural beliefs, etc.). We have come to this conclusion for two reasons. First, while ecological adjustment of animals and plants over long periods of time in any geographical area tends to be perfect, in the sense that those who fail to make it have either to die out or move out, that of human beings is always imperfect.

Human inhabitants as a rule have problems of garbage, refuse, debris, ruins, or depletion of resources wherever they are, while animals rarely concentrate or reproduce themselves in any geographical area to the extent that these become a continuing problem. Human beings in many parts of the globe are either suffering from chronic malnutrition, endemic diseases, recurrent devastations of war and famines, or have such good health that they have to seek happiness in dissipation, and so much wealth that they have to engage in conspicuous consumption or potlatches on a fantastic scale. On the other hand, human beings everywhere have experienced new inventions, new discoveries which increase the potential uses of their talents and expressions of their power, or novel ideological developments which propel them toward new conquests of the physical or human environment or more severe submission to it; these are unmistakable signs of imperfect adjustment between men and their physical environments.

The other reason why the human part of the environment is far more important than the physical part is that there are, up to this point, no valid criteria for evaluating the role of the physical environment in the development of human institutions and ways of life. Homan's description of the Tikopian village, district, and household, and his cursory mention of farms and forest near Hilltown in New England have no intrinsic relationship with the rest of his analysis. Basically he explains social decline or super-ordination-subordination relationships by rates and kinds of interaction, and so on, but not by such factors as humidity and barrenness of the soil. Many human societies in very diverse physical environments share similar social organizations, religious beliefs, economic practices, and political ideologies; while conversely, many other human societies in similar physical environments exhibit very different cultural ways.

To say all this is not to say that the physical part of the environment has absolutely no effect on the behavior patterns of individuals and on the culture characteristics of groups. It may very well have real effects which are not yet deciphered. But there are specific and relatively obvious ways in which the human part of the environment operates to give shape and direction to the human group; these can help us to explain many group characteristics. At some remote date investigators may be able to demonstrate a more consistent relationship between the physical part of the environment and human affairs, but until then it is only practical that we consider more thoroughly the factors which hold for us some degree of immediate promise for comprehending the human group.

A THEORY OF THE HUMAN GROUP

We are now in a position to state a hypothesis on the relationship between the human individual and his group, based partially on Homans' theory, but with a revised focus on the most relevant factors.

The three cardinal factors in our hypothesis are (1) the general environment, (2) the individual's needs, and (3) the human group or groups through which the individual achieves fulfillment of his needs within the general environment consisting of physical, technical, and social elements as defined and conditioned by his culture. While the three factors in our hypothesis are obviously interrelated, we must begin at some point. The point at which we choose to begin is the individual.

Every human individual has two varieties of needs: (1) biological needs and (2) social needs. The term "need" is used in Henry A. Murray's sense, as a construct or a hypothetical concept, which "stands for a force (the physicochemical nature of which is unknown) in the brain region, a force which organizes perception, apperception, intellection, conation and action in such a way as to transform in a certain direction existing, unsatisfying situations."[30] The biological needs refer to those for food, sex, air, bodily protection, and gravitation. These needs are evidently of great importance to man. But for them he can hardly exist. Every society and culture must deal with them. For this reason some social scientists, notably B. Malinowski, postulated them as a basis of human cultures. It is no accident that this kind of postulate led to no significant gains in our understanding of human behavior. It is one thing to say that all humans have to eat but it does not follow that the need for food has generated the particular ways in which different groups of humans produce, distribute, exchange, and consume food. The biological needs are shared by humans and animals alike, and they cannot, therefore, account for behavior patterns which are peculiar to human beings.[31] For the latter purpose we must look into needs which are more exclusively human; we must start by observing that humans begin, carry on, and end their lives as part of a network of human relationships. Food, sex, physical protection, etc., are substances of life, without which there will be no life, animal or human. But the needs which give meanings to life are the social needs without which human life would be undistinguishable from animal life. These social needs are the basic fountainhead of the individual's existence as a *human* being, in a society and following a given pattern of culture, as distinguished from his existence as a *physical* being, with no necessary tie with any society and no identification with any culture. Fairy tales notwithstanding, the efforts of animals are primarily directed toward the satisfaction of biological wants. In spite of the fact that humans have to tend to their biological needs, their efforts are, on the other hand, primarily directed toward the satisfaction of social needs: to be with other human beings, to be related to them, and to be of importance to some or all of them.[32] *

We have observed that while Homans speaks of *sentiments,* he declines to clarify them by giving them substance. Consequently he oscillates, in his use of the concept, between altruism and self-interest. There is a strong affinity between what Homans means by sentiments and what we postulate as social needs. Sentiments are simply what every human individual expresses, consciously or unconsciously, as what he loves, desires, prefers, idealizes, regards as a "must," or what he hates, fears, wishes to avoid, considers evil, regards as taboo. Seen in this light Homans' sentiments are related to what Talcott Parsons designates as "the cathectic orientation of the actor" (individual) which "is his set of need-dispositions toward the fulfillment of role expectations, in the first place of other significant actors but also his own." Parsons goes on to say:

> There is, in the personality structure of the individual actor a "conformity-alienation" dimension in the sense of a disposition to conform with the expectation of others or to be alienated from them. When these relevant expectations are those relative to the fulfillment of role-obligations, his conformity-alienation balance, in general or in particular role contexts, becomes a central focus of the articulation of the motivational system of the personality with the structure of the social system.[33]

But though Parsons discusses the "genesis of deviant motivation," he never goes beyond the "directions" or "solutions" of resolution of the strains, and how they may be aggravated by a vicious circle, after the strains have begun.[34] All he ever says about the "genesis" of the strain is, "Let us assume

---

* It may be argued that human beings innately meet their biological needs in culturally learned ways and that these culture patterns teach them social needs as prerequisites for satisfying biological needs. That is to say, one does not want a theater ticket for its own sake, but he often buys one because he wants to see the show. Certainly it is possible (and probable) that people do learn in early childhood that certain kinds of social behavior or situational qualifications (such as status) are tickets to the satisfaction of biological needs. What such an argument does is to underline the primariness of the biological needs but it does not negate the fact that a general characteristic of human culture is its tendency to become tool oriented rather than task oriented, to focus on the ticket rather than on the show. Thus these instrumental social needs in time become ends in themselves. The question of the universality of the three social needs proposed in this chapter cannot be answered till it is tested cross-culturally on a wide scale.

that, from whatever source, a disturbance is introduced into the system, of such a character that what alter does leads to a frustration, in some important aspects, of ego's expectation-system vis-à-vis alter."[35]

The difficulty encountered by Parsons in locating the true genesis of deviance can be avoided in our analysis of human behavior if we see Homans' sentiments and Parsons' "need-orientations toward the fulfillment of role expectations" in terms of social needs which propel human behavior. But before we proceed to explain our postulate of social needs we must digress momentarily to deal with some objections to such postulates. Some students, such as Alfred R. Lindesmith and Anselm L. Strauss, think that need postulates are futile and should really be abandoned. They have come to this view because needs, according to them, are diverse and tend endlessly to increase or change as external conditions of life progress from the simple to the complex; and classification of social needs into a relatively few basic types "does not all explain the behavior."

> Thus, if a husband is said to be unfaithful to his wife because of the "wish for new experience" and another husband is faithful because of "the wish for security," we must still ask why one is unfaithful and the other is not. To label behavior in such terms is quite arbitrarily to impute to the individual abstract and unverifiable motives which are conceived of as the forces or causative agents behind the overt acts. A need as such is not directly perceived; all that can be observed is behavior itself. Hence the need is first inferred from the act and then used to interpret and explain it. Such explanations are circular or tautological because they do nothing that cannot be accomplished by a simple description of the behavior.[36]

All three bases of Lindesmith's and Strauss's argument—namely, (1) that since motives are multifarious, they cannot be successfully classified into a few basic types, (2) that since motives cannot be seen, they are arbitrary and unverifiable, and (3) that since motives are inferred from the act, they cannot be used to interpret and explain it—are untenable. First, the cardinal rule of science is to arrive at fewer and fewer theories to cover more and more facts. Science cannot progress unless the scientist attempts to reduce multifarious facts to more basic categories. In doing so, he must, of course, be fully aware of the level on which his classification rests. Second, unseen facts may be as real as overt acts and are just as verifiable. The entire field of psychology depends upon the unraveling of the unseen forces. Furthermore there are many forces, even in the physical universe, which, by their very nature, can never be seen. Electricity is one of them. Gravitation is another. No reasonable student can deny the important role these concepts have played in the physical sciences. Finally, having described or summarized the unseeable forces or factors in certain terms, the scientist has not completed his work but has just begun it. He is now ready to investigate their characteristics, their relationship with other forces or factors, their intensity, and their effects. The descriptive or summary concepts serve as convenient tools with which to *build* explanations, not as explanations themselves.

With these qualifications in mind, we propose that the basic social needs of man are sociability, security, and status. Status gives the individual his sense of importance among his fellow men in all or most situations which concern him. It is the evaluation of the individual vis-à-vis the group or groups of which he is a part. To state it differently, status is the rank or position occupied by an individual in his group or groups, with specific attitudes, duties, and privileges between him and his fellow men who acknowledge his rank or position. Status can be seen in sports, in economic pursuits, in the professions, in politics, among churchmen as well as hunters, valued by students no less than by warriors. The Chinese concepts of face and of propriety and the American sensitivity to prestige and superiority are familiar expressions of the same need.

Security means the individual's certainty of his bonds with his fellow men. It is provided by the circle or circles of human beings to which the individual belongs. To put it in another way, security refers to a condition of the individual in which he can with certainty and without fear of repudiation claim that a number of his fellow human beings belong to him, are of the same kind as he, share with him certain aims, thought or action patterns. In time of need he can count on their moral or material support just as they can count on his. Sources of security for the individual are numerous: family, friendship, trade union, club, national state, political party, church or temple, gang and clique, the Royal Society of England, and exclusive suburbs surrounding large industrial cities of the United States.

Sociability signifies the individual's enjoyment of being with his fellow men. It means the desire on the part of the individual to maintain friendliness, affability, and companionship with his fellow human beings. It includes the individual's desire to seek contact with fellow human beings, to promote group relations, or to enter into sexuality, aggression, submission, intrigue, etc., in a social context. Concrete expressions of sociability found in human societies are social gatherings, hospitality, dances, marriage, fox hunts and other society events, fairs, sexual intercourse (other than for begetting children or for material gain), family and clan relations, parades, public appearances by heroes, warriors, kings, presidents, and the tumultuous crowds which cheer them, Times Square on New Year's Eve, and all forms of communal activities which are not tied to any other purpose.

Sociability, security, and status beget or are closely related to each other. A man with higher status is likely to possess greater opportunities for security and sociability. He is likely to be more sought after by his fellow men than a man of lower status. He can better afford to be tired of parties than the other. Similarly, other things being equal, a man with greater ability to socialize is likely to reach higher positions which will give him more security and more status. He is likely to have developed more connections with men and women of consequence than another man less endowed in this regard. In fact few of the examples given above refer each to a single variety of needs. A romance between a man and a woman may combine pure sociability with status. A club or a residential area may serve all three needs of security, status, and sociability. Finally there are reasons to believe that the needs for security and status are probably more important than that for sociability, for sociability tends to be affected by security and status far more than security and status by sociability.[37]

Our reasons for postulating these three as man's basic social needs are relatively simple. There are a number of lists of needs proposed by various social scientists. Those which readily come to mind are the "psychic needs" of Ralph Linton, the components of A. H. Maslow's higher-order needs, the "needs" in the "fundamental interpersonal relations orientation" ("FIRO") scheme of William C. Schutz, the "motives" of McClelland, Klineberg's "motive" or "drive," the "engrams" ("sentiments and complexes") of Raymond B. Cattell, the famous four "wishes" of W. I. Thomas, the "socializing forces" of Sumner, and the "values" of Arens and Lasswell.[38] But if we examine the contents of these lists, we shall preceive that, apart from the obviously biological needs such as Sumner and Keller's hunger and fear and Klineberg's sex and organic needs, which we exclude in our scheme because they are shared by human beings and animals alike, most of them can be grouped under one or another of the three categories we have postulated. For example, Maslow's "esteem," Schutz's "control," Sumner and Keller's "variety," Arens and Lasswell's "wealth," "respect," "rectitude," "skill," and "power," McClelland's "achievement," Klineberg's "aggressiveness," "acquisitiveness," and "self-assertiveness" all bear clear resemblance to our "status," while Schutz's "inclusion," McClelland's "affiliation," Sumner and Kelly's "love," Klineberg's "gregariousness," Arens and Lasswell's, Schutz's and Maslow's "belonging" and "affection" all refer in one way or another to our "security" or "sociability."*

Another reason for postulating sociability, security, and status as the basic social needs of man is that they are substantially the same as three of Thomas's four "wishes": "response," "security," and "recognition," but not "new experience." Thomas's "new experience" and Maslow's need for "self-realization" are both culture-bound concepts. They spring from the same sort of facts which prompted George Homans to remark that "intel-

---

* An intensive analysis of the similarities and differences between the various postulates will be made in a later publication.

ligent men have always found small-town life dull." We examined Homans'
observation above, and we shall see the importance of such facts in *American*
culture later in Chapters IX and X. In the meantime we must note that
Thomas's four "wishes" constitute the earliest of the postulates on motivation or need in modern social sciences. They have not become more useful
in the study of human behavior for two reasons. On the one hand, the
tendency to proliferate new concepts makes it difficult for any one set of
concepts to undergo adequate analysis and testing.* On the other hand, the
mistaken notion that need or motivational postulates mark our ends in
scientific analysis instead of its beginnings foredooms the scientific usefulness of any of such postulates. Without adding to the already great proliferation we shall simply make use of the best-known set of postulates not
as final explanations but as tools to help us in our attempt to understand
human behavior.†

With the postulate of the three social needs as the motivating factor, we
shall be able to deal with the genesis of conformity-deviance balance without psychiatric or ethical overtones. The individual tends to conform to the
rules and disabilities of his group if, in his view, he is achieving the fulfillment of his social needs essential to make his life meaningful or satisfying.
He will tend to be alienated from the group and to seek other group attachment or attachments if, in his view, he is not achieving it or is achieving
it not as much as he deems necessary or desirable. We are more free from
psychiatric or ethical overtones because deviance, in this framework, is related to those psychocultural forces which make for social dynamism or
change in general. The intrinsic expression of dynamism of a society is
change, and change is likely to be imperceptibly slow unless the society's
members are prone to the formation and enlargement of groups beyond the
family and kinship circles. In our formulation, then, the more easily members of a society can find satisfaction of their social needs in their primary
groups the less likely they are to attempt to seek their satisfaction in other
human circles of a secondary nature, and the less likely they are to pursue
deviance. Conversely, the less easily members of a society can find satisfaction of their social needs in their primary groups the more likely they are to
attempt to seek their satisfaction by attaching greater importance to secondary and other groups.

The reason social needs are basic to human beings is not hard to understand. Each individual begins life and grows up with other human beings,

---

* We use the term "sociability" instead of Thomas's "response" because the former is
broader. It is also a term used and well expounded by Georg Simmel.[39] We use the
term "status" instead of Thomas's "recognition" because the former is more commonly
understood.

† Though employing these postulated needs as present working tools, we do not preclude the possibility that other needs may serve as better working tools in the future.

especially his parents, relatives, and guardians. The social system in which he is born may vary a good deal, in accordance with descent, residence, and succession rules; the family in which he is reared may vary greatly, according to composition and size of the unit; and so on. No human being is born and reared in isolation, but is, on the contrary, invariably surrounded by a large or small number of other human beings who are interested not only in feeding and clothing him but also in guiding and channeling his activities— marital, religious, occupational, ideological, etc.—so that he will grow up in their image. In these processes of socialization and enculturation, he not only acquires the beginnings of his language, manners, and aspirations, but he also forms with his parents and other individuals emotional relationships which are intertwined with the business of life itself. While there are some indications of inborn variability in taste, sensitivity to light, etc., there are much stronger evidences in support of the fact that the unit of human existence is the group. Living, as distinguished from existing, means for the human individual his ties with circles of fellow human beings, among whom he finds satisfaction of his social needs. Human existence is inconceivable without groups, just as every item of human behavior, except for completely involuntary movements, must operate within a field which is either its origin or its audience, consciously or unconsciously, symbolically or literally. That is why solitary confinement tends to be the most severe punishment next to death.

This is what Walter Cotu means when he describes, in his book *Emergent Human Nature*, the human personality as "TINSIT" or "tendencies-in-situation."[40] As the individual grows older his circles of contact and identification may widen but his later patterns of interaction with fellow human beings are at least conditioned, though not completely determined, by his earlier social and psychological constellations. In fact, his later needs for fellow human beings, though no longer identical in form, content, and function with those of his earlier years, remain urgent and predominant in his personality composition. Not only do the human individual's likes or dislikes, fears or loves, anxieties or aspirations originate from the ways he interacted with his fellow human beings in his early years, but the continuation of his early personality trends and performance of his social roles according to those trends depend largely upon the human situations in which he finds himself in time and place. From his fellow human beings the individual learns to be a human being, to be a particular human being, to acquire particular social and cultural identifications; and in association with his fellow human beings he continues these trends or modifies them.

It is not necessary to show how every one of the "sentiments" ever mentioned by Homans, from sadness to wage quest, is but an expression of one or another of the needs for sociability, security, and status. This would be an exercise in redundancy. We must move on to the next factor in our hypothesis.

This is the group in which every individual must seek to satisfy his social needs. The human being in every society starts life in some sort of family. It is in this first group that the individual not only begins his or her existence, but is related to a small or large number of human beings. As the individual grows up he or she will become aware of or come into contact with other modes of grouping: neighborhoods, schools, clan, scouts, churches, professional associations, cause-promoting organizations, political parties, evangelical movements, racial affiliations, caste, colonies, and so on, and finally the national or tribal boundary which embraces all of these groupings.

While these are all possible groupings within which the individual will seek to satisfy his three social needs, the extent to which he cares about or wishes to exert himself in order to enter any of them will be dependent upon the extent to which he can find fulfillment of his three social needs in his first grouping, the family and immediate extensions of it. The family establishes for the individual his first connection with his fellow human beings and it is certainly the basis for his subsequent approach to other fellow human beings. This part of our hypothesis is that, if the individual can fulfill his social needs in his family, he will have little urge to reach for other groupings. At most such an individual will be interested in groupings which are immediate extensions of the family, such as clan, but not in nonfamilial associations. If the individual cannot fulfill his social needs in his family, on the other hand, he is likely to reach out for, work toward, and even form nonfamilial groupings where the satisfaction of his social needs has a greater chance. In short, where the individual fails to find satisfaction of his social needs in the grouping of which he forms a part, he tends to seek greener pastures elsewhere. The frustrated drives will, as Spiro points out, either "lead to serious dysfunctional consequences for personality . . . or to the breakdown of social control, resulting in crimes and revolutions, or provide motivational source for social-cultural change."[41]

This means, in Homans' terms, that frustration within the internal system will lead at least some members sharing that system to spill over outside of it where they will have to fortify themselves either by joining existing groups or forming new groups by means of which they hope to meet the frustrated social needs. From this point of view, the differentiation by Homans of the human group into the internal and external systems is nebulous and inadequate for our analytic task at hand. In Homans' scheme, internal and external systems are two aspects of every group, and therefore a specific group is the basic unit for analysis. But the sentiments, etc., in his external system do not exist in mid air, as it were, but must be entertained or expressed by individuals who are part of some human grouping or groupings. In our hypothesis, the starting point for analysis is the dynamic interrelationship between the individual and the group or groups in which he seeks the satisfaction of his social needs. The group of his affiliation will remain unchanged or change drastically as the individual finds in it, or fails to find in it, the satisfaction of the social needs we postulated. But whether the individual leaves his group or not, he will be reacting to Homans' external system in terms of the human actors in it, and if he leaves his group he must seek to enter other groups which previously formed, at least in part, his external system before he made the move. In our analysis it is therefore necessary to think of both the internal and the external systems in terms of human groups. At any given point in time, the solidarity of the internal system of a human group is not a fixed entity. In the interaction between the internal and external systems, the centrifugal forces of the internal system may be far greater than the centripetal forces, making the internal system primarily a base from which the individual is ejected into a group or groups forming the external system.*

This part of our hypothesis presumes that the process of seeking satisfaction of the unfulfilled social needs is an ongoing one. When the individual has broken out of his affiliation with one group into one or more other groups where he hopes to meet his social needs, he will not stop there if these secondary groups do not live up to his expectations. When he finds that his needs are not met in these new groups, he may seek still other newer groups. Under such a condition the society will develop a multitude of groupings between the family and the tribe or nation, and it will be far more dynamic than another society in which such pressures are not present.

However, the completion of our hypothesis requires yet another and last factor. This factor is culture, which conditions the environment, whether social, technical, or supernatural, of the individual and colors or gives substance to his social needs. While the individual in all societies seeks sociability, security, and status, the specific contents of what he regards as being satisfactory sociability, security, and status differ from society to society. Similarly, the ways in which these social needs are fulfilled differ from society to society. It is imperative to examine how the activities and interactions are viewed through the culture of each society. It is equally imperative to see the levels of the individual's aspirations with reference to these three needs. For the modes and criteria of fulfillment of the needs differ according to the culture pattern in which the individual is reared, just as

---

* Homans' dichotomy between the internal and external systems in human groupings is not to be confused with the distinction, which we shall make in Chapter X, between the inner and outer worlds in the culturally conditioned outlook on the part of the individual.

the object of his self-interest and the extent of inclusiveness of his self-interest also vary greatly from society to society.* These variations, in turn, cannot but have profound consequences in the modes and criteria of the activities of societies and their interactions with each other. What Homans has done is to mix the American culture pattern inherent in the self-interests, activities, and interactions exhibited by his *American* subjects into a theory which is supposed to be applicable to all mankind.

Our hypothesis presumes that it is the culture which not only determines the rate and pattern of interaction between the individual and his fellow human beings as members of any social group, but also greatly influences the individual's views of what constitutes satisfactory levels for his social needs, which group or groups will satisfy his social needs best, and whether he should or should not seek their better satisfaction in a group or groups other than the ones he is already affiliated with. How this hypothesis can aid our understanding of the Chinese behavior in clan and the Hindu way in caste will be dealt with in the next chapter.

NOTES FOR CHAPTER VII

1. To those readers who may wonder why we begin with the nature of human group and not the nature of human nature, I must point out that one of the basic findings of the science of man is that human beings always exist in groups and not as single individuals. Society and not the individual is the basic unit of human existence.

2. George C. Homans, *The Human Group* (New York: Harcourt, Brace, 1950).

3. *Ibid.,* p. 88.

4. *Ibid.,* p. 90.

5. *Ibid.,* pp. 109–110.

6. *Ibid.,* p. 247.

7. *Ibid.,* pp. 355–368.

8. *Ibid.,* p. 232.

9. *Ibid.,* pp. 37–40.

10. Raymond Firth, *We, the Tikopia* (New York: American Book Company, 1936), p. 160. Quoted in Homans, *op. cit.,* p. 241.

11. Homans, *op. cit.,* p. 100.

12. *Ibid.,* pp. 95–96.

13. F. L. K. Hsu, "Incentives to Work in Primitive Communities," *American Sociological Review,* VIII, No. 6 (December 1943), pp. 638–642.

14. Homans, *op. cit.,* p. 125.

15. For a discussion of the three uses of the concept value see Charles Morris, *Varieties of Human Value* (Chicago: University of Chicago Press, 1956), pp. 10–12.

16. Homans, *op. cit.,* pp. 121–128.

* Most anthropologists know these facts so well that some of them may accuse me of elaborating the obvious.

17. *Ibid.*, pp. 128–192. Homans maintains, in contradiction to Warner, that the three systems have nothing in common. "The technical and social systems are parts of overt behavior; Warner's religious system is partly overt behavior and partly inferred from it, especially from what people say." But the social systems are not all open to observation. They are also partly inferred from overt behavior, namely, what people say. Even the technical system cannot escape this. At one point Homans writes of the sexual act as follows: "Let it never be said that in describing systematically the relations between the elements of behavior we are afraid of the obvious; and so, with straight faces, let us point out that even the satisfaction of sexual desires demands cooperation between a man and a woman in accordance with a technique" (p. 234). How do the students acquire any knowledge about the technique of sexual intercourse in general besides their own personal experiences and inferences from what other people tell them? The two Kinsey reports are entirely based on the latter source.

18. *Ibid.*, p. 129.

19. F. L. K. Hsu, "Kinship, Ancestor Worship, and Kingship," in preparation.

20. Homans, *op. cit.*, p. 247.

21. The difference and some of its implications are explained more fully in F. L. K. Hsu, *Americans and Chinese: Two Ways of Life* (New York: Abelard-Schuman, 1953), pp. 181–183.

22. Homans, *op. cit.*, pp. 359–360.

23. *Ibid.*, pp. 360–368.

24. *Ibid.*, p. 359.

25. *Ibid.*, p. 454.

26. F. L. K. Hsu, *Americans and Chinese.*

27. An interesting question is: Would the traditional Chinese, with their culturally conditioned internal system as it was, have departed from their native communities as did the Hilltown Yankees if they were suddenly confronted with the American environment, without ancestor worship but with Puritan ethics, individual self-reliance, industrialism, and a high standard of physical living? It is possible that they might have wanted to move out of their native communities as did the Hilltowners. But the facts would seem to argue against such a possibility. One indication is that the Chinese, in spite of being long plagued by natural disasters, human disturbances, and overpopulation, have emigrated very little. The Chinese in the South Seas mostly originated from a few districts in Fukien and Kwangtung Provinces. The Chinese in the United States mostly came from a few districts in Kwangtung Province. Another indication is that the Chinese who emigrated to the United States remained for long in Chinatowns and had their hearts set on retiring and being buried in their native villages. Even in the South Seas and among peoples who cannot always physically be distinguished from them, the Chinese have never become identified with the local populations as early Spanish settlers in Mexico did with the native Indians, the former joining forces with the latter to fight against Spanish newcomers for Mexican independence. Furthermore, if the traditional Chinese could have left their native communities as easily as Yankees left Hilltown, the process of Chinese modernization and industrialization would have gained far greater momentum than it did before the arrival of the Communists.

28. E. D. Chapple and C. S. Coon, *Principles of Anthropology* (New York: Henry Holt, 1942).

29. Julian Steward, *A Theory of Cultural Change* (Urbana: University of Illinois Press, 1960).

30. Henry A. Murray *et al.*, *Explorations in Personality* (New York: Oxford University Press, 1938), pp. 123–124. Some psychologists differentiate between the dynamic and nondynamic meanings of the term. According to the latter, need leads to no compensatory action while, according to the former, it does. See Paul T. Young, *Motivation and Emotion* (New York: John Wiley & Sons, 1961), pp. 123–124. Our use of the term in this book is based on its dynamic meaning.

31. The shortcomings of any theories of human motivation based on biological needs have been well exposed by David McClelland, John W. Atkinson, Russell A. Clark, and Edgar L. Lowell in *The Achievement Motive* (New York: Appleton-Century-Crofts, 1953), pp. 13–18.

32. There are evidences which indicate that infants who are not cared for by humans with love and affection do not grow well physically (Robert Watson, *Psychology of the Child*). There is also evidence from experimental psychology that the behavior of adult rats which have been subjected to electric shocks and that of those subjected to gentle handling during infancy cannot be distinguished from one another, but both can be easily distinguished from that of adult rats which have not been subjected to either. The former two kinds of rats will freely explore the space when placed in the unfamiliar but otherwise neutral surroundings of a transparent plastic box, while the latter will crouch in a corner of it. (See Seymour Levine, "Stimulation in Infancy," *Scientific American*, May 1960, pp. 81–86.)

33. Talcott Parsons, *The Social System* (Glencoe: Free Press, 1951), p. 32.

34. *Ibid.*, pp. 251–256.

35. *Ibid.*, p. 252.

36. Alfred R. Lindesmith and Anselm L. Strauss, *Social Psychology*, rev. ed. (New York: The Dryden Press, 1956), pp. 280–281.

37. Needs, whether of a biological or social nature, are not always consciously felt. "Needs may be recognized by some persons and not by others; by some groups and not by others. They may be recognized and not adopted, or adopted and not recognized (unconscious needs). Needs may be imputed but not accepted; they may be imputed by some and disputed by others. There are all sorts of conditions of needs in social fields. An imputed need is always a felt need of the person or group imputing it to others, but it is not necessarily a felt need of those to whom it is imputed. A felt need is always experienced as tension of some degree, but all tensions may not be identified by self or others, or they may be identified by others and not by self, by self and not by others, by neither or both"—Walter Cotu, *Emergent Human Nature* (New York: Alfred A. Knopf, 1949), p. 228. In our present hypothesis the distinction between recognized and unrecognized needs is not made, but the existences of all needs are primarily deduced from the behavior patterns of the peoples concerned. However, it is understood that some of the needs are encouraged more in some societies than in others. For example, in contrast to the Eskimo way of life, that of the Samoans induces a greater status quest. In contrast to the Hindu way of life, that of the Americans induces a greater sociability quest. The universally observable means by which individuals in all societies reach for the satisfaction of these needs are *Identity* and *Role*. *Identity* answers the question, "Who am I?" *Role* answers the question, "What am I doing?" The most common example of an identity is an individual's personal or family name. The most common example of a role is an individual's job or profession. It is possible for the two to be separated, but it is unlikely that one does not imply the other except in rare extreme cases. The hobo may have identity but

little role. The ghost writer may have role but scarcely identity. Similarly we can think of the dethroned monarch who lives an aimless existence in Paris as against the circus clown whose identity is concealed by a time-honored mask. But even in such one-sided cases, the other component is never completely absent. The dethroned monarch could be a big spender for Paris merchants and a good tool for wealthy persons interested in social climbing. The circus clown must also be known to his employer and to his family, friends, and neighbors by name and trade. Every individual tends to have more than one role and identity but tends to give those roles and identities greater prominence which will enable him better to satisfy his needs in sociability, security, and status.

38. Ralph Linton, *The Cultural Background of Personality* (New York: Appleton-Century-Crofts, 1945), pp. 6–7; A. H. Maslow, *Motivation and Personality* (New York: Harper and Brothers, 1954), pp. 82–83, and "Deficiency Motivation and Growth Motivation," in M. R. Jones (ed.), *Nebraska Symposium on Motivation* (Lincoln: University of Nebraska Press, 1955); William C. Schutz, *FIRO* (New York: Rinehart, 1958); David C. McClelland, J. W. Atkinson, R. A. Clark, and E. L. Lowell, *The Achievement Motive* (New York: Appleton-Century-Crofts, 1953); and David C. McClelland, *The Achieving Society* (Princeton: Van Nostrand, 1961); Otto Klineberg, *Social Psychology*, 2nd ed. (New York: Henry Holt, 1954), Chapters V and VI, pp. 76–169; Raymond B. Cattell, *Personality and Motivation, Structure and Measurement* (Yonkers-on-Hudson: World Book Company, 1957), Chap. XIII; William I. Thomas, *Social Behavior and Personality* (New York: Social Science Research Council, 1951), pp. 111–144; William Sumner and A. G. Keller, *Science of Society* (New Haven: Yale University Press, 1927), Vol. 1, pp. 21–28; and Richard Arens and Harold Lasswell, *In Defense of Public Order* (New York: Columbia University Press, 1961), pp. 12–23.

39. Georg Simmel, *The Sociology of Georg Simmel*, translated, edited, and with an introduction by Kurt H. Wolff (Glencoe: Free Press, 1950), pp. 40–57.

40. Walter Cotu, *op. cit.*, pp. 18–19, pp. 174–209.

41. Melford E. Spiro, "An Overview and a Suggested Restoration," in Francis L. K. Hsu (ed.), *Psychological Anthropology: Approaches to Culture and Personality* (Homewood, Illinois: Dorsey Press, 1961), pp. 480–482.

Chapter VIII

THE PSYCHOLOGICAL BASIS
OF CASTE IN INDIA

As WE NOTED in Chapter VI, while the Chinese way in clan is an automatic extension of the cohesiveness of the Chinese family, there is a real contradiction between the centrifugality of the Hindu family and the self-enclosing as well as divisive tendencies of Hindu caste. Our task is now to see to what extent our hypothesis concerning the individual and his social group can shed some light on the differences between the Chinese and Hindu situations and especially to explain the contradiction between Hindu family and Hindu caste.

As a starting point, we shall begin with the assumption that the same sociability, security, and status, which we shall use as tools to analyze the Chinese situation, also apply to the Hindus. We shall presume that the Hindu individual, like his Chinese counterpart, must seek the satisfaction of these needs in some human group of which he forms a part. Since the first human group to which Hindu and Chinese individuals have access is the family, it is obvious that the Hindu no less than the Chinese can be expected to seek the fulfillment of his needs in the family.

SITUATION-CENTERED ORIENTATION AND INDIVIDUAL NEEDS

The most basic psychological foundation of the Chinese situation-centered orientation of life is mutual dependence. This, and the link between mutual dependence and the predominance of the father-son axis in the Chinese kinship structure, has been explained in Chapter III. In understanding the psychocultural orientation, individual needs, and social grouping in the two societies the reader will do well to refer to the diagrams accompanying this analysis (Diagrams II and III). Our starting point in the Chinese situation is mutual dependence. From that starting point our analysis fans out in three directions: direction of ideal life (A, C, D, in Diagram II); direction of actual life in society (A, B, E, F); and the life of the individual in society

162

DIAGRAM II   CHINESE ORIENTATION
Kinship takes precedence over all other ties

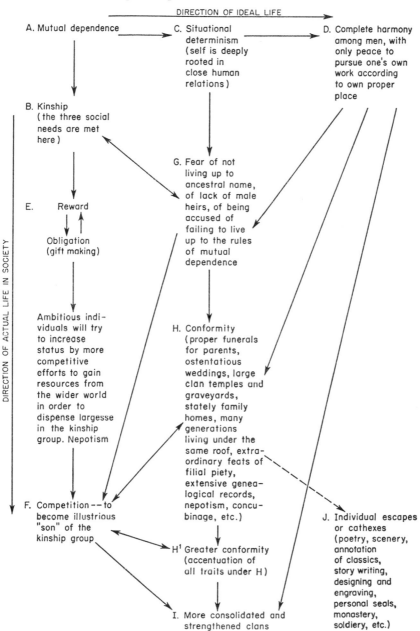

DIRECTION OF IDEAL LIFE

A. Mutual dependence

C. Situational determinism (self is deeply rooted in close human relations)

D. Complete harmony among men, with only peace to pursue one's own work according to own proper place

B. Kinship (the three social needs are met here)

G. Fear of not living up to ancestral name, of lack of male heirs, of being accused of failing to live up to the rules of mutual dependence

E.   Reward

Obligation (gift making)

Ambitious individuals will try to increase status by more competitive efforts to gain resources from the wider world in order to dispense largesse in the kinship group. Nepotism

H. Conformity (proper funerals for parents, ostentatious weddings, large clan temples and graveyards, stately family homes, many generations living under the same roof, extraordinary feats of filial piety, extensive genealogical records, nepotism, concubinage, etc.)

DIRECTION OF ACTUAL LIFE IN SOCIETY

F. Competition -- to become illustrious "son" of the kinship group

H¹ Greater conformity (accentuation of all traits under H)

J. Individual escapes or cathexes (poetry, scenery, annotation of classics, story writing, designing and engraving, personal seals, monastery, soldiery, etc.)

I. More consolidated and strengthened clans

with a particular ideal (B, C, G, H, I, J). The first leads to greater and greater idealization of the Chinese view of the meaning of life. The ultimate of this ideal* is expounded elegantly by Confucius and by Tao Yuanming in his well-known little piece on utopia *Táo Hwa Yuan Chi* (Record of the Source of Peach Blossoms). Confucianism is a system of ethics aimed at harmony among men, which exhorts the individual to keep to his proper place and discharge his customary duties. It shuns supernatural thoughts. It has little concern with metaphysical questions. *Táo Hwa Yuan Chi* has been part of the standard reading material of Chinese school children for many centuries since its author wrote it in the fourth century A.D. It tells of the author's brief experience with a lost community in some obscure mountainous region. He saw their men tilling the soil, their women busy with household chores, children frolicking in the green fields—a picture of peace and bliss in which there was no jarring note of quarrel or hatred. This is the Chinese view of the ideal world.

In terms of interpersonal relations this approach may be described as "situational determinism" (C in Diagram II), in which the self views the external world according to its place among fellow human beings. First, there is the sharp differentiation between those who are members of any kinship group and those who are not. Within this kinship group are men and women who belong to him and whom he can count on with certain differentiations, unconditionally. Without his kinship group are men and women who have no definite claims on him and on whom he has no definite claims. There are secrets within this group which must never be divulged to people who are outside it. By the same token one recognizes that the ways of other individuals who belong to other kinship groups than one's own are bound to be limited by their separate kinship affiliations. Second, generalizing from this sharp line of differentiation, the self's view of the world at large is regulated and conditioned in every major sphere. The key Chinese saying in this connection, which parents and elders use again and again everywhere in educating the young, is *jen ch'ing shih ku,* or roughly "human relations and accepted traditions" (or usages). A good and respected man is one who, in his judgments and actions, takes adequate cognizance of *jen ch'ing shih ku.*

The best way to explain this idea is to think of multiple (not double)

---

* Throughout this analysis the term *ideal* (D in Diagrams II, III, and IV) may be equated roughly with the term *value* as used among many anthropologists (see Walter R. Goldschmidt, *Man's Way: A Preface to the Understanding of Human Society,* New York: Henry Holt and Co., 1949, pp. 72–81). However, our ideal in each culture refers to the consciously held portion of the value orientation, or what Charles Morris would designate as *conceived value.* On the other hand the ideal as applied to interpersonal relations in our scheme (C in Diagrams II, III and IV) refers to the more covert and/or unconscious aspects of the value orientation, or what Charles Morris would designate as *operative value* (see Charles Morris, *Varieties of Human Value,* Chicago: University of Chicago Press, 1956, pp. 10–12).

standards of conduct; the differing standards prevail according to the differing varieties of human grouping in which particular events occur. Even in Western society a certain amount of situational determinism is unavoidable to some extent. Thus there are conversations which a male can carry on with another male but not another female; parents, especially fathers, are supposed to appear on the whole dignified to their children; jokes are out of order during any church service. But the Chinese situation-centered approach to life goes much further and is much more pervasive. All human affairs, all higher principles, all matters of the supernatural and even the basic worth of the individual are affected by the respective places in the human web of relationships of one man with reference to another. When a son kills his father, the punishment is far more severe than when a father kills his son, regardless of the circumstances. Their respective places in the kinship structure will determine their respective rights with reference to each other forever.

The A, B, E, F line in Diagram II represents the direction of actual life in society. The idea of mutual dependence is the backbone of a kinship structure dominated by the father-son axis. As we have seen before, the basic attributes of this axis consist of inclusiveness and continuity. The overall tendency is centripetality among men. The result is that the family, which is the individual's first grouping, and the clan, which directly extends from the family along the father-son axis, are the groupings within which all the individual's social needs are met. The central concern of the individual in this situation is to fulfill the obligations befitting him and receive the rewards due to him as a member of this everlasting corporation. As the Chinese individual moves forward in life his family, his living relatives, his departed ancestors, and his unborn descendants form his permanent and continuing circle or circles of human groups in which fulfillment of his needs is a foregone conclusion. His cultural ideal tells him that the family and its extension are the first and last things of human living. He must do his best for them, but they will also not fail to nurture him, claim him, and honor him.

In this kinship scheme one's obligation tends in time to equal one's reward (E in Diagram II).* The words "in time" are used advisedly, for when parents oblige themselves by rearing their sons they do not lay down the exact amount of the reward they expect to receive from the young ones as a condition for accepting their burden. The same applies when an uncle helps a nephew, or one cousin helps another. All the same a son who refuses to support the parents in their old age, or a relative who refuses to be

---

* Obligation and reward here and in subsequent chapters refer, in the first place, to tangible goods and services. But the worth of such goods and services is, of course, measured by the extent to which they satisfy the social needs of the individuals concerned.

as obliging to a relative who had been benevolent to him earlier, are objects of severe censure not only by the relatives who expect to benefit but also by all. What the members of a Chinese kinship group do to one another in this connection can be compared with gift-making as contrasted to any businesslike exchange. The gift-makers know when and about how much they are expected to give. In doing so they do not tell the recipients that they want such and such a return at such and such a time. In fact they usually protest the smallness and the worthlessness of their gifts and are against all ideas of any return. But in spite of such protests they will be mightily surprised, annoyed, and even angry if later, at the proper time and under the appropriate circumstances, they fail to receive the well-expected return. The giving is dictated by kinship rules. The return later on is also governed by the same rules.

However, in spite of the fact that all members of the kinship group have the reasonable expectation of achieving all their social needs in time, not all of them can do so (see G in Diagram II). There are, for example, those members of the family and clan who may be, as I described them elsewhere, "in the penumbra."[1] That is to say, if benefits of the family and clan spread over the individual like the shadow of a tree, those who are without lineal descendants are on the margin and therefore less fortunate than others. Their fear of lack of male heirs is both insistent and real. Adoption of sons of brothers or cousins ameliorates this situation but it does not make the position of the adopting parents as enviable as those who have natural heirs. Then there are others who fear that they are failing to live up to the illustrious names of their ancestors. The burden of this is especially heavy on those whose lineal ancestors achieved wealth and distinction. Many households have plaques decorating the lintels of their family homes. These plaques are either indications of successes in imperial examinations or special decorations or commendations bestowed upon the past or present members of this kinship group. If the illustrious members of the group lived recently or are still living, their honor and their wealth are naturally shared according to rules of kinship propinquity. If the illustrious ones lived many generations ago, their importance is likely to have become clanwide, and the descendants who do badly will simply be regarded as the poorer branches of an illustrious clan. But the fear of failing to live up to an illustrious ancestral status is most pressing when the illustrious ones lived far enough back to have exhausted their direct benefit on the immediate descendants but not far back enough to be forgotten. Finally there is the fear on the part of all adults of failing to live up to the rules of mutual dependence. Especially since there are no expressly stated terms for rewards and obligations there is some room for ambiguity and therefore for the possible accusation of taking too much but giving too little. These people are most certainly described as ignorant of *jen ch'ing shih ku*. There are other anxieties in this system; but we must move on in our analysis.

These anxieties lead directly to conformity (H in Diagram II) and feed the forces of competition (F in Diagram II), and are in turn fed by them. Although rewards and obligations in this system are supposed to be equal in time, ambitious individuals will try to increase their personal status as well as the prestige of the entire clan. Whether we look at China, India, or other societies in the world, including the Apollonian Zuni described by Ruth Benedict and the "effeminate" and cooperative Arapesh documented by Margaret Mead, we find some ambitious individuals who wish in some ways to excel over or differ from their fellow human beings. In the Chinese way of life the ambitious ones strive to become the most illustrious "sons" of the family and the clan and, in so doing, make their clan more illustrious than other clans. The primary way of doing this is to upset the balance of long-run equality between obligations and rewards, by making one's obligations much bigger than one's rewards. In the same sense as a departed ancestor shading his descendants like a tree, a living man who can spread his personal shade to cover a large number of clansmen (and others if he is in a position to do so) is a more important man in the kinship group than another man who is unable to do so. For this purpose the ambitious individual attempts to gain resources by competitive efforts from the outside world in order to be able to dispense greater largesse among members of his own kinship group. This is the foundation of the well-known Chinese phenomenon of nepotism. The more resources (jobs, money, influence, etc.) he can command outside the kinship group, the larger and better the sort of *dependence* he will be in a position to dispense within his kinship group. In this relationship the illustrious "son" of the clan does not ask for material return from his numerous "dependents" within the clan. His material return comes from what he can mobilize from outside the kinship group, especially from those who hope to curry his favor. It is a well-known fact in China, as I have documented elsewhere, that the offer of extraordinarily expensive gifts or huge sums of money by lower officials to higher officials, by the less powerful to the more powerful, has always been the "expected usage" in Chinese bureaucracy and society.[2] The importance of the kinship principle in this system is so great that the donors and recipients of such gifts and money often establish between them some sort of ritual or pseudo-kinship relationship.

Even without any notable ambition the anxieties of failure in general tend to support conformity. However, while the forces for conformity are one of the common features of all organized societies, conformity itself is a neutral term. The object or content of conformity is determined by the psychocultural orientation of every society. In the Chinese system, conformity means strict adherence to the rules of mutual dependence within a centripetal kinship group and under the cultural ideal of complete harmony among men—thus, extravagant funerals for departed parents, advantageous marriages for the children, stately clan temples and graveyards, expensive family homes, the ability to keep a large number of generations under the same roof, fantastic feats of filial piety, extensive genealogical records, good deeds, nepotism, and so on.

Competition and conformity feed each other just as competition and fear of failure feed each other. The greater the competitive effort on the part of ambitious individuals, the more widespread is likely to be the fear on the part of many who fail to live up to such standards, and the greater will be the pull toward conformity. Both conformity and the fear of failure have the sanction of the cultural ideal of harmony among men. The competitive efforts of ambitious individuals, instead of leading toward fission of the clan, move in the direction of further consolidation of it. For if one's prestige is increased by one's enlarged "shadow" within the clan, one's prestige is likely to be greatly enhanced by "shadowing" over a larger clan. Therefore, for centuries, one of the important steps to be taken by many a man recently become illustrious was to endow a genealogical bureau composed of hired experts who would trace and investigate the connections between his clan and all possible branches of it however widely these might be scattered or however remotely connected with it they might seem. This search for horizontal connections between hidden branches of a clan is the necessary counterpart of the search for vertical connections for ancestors of greater and greater antiquity. All other kinds of efforts, whether in competition or conformity, lead to the same result: a gradual enlargement and strengthening of the bonds of the clan, greater clan consciousness and greater importance of the clan as a corporate group (I in Diagram II). In this situation the ambitious members of the family and clan will achieve greater status in their active years than others, while the less capable ones will enjoy more security by being dependent upon them, also as followers in all societies tend to do. Other things being equal, leaders the world over derive status from their followers while they provide their followers with security. However, the highly structured nature of the Chinese kinship system enables even the less capable ones in time to be elevated by the achievement of their sons, grandsons, and later descendants in the generations to come.

As pointed out in Chapter III, the early integration of the Chinese male child into the realistic world of his father leaves little doubt in his mind as to the center of gravity of the world to come and his place in it. That world and his place in it are specific, concrete, and practically automatic, if he follows the rules. He has little or no need to seek sociability, security, and status outside the kinship bonds. He is free to seek them outside the kinship bonds to the extent that they will not harm or destroy such bonds. But he is welcome and expected to fall back on the kinship bonds whenever the going is difficult outside, or just as a matter of the normal course of events.

In dealing with emergencies, such as a cholera epidemic, a flood, a drought, banditry, or encroachment by the wider political power, members of a village or of several villages will definitely band together and cooperate. This form of cooperation is common to peasants all over the world, wherever they live in villages, and is not a distinguishing characteristic of the Chinese. What distinguishes the Chinese is the permanent solidarity and mutual help prevailing within their clan and the family. For them even during such emergencies there is no question but that loyality to the clan and the family has priority over loyalty to the village or any larger local aggregate. This is to say that the Chinese family and clan are more centripetal than centrifugal. The individual can more easily achieve within them the satisfaction of his social needs than he can do outside of them. Except for occasional instances of outside adoption, membership in Chinese clans is based on birth for the male and marriage for the female.

There is little room for dispute as to who belongs to the clan and who is outside it, especiallly since there are always detailed genealogical records. Furthermore, because of the strong sense of solidarity between the dead, the living, and the unborn, fostered in the family and buttressed by supernatural beliefs, there is little encouragement or desire on the part of the individual to claim affiliation with a clan other than his own. Even occasionally when a man takes a wife in the matrilineal and matrilocal pattern, at least one of his sons will be returned to the clan of his origin, in order to continue his own patrilineal line. And none but a male in very straitened circumstances would consent to enter into this last form of marital union in any case. One's membership in the family and in the clan reinforce each other. Improvement of the status of the one means a corresponding improvement in the other. Consequently the Chinese can be cohesive and inclusive toward his clan without being divisive and demonstratively exclusive toward outsiders, because his membership in the clan is not subject to encroachment and cannot be taken away from him. He has no need to prove that he belongs to it, or to proclaim to his exalted place. In Homans' terms, since the internal system composed of family and clan can in the normal course of events satisfy the social needs of the individual, the culturally conditioned institutional framework of the Chinese gives him no necessary incentive to sever his permanent relationship with his primary groups and to venture widely into the external system to seek permanent affiliation with other and new circles of human beings. Because of circumstances, such as the need for livelihood, war, or natural calamity, he may leave the internal system, but he will attempt to return to it if at all possible.

As shown in Diagram II there is in this system remarkably little need for individual cathexes (J) as avenues of escape and almost a total absence of reaction against conformity. The overall ideal of the culture (D) lends no support to the latter reaction and the operation of the system itself tends to pull a majority of the individuals toward the center rather than away from it. From historical records and district histories in diverse parts of China we learn of occasional Chinese who were hermits, who traveled about the country enjoying varieties of magnificent scenery, who found solace in poetry or painting or engraving personal seals. There were also Chinese who became priests, monks, and even soldiers. But if we look closely we shall find all of the Chinese hermits lived in seclusion with their families and many of them were disappointed men, with frustrated ambitions. Many of them, like the famous strategist Chu Ke Liang of the first century A.D., made famous by the novel *The Romance of the Three Kingdoms,* were simply waiting for some ambitious political leader or emperor to discover them and to persuade them to come out. Monks and priests have always been treated in China more or less as the scum of the society. They would be needed for such emergencies as funerals and sickness and for exorcism, but any family which fraternized much with them was, according to popular thinking, either disreputable or in for trouble. Soldiers were always regarded as outcasts. Chinese became soldiers generally because they were hard up and had no other means of making a livelihood, or because they were outlaws and found in soldiery a way of escaping punishment. Soldiery and banditry have had a long association in the mind of the public throughout China.

SUPERNATURAL-CENTERED ORIENTATION AND INDIVIDUAL NEEDS

To the Hindu individual, the meeting of his social needs through the forward movement of life presents many problems. His relationships with his relatives, his ancestors, and his unborn descendants are far less structured than is the case with the Chinese, and therefore provide him with no corresponding permanent and continuing circles of cohesion and continuity. For the family is neither first nor last. He must find affiliation in wider and higher circles of beings and powers. In fact, at the refined level of Hindu thought his affiliation with Ultimate Reality is a foregone conclusion and he has no escape from it.

In our analysis of caste we have already seen its two characteristics: the tendency toward fission and insulation behind socially and ritually closed walls, and the recurrent claims of superiority on the part of one caste group over another. Superficially these two tendencies would seem to be contradictory but in fact the former is a function of the latter. Insulation behind self-enclosing walls and fission may have other foundations but in the Hindu cultural contexts they are best interpreted as means to superiority in status claims. The greater the stress on status and hierarchy the more prolific will be the efforts at self-insulation on the part of groups which wish for a greater superiority or are dissatisfied with their present inferiority.

The dynamics of the interrelationship among the psychocultural orientation, individual needs, and social grouping in the Hindu situation is schematically represented in Diagram III. Our starting point here is unilateral dependence. As in Diagram II our analysis here again fans out in three directions from that starting point: direction of ideal life (A, C, D); direction of life in society (A, B, G, H, K); and direction of the individual life (A, F, I, J, L, M, N). The first leads to greater and greater idealization of the Hindu view of the meaning of life. The ultimate of this ideal insists that all finite phenomena, including all men and all things, spring from and inexorably return to the great Atma which is the all-embracing Ultimate Reality or God. An eloquent exposition of this ideal is given by Dr. S. Radhakrishnan:

> Strictly speaking we cannot give any description of Brahman. The austerity of silence is the only way in which we can bring out the inadequacy of our halting descriptions and imperfect standards. The *Brhadāranyaka Upanisad* says: "Where everything indeed has become the Self itself, whom and by what should one think? By what can we know the universal knower?" The duality between knowing and knowable characteristic of discursive thought is transcended. The Eternal One is so infinitely real that we dare not even give It the name of One since oneness is an idea derived from worldly experience (*vyavahāra*). We can only speak of It as the non-dual, advaita, that which is known when all dualities are resolved in the Supreme Identity. The Upanisads indulge in negative accounts, that the Real is not this, not this (na iti, na iti), "without sinews, without scar, untouched by evil," "without either shadow or darkness, with a within or a without." The *Bhagavadgītā* supports this view of the Upanisads in many passages. The Supreme is said to be "unmanifest, unthinkable and unchanging," "neither existent nor nonexistent." Contradictory predicates are attributed to the Supreme to indicate the inapplicability of empirical determinations. "It does not move and yet it moves. It is far away and yet it is near." These predicates bring out the twofold nature of the Supreme as being and as becoming. He is parā or transcendent and aparā or immanent, both inside and outside the world. . . .
>
> In the *Upanisads*, we have the account of the Supreme as the Immutable and the Unthinkable as also the view that He is the Lord of the universe. Though He is the source of all that is, He is Himself unmoved for ever. The Eternal Reality not only supports existence but is also the active power in the world. God is both transcendent, dwelling in light inaccessible and yet in Augustine's phrase "more intimate to the soul than the soul to itself."[3]

DIAGRAM III HINDU ORIENTATION
Hierarchy overrules kinship ties

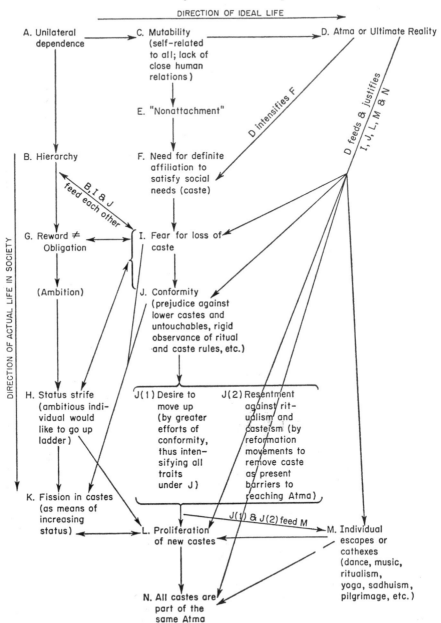

DIRECTION OF IDEAL LIFE

A. Unilateral
   dependence

C. Mutability
   (self-related
   to all; lack of
   close human
   relations)

D. Atma or Ultimate Reality

E. "Nonattachment"

B. Hierarchy

F. Need for definite
   affiliation to
   satisfy social
   needs (caste)

D intensifies F

D feeds & justifies I, J, L, M & N

DIRECTION OF ACTUAL LIFE IN SOCIETY

B, I & J feed each other

G. Reward ≠
   Obligation

I. Fear for loss of
   caste

(Ambition)

J. Conformity
   (prejudice against
   lower castes and
   untouchables, rigid
   observance of ritual
   and caste rules, etc.)

H. Status strife
   (ambitious indi-
   vidual would
   like to go up
   ladder)

J(1) Desire to
   move up
   (by greater
   efforts of
   conformity,
   thus inten-
   sifying all
   traits
   under J)

J(2) Resentment
   against rit-
   ualism and
   casteism (by
   reformation
   movements to
   remove caste
   as present
   barriers to
   reaching Atma)

K. Fission in castes
   (as means of
   increasing
   status)

J(1) & J(2) feed M

L. Proliferation
   of new castes

M. Individual
   escapes or
   cathexes
   (dance, music,
   ritualism,
   yoga, sadhuism,
   pilgrimage, etc.)

N. All castes are
   part of the
   same Atma

The importance of this ideal in Hindu society cannot be overestimated. This is not to deny that many Hindus are very material-minded and not at all otherworldly and, as we have already noted, that many Hindus do not live according to the classical four-stage plan of life. It is also true that many Hindus in different parts of the country are excessively tied down by obligations to and claims of family members and relatives so that some are practically enslaved and resent the situation. But compared to the Chinese and the Americans, the Hindus pay far more attention to supernatural matters; they spend greater amounts of time, energy, and money in propitiating the gods, in taking care of them, in deriving darshan from them, in asking boons of them, in dramatizing their superhuman deeds, and simply in singing their praise. Furthermore, these remarks are true of the high and the low, the pandit and the peasant, the rich and the poor, a majority of the modern educated and all of the traditionally brought up. Finally the very fact that some Hindus are nearly enslaved by obligations to relatives is indicative of the unilaterality and the peculiar diffusedness of human relationships in which rules and measures governing rewards and obligations are unclear—a corollary of the supernatural-centered way of life explained at the end of Chapter III.

In interpreting Hindu thought Dr. Radhakrishnan makes some comparisons with Chinese thought and numerous comparisons with Western Christian thought. In connection with the first sentence in the first quotation just given, he refers to Tao Te Ching, the scripture of Taoism, as well as to Jesus and Plotinus, and shows that Lao Tze's and Jesus' conceptions of the Ultimate Reality (Tao) are the same as its Hindu counterpart, namely silence:

> Cp. Lao Tze: "The Tao which can be named is not the True Tao." "The reality of the formless, the unreality of that which has form—is known to all. Those who are on the road to attainment care not for these things, but the people at large discuss them. Attainment implies non-discussion; discussion implies non-attainment. Manifested Tao has no objective value; hence silence is better than argument. It cannot be translated into speech; better, then, say nothing at all. This is called the great attainment." Soothill: *The Three Religions of China*, second edition (1923), pp. 56–7. The Buddha maintained a calm silence when he was questioned about the nature of reality and nirvāna. Jesus maintained a similar silence when Pontius Pilate questioned him as to the nature of truth.
> Cp. Plotinus: "If any one were to demand of nature why it produces, it would answer, if it were willing to listen and speak: You should not ask questions, but understand keeping silence as I keep silence, for I am not in the habit of speaking."[4]

But what we must realize is that Tao Te Ching has for the last two thousand years been an obscure and nearly forgotten classic to nearly all

Chinese, while the Hindu scriptures, from the Vedas and the epics to the shastras and Puranas, have been and still are everyday reading or listening materials for a majority of Hindus. Except in rare instances Chinese thinkers and the general public paid utterly no attention to Lao Tze's teachings. Such "Taoism" as prevailed in China appeared in the form of alchemy, healing arts, exorcism, and so on, which occupied the bulk of the missionary Henry Doré's monumental work entitled *Researches into Chinese Superstitions.* Those Chinese who could not read and write left it up to the priests to perform the right rituals for them. Those Chinese who were literate occupied themselves with Confucian analects and other writings along the same line. It was no accident that I, though born and raised largely in China and Chinese schools, had never had occasion to learn anything about the Tao Te Ching till I visited in 1956 the residence of Professor Suniti Kumar Chatterjee, a well-known linguist, in Calcutta. In his living room are, engraved on stone in their original languages, quotations or paraphrases from the scriptures of many of the world's religions, living or dead. There, in Chinese, I came for the first time upon a passage of the Taoist scripture concerning the origin of the universe. It was no accident that, of the many contending schools of philosophy, only Confucianism triumphed in China. For the Chinese have never been interested in the primeval origin of the universe, nor have they been much concerned with where mankind in general would go after passing from the world of the living.

Similarity in some respects between Hindu and Western conceptions of the Ultimate Reality is undeniable. But this similarity is more indicative of the historical connection between India and the West from the remote past rather than their psychological affinity at present. It is interesting that Dr. Radhakrishnan, after noting the fact that the idea of avatara or incarnation was also a subject of discussion in Christian theology, has the following to say:

> . . . what is said about the Incarnation of Jesus Christ: "Whilst all things were in quiet silence and night was in the midst of her swift course; thine Almighty Word leapt down from heaven out of thy royal throne. Alleluia." The doctrine of the Incarnation agitated the Christian world a great deal. Arius maintained that the Son is not equal of the Father but created by Him. The view that they are not distinct but only different aspects of one Being is the theory of Sabellius. The former emphasized the distinctness of the Father and the Son and the latter their oneness. The view that finally prevailed was that the Father and the Son were equal and of the same substance; they were, however, distinct persons.[5]

The latter part of Dr. Radhakrishnan's comment here shows the evolution of the Western conception of God away from its ancient starting points. In spite of differences of opinion among early Christian thinkers it was the view that "the Father and the Son were equal . . . and were . . . distinct persons" which finally prevailed in the West. The ideal of the Western way of life, as we shall see in the next chapter, is complete freedom of the individual and not God or union with God. The latter is a peculiarly Hindu ideal of life.

We have already seen how the Chinese and the Hindus are similar in that their respective cultures do not abhor dependence. On the contrary the individual in either culture is encouraged to seek dependence and to submit to authority on which he can depend. But while dependence and submission in the Chinese situation operate in a concrete framework with concrete points of reference, dependence and submission in the Hindu situation are found in a far more uncertain field. For the situation-centered Chinese his psychocultural pattern of mutual dependence among men enables him to be satisfied with achieving sociability, security, and status within the first grouping he comes across in life and in its immediate extension. For the supernatural-centered Hindu his psychocultural pattern of dependence upon higher powers attracts him away from his family and its extension, the clan.

It is not that the Hindu will completely fail to find satisfaction of his social needs in the kinship organization. To a certain extent he does. To Western observers who come from individual-centered cultures the Hindu seems to be enmeshed in his kinship situation to an extraordinary degree. We have seen in some of the foregoing chapters how erroneous this Western impression is. What differentiates the Hindu from the Chinese is the presence among the former of a higher degree of mutability (C in Diagram III) among all things and the stress on hierarchy (B in Diagram III) among all men, both of which are undergirded by the ideal of the Atma or Ultimate Reality (D in Diagram III). Mutability is the ideal of Atma translated into an approach to interpersonal relations. Extreme mutability will negate the difference between life and death, between one and many, between men and things, between ego and alter, etc. It is a view that the self is exposed to all or at least related to all. Unlike the Chinese, who differentiate strongly between the inner group of kinship relationships and external groups of other relationships, the Hindu ideal tends to eliminate or at least minimize that differentiation. Consequently since the self is related to all it tends to lack definite associations with any. The situation can be compared with a man who wears a robe as big as the house and consequently feels that he is not wearing any robe at all. The Hindu solution for this lack of close human relations is the much-expounded doctrine of nonattachment (anāsakti or asakti) (E in Diagram III). This is the most significant theme of the Bhagavadgita, or Song of God, which forms part of the great Hindu epic, the Mahabharata. It is impossible to overestimate the importance of this theme in Hindu life. "The poem so brims with the spirit of Hinduism that every school of philosophy and every sect believes that it teaches their particular doctrine. The Advaitin, the Vishishtadvaitin, the Yogin, the Sannyasin, the soldier, the saint and even the common rogue will quote the Gita as his authority; so thoroughly does the work represent the Hindu view of life."[6] This is also the view of one of the most astute students of Indian history in modern times, A. L. Basham:

> The teaching of the Bhagavad Gita is summed up in the maxim "your business is with the deed, and not with the result." . . . The inspiration of the Bhagavad Gita has been widely felt in India from the time of the Guptas to the present day, and it has been commended by the Christians and Moslems, as well as the Hindus, whose most influential scripture it is. No one has so ungrudgingly admitted his debt to its doctrine of tireless and unselfish service as Mahatma Gandhi, who so strongly opposed the two features of ancient Indian society which the Gita itself was in part written to defend—militarism and the class system.[7]

Regardless of how it was intended, this doctrine of nonattachment goes well with the ultimate Hindu ideal of Atma and is calculated to help the individual in his actual relations with fellow men, things, and events, while at the same time not violating the spirit of the ultimate ideal. The sense of mutability of all beings, things, and events can but lead the individual to diffused reactions to his environment and to lack of concern for any concrete lines of action. The doctrine of nonattachment aims at channelizing the individual towards certain concrete lines of action or objectives while at the same time keeping him mindful that all are equal to all or to nothing.

However, the doctrine of nonattachment does not really solve the problem of the Hindu individual's need for definite affiliation as a means of achieving his sociability, security, and status. As parts of an ideal the concept of the mutability of all finite phenomena embraced in an ultimate Atma and the concept of efforts without regard for reward are fine for discussion, eulogy, and admiration. At least they need not at that level be cause for significant difficulties. Applied to concrete life situations they will, however, create acute impracticalities. In the first place, living means decisions. From morning to night, from one day to another, all human beings are confronted with and must make decisions. Decisions are impossible or at least difficult if the individual views the different alternatives with too strong a feeling of changeability among all or most of them. The landmarks for decisions are lacking.

In the second place, since the unit of human existence is the group, living as a human being means that every individual has to deal with fellow human beings who are members of the same group. A diffused outlook founded on the mutability of the finite phenomena of the world will inevitably be correlated with a strong feeling of mutual uncertainty and even distrust among men.

The individual who regards all men and things as changeable, when compared with another with a different outlook, tends to see little reason why he should be bound by rules of conduct, equivalence of obligations and repayments, and deep convictions or loyalties. The main question before him, if he is bent on a course of action, is whether he can overcome the hindrances in his way or whether these hindrances are insurmountable.

Some students look on Western cultures as being undergirded by guilt, in contrast to Oriental cultures, which are supposed to be undergirded by shame.[8] Elsewhere I have shown that the guilt-shame contrast is better understood as an expression of the contrast between a repression-dominated and a suppression-dominated way of social control.[9] In control by repression the rules of behavior are mostly within the individual's mind, usually the unconscious part of his mind, while in control by suppression the rules of behavior are more strongly dependent upon the external situation, owing to the nature of the particular group of human beings who compose his human environment. It is not alleged that any society can be wholly governed by only one of these mechanisms of control. There is evidence to indicate, however, that the mechanism of repression is more characteristic of Western societies such as the United States of America, while the mechanism of suppression is more characteristic of Oriental societies such as Japan and China. Following the same line of thought, the cultures of Hindu India must be regarded as dominated by the mechanism of impediment, and its most significant expression is neither guilt nor shame but rather effusion, passivity, or irascibility.

Suppression means generalized restraints on thought and behavior which are rooted in the external social contexts in which the individual finds himself. The act or thought of violating some of these restraints is more likely to call forth in the individual the feeling of shame than anything else, when he thinks of his fellow human beings. Repression means generalized restraints on thought and behavior implanted in the psyche of the individual throughout his development. The act or thought of violating some of these restraints is more likely to lead more to a feeling of guilt than anything else, with reference to the superego. Impediment means restraints on thought and behavior which are based on particular external barriers, human or physical or supernatural, that make an intended act or thought difficult or impossible. The act or thought aiming at overriding such restraints tends to result in effusion, passivity, or irascibility. Effusion combines excitability and mental and physical activity. Under its influence the individual tends to pour out his emotions freely, to be unduly demonstrative, and to stop at nothing. Passivity is the well-known state of receiving or enduring without resistance, often linked with concepts such as patience and obedience, and needs no elaboration. Irascibility bears resemblance to irritability, petulance, and related concepts. The irascible is prone to anger and galvanizable into uncontrolled action with relative ease. Effusion prevails with success, because the individual's feeling of the mutability of all things is reaffirmed and he is unlikely to stop at the present success. Passivity and irascibility are both well-known Hindu methods of dealing with authority or higher powers. Passivity is evident in sit-down strikes and fastings, sometimes to the point of death; irascibility is easily discernible in mob scenes and riots.

The fact that India, with its well-known technique of passive resistance and general cultural emphasis on peace, should be given to so much uncontrollable mass violence before and during the first years of independence has led many observers to wonder. Mrs. Lois Murphy suggests that this violence is rooted "in the lack of opportunities in childhood for group thinking and planning" as well as "in the later lack of methods of resolving conflicts between groups."[10] In the light of our present analysis Mrs. Murphy has touched upon an important point, but the link between the extensive and observable passivity on the one hand and the uncontrollable violence on the other in Hindu life is the relative importance of impediment or effusion, rather than suppression or shame and repression or guilt as mechanisms of social control.

Both suppression and repression consist of generalized rules which are concrete points of reference for members of the same society in their dealings with each other. But impediment recognizes only that human, physical, or supernatural obstacles can make a given act possible or impossible. In the crudest terms this means that human relationship is governed by how far one can go with reference to another. It tends to foster distrust among men based on a generalized fear of the unknown. For when the self sees no limit in its thoughts and actions, projection of the same psychology into others is inevitable.

Besides the problems of decision and of unsureness among men, the final problem of the Hindu situation comes from the human tendency to attachments. In our hypothesis on the human group we posited the three universal needs of sociability, security, and status on the part of the individual vis-à-vis his fellow human beings. Underlying all these needs is attachment. The infant will be attached to his material surroundings, to specific objects in them, and to his mother or nurse. It is a central point of our hypothesis that as an individual grows his attention will increasingly be trained toward the human beings who come into his life, by seeking varying degrees of satisfaction of the three needs specified above. And if these needs remain unsatisfied in the primary group, the individual is likely to go on searching for secondary circles of allegiance and alignments. Whichever way he turns, he will be attaching himself to some objects, human or animal, animate or inanimate, but always with the highest preference to humans.

This is the basic reason for the universality of the human group as well as of the concept of property. This is also the reason for the ancient custom found in many lands of burying slaves and concubines and the universal custom of burying at least articles of personal use with the dead. The survivors, projecting their own psychology of attachment to the dead, cannot conceive of the soul as being entirely freed from attachment. The Hindu ideal of nonattachment (anāsakti or asakti), as explained in the Bhagavadgita by Lord Krishna to the warrior Arjuna just before the great battle described in the Mahabharata, asks of the individual that which is not possible, however strongly this sentiment is buttressed by its linkage with caste dharma or duty. It is asking the individual virtually to give up life itself. For life means attachment.

The Hindu individual, as he goes through life, is therefore confronted by a series of dilemmas. Like all human beings he must make decisions, must feel sure about the intentions of the individuals who in one way or another have something to do with him, and must be attached to well-defined circles of human beings among whom he can enjoy his sociability, security, and status. But his supernatural-centered culture militates against decisions, certainty among human beings, and attachments to them. Instead it exhorts him to gravitate in the direction of imponderables such as the Atma or the Universal Soul which is formless, tasteless, colorless, nameless, and so on. The Universal Soul has all the attributes that man can experience yet is none of them.

THE PSYCHOLOGICAL BASIS OF CASTE

Much of the Hindu's need for definite affiliation to achieve his sociability, security, and status is met in caste (F in Diagram III). We observed earlier that the two outstanding characteristics of caste in India are (a) its tendency to fission into separate groups, each trying to fortify itself behind self-imposed walls, and (b) the tendency of each caste to claim superiority over the others. Various scholars have considered other features of caste, such as the intercaste relations and the economic privileges in the jajmani, as being of primary importance. We have examined these positions and have found them lacking in the theoretical significance claimed on their behalf. On the other hand, both of the outstanding characteristics of caste we have named here can be shown to possess intrinsic relationship with unilateral dependence, mutability of all finite phenomena, and the ultimate ideal of Atma. The fact that caste is an extrafamilial grouping which satisfies the Hindu's need for sociability, security, and status is not hard to see. In Homans' terms, since the family, and its extension the clan, as the internal system cannot in the normal course of events satisfy the social needs of the individual, the Hindu seeks permanency in another grouping in the external system—the caste. Caste (F in Diagram III) is thus a device to compensate for the diffusedness of the supernatural-centered way of life, for impermanency in the kinship situation, and for the lack of definable landmarks due to the mutability of all things.

If all human beings and all other phenomena of the world were completely immutable, then each death or decay would be an irreparable disaster to all individuals who hold the dead person or decayed article dear, and the life of the society would be difficult to continue. For the physical as well as the human world is full of change. But if all human beings and all other phenomena of the world were completely mutable, then no individual would develop any loyalty for another nor even a sense of duty toward another or obligation or attachment to another. Complete mutability means that everything is subject to change at all times. Such a state is, in fact, an antithesis of organized society. However, while complete immutability or complete mutability does not prevail in any human society as a fact, the Hindu situation promotes a far greater sense of inconstancy among men, and among all phenomena, than does the Chinese pattern. As an ideal it is highly laudable. But in practice the individual who is given to the idea of changeableness of all phenomena must also be subject to the contrary urge for some area of life where his relationship with his environment is far more certain or far more reliable. A society which confronts the individuals born into it with a pervasive ideal of the mutability of all phenomena will also force them to seek refuge behind some wall where they will at least find their bearings.

If need for definite affiliation were the only requirement, we should, however, have only relatively few stable castes in India which would show no tendency to fission. But the essential characteristics are not merely that its members entrench themselves behind its walls, but also that they constantly seek to break out of one set of walls into another for which they claim superiority. These two tendencies are part and parcel of each other. The stronger the urge to claim superiority, the greater the tendency to fission within existing groups. In other words status need is paramount and, in the struggle for status, security is given second place while sociability is either curtailed or used as a means to gain or buttress that claim to superiority. Status or hierarchy (B in Diagram III) is indeed the most basic ingredient in the Hindu way of life in its actuality. Its link with the supernatural-centered ideal is not only that the universally demanded status in India is *ritual* status but also that Atma is the apex of all statuses toward which all must unceasingly strive and toward which no living being is ever near. The Atma is the ultimate goal which sets the unknown ceiling of Hindu hierarchy and which, therefore, inspires unceasing efforts to reach it. In this atmosphere dissatisfaction with the status quo is a foregone conclusion.

There is no question but that one's status in the caste hierarchy is the most crucial concern of Hindu children and adults alike. In the Chinese process of growing up the ubiquitous question the child is enjoined to ask himself is whether his action is going to please his parents or to anger them. In the Hindu process of growing up the ubiquitous question the child is taught to mull over is whether his action is going to raise, maintain, or lower his caste status. It is not that the Hindu child will be insensitive to his parents' pleasures or displeasures, or lack close relationship with them. On the contrary. But what the Chinese child knows is that his parents, and through them his departed ancestors, are the final judge of his actions, while what the Hindu child learns is that, if he violates the status rules of the caste hierarchy, his parents can do little for him. In fact they will go down forever with him. In other words, there is a wider force which cuts through the kinship system and every other kind of relationship among men, things, and gods. This is why, as we have already observed, the characteristics and decisive features of caste have nothing to do with ritual purity or kinds of food as such. Ritual purity or food taboos are two of the most ubiquitous but arbitrary signs limiting, demarcating, and defining specific boundaries of sociability, belonging, and status. As soon as one sign for ritual purity or food taboo is eliminated, another will take its place unless there is basic change in the idea of hierarchy and attitude toward it.

The stress on status or hierarchy, especially ritual status or hierarchy, permeates the entire Hindu social organization. It is the principle which regulates nearly all conduct and affects nearly all evaluation of it. Its link with the pattern of unilateral dependence (A in Diagram III) is no less clear than its link with the ultimate Atma. Any dependence of one human being upon another involves a degree of differences in strength, capability, wealth, maturity, wisdom, or other factors. To that extent dependence implies a high-low relationship. But such differences may be compensated by stipulated return or payment within certain time limits or by understood future favors or obligations. The former form of compensation occurs where the contract principle is dominant, as in the American world, which we shall deal with in Chapters IX and X. The latter occurs where the kinship principle is dominant, as in the Chinese world, which we have already examined. Though the Hindu usage within the kinship situation is not dissimilar to that found in China, it is heavily weighted by the principle of hierarchy. Hierarchy cements different persons or groups together under obvious conditions of inequality. Under it reward and obligation among the parties concerned are, as a rule, unequal. Guided by an active ideal of union with the Ultimate Reality this unequal relationship between the high and the low turns into unilateral dependence in general. Dr. S. Radhakrishnan explains this relationship succinctly: "While the world is dependent on Brahman, the latter is not dependent on the world. This one-sided dependence and the logical inconceivability of the relation between the Ultimate Reality and the world are brought out by the word 'māyā'."[11]

Some hierarchic relationships and situations are found in every organized society. Where self-reliance is the basic idea, as in the American way of life, inequality between reward and obligation is denied or deplored or, when permitted, the reward-obligation ratio is in favor of those of higher status than others. For the ability to pull down more resources outside the self signifies success on the part of the self-reliant man. Where mutual dependence is the basic idea, as in the Chinese way of life already analyzed, inequality between reward and obligation is justified on the grounds of past or future balances, and where it is extended, the reward-obligation ratio is in favor of those in lower status than others. For the ability to confer benevolence on a multitude of others is a sign of greatness on the part of the man reared in the ideal of mutual dependence. But where unilateral dependence is the basic idea, as in the Hindu way of life, the reward-obligation ratio may lean in either direction; i.e., the reward could be greater or smaller than obligation for those situated on any level. What determines the reward-obligation ratio is not past or future balances in any interpersonal sense, but dharma according to an all-embracing supernatural design culminating in the Ultimate Reality. The lower castes have to perform manual services to the higher castes even if they do not wish to do so because it is their dharma according to the supernatural design. The higher castes are sometimes benevolent toward the lower castes because it increases their dharma according to the same supernatural design. All castes are obliged to give alms to the Brahmans because they want to increase their own dharma according to the same supernatural design. And finally any member of the lower castes, including the untouchable, can make himself a holy man and turn the tables on the higher castes so that all will have to support him. This is why begging is not only such a common phenomenon in India but is also an activity which is given the highest ritual and social esteem. Anyone can and should beg: the king does it symbolically, the Brahman by design, others by necessity. Begging is the expression of utter dependence by the prospective recipient on the prospective giver without any implication of personal reciprocity.

As in the case of the Chinese system, ambition on the part of some individuals leads some men to desire a higher status than the one they occupy or than others (H in Diagram III). In any society some individuals are more ambitious than others. These ambitious individuals will try, as we noted before, to achieve more status than others. In the American system enhancement of status is achieved by securing more rewards than obligations. In the Chinese system enhancement of status is achieved by spreading more obligations than rewards. In the Hindu system enhancement of status is achieved by securing ritual purity, or any other symbols or substance, which will raise the individual's place according to the all-embracing supernatural design. Where the principle of hierarchy prevails the strife for status tends to be far more general among all sections of the society than where it does not prevail. Therefore, while the idea of status as more important than security is found only among a relatively few ambitious Chinese, this tendency is likely to be true to a majority or even all Hindus on all levels of the society. Where hierarchy is the basic principle, even those enjoying highest status in the society must strive for still higher status. In this strife for status, the reward-obligation ratio is relegated to a secondary importance. This is why, as we noted earlier, economic advantages, though not without importance in any society, may be sacrificed for caste status in India or may be totally beside the point in strife involving caste status.

The hierarchical principle, the unequal reward and obligation, and the strife for status (B, G, H, in Diagram III) all feed and in turn are fed by the fear of loss of caste (I in Diagram III). There is no question but that the fear of loss of caste is universal in India. This fear is expressed in many forms: fear of ostracism, of expulsion by the caste or village panchayat, of ritual impurity, of pollution, and so on. The political power of the Kshatriya in punishing violation of caste rules only intensifies this fear among the multitudes. The natural outcome of this fear is conformity (J in Diagram III). Conformity is a neutral word the content of which is dependent upon the orientation of the culture. That is to say, the object of conformity in the Chinese type of society, where the kinship principle prevails, leads to thoughts and actions which are designed to better one's place in the kinship structure. This means, as we have already seen, great clan temples, pompous funerals for deceased parents, and the like. Conformity in situations of the Hindu type, where the hierarchical principle prevails, leads to thoughts and actions designed to buttress one's place in the caste hierachy. This means rigid observance of rituals and caste rules, stringent exercise of caste prerogatives, invention of new caste rules and rituals which may increase or at least buttress one's status, prejudice against those in lower stations, and so on.

Conformity in the Hindu system generates two types of sentiment (J_1 and J_2 in Diagram III). On the one hand there will be the desire to be ranked higher on the same hierarchical ladder. On the other hand there will be resentment against ritualism and casteism. The desire to be ranked higher on the same ladder is simply intensified conformity. The resentment against ritualism and casteism is in line with the Hindu idea of the great Atma (D in Diagram III). Sentiments of both types are aggravated by the status strife of ambitious individuals and probably also serve, at least for some individuals, as defense against the fear of loss or lowering of caste. The ideal of the great Atma is a concept which pronounces all beings and things in the universe to be expressions of the same Universal Soul (or Ultimate Reality) and declares that all will inevitably and eventually return to that Universal Soul. The exact mechanism by means of which the Universal Soul came to turn itself into the multifarious finite phenomena, as well as the provision for the eventual return of the finite phenomena into the great Universal Soul, varies with different schools of theology. But the aim of all Hindu schools of thought is the liberation of the individual from his finite confinement by the physical body, from his need for nourishment, from his kinship ties and worldly attachment, so that his soul may unite with the Universal Soul now or in the future. The more reformationist movements such as Jainism and Buddhism emphasize the immediate union with the Universal Soul regardless of caste. But the more orthodox Hindu sects emphasize union with the Universal Soul at a more remote date after the individual's soul has gone through many reincarnations of an ascending nature.

The strife for status (H in Diagram III) leads to fission in castes. Splitting from an existing caste group is simply a means of raising the status of the splintering group. This has been so well demonstrated and is so well known that it needs no elaboration. But fission in castes is also fed by the fear of loss of caste, conformity, and the desire to rank higher on the same caste ladder (I, J, J_1 in Diagram III). And whether it is fission in castes as a means of increasing one's status on the caste ladder, desire to rank higher on the same caste ladder, or resentment against ritualism and casteism, the result is the same—namely, the proliferation of new castes (L in Diagram III). Here the Indian ideal of the Universal Soul compels consequences which are totally different from those of its Chinese counterpart. The ideal of the Universal Soul and its accompanying nonattachment intensify the need on the part of the individual for definite affiliation to satisfy his social needs. But the ideal of the Universal Soul also feeds and justifies the fear of loss of caste, conformity by intensification of casteism, desire to rank higher on the same caste ladder, and resentment against ritualism and casteism, as well as the proliferation of new castes. It feeds the fear of loss of caste because it is the ultimate destination in a hierarchy which no one can reach. It feeds conformity because its essential operational theology is that the individual will come near it by intense devotion to the various rules embodied in the sacred books. It justifies the desire to rank higher on the same caste ladder because it enjoins the individual to rise through good works and reincarnation. It justifies the proliferation of new castes because it sanctions avoidance of pollution, ritual purity, and other characteristics of high caste as a means of greater proximity to it. It combines anything with everything: the similar with the dissimilar, the commensurable with extreme opposites. As a matter of fact, and in addition to the many expressions described above, the Hindu ideal of Atma also sanctions a variety of individual cathexes (M in Diagram III). These cathexes range from indulgence in dance, music (both regarded as means of reaching God), ritualism, continuous pilgrimage, and yoga to individual seclusion and spiritual concentration, either in one's own home or on the slopes of the Himalayas.

This is not to say that Hindu society is the only society which embodies sharp contrasts. Some sharp contrasts can be found in any society anywhere. Universally there are always the old and the new, the traditional and the modern, the very fast and the very slow, and the honest and the crooked. But the contrasts in Hindu society are far more startling than their counterparts elsewhere. Here we find extremely universalized thoughts side by side with extremely parochial defenses; extremely vague ideals side by side with extremely concrete prescriptions; extremely diffused theories side by side with extremely specific injunctions. Furthermore, none of these contrasting thoughts is even designed, in the theoretical sense, to overcome or replace any other.

This startling contrast is most evident in religion, which penetrates into every other area of life. The Hindu approach to religion is the most monotheistic in the world. The purest Hindu contemplation of the supernatural affirms the attributeless yet all-embracing Universal Soul which can only be represented by the syllables AUM or OM in Sanskrit. "A" and "M" are the first and last sounds human beings can utter. "U" links them. AUM or OM is a suitable sign of the Universal Soul for two reasons. First, since all forms of phenomena in the universe are known to man by their names, AUM, by virtue of the fact that it embraces all sounds man can utter, embraces all phenomena in the universe. Second, AUM is purely symbolic, unattached to any specific being, thing, or phenomenon. It is the utmost in abstraction the purist can demand.

As against this extremely abstractionist, broad, and universalist approach in the Hindu religion, we have no trouble at all in finding the most concrete, specific, localized, and detailed, almost profane ways of dealing with and representing the gods. First, though all gods and goddesses are but phases or aspects of the same godhead, they are not only given elaborately different names, different attributes, and different appearances, but also varieties of localized powers to deal with specific diseases, calamities, and other problems. Second, though great gods like Siva and his consorts are often discussed in higher religious circles as symbolic of universal principles, their effigies in many family shrines are literally put to bed every evening and raised from it every morning by Brahmans regularly hired for this purpose. In the great Meenakshi temple of Madurai in the State of Madras, the marriage of the Lord Siva and his wife is celebrated each month of the year in an affair lasting over twenty days. Third, though extolling nonattachment and unity of all in the Atma, the ritual details are given the greatest care everywhere. It is not uncommon to find, as already noted, in a wedding the priest of the groom's family quarreling repeatedly with that of the bride's in the protracted observances for such occasions.

It is, of course, natural for the theory and practice of any religion in any society not fully to coincide. The Christianity or Judaism discussed by learned theologians and rabbis is bound to be divergent from the Christianity or Judaism known to common men. But the contrasts in the Hindu scene are more striking than those to be found elsewhere. They are more striking because extreme abstraction and extreme realism in worship are combined even among the learned Hindu pandits. They are more striking also because, while in Christianity protestantism tends to simplify the worship by reducing dogma and rituals, protestant movements in Hinduism have simply created more sects, more religious practitioners and followers along the same lines. Jainism, Buddhism, the Lingayat movement, Bhaktism, and others are all expressions of Hindu protestantism. They have simply become parts of the same religious system or, as in the case of Buddhism, have no significant place on Indian soil. This fact has often been noted as indicating the strength or tolerance of Hinduism. Hinduism is indeed the most tolerant of religions in Western terms. In my view this is not mere tolerance. By definition tolerance means the permission to exist granted by those who are superior to those who are inferior. But the Indian ideal equally sanctions not only different caste groups but also the extremely opposite, the extremely incongruous, the extremely irreconcilable. Even the Vedanta or Ramakrishna Mission is no exception to this rule. What the Vedanta movement has, compared with the earlier protestant movements already mentioned, is a greater *addition* of Western Christian practices grafted onto the Hindu religious body, with no significant synthesis between them, and no significant efforts at eradicating the traditional elements.

Individual cathexes may, of course, lead to religious or ritual movements, but this eventuality is far more likely in India than in China. Chinese individual devotees are often regarded by other Chinese as peculiar individuals or at any rate out of the main stream of society. Except for widows or very old people, those who devote most of their time to pilgrimage would be pressured by relatives and friends to pay more heed to their earthly duties and responsibilities. The Chinese individual is likely to be sensitive to such pressures also because the rewards for such ritual activities are scarce in the wider society. He will have little sympathy from others and certainly no following, except in folktales and novels in which there is a role for devotees of ritual similar to that of Superman or Mighty Mouse in American comic strips.

The situation for the extreme devotee in India is quite different. Devotion to God, ritualism, or pilgrimage means not only supernatural power or closer union with the Universal Soul but also earthly power through the command of enormous wealth and following. The devotee's following may range from a few hundred to millions. There is an unimpressive little man who started life as a sadhu some thirty years ago on the east bank of the Hooghly River just behind the Dakineshwar Temple in Calcutta. He started unobtrusively, but as the years went by some devotees started following him. Then more came. When I saw him in 1956 a number of devotees had already built for him a modest little house of brick and cement. I sat on the floor opposite him one afternoon. Streams of well-dressed and gift-bearing devotees kept coming in and going out. Among these devotees were the unemployed, peasants, laborers, and middle-rank government officials, as well as wealthy ladies with their husbands and children. At the other extreme are modernized holymen such as Swami Vivekenanda of another generation and Swami Shivananda today. These are English-speaking preachers as well as Sanskrit scholars. They can use the microphone and make brilliant sermons to hundreds and thousands at a time. They are usually far more conversant with Western religions and theologies such as Christianity and Judaism than Western ministers or rabbis would be with Hinduism or Islam. Between these extremes we have Paglababa (mad father) near Serampore, West Bengal, and Anukul Thakur of Deoghar, in Santal Parganas of south Bihar. Both of these have larger followings than the diminutive gentleman behind the Dakineshwar Temple in Calcutta, but less following than the internationally known Swami Vivekenanda. Paglababa is married and at the age of over seventy has two or three little children. Anukul Thakur is not only married but has many wives. Among his followers are one American and Sri Benodananda Jhan who succeeded Sri Sinha upon the latter's death as Chief Minister of Bihar. As soon as Sri Benodananda assumed office he ostensibly went to receive the holy man's blessing, the proceedings of which were prominently reported in the newspapers.

The rewards for these individual devotees are truly great. Many of them become heads of new sects with new forms of worship, new taboos, and new rituals. The Universal Soul not only sanctions the proliferation of new castes but it also firmly insists that all castes and sects, however different and divergent, are part of it. As the individual devotees gain in spiritual nearness to the great Atma and in earthly following, they tend to become heads of new sects which in turn simply develop into castes within the same all-inclusive framework of the Universal Soul. This, as we have seen before, is the fate of all religious reform movements in India except for Buddhism, which left its motherland and flowered elsewhere. The modern Indian tendency is to welcome Buddhism back to India. In 1956, some 2500 years after the Lord Buddha reached Nirvana in Bodh Gaya, a most elaborate Buddha Jayanti celebration occurred throughout all India. Some observers have tended to regard this as at least partially political in motive. Independent India, which hopes to assume a strong leadership among nations of Asia, may conceivably wish to use Buddhism as the cementing factor in strengthening its solidarity with Asian nations. But from what we know of the pattern of the Hindu way of life, the welcoming back of a protestant movement such as Buddhism to its mother religion is perfectly natural. The Buddhists are simply another caste group as are the Lingayats, the Sikhs, the Christians.

Caste in India expresses the basic conflict inherent in the Hindu way of life. Caste is based on the theoretical position of oneness of all living beings. It regards the multiple self-enclosed caste walls merely as part of the total fabric, using individual improvement through reincarnation as the bridge across them. Casteism is, therefore, not a defect to be remedied even in some future time, however remote. It expresses a conflict which allows no permanent solution. In the face of the diffuseness of nonattachment, man seeks to fortify himself behind the closed walls of caste. But since all differentiations and existences are ultimately subject to change, the pressure for satisfaction of his social needs cannot be confined by any particular barriers. There is then an unceasing inquiry into the universal and the ultimate in which all differences disappear, side by side with an unceasing search for the particular and the immediate in which the only considerations are specific circles of friendship, signs of belonging, and symbols of prestige.*

We thus understand the Hindu caste system in a new psychosocial per-

---

* Sadhus, sanyasin, or holy men are often, though not always, of low caste origin. There is no doubt that some of them choose their careers to renounce the world, including caste with all its privileges and restrictions. Since the professed preoccupation of the sadhu is with the Atma, it can be argued that supernatural orientation is in fact a reaction against, and therefore contradictory to, casteism; religious devotion is "individualistic" in contrast to caste privileges and disabilities, which are matters of orthodoxy. This argument is wide of the mark in several respects. First, it is clear that, while a few outstanding men like Buddha and Ramakrishna may truly seem to renounce caste along with everything else, a majority resort to sadhuhood as an obvious means of escaping caste disabilities, of rising in caste hierarchy, or of achieving other forms of worldly gains. This is a fact that we noted before and which has often been remarked on by other observers, including Mahatma Gandhi. The many disputes and acts of strife among different orders of sadhus are also indicative of this (see G. S. Ghurye, Indian Sadhus, Bombay: The Popular Book Depot, 1953). Second, the caste system itself is part and parcel of the same complex supernatural belief which induces this very renunciation. Finally what links the "individualistic" religious devotion to the group characteristics of the caste system is the social needs which everyone seeks to satisfy. In this effort the individual not only has to surrender much of his individuality but is also confined to culturally provided avenues for its attainment. Union with the Atma is the major cultural avenue open to Hindus, being what complete freedom of the individual is for Americans and what eternal harmony among men is for Chinese.

spective. To carry on life's activities the Hindu finds in caste a circle of interaction beyond the biological family, in which he can find the sociability, security, and status that he needs. But, since the hierarchical principle dominates the entire social organization, the status strife, the fear of loss of caste, the resulting greater conformity, and the resentment against casteism keep the caste system in a state of dynamic animation. The individual can never be satisfied with the status quo. He will try to change the name of his caste; he will develop new subcastes; he will find justification in obscure myths, folktales, and sacred scriptures for raising the status of his caste; he will invent new rules based on old models (such as forbidding widow remarriage) to make his subcaste different from, or higher than, other subcastes. These are unending processes in Hindu society.

The self-containment behind one's own caste walls and the endless processes of fission into new subdivisions and disputes over old statuses are therefore the outer responses to an inner contradiction inherent in the Hindu supernatural-centered orientation of life. These processes are, in addition, complicated and probably accelerated by the fact that the nature of the bases for caste membership in the Hindu caste and subcaste are, compared with those for membership in the Chinese clan, much more arbitrary and subject to dispute. To be sure caste membership is also rooted in the family because one is born into a caste or subcaste in a certain locality. But as soon as there is a little contact among inhabitants of the different localities there are chances for dissatisfaction with one's own status and for imitation of persons of higher statuses by persons of lower ones. This, as we have noted already, must have happened again and again long before the impact of the West or of Islam. The Hindus have to be more demonstratively divisive and exclusive rather than inclusive and cohesive, because their caste membership is constantly threatened by divisions from within, and the status of their group *vis-à-vis* other groups is constantly threatened by disputations from without. Even an Untouchable must be constantly on guard for his status, for there is a possibility that he will sink still lower by splintering movements among his own Outcaste mates. The net result of these processes, from the point of view of the larger Indian society, is division rather than cohesion.[12, 13]

It is now easy to see how this hypothesis is different from the previous ones. Certainly it is not unusual to find societies in which occupational differences, the consumption of different foods, and the enjoyment of services are associated in some ways with class differences, sex differences, or other status differences. The idea of occupational differentiation into higher versus lower grades, and the idea of purity versus impurity in foods and services, might have been associated with the caste system from earliest times. And it would not have been difficult for the search for caste differences to be identified with what in the first instance were class or other differences. But that is far from saying that occupational differentiations or differences in purity are intrinsic to caste as such. Take occupational differentiations, for example. Every society must have some division of labor. If we cannot reasonably suppose that caste is older than division of labor among men, then it becomes obvious that caste or any other type of social, religious, or political differentiation which comes after division of labor may be attached to or fused with division of labor. For the new development in any society must be related to its old elements and use some of them for its expression. Division of work, being much older and much more nearly universal than caste, was simply one of the elements in Hindu society used as a tool for expressing and elaborating the relatively new idea of caste or hierarchy. The Hindu psychology of caste would find no way of giving itself expression except in particular historical and cultural contexts. That psychology would have found other means of giving itself expression if occupational differentiation were not available. Indeed in the actual boundaries drawn among the castes with their myriad and trivial caste-differentiating signs or symbols, division of work is not often in the picture.

Our hypothesis does not, therefore, begin with the idea that differences in purity, occupational differentiations, the powers of the Brahmans or of Kshatriyas, or any of the tools of casteism gave rise to the caste system or were even the basis of it. Our hypothesis takes into full account the interrelatedness among the overall ideal, the organization of the society, and the needs and aspirations of the individual. Our analysis shows that the caste system is the expression of the contradictions inherent in the supernatural-centered world, in which the symbols of hierarchical differentiation may be purity versus impurity, higher occupations versus lower occupations, one variety of foods versus another, or any other distinction of a symbolic nature the cultural and historical context can provide. The exact nature or substance of the symbols is immaterial. The essence of the Hindu caste system consists of the tendency on the part of the individual, in his search for circles of sociability, security, and status beyond the kinship group, to fortify himself behind self-imposed social and ritual walls, and the conflicting tendency to break through those walls for the purpose of raising himself to a higher status. Under modern conditions new caste symbols have already arisen and more of them will undoubtedly appear as time goes on. Vegetarianism may be changed to meat-eating; the sacredness of Brahmanism may be replaced by industrialism; but to understand caste our primary task is to unravel the psychocultural forces bearing on the Hindu way of life and not the meanings of the ever-fluid and never-consistent symbols of status. The symbols, whether in terms of static attributes or of dynamic interactions, are tools. The social needs and the manner of their satisfaction through cultural means are the power which manipulates the tools and provides them with direction and significance.

NOTES FOR CHAPTER VIII

1. Francis L. K. Hsu, *Under the Ancestors' Shadow* (New York: Columbia University Press, 1948), pp. 249–255.
2. Francis L. K. Hsu, "A Closer View of China's Problems," *The Far Eastern Quarterly*, November 1946, p. 54, and *Americans and Chinese: Two Ways of Life* (New York: Abelard-Schuman, 1953), pp. 188–195.
3. S. Radhakrishnan, *The Bhagavadgītā* (London: George Allen and Unwin, 1948), pp. 21–22 and p. 23.
4. *Ibid.*, p. 21 (footnote 1).
5. *Ibid.*, p. 35 (footnote 1).
6. P. Thomas: *Hindu Religion, Customs and Manners*, 2nd Indian ed. (Bombay: D. P. Taraporevala Sons, undated), p. 49.
7. A. L. Basham, *The Wonder That Was India* (London: Sidgwick and Jackson, 1956), pp. 341–342.
8. G. Piers and Milton B. Singer, *Shame and Guilt: A Psychoanalytic and a Cultural Study* (Springfield: Charles C Thomas, 1953).
9. Francis L. K. Hsu, "Suppression Versus Repression, A Limited Psychological Interpretation of Four Cultures," *Psychiatry*, XII, No. 3 (1949), pp. 223–242.
10. Lois Murphy "Roots of Tolerance and Tensions in Indian Child Development" in Gardner Murphy, *In the Minds of Men* (New York: Basic Books, 1953), p. 56.
11. S. Radhakrishnan, *op. cit.*, p. 38.
12. Writers on Hindu caste often speak of the fact that the hierarchic arrangement of the different castes and subcastes makes all of them parts of a wider system. (See H. N. C. Stevenson, "Caste [Indian]" in Encyclopedia Britannica, p. 982.) This is certainly true, but such a view completely fails to take into account the fissiparous characteristic of the caste system.
13. I. Desai and Y. B. Damle in their essay, "A Note on the Change in the Caste," in K. M. Kapadia (ed.), *Professor Ghurye Felicitation Volume* (issued under the auspices of the Ghurye 60th Birthday Celebration Committee, Bombay: 1954), pp. 266–276, came close to probing the psychological roots of caste, but these authors did not go further than mentioning the possibility.

Chapter IX

COHESION AND DIVISION IN THE
AMERICAN WORLD

THE BROAD OUTLINE of our hypothesis so far is that, while presuming that the needs for sociability, security, and status are as applicable to the Chinese as to the Hindu, their respective manners of satisfaction are dissimilar. The Chinese pattern of mutual dependence embodied in the ideal of complete harmony among men enables the individual to find satisfaction of his needs within the kinship sphere so that he is under little pressure to go outside it. The Hindu cultural pattern of unilateral dependence rooted in the ideal of union with the Ultimate Reality, on the other hand, makes such satisfactions vaguer and more problematical, so that the individual is forced to find some nonkinship circles such as caste for anchorage. In the Chinese situation the relationship between the individual and his kinship groups where he finds his sociability, security, and status is a relatively static affair while the corresponding relationship in the Hindu's world is far more dynamic. The Chinese individual looks forward to a fairly straightforward line of advancement and affiliation as he grows old. His place in the family, the family shrine, the clan hierarchy and temple is automatic, permanent, and a foregone conclusion. There is no fear on his part of possible loss of that place, nor is there much room for him to change it. But as the Hindu individual matures, his destination is not so clear and foreordained. He must move outside his family and he also has to defend his caste against oppression from above, against cleavage from within, and against encroachment from below.

In some of the foregoing analyses we have occasionally touched upon the American world. How does our hypothesis, one which has so far been tested in Chinese and Indian cultural contexts, stand up when scrutinized in the light of life in the United States? To this question we shall now address ourselves.

CHARACTERISTICS OF THE AMERICAN FAMILY

The structural ideal of the family in the United States is entirely different from that of China or India. In the American family system descent is is patronymic, virilocal, and neolocal, and authority is nominally in the hands of the father and husband. But universally, the ideal of the individual family prevails, and it is almost universal in reality. The normal custom among the overwhelming majority is for a young man and his wife to begin married life in an independent household. Even if they have to begin their married life under the same roof with his or her parents, as sometimes happens during a housing shortage, they will consider such an arrangement to be an emergency measure and therefore temporary. As soon as it is possible, they will set up an independent household of their own. If for some reason they are unable to do this and if in the ensuing months or years there are some marital difficulties, the first advice a marriage counsellor or a Dorothy Dix will give them is that they should move out from under the parental roof.

In theory, there is no question of specific forms of expressly stated preferential mating, such as that between cross-cousins. In reality marriage within the same religion and within the same sect of the same religion, within the same race, and within the same subethnic group (e.g., between those of Polish origin or of northern European origin) are deemed more desirable than outside them. There is even endogamy of a sort among people who are highly mindful of their social or class status, although this is not clearly expressed, and when confronted with it, many will be embarrassed to admit it. Within the family the *de facto* structural arrangement for a majority is for the father to be the breadwinner and playmate of the children, and the mother to be the housekeeper and the disciplinarian, not only of the children but also of the husband. This pattern is especially true of the "middle classes" with which a majority of Americans, as shown by the public-opinion polls and other sources of information, claim affiliation.

The laws of inheritance vary somewhat in the different states, but the man usually has a free hand in making his will, although in general he can disinherit only his children, not his wife. The question of what proportion of a mate's estate goes to his surviving children only occurs if he dies intestate. There is a theoretical equality between the sexes and the ages, and this is also close to reality. Men and women can marry as often as they are widowed or divorced, and there is no significant stigma against either. In fact, there are statistical indications that, age for age, divorced and widowed males and females stand a much better chance for remarriage than men and women who have never been married before.[1] Plurality of mates is totally forbidden by custom and by law. The nearest to it is a sort of "serial polygamy" often practiced in some sectors of the population, of which "show people" are the stereotype. The individual is educated not primarily for duties and obligations, but to exercise his freedoms and his rights. Consequently, the pattern of conduct within the family is not clearly delineated by specific rules, but revolves around the word "adjustment," a word which is found in greater circulation every day.

All these are structural differences between the American family on the one hand and the Hindu and Chinese families on the other, but there are other profound structurally related differences in content.

The structural relationship most elevated in the American family is that between the husband and wife. All other relationships are either subordinated to this central one or are patterned after and modified by it. Unlike those of the father-son relationship, the attributes of the husband-wife relationship are exclusiveness and discontinuity. It is discontinuous over the generations because each husband-wife relationship has no necessary link with other such relationships. Children become independent when they marry or reach majority. It is exclusive of other individuals because each husband-wife relationship is not only complete in itself but is intolerant of intrusion by any third party. It is, therefore, necessary to have monogamy as an absolute ideal. The three most important elements of this kinship content are Romantic Love, worship of the young, and self-reliance. These three elements are closely interrelated, with self-reliance at the core.

Romantic Love is an expression which embodies unaccountableness of choice, exclusive possession, freedom for the partners from interference by other human beings, and complete lack of definite ties with other relationships whether they be parent-child or fraternal. In contrast to the Chinese situation, where the father-son relationship symbolizes all that is "forever," and to the Hindu situation where Atma symbolizes all that is "forever," the society of the United States is one where only the husband-wife relationship is described as being "forever."

Worship of the young is obvious in American society wherever one looks, exactly as worship of the old is plain for all to see in the culture pattern of traditional China. In fact no other country accords so much attention to infancy or so many privileges to childhood as does the United States. There are many expressions of this. Americans are very verbal about their children's rights. There is not only state and federal legislation to protect the young ones, but there are also various juvenile protective associations to look after their welfare. Not only is infanticide classified as murder, but parents can get into legal trouble and even social difficulties if they discipline their children with "undue" enthusiasm. It is literally true that from the point of view of American children, parents have practically no rights. American parents not only wish to help their children according to their own experiences, but they also must find out through elaborate research what the youngsters really want so that the elders can better satisfy the youngster's individual predilections. They handsomely support a tremendous number of child specialists to supply them with advice on what children like best. Juvenile literature and the toy industry are both big businesses. The toy industry was boosted from an annual business of a mere 150 million dollars in 1949, to 750 million dollars in 1951, and over 1300 million dollars in 1961. The annual business catering to all infant needs had reached in 1951 an astronomical five billion dollars. Television today provides, as radio did for years, scores of programs designed for children. The announcers advise kiddies to tell their parents that they will eat nothing but Snapcrackles for breakfast or want only Firebird 77 for a toy. The children do so, and in many cases their parents obey by procuring the desired products. The important thing in the minds of American parents seems to be what they should do for their children, but the situation is not generally vice versa. It is no exaggeration to say that while the Chinese glorify their ancestors and the Hindus glorify their gods, the Americans glorify their children. The American family thus fosters an overwhelming sense of self-importance in the growing children, and it correspondingly minimizes the importance of the older people who are responsible for bringing them up.

The third and the most dominant element in the American kinship content is self-reliance. The individual is conditioned to think in terms of the first person singular, here and now: his own rights, his own pleasures, and his own privacy; his own status, and his own chances for advancement or dangers of regression. For he is trained to regard the human world around him as impermanent. He has no inalienable place in the scheme of things except that scheme he himself initiates and constructs. Given this premise it is a foregone conclusion that the individual has to seek a mate on his or her own merits and to cut himself adrift from those who have brought him into the world and been dear and close.*

* This pattern is graphically confirmed in a study of 200 young women students by Helen Codere at Vassar College. Codere concludes: "In conclusion, the kinship system set forth and detailed by the genealogies of these students of high socioeconomic status seems to have minimal definition, in comparison to that of any other known system in any culture that is a going concern. Moreover, the kinship system described seems to be permeated to a far greater degree than any other known system by the process of individual choice-making as a way of setting up interpersonal relationships. So minimal a system cannot perform many of the functions of a social organization, and can only form and be formed by a social organization in which there is a great degree of social mobility and individual self-dependence. In other words, it is a kinship system that supports and is supported by classical American attitudes about freedom and opportunity for the individual. The minimal kinship system described both guarantees to the individual this classical freedom and offers him, as accompaniments, problems of social security and of making and maintaining interpersonal relationships. It is not surprising that a group that is significantly distinguished from the United States population as a whole only by higher

Psychologically this American pattern offers for speculation a possible contrast with that of India. I suggest that, if the Hindu pattern of mother-dependence is correlated with a feeling of the mutability of all men, the American pattern of self-reliance can be expected to be correlated with a feeling of immutability of all men. The general effect of the all-answering and all-embracing mother on the child is, as we have seen, the minimization of distinctions not only among different stimuli but also possibly between the self and nonself. The general effect of a situation in which the child is encouraged to think and act for himself is likely to be the heightening of distinctions among different stimuli as well as possibly between the self and nonself. The testing of this hypothesis, in the light of the existing studies of the psychosocial development among western infants and children by well-known scholars such as Gesell, Spitz, Murphy, Piaget, and others, remains for the future. What I wish to suggest at this juncture is that employing this hypothesis may help us to understand many characteristics of the American approach to human relationship.

It is perhaps not difficult to see how the idea of immutability is a large, perhaps primary, ingredient in Romantic Love, the separation of the generations in favor of the young, and self-reliance. The outstanding contrast between marriage through Romantic Love and marriage by parental arrangement is that in the latter case mate-selection is expressly determined by calculable factors such as money, virtue, social standing, and personal appearance, but not necessarily by the attraction of the married partners for each other; in the former case every individual has, at least in theory, only one suitable mate for whom he or she should personally fall without rhyme or reason: this in spite of the fact that, the demands of Western marriage being what they are, the actual number of possible mates is very small. Separation between the generations contrasts sharply with continuity between them. In spite of the common American expression, "a chip off the old block," the prevailing search in America is for something new and different, and hence the young know best because they really do not have to learn from the old and therefore have little or no reference to the old. Self-reliance is indeed the epitome of immutability of stimuli, by its insistence on autonomy and the uniqueness of the individual. Romantic Love and worship of the young are in fact merely two outstanding expressions of it. For the individual brought up under this pattern the world tends to be dichotomized: on the one hand, the self and all beings and phenomena affiliated with or pos-

---

socioeconomic status does not differ very much from the total culture as it is usually described, although this would seem to contradict those social scientists who have indicated that a social class analysis of United States culture is of fundamental importance." (Helen Codere: "A Genealogical Study of Kinship in the United States," *Psychiatry*, XVIII, No. 1 (Feb. 1955) p. 79.)

sessed by the self; and on the other hand, the nonself. There is a deep gulf between these two parts that cannot easily be bridged. Since projection is a commonplace fact of human psychology, it is reasonable to expect that the nonself portion of the world will be regarded by the individual in this pattern, consciously or unconsciously, as also dichotomized by each and every one of the human beings living in it. These observations to which our analysis leads us seem to be partially confirmed in the work of Kurt Lewin, though not in the same terms. In his study Lewin finds "the educational situation in the United States, as compared to Germany, to be characterized by regions of very different degrees of freedom [life space] and sharply determined boundaries of these regions," which make for "great qualitative differences" between them. Lewin further observes that this structure of American education is "an expression of American style of living," in which extremes abound.[2] In terms of personality structure Lewin observes that the social distance between different individuals "seems to be smaller in the United States" than in Germany with reference to the "peripheral regions," but that it is far greater than in Germany with reference to the "central regions."[3]

> Germans entering the United States notice usually that the degree of friendly and close relation, which one may achieve as a newcomer within a few weeks, is much higher than under similar circumstances in Germany. Compared with Germans, Americans seem to make quicker progress towards friendly relations in the beginning, and with many more persons. Yet this development often stops at a certain point; and the quickly acquired friends will, after years of relatively close relations, say good-by [sic] as easily as after a few weeks of acquaintance.[4]

Dealing only with the Germans and the Americans, Lewin sees principally their differences. Had he viewed the two peoples from a wider perspective he would have seen that their similarities far outweigh their differences, for both peoples share the same basically individualistic way of life rooted in a kinship organization structurally anchored in the husband-wife relationship. The differences between the Chinese and the Hindus, or between the Chinese and the Americans, as we have noted in the foregoing chapters, are essentially qualitative and a matter of kind; but the differences between the Germans and the Americans, noted by Lewin, and by others such as Erik Erickson, are primarily quantitative and therefore a matter of degree.[5] For our analysis in the present chapter, Lewin's observations on "sharply determined boundaries," "extremes," and the difficulty of access into the "central regions" of personality in social relations fit well with our conclusions on the tendency toward immutability in human relations and toward dichotomization of the world into the self and the nonself.

Needless to say, this pattern affects the old no less than it does the young.

To the young it means independence and search for new frontiers, but to the old the picture is considerably different and often leads to results contradictory to what is favored by the young. To understand this we need to begin with the observation that, though promoting independence and self-reliance in their children, Americans have at the same time complete and exclusive control over their minor children. This is in sharp contrast to the condition of Chinese and Hindu parents who, though expecting and receiving utmost respect and complete obedience from their children, do not have exclusive and complete control over them even before the youngsters are of age.

The roots of this contrast are not to be found in the differing sizes of the family but in its differing contents. The average size of the American family is somewhere between three and four persons and the average size of each of the two Asian families is about five. We have seen before that the smallness of the average Chinese and Hindu family is due to the fact that the majority in both Asian societies is poor and not able to live up to the joint-family ideal. The details as to why this is so need not detain us here. But this means that whether it is in China, India, or America, the elementary group in which most newborn infants find themselves is the nuclear family composed of parents and their unmarried children.

However, the differences in kinship content between the two Asian societies and America are truly profound. In the first place, when an American speaks of a family, he refers to and thinks of the nuclear group, whereas the Chinese or the Hindu will include in it grandparents and in-laws as well. Even if Chinese grandparents and in-laws do not live under the same roof, they usually reside in the same village, a neighboring village, or at the farthest, a neighboring district. On the other hand, Americans related by blood or marriage often live so far from one another that this broader group does not come together except on such occasions as Easter, Thanksgiving, Christmas, or other holidays. The Asian children grow up amidst continuing or frequent contacts with a number of relatives besides their own parents and siblings, but American children grow up in much greater physical isolation from them.

Far more crucial, however, is the manner of interaction between the growing child and the individuals other than those belonging to his immediate family. American parents are the sole agents of control over their children until the latter are of age. Even if grandparents and in-laws share the same roof, they do not ordinarily have any disciplinary role. When grandparents or in-laws take over during an emergency, such as sickness or childbirth, they are supposed to do no more than administer the laws laid down by the younger couple, more especially by the woman. Thus the American parental arm exercises control over the children even in its absence.

This is in sharp contrast to the patterns prevailing in the two Asian societies. This contrast is put in bold relief by the manner in which parents of the three societies will react to outside interference. In America strangers can interfere with parents if they think that the parents are mistreating their offspring. They can call the S.P.C.C. about it or report it to the police. In some instances I have heard of and witnessed direct intervention by strangers. Toward this kind of interference American parents may be resentful, but they cannot do anything about it. With the society's emphasis on the protection and glorification of children at all costs, the parents will at best be on the defensive. But a different kind of interference will bring down nothing but wrath on the part of the parents and condemnation from others. This happens when a stranger, noticing that a child is doing something that he should not, perhaps even breaking the law, decides that he should stop the young culprit by bringing him to his mother. The result is predictable. The mother will most likely tell the outsider to mind his own business. If they were friends before, the friendship will come to an abrupt end. American parents are so touchy about their prerogatives regarding their children that they will often regard even as enemies those who commit the deadly sin of being even unwittingly uncomplimentary toward their children. This omnipresent parental control over their children is, like the emphasis on children's independence and self-reliance, unknown in China and in India.

Thus the American family exercises on its children two contradictory influences. On the one hand, the children are made to feel that they are all-important, while the adults are mere caterers to their wishes and comforts. On the other hand, they soon realize that, before reaching maturity, the same adults are the sole sources of law. Therefore, if and when they can get away from their parents there will seemingly be no further limitations on their conduct.

Neither Chinese nor Indian children are subject to this conflict. In China, they submit to the parents and their ancestors for life, and expect similar treatment from their descendants. In India, they are reared to follow their parents and, after their parents, their gurus and the gods. At all times the growing Chinese individual is subject to a multiplicity of authorities besides that of his parents. Since the different sources of authority often conflict with each other, the parental authority tends to vary with circumstances. Instead of being all-powerful, the parental image in the mind of the growing child must necessarily share the spotlight with other images held in much higher esteem, such as grandparents in China, or gurus and gods in India.

The conflicting forces bearing on American children tend in any event to lead to deep emotional involvement between them and their parents. Since parents are all-powerful, their images in the mind of the growing child naturally are elevated above all else. To the extent that they are the only objects of worship, they also are liable to become the only oppressors. The feeling of oppression is likely to be heightened by the fact that the children have been trained to be self-reliant. Consequently, when an American child likes his parents, they are his idols, but when he dislikes them, they are his enemies. A conscious or unconscious attachment to one parent at the expense of the other, the condition of mind which gave Freud grounds for postulating his well-known Oedipus complex, is the extreme expression of this situation.

Under the Chinese circumstances, the need for strong feelings is less. When a child likes his parents he is not so likely to worship them; when he dislikes them he can afford to vent his displeasure with some reserve. Theoretically at least there is far less reason in the Hindu and especially the Chinese situation for the Oedipean triangle.

PRIVACY, HUMAN RELATIONS, AND PEER GROUP

As the American child grows older and begins to enter school life, the results of his early familial experiences are intensified. We have seen how, on the one hand, the American child has been encouraged to be independent and to think for himself—in other words to be self-reliant—while, on the other hand, the parents seem firmly to refuse to let the youngster enter the real world of the adults. This is especially common in the middle classes, to which a majority of Americans claim affiliation. For one thing, American parents leave their children with sitters when they go to their own parties. If they entertain at home, they put the youngsters to bed before the guests arrive. Children have little part in parents' social and other activities. The youngsters tend to develop a world of their own especially since the parents foster the idea of privacy for all individuals.

Many are the expressions of this emphasis on privacy. For example, the social and commercial activity of American parents is their private reserve, and no trespassing by children is allowed except on those rare and eventful occasions when an explicit invitation is extended. Newspaper "psychologists" frequently advise that a well-adjusted personality will result if parents do not burden their children with adult difficulties. By the same token, parents are also supposed to refrain from prying or even entering into the activities of their youngsters, especially of the boys. These same advisers admonish worried mothers to disappear when their teenage daughters entertain at home.

The line of demarcation between the grown-up and the juvenile worlds is drawn in other less explicit ways. For instance, many American parents may have no use themselves for the church and are atheists or agnostics, but they send their children to Sunday schools and help them to pray. American parents struggle in a world of tough competition where cunning and false-hood are often rewarded and respected, but they feed their children with nursery tales in which the morally good invariably triumphs over the bad. When American parents have serious domestic troubles they tend to main-tain before their children a front of sweetness and light. Even after a major business catastrophe they feel obliged to fake a smile, with a "Honey, every-thing is all right." Americans usually hold off telling children when their parents have been killed in an accident, or conceal the facts from them when one of the parents goes to jail. In sum, American parents face a world of reality while their children live in the near-ideal realm of the fairy tales where the rules of the parental world do not apply or are watered down or are even reversed.

Thus, although by adolescence most Chinese and even Indian children have already entered into adult circles, their American counterparts at this time are often unworried and starry-eyed youngsters who understand little of the world of human reality which awaits them. Except among the very poor, a large section of the Negroes or immigrants from southern and eastern Europe, American youngsters at the threshold of adolescence have generally led an existence quite distinct from that of their parents. The self-reliance which is emphasized in family training undeniably encourages be-havior superficially imitative of adult life. But this simulation of adult roles is a totally ineffective substitute for a real initiation into adult life, since the sole concern of the children is with the surface aspects of adult life. The crucial determinant of maturity is an exposure and a realistic introduction into what are commonly called the ways of the world.

The teaching of self-reliance has another and far more significant con-sequence: as children grow, the gulf between them and their parents pro-gressively widens. From the first, the elders have interests which they pur-sue while the children remain with a sitter. Having no integrated place in their parents' doings, the youngsters soon find in their playmates a society that is equally exclusive and in turn unconcerned with the world of its elders. With these beginnings, there is little reason for children and parents to come closer together at a later date. It is therefore vain to hope, as some educators and parents presently do, that television may restore that family unity which they say has been undermined by the attractions of nonfamily commercial amusements. The American family bond just has not been weak-ened or destroyed by the absence of home entertainments, and its strength will not be restored by such artificial solutions.

It is not surprising, considering all this, that the majority of Americans enter adolescence with a romantic concept of life. Unprepared for the im-perfections of the real world, they tend to be easily disillusioned. Humanity's inconsistencies and weaknesses, especially when discovered in persons whom these adolescents have idolized, confuse or shock young persons whose idealized view of life's ways proves no guide to its true twists and turns.

American parents, on their side, tend to erect barriers to independence of their offspring. The first direct appearance of this conflict is seen at school age. When children enter adolescence, the struggle becomes more pronounced. For the parents, at this time, see before them the threat of complete relegation to the background. They tend, naturally enough, to react by intensifying their efforts to delay or prevent their children's self-reliance. In this campaign the elders have a variety of resources at their disposal: love, money, persuasion, and personal or legal force.

The resulting situation is often unbearable for the American adolescent. Having been raised to be self-reliant, it is now too late for him to turn back from his self-seeking activities. Two problems face him. On the one hand, the highly competitive American society demands that the self-respecting individual achieve success as quickly as possible. On the other hand, having been taught to feel that the parental family is no bulwark for his protection as an adult, he has to find belongingness in a peer group or groups. These two actions are interrelated. If he is admitted to a peer group which has high prestige, he is a success according to one criterion. If he is successful in competition, his also automatically a member of an elite peer group. These two social pressures which affect American youth are totally absent in the environment of his Asian counterpart. Asian adolescents, like Asian children, are essentially oriented toward a vertical relationship rather than a horizontal one, being more intimate with and more sensitive to their elders than to their peers. American adolescents, like American children, are essentially oriented toward a horizontal relationship rather than a vertical one, being more intimate with and sensitive to their peers than to their elders.

This American pattern is substantiated by recent researches, one of which is the Cornell Study of Student Values, which covers a total of 2,760 undergraduate men and women attending Cornell and 4,585 undergraduate men and women attending ten universities (The University of California at Los Angeles, Dartmouth, Fisk, Harvard, Michigan, North Carolina, Texas, Wayne, Wesleyan, and Yale). Suchman, in his summary report, concludes that "much of the student's development during four years in college does *not* take place in the classroom. The conformity, contentment and self-centered confidence of the present day American students are not academic values inculcated by the faculty, but rather the result of a highly organized and efficiently functioning extracurricular social system."[6, 7]

Up to this point the restraint on the activity of the American adolescent has been primarily that of his parents. Now he begins to run up against the boundary between legality and illegality as defined by the society at large. The successful, and therefore respected, businessman often prides himself on openly operating "just within the law." To the adolescent who is in the twilight between parental restraint and legal restraint, this tends to be reduced to the principle of "anything goes so long as you don't get caught." It is a well-known fact among school youngsters, even at the college level, that the basic criterion for mutual evaluation among them is smartness, which means being able to get away with things without getting caught; morality, the conducting of oneself according to the ethical principles of the society, is not so important. Disillusioned by the inconsistencies of the real adult world and innocent of its intricacies, but pressed by the desire to achieve success in a hurry, the American adolescent finds himself in far greater difficulties than he experienced during his grade-school days. His determination to be independent from his parents is now heightened. His insecurity is also increased because he is now more exposed to reality. Retreat is impossible without loss of self-respect.

The result is emotional turbulence. Since individuals differ widely, this turbulence erupts in diverse ways. The milder reactions are sulky moods, quarrelsomeness, incorrigibility, hostility to parents, and other forms of misconduct. The more extreme reactions are criminal, ranging from joy rides in stolen autos and robbery to sex orgies, narcotics addiction, and apparently unmotivated murder.

The American society today is faced with an unusual problem of adolescent crime throughout the country. The sociological interpretations of this phenomenon have by and large followed the established line that juvenile delinquency is a function of slums, poor housing, absence of mothers from home, and poverty in general. Reactions of two other types seem to greet any quantitative evidence of rising crime. One type would dismiss any such rise by maintaining that it is simply a result of better reporting and recording of juvenile court coverage. The other type seeks excuses. A few years ago a sensational "new discovery" was made linking juvenile violence with comic books, and for the last few years, a target has been the sale and viewing of smut literature and pictures.

What people in general have failed to realize is that the fundamental condition fostering juvenile delinquency in America consists of the twin pressures for individual success and for nonfamilial peer group affiliations. Those who have made it can gloat over their successes and exclusiveness with condescending pride, but those who have not made it, or those who because of race, religion, ethnic origin, or social class do not even have the chance to begin to compete, can only view the situation with disgust and resentment. The story is as obvious as that.

Juvenile delinquency is not, however, the concern of the present book. At any rate, and fortunately, a majority of American youngsters, even under such great pressures, still operate within legality, and grow up by assuming

more socially acceptable means of achieving success. But the general result of the pressures is a strong centrifugal outlook on the part of all or a
majority of individuals growing up. This tendency is similar to that found
among the Hindus but in sharp contrast to that found among the Chinese.

The Chinese have no compulsion to leave their kinship organization. The
widest grouping with which they have intimate affiliation and within which
they find satisfaction of their social needs is the clan. Their centripetal
tendency provides them with very little curiosity about the outside world
and thus the Chinese affiliation is with the family and its extension, the clan.

The Hindus have a great deal of compulsion to leave their kinship organization. For this reason their "clan" is mostly nominal. The widest grouping with which they claim intimate affiliation is the Universal Soul which
embraces all creatures under heaven. Since such a grouping is too vague
to be the individual's practical point of reference through the journey of
life, the Hindu seeks to satisfy most or all of his needs for sociability,
security, and status in a nonkinship but localized grouping, the caste.

The Americans have practically no kinship organization beyond the individual family. The clan is nonexistent. Not only will the individual find
no permanent and continuing affiliation with the kinship group in which he
is born and grows up, but his society's very definition of adulthood and even
normality includes his ability to cut off parental ties and to strike out on his
own. Ancestor "worship," even when so designated, is never more than the
mere pride in a distinguished genealogy and is never calculated to benefit
the dead. In fact, death severs the relationship among men, for the spirits
of the dead have no more interest in the living, while the living remember the
dead only if there is individual affection. The individual American has no
alternative except departure from his kinship group and the seeking of satisfaction of his needs for sociability, security, and status in that which I designate as *club*, a term to be explained below.

INDIVIDUAL-CENTERED ORIENTATION AND INDIVIDUAL NEEDS

The dynamic interrelationship among the psychocultural orientations, individual needs, and social grouping in the American situation is schematically
represented in Diagram IV. Our starting point here is self-reliance. From
this point our analysis fans out in three directions: ideal life (A, C, D); life
in society (A, B, G, H, K); and individual life (A, F, I, J, etc.). The first
line leads to greater and greater idealization of the American meaning of
life. The ultimate of this idealization is epitomized by that famous saying of
Rousseau: "Man was born free and everywhere he is in chains." The importance of this ideal for American society in particular and the West as a
whole cannot be overestimated. A most recent exposition of it is given by
Professor Shepard B. Clough of Columbia University who wants to make

DIAGRAM IV AMERICAN ORIENTATION
Contract relationship dominates all others

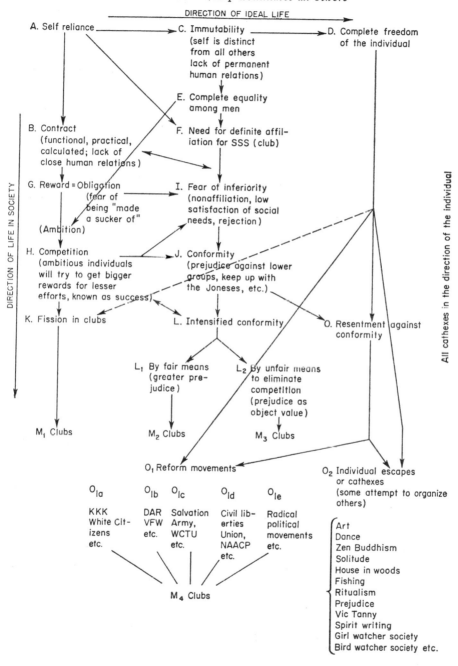

DIRECTION OF IDEAL LIFE

A. Self reliance

C. Immutability
(self is distinct
from all others
lack of permanent
human relations)

D. Complete freedom
of the individual

E. Complete equality
among men

B. Contract
(functional, practical,
calculated; lack of
close human relations)

F. Need for definite affiliation for SSS (club)

DIRECTION OF LIFE IN SOCIETY

G. Reward = Obligation
(fear of
being "made
a sucker of"
(Ambition)

I. Fear of inferiority
(nonaffiliation, low
satisfaction of social
needs, rejection)

H. Competition
(ambitious individuals
will try to get bigger
rewards for lesser
efforts, known as success)

J. Conformity
(prejudice against lower
groups, keep up with
the Joneses, etc.)

K. Fission in clubs

L. Intensified conformity

O. Resentment against
conformity

All cathexes in the direction of the individual

L_1 By fair means
(greater pre-
judice)

L_2 By unfair means
to eliminate
competition
(prejudice as
object value)

M_1 Clubs

M_2 Clubs

M_3 Clubs

O_1 Reform movements

O_2 Individual escapes
or cathexes
(some attempt to organize
others)

O_{1a} O_{1b} O_{1c} O_{1d} O_{1e}

KKK
White Cit-
izens
etc.

DAR
VFW
etc.

Salvation
Army,
WCTU
etc.

Civil lib-
erties
Union,
NAACP
etc.

Radical
political
movements
etc.

Art
Dance
Zen Buddhism
Solitude
House in woods
Fishing
Ritualism
Prejudice
Vic Tanny
Spirit writing
Girl watcher society
Bird watcher society etc.

M_4 Clubs

M_5 Clubs

explicit "our way of life"—a way of life that "we in the West claim should be defended to the death."[8] The author quotes the eloquent declaration of the Four Freedoms, a document drafted by Franklin D. Roosevelt and Winston Churchill shortly after America's entry into World War II, presented to Congress on January 6, 1941, and so well known throughout the world:

> In the future days, which we seek to make secure, we look forward to a world founded upon four essential human freedoms.
> The first is freedom of speech and expression—everywhere in the world.
> The second is freedom of every person to worship God in his own way—everywhere in the world.
> The third is freedom from want—which, translated into world terms, means economic understanding which will secure to every nation a healthy, peaceful life for its inhabitants—everywhere in the world.
> The fourth is freedom from fear—which, translated into world terms, means a worldwide reduction of armaments to such a point and in such a thorough fashion that no nation will be in a position to commit an act of aggression against any neighbor—anywhere in the world.[9]

This is not to say that Americans do attain the complete freedom that their ideal signifies. Any ideal, whether it be the Chinese one of complete harmony among men or the Hindu one of union with the Atma, is unattainable, for that is the very nature of ideals. But the great importance of ideals resides at least partly in their unattainability, and thus they serve as objects for endeavor among those who treasure them. There is no doubt that complete freedom of the individual is the ideal which inspires America more than any other society. It is literally the magic word. The question of freedom of the individual is written in every conceivable book and resorted to on every conceivable occasion, often for issues which support it as much as for those which contradict it. This ideal is completely absent in Chinese thought and is present in Hindu thinking only in connection with the ultimate liberation of the individual soul from the burden of reincarnation.

In terms of interpersonal relations, self-reliance and complete freedom of the individual signify that the self is distinct from all others, or immutable from them (C in Diagram IV). We have already in this chapter described this concept and shall observe here that a necessary corollary of immutability of the individual is the relative lack of permanent human relations. Since each individual tends to erect "sharply determined boundaries" which increase the difficulty of access by other individuals into the "central regions" of his personality, close interpersonal relations can only be achieved at the risk of cracks in those boundaries which each individual zealously guards. In the American culture, individuals who allow others to make serious inroads into the central regions of their personalities are likely to be dependent types (who need psychiatric care) or partners to intensively binding marital unions (which have little to do with other forms of relationships).

Ideologically the American remedy for this lack of permanent human relations is complete equality among men (E in Diagram IV). In my view this idea of universal equality is the American counterpart of the Hindu idea of "nonattachment" which is designed to enable the individual to develop enthusiasm for worldly objectives and duties in spite of the mutability of all under the ideal of Atma. The Western idea of universal equality at least delimits one general basis on which otherwise completely free individuals may be related. However, equality among men does not provide men with adequate means of relating to each other and satisfying their needs for sociability, security, and status. For one thing human beings are unequal in age, physical attractiveness, ability, and experience, to name but a few points. We have yet to find any human society where those who are in some obvious ways superior can easily be induced to remain content with being equal to their inferiors. Another problem is that, in spite of the stress on universal equality, not only those who are equipped with some points of superiority but even those who are not so equipped tend often to demand not *mere* equality with others but *more* equality than others. And finally, the needs of sociability and security require that human beings form close ties with each other, not simply equality with each other.

I submit that these needs are met by free associations or clubs (F in Diagram IV) and that the fundamental principle governing such affiliations is contract (B in Diagram IV).

The term *club* is used in this book, as indicated in Chapter I, in its widest possible sense to denote any sort of free association consciously organized for any purpose whatever. Lowie and others designate all social units not based on the kinship factor as associations.[10] From time to time other terms, such as society or sodality, have been applied to it. In the present chapter we shall confine ourselves to the term club.

Associations or clubs are of two kinds: voluntary and involuntary. The distinction is not absolute. A conscripted army is an involuntary club and a sorority is a voluntary one. Their distinction on this basis is unlikely to be cause for dispute. But it is very difficult to put labor unions with, for example, the Y.M.C.A., and describe both as voluntary associations. Membership in a union is voluntary in principle, but a worker who refuses to belong to the union designed for workers in his trade is likely to find his livelihood in jeopardy. We might simply observe here that an overwhelming majority of the groupings found in American society are voluntary in nature, though the distinction has no significant bearing on our present analysis.

The characteristics of the principle of contract are that it is functional, it is practical and it is calculated. It is functional and practical because no party to a contract will enter into the relationship unless he thinks he is gaining some advantage that he cannot gain outside of the contract. It is calculated because every contract as a rule stipulates the commencement and termination dates of the relationship as well as the terms and conditions of the agreement. The contract principle can also operate to a certain extent in the Hindu society where hierarchy is the dominant principle of social organization and in the Chinese society where kinship is the dominant principle of social organization. But in its barest structure it presupposes the entrance into a relationship by two or more free parties who are equal to each other. The contract principle satisfies the need for definite affiliation on the part of the individual but at the same time provides him with the reins with which he can control the extent of his involvement in the relationship.

The lack of permanent human relations, the idea of complete equality among men, the contract principle, and the need for definite affiliation to achieve sociability, security, and status combine and generate a situation in which club life is of the essence of existence.

Even a brief look at American schools and colleges is enough to convince anyone of this. At the grade-school level the peer groups are already important but they are mostly unorganized. Even if organized they are not yet exclusive in membership. There are the Brownies and the Girl Scouts; the Cubs and Boy Scouts; Sunday schools and fellowship groups. Though there may be undercover discrimination of a sort, membership in these clubs is open to anyone who wishes to belong to them, provided that he or she is already a member of the particular church or school, or a resident of the particular neighborhood.

At the high-school level clubs become more numerous, but their memberships are still by and large based on talent and interest, and are therefore not primarily exclusive in nature. In some high schools exclusive sororities and fraternities have appeared, but in many places such exclusive groupings are banned. It is in the colleges and universities that America has outdone all the educational institutions of the world, in the multiplicity of its exclusive sororities and fraternities. In most of them membership is expressly exclusive, based on considerations of race, ethnic origin, religion, and economic status, and, when other things are more or less equal, personal beauty or charm, which will at least compensate for economic inferiority. On a large number of American campuses of higher learning, these exclusive clubs dominate the social and political life of the student body. This fact is no secret; it is ascertainable by asking an average student on an average campus. The pattern varies somewhat from region to region. For example, in some exclusive schools of the East, there is less pressure for exclusion by sororities and fraternities than in most sections of the Middle West. Membership in these exclusive groups means success, and a hierarchy among these exclusive groups will differentiate the greater successes from the lesser ones.

Some religious, racial, and ethnic minorities who are barred from this race for success and belonging respond to their exclusion by forming hierarchic and exclusive clubs of their own.

What we see on the campuses is but a small fraction of what we see in the American society at large. Of the role of club life in America, I cannot do better than quote W. Lloyd Warner.

> Secret societies, fraternities, and civic organizations have been prominent and important features of American life from the very beginnings of the Republic. These voluntary associations permeate every aspect of the society. Whether for trivial and ludicrous or serious and important purposes, Americans use associations for almost every conceivable activity. Sinclair Lewis' middle-class Babbitt joins and is active in associations with the same zest and faith as John Marquand's "Boston Brahmins." When "something needs to be done" or "a serious problem must be solved" in the United States, private citizens usually band together in a new association or use one already available. They do this with the same ease and lack of thought as primitive peoples might when acting within the traditions of an ancient folkway. The association is the perfect social instrument for those Americans who wish to be private citizens and free individuals and yet, at the same time, public men who are socially bound in their daily lives.[11]

We do not necessarily agree that all or even most of these associations are formed and joined when "something needs to be done" or when "a serious problem must be solved" or that "the association is the perfect social instrument for those Americans who wish to be private citizens and free individuals and yet, at the same time, public men who are socially bound in their daily lives." Our analysis so far shows that Americans form and join associations for solving specific problems or as an expression of interest in public affairs as much as for the satisfaction of their basic needs for sociability, security, and status. We shall see presently that even Warner's own evidence from Yankee City seems to give weight to this conclusion. In connection with a research project at the Center for the Study of Leisure at the University of Chicago, 183 graduating seniors of the class of 1955 (including graduates of Harvard, Princeton, Notre Dame, Williams, Dartmouth, Georgia Tech, the Universities of Houston, Michigan, and Wisconsin) were asked the question as to what they expected their life to be in fifteen years, i.e., 1970.

David Riesman reports that one Princeton senior was so very explicit about his expectations that he (Riesman) first thought the interviewee must have been pulling the interviewer's leg. However, after reading all the interview material Riesman came to the conclusion that what this Princeton senior said only highlighted a norm. This was a senior going into law, and he declared:

I'll belong to all the associations you can think of—Elks, V.F.W.'s, Boy Scouts and Boys' Clubs, Y.M.C.A., American Legion, etc. It will keep me away from home a lot. But my wife (a purely hypothetical wife, remember) won't mind. She'll be vivacious and easy with people. And she will belong to everything in sight too—especially the League of Women Voters. I won't marry her until I'm twenty-eight, and so when I'm thirty-six we will have only two of the four children I hope for eventually. We'll be living in an upper-middle class home costing about $20,000 by then, in a suburban fringe. . . . We'll have two Fords or Chevies when I'm thirty-six, so we can both keep up the busy schedule we'll have. But in addition to this public social life, we'll have private friends who don't even live around Toledo—friends with whom we can be completely natural and relaxed. That's where Princeton friends will be very important.[12]

This senior's expectations on family size, cars and house, need not detain us here, but his craze for clubs accords truly well with our hypothesis. Having been trained to be independent from the family and self-reliant *vis-à-vis* the world, the individual attempts to satisfy his psychosocial needs, best expressed in the American term *success*, by joining clubs. If the individual needs associations in college, his need for them becomes much greater at the threshold of his entrance into society. This is why the Princeton senior's compulsion for joining appears promiscuous at this time. Not yet certain of the path of personal advancement, the young man wants simply to make sure that all paths will be open to him when he is ready.

We must now examine to what extent associational life engages the time and energy of Americans. Here we rely heavily on the work of Lloyd Warner and his associates. In Yankee City, a community of only 17,000 persons, Warner and his associates found somewhat over 800 associations. Warner states that not all of these associations existed simultaneously, that some were formed during the period of their investigation, and others disappeared, and that many associations have a very ephemeral life, since some of them are designed for a specific purpose and therefore have a very short existence.[13]

Narrowing their scope, Warner and his associates studied, learned the membership, and observed the activities of 357 associations. If we take the figure of 800, the average associational membership is 21; if we take the lesser figure of 357, the average membership is 48. The specific number of individuals figuring in the average is not as important as the fact of the proliferation of clubs, but it is interesting. The picture of Yankee City tallies well with that of the Middletown studies of the Lynds. In 1890, Middletown had roughly 92 clubs, or one for every 125 people. But in 1924, the Lynds found 458 active clubs, or one for every 80 people.[14] When the Lynds revisited Middletown ten years later, they unfortunately did not secure the exact number of clubs in the community, but they offered the following comment from which we can surmise that the number of clubs must have substantially increased:

> As one passes from these unorganized ways of spending leisure—gardening in one's back yard, going to the movies, listening to the radio, driving about in one's car, or reading, playing bridge, or drinking—nothing about the organized life of Middletown at play strikes the returning investigator more forcibly than the hardy persistence of the city's club life. Asked about any changes in local club life, a veteran Middletown woman exclaimed, "Goodness! we have more than ever."[15] *

The town of Jonesville studied by Warner and associates tops them all. In the 1940's it had one club for every twelve individuals if all clubs were included and one club for every sixteen individuals if only adult clubs were included.[16]

What do members of these clubs do? Lloyd Warner and associates systematically studied the activities of Yankee City associations for a period of two years. They have records of 5,800 events or activities. The records include everything, from the most sacred to the most profane, and "from the most reasonable and sensible behavior to the ultimate in triviality and nonsense." Warner states that much, if not all, of the behavior in these events is directly or indirectly, consciously or unconsciously, symbolic, since what they say and do in a given activity usually stands for something else. But separating those activities which are consciously used by the association for ritualistic purposes (of which there are four types), Warner classifies the other activities into fifteen categories. In all, the ritual or purely symbolic type of behavior composes about one-fifth of the activities of the association in Yankee City, and is by far the most important of all the activities. Following the ritualistic group of activities closely, there are, in order of importance, drama and talent exhibitions (14.28%), speeches (12.83%), organization (9.78%), eating (8.60%), and fund-raising (8.60%). The remaining categories, which occupy 27% of the totals, are gifts, sedentary games, hospitality, contests, athletic games, crafts and skills, socials, outings, teaching and learning, and social dancing. From this summary account, it is obvious that the overwhelming majority of the clubs are formed and joined for purposes other than the solution of specific problems.

That the club activities in America exist primarily for the purpose of belonging and success-seeking is also evident from other facts. In Yankee City, club affiliation is quantitatively linked with class. According to Warner:

---

* It should be noted, however, that the clubs referred to in Warner's and Lynds' studies do not include the large professional associations of national or regional scale such as the American Medical Association and the American Association for the Advancement of Science, various pressure groups in Washington, D.C., and state capitals, and churches.

Approximately 72 per cent of the people in the upper classes belong to associations, 64 per cent of the upper-middle class, and only 49 per cent of the lower-middle class. The percentages continue to drop as one moves down the class levels, for only 39 per cent of the upper-lower and 22 per cent of the lower-lower class are members of associations. The percentages for the two lower classes are somewhat misleading, since they are heavily weighted with members of ethnic groups who belong to ethnic associations. The lower-class old American is not a joiner. More often it is the members of the classes above the Common Man Level, particularly the upper-upper old families, who are members of associations. They are the joiners. Associations aid them to control the social life of the community.[17]

In both volumes on Middletown, the Lynds discuss club life in connection with the use of leisure. From the contexts of their discussions, it would seem that they regard the increase in the number of clubs as being attributable to an increase of leisure in the decade which separated their two studies. Comparing the Lynds' discussions with Warner's facts just presented, one might interpret the class differences in associational activity in Yankee City as being due simply to the fact that the upper classes have more leisure, while the lower classes have less of it. In the light of our hypothesis and of the known facts, such an interpretation is unjustified. In the first place, it is a well-known fact that membership in the right clubs is an established method of attaining and maintaining social prestige in any urban or suburban area of the United States. In the second place, not only do Warner and associates point out that the upper classes are joiners because "associations aid them to control the social life of the community," but they also provide us with the following episode to demonstrate "how fund raising functions and how money conspicuously spent for worthy causes can advance the social aspirations of those who spend it," "how individual social mobility is related to joining a club and how money as such must be translated into behavior in an association which meets the approval of the class above in order to advance a mobile man":

This . . . is supposed to be a true story of what happened to a Mr. John Smith, a newly rich man in a far western community. He wanted to get into a particular social club of some distinction and significance in the city. By indirection he let it be known, and was told by his friends in the club they had submitted his name to the membership committee.

Mr. Abner Grey, one of the leading members of the club and active on its membership committee, was a warm supporter of an important philanthropy in this city. It was brought to his attention that Mr. Smith, rather than contributing the large donation that had been expected of him, had given only a nominal sum to the charity.

When Mr. Smith heard nothing more about his application, he again approached one of the board members. After much evasion he was told that Mr. Grey was the most influential man on the board and he would be wise to see that gentleman. After trying several times to make an appointment with Mr. Grey, he finally burst into Grey's offices unannounced.

"Why the hell, Abner, am I being kept out of the X club?"

Mr. Grey politely evaded the question. He asked Mr. Smith to be seated. He inquired after Mr. Smith's health, about the health of his wife, and inquired about other matters of simple convention.

Finally, Mr. Smith said, "Ab, why the hell am I being kept out of your club?"

"But John, you're not. Everyone in the X club thinks you're a fine fellow."

"Well, what's wrong?"

"Well, John, we don't think you've got the *kind* of money necessary for being a good member of the X club. We don't think you'd be happy in the X club."

"Like hell I haven't. I could buy and sell a half-dozen of some of your board members."

"I know that, John, but that isn't what I said. I did not say the amount of money, I said the kind of money."

"What do you mean?"

"Well, John, my co-workers on the charity drive tell me you only gave a few dollars to our campaign, and we had you down for a few thousand."

For a moment Mr. Smith was silent. Then he grinned. So did Mr. Grey. Smith took out his fountain pen and checkbook. "How much?"

At the next meeting of the X club Mr. Smith was unanimously elected to its membership.

Mr. Smith translated his money into philanthropy acceptable to the dominant group, he received their sponsorship, and finally became a participant in the club. The "right" kind of house, the "right" neighborhood, the "right" furniture, the proper behavior—all are symbols that can ultimately be translated into social acceptance by those who have sufficient money to aspire to higher levels than they presently enjoy.[18]

THE DYNAMICS OF THE AMERICAN SOCIETY

We are now in a position to pursue still further the dynamics of the American society based on the ideas of immutability of the individual and equality among men, the principle of contract, and the fulfillment of the need for definite affiliation in free associations or clubs. We noted in the last chapter that in the Hindu situation reward is unequal to obligation while in the Chinese situation reward tends to be equivalent to obligation in a roundabout manner and in the course of time without, however, explicit statements in any particular relationship and at any particular time as to who owes how much to whom. In the American system reward is scrupulously equivalent to obligation; that is to say, the individual cannot ask anyone to do anything that he cannot do himself or pay for in a manner that the other person will regard as equitable (G in Diagram IV). In fact the equivalence in quantity and quality between reward and obligation is usually expressly stated before the entrance of all parties into the relationship. If we compare the reward-obligation equivalence in the Chinese system with gift-making we must compare the relationship between reward and obligation in the American system as a commercial transaction—that is, buying and selling. The need for definite affiliation, the functional and calculated contract principle, and the scrupulous equivalence between reward and obligation combine to foster the fear of inferiority. Since membership in clubs is not automatic and is dependent upon individual efforts, there will be the fear of nonaffiliation on the part of those who have failed to make such membership. Furthermore even for those who have achieved some sort of affiliation in clubs, there will still be room for the anxiety that they have not made the kind of affiliation that will afford them the higher status that others enjoy. Finally, since the contract principle emphasizes the equivalence between reward and obligation, there will be those who are affiliated but who fear that they are being made a sucker of, for the hidden details may have caused them to receive less reward for their obligation than they thought was coming their way.

We noted in the last chapter that ambition characterizes some members of every society. We further noted that the ambitious individuals in every society tend to be actively oriented toward status by trying to get a larger share than others of whatever it is that the society most values. In the Chinese system the ambitious individuals tend to try to upset the reward-obligation equivalence by working toward a situation in which their obligation is larger than their reward. The more people who stand in a dependent relationship to them, the higher their status. In the Hindu situation the ambitious individuals tend to be active in the securing of ritual purity, or any other symbols or substance, which will raise their place according to dharma or the all-embracing supernatural design. In the American society the ambitious individuals will compete to get bigger rewards for lesser efforts than their fellow men (H in Diagram IV). This is success in popular American terms. The bigger the rewards one can command, the larger the number of people he is able to control and influence, the more magnificent his success.

However, while the status quest of the ambitious Chinese tends to be limited by the kinship principle, and that of the ambitious Hindus tends to be limited by the hierarchical principle, the ambitious Americans under the contract principle tend to be confined by no ultimate boundary. That is to say, the ambition of the Chinese and of the Hindu may be as great as that of the American, but the effective human fields in which they can act out their ambition are far smaller than that available to the American. From the Chinese point of view all statuses must refer ultimately to the family and clan. One cannot rise without it and one must return to it after one has arrived. The road to advancement is straight and narrow and, though no one is forever barred from advancement, the differences at any given point of time between those who can reach for high status and those who cannot are obvious and great. Ambition tends to remain the prerogative of the relatively few while the vast majority of others tends to feel the necessity of keeping to one's place and lot. From the Hindu point of view all statuses are rooted ultimately in the Atma, for all statuses are ritually based. The only road to the highest status is the slow process of dharma or sacred law. Effective interaction and combination between people of high and low status are forbidden, curtailed, or severely regulated according to rules of ritual purity. It is true that the hierarchic principle tends to propel a much larger number of Hindus than Chinese to be dissatisfied with the status quo, but dissatisfied and ambitious individuals seek widened circles of dependence along the same traditionally accepted lines. In the American system the ambitious individual is not tied down to his kinship group and not prevented from entering into any area of activity which he calculates will yield status. Furthermore, with self-reliance, equality, and the ultimate ideal of complete personal freedom, each individual tends to look forward to his personal empire and consequently the number of individuals likely to be ambitious in the American system is bound to be enormously larger than in the other two systems. In fact, competitive efforts in the American system seem to be nearly universal.

Competitive efforts on the part of ambitious individuals tend to increase, or at least aggravate, the fear of inferiority on the part of other members in every society. The more widespread is ambition, the more widespread will be the fear of inferiority. These lead to an unceasing struggle in and among clubs in America for more supremacy or at least for less inferiority. Within each club this struggle takes the form of a constant tendency to fission into more exclusive, or at any rate different, clubs (K and M_1 in Diagram IV). Being a member of a club may satisfy the individual's need for status for the time being. But the self-reliant man demands that he be a greater success than his fellow club members. The dynamic expression of a solution to this conflict is the fact that, in every major association, however exclusive it is, there tend to form within it smaller clubs, often not expressly publicized but invariably understood by all concerned, which are more exclusive than the already exclusive larger entity. We have already referred to Warner's observation that the upper classes are great joiners because "associations aid them to control the social life of the community." We may now observe that the more ambitious climbers within any club are great initiators of exclusive cliques because such exclusive cliques aid them to control the social life of the association. In time the exclusive cliques will break out of the mother group and form new clubs which will be more exclusive than the mother group. This feeds the fear of rejection on the part of those already affiliated, resulting in tensions, anxieties, and greater determination on their part to redouble their efforts in defending their self-respect by mobility of some sort. In America social mobility has taken typically two directions. Vertical mobility is the goal most desired by every individual. But if vertical mobility is out of reach for the time being, then horizontal mobility either by the formation of a parallel club or moving into another club or locality is at least a temporary palliative.*

We have just noted that in the American system competition tends to be universal since the ambition of the few is likely to be generalized among all. We must now turn to the fact that universalized competitive efforts also tend to make competition more severe and, consequently, the fear of inferiority in the form of nonaffiliation, low satisfaction of social needs, and rejection tends also to become more intense than in other societies. These are at the root of conformity (J in Diagram IV).

Much ink has been spilt over the subject of conformity in America. Superficially conformity is contradictory to self-reliance. David Riesman tries to explain this contradiction in terms of change of national character. According to Riesman, Americans inherited from their European forefathers the inner-directed orientation, which propels the individual to determine upon an unyielding drive toward personal goals; in the inner-directed way, the society is characterized by personal mobility, expansion in production, exploration, colonization, and imperialism. This type of person, Riesman claims, began to emerge in Europe during and after the Middle Ages and has been predominant in Western society since the Renaissance and Reformation. Riesman thinks that the inner-directed orientation of life has undergone very serious changes in America. These changes point toward an other-directed orientation. Compared with the inner-directed individual, the other-directed man is "shallower, freer with his money, friendlier, more uncertain of himself and his value, more demanding of approval." The individual bred in this way of life is capable of a "superficial intimacy with and response to anyone." This characteristic emphasis on conformity is the basic element determining the character type emerging in the larger American cities. The type is most noticeable at this time among "the upper-middle class," "the young," the "bureaucrats," and "the salaried employees in business."[19] What is referred to by Riesman has been observed by other students.[20] William H. Whyte, Jr., in The Organization Man,[21] has since related conformity to the pernicious effect of Organization. William J. Lederer laments the fact that Americans have become a nation of sheep. On the other hand the pendulum seems to have swung back. More recently Stanley Milgram, a social psychologist, after some experiments comparing conformity among Nor-

* The recent (1961) suggestion by former President Herbert Hoover that the United States attempt a separate world organization outside the United Nations and away from the Communist countries is a projection of this psychology into the international sphere.

wegians and the French, observes that conformity is not exclusively a U.S. phenomenon.[22]

Riesman errs because he places his classification in time, via demography, when in fact he should have made a monochronic study. What has actually happened is that the American orientation remains one of self-reliance; as self-reliance gains momentum, however, it forces the individual to be even more conformistic than if he was not oriented toward self-reliance in the first place. According to our analysis conformity is the extremely self-reliant man's defense against the fear of inferiority. In fact, we can truly say that, other things being equal, the more a culture stresses self-reliance, the more it will generate the fear of inferiority on the part of the individual, and the more it will compel him toward conformity.

Those who show that conformity is also present in Norway and France or other societies do not lead us far either. It is obvious that a degree of conformity is essential for every organized society. Furthermore, apart from long-standing habits built in every individual since childhood, the fear of inferiority and competitive efforts of ambitious individuals will intensify conformity in every society. But what distinguishes America in this regard is not conformity as such but, on the one hand, the severity of it in spite of the stress on individual freedom* and, on the other, the *protest* against it.

In the Chinese and Hindu situations the fear of the individual of inferiority is alleviated by the basic psychological factor of dependence (A in Diagrams II and III). With its aid the individual need have no qualms about seeking shelter behind existing human walls. In the American situation not only is the fear of inferiority greater because ambition is more generalized among the population, but the individual must largely rely upon himself to deal with the pressures which threaten him. He must, if he can, try to find walls that he himself can construct in defense against his fear of inferiority. Having no handy human walls for protection means that the American's task in achieving the satisfaction of his social needs is harder than that of the Chinese and Hindu. At the same time it also means that the American is freer from many of the restraints which shackle his counterparts in the other two societies. In our schematic analysis the former expresses itself in intensified conformity (L in Diagram IV) and the latter in resentment against conformity (O in Diagram IV).

The general aspects of conformity, such as "keeping up with the Joneses,"

---

* In a previous connection we discussed conformity among teenagers and college students in America. On the adult level one obvious illustration of this is found in the pattern of residence. It is common in China and India to find houses of the rich situated side by side with abodes of much humbler citizens and even shacks, whereas in the United States the residential pattern tends to be astonishingly segregated among the whites according to income and among all groups according to income, race, and religion.

and acceptance of views according to the dictates of whatever group or groups to which one belongs or hopes to belong, need no elaboration. What is not usually seen is the psychological connection between intensified conformity and prejudice as well as extreme bigotry. Generalized competition raises everyone's sights so that no one's walls are permanent. In his fear of inferiority the self-reliant man envies those who have climbed above him and dreads the encroachment of those struggling below him. The greater the envy of those above, the more serious is his apprehension of encroachment from below. These sources of perpetual insecurity generate not only the passion for conformity but also the impulse for persecution. The greater the desire to conform to those "who belong," the more severe the tendency to persecute those who do not. In fact the latter is often a direct result of the former, for those who are not sure of their position often are inclined to outdo others as insurance against rejection.

Our failure to recognize the intimate connection between conformity and prejudice is partly due to our failure to differentiate what I designated elsewhere as violent acts of prejudice, active nonviolent acts of prejudice, and passive nonviolent acts of prejudice.[23] A majority of Americans is not involved in any act of violence against Negroes or bombing of synagogues (in fact, they would be horrified by the thought of it), and does not even have any intention of being discriminatory toward Negroes or other minority groups (in fact, they can honestly deny such intentions). Nevertheless they *consciously* avoid having social relations with Negroes and scrupulously maintain the "right" views on subjects involving education, residence, employment, marriage, etc., where race and religion are concerned because they fear rejection by their peers and hence inferiority. The self-reliant man's best defense against the fear of inferiority is to move up. If he cannot move up, at least he must maintain the position he has already attained. The fastest way to lose his place is to entertain attitudes unpopular among his peers or associate with people his peers regard as inferior or unacceptable. These passive, nonviolent acts of prejudice resulting from fear of inferiority, though superficially having nothing to do with violent acts of prejudice, are in fact linked with them through competition which fosters intensified conformity (L in Diagram IV). If "keeping up with the Joneses" is an expression of conformity, "out-doing the Joneses" is an expression of intensified conformity. Similarly if passive nonviolent acts of prejudice are a matter of conformity, active nonviolent acts of prejudice are more of an intensified sort of conformity. In other words competition, which propels the individual to increase his efforts in getting desired objectives will, in the present instance, simply lead him to expand and strengthen those activities and attitudes which support conformity. For the competitive individual intensified conformity simply becomes a means for higher status. He will either be more competitive as a means of greater conformity or more conforming as a matter of adding to his competitive efforts.

Intensified conformity can be achieved by fair means (L_1 in Diagram IV) or by unfair means (L_2 in Diagram IV). What are some of the fair means of intensifying conformity? If "bigness" is the thing to achieve, merger or continued enlargement of membership is one of these means. If "image" is a popular asset for success, organizational mechanisms to ensure that no other considerations interfere with it are another one of these means. Playing up the religious angle, the underdog angle, the sex angle, or giving people anything they want to have and hear are all fair means to intensified conformity for greater success. Applying the same criteria to the area of prejudice, intensified conformity easily leads the individual from passive nonviolent acts to active nonviolent acts. "If we hire Negroes we will lose friends and customers" is an expression of prejudice of a passive nonviolent nature. When the competitive manager of a company decides to make sure that this never happens by making it a matter of policy, the same expression of prejudice has become actively nonviolent in nature.

Unfair means of intensifying conformity are found in many situations: when leaders or would-be leaders of rival unions resort to murder and mayhem against each other, when giant corporations enter into price-fixing arrangements among themselves to crowd out smaller concerns, when manufacturers and contractors engage in fraudulent means to spiral profits, or when hate groups use smear or bodily harm as weapons to intimidate those who choose to disagree with or oppose them. These means range from the obviously violent to the infinitely subtle; but they generally aim at outright or speedy elimination of competition, or at least at making their job of meeting competition easier, rather than winning battles in competition, although the latter can lead to the former.

On the surface fair and unfair means of intensifying conformity seem totally different from each other. In fact they often overlap. Obviously reputable firms and organizations will not hire hoodlums to destroy the businesses or lives of rival groups. But the recent revelations and indictments involving some of the biggest electrical and other firms of the country indicate that the final lines between these two types of means in competition are indeed difficult to ascertain. Price-fixing and influence-purchasing must be on the conscience of the officials of many big organizations. The Bernard Goldfine case under the Eisenhower administration and the Billy Sol Estes case under the Kennedy administration are but outer symptoms of conditions which have much wider and deeper currency. Whatever the means, the end results are the same. They lead to bigger and more efficient organizations or clubs (M_2 and M_3 in Diagram IV) which tend to make newer organizations and smaller clubs harder to establish and harder to sustain.

We must now turn our attention to the other development connected with conformity in the American system, namely resentment against conformity (O in Diagram IV). We noted earlier how observers who decry conformity in American society as well as those who tell us that conformity is not peculiar to American society fail especially to appreciate the significance of active resentment against conformity in American society. Here the American system contrasts sharply with the other two systems. In the Chinese situation there has never been any significant protest against conformity. Conformity in that system simply strengthens the existing kinship structure from family to clan. In the Hindu system conformity is followed by either the overwhelming strengthening of the existing grouping or by a continuous fission of it without any significant change in the caste framework. Resentment against conformity is as characteristic of the American system as it is unrepresentative of the other two. American conformity is fundamentally different from Chinese or Hindu acquiescence to tradition. The Chinese or Hindu who follows tradition has been taught from childhood that this is what he should do. He does so without a sense of inner conflict. The American who is obliged to conform has been brought up to be the master of his own destiny. He has been brought up in a social atmosphere and an educational system which encourages him to find himself. With such a background, he cannot but resent conformity or at least feel guilty about it at some point or other. In more ways than one he is likely to feel that conformity has dented his self-respect. Furthermore his resentment against conformity has the overwhelming support of the American ideal, namely, complete freedom of the individual (D in Diagram IV), which is expressed in almost every generation in the writings and utterances of those who extol rugged individualism. This is why Whyte, after dissecting the deleterious effects of Organization on the individual, offers no more than the advice that he should fight it. What Whyte has done here is no more than reiterate the age-old American ideal. But this American resentment against conformity in fact leads to two types of actions, both of which are of the greatest importance to the development of the American society and culture. On the one hand it leads to reformatory and revolutionary movements; on the other hand it leads to individual escapes or cathexes (O_1 and O_2 in Diagram IV).

We saw before that, although there were reformatory movements in the Indian system, they tended to end up as parts of the same unchangeable basic social fabric. In the Chinese system such reformatory movements were extremely rare. Before contact with the West in neither India nor China was there any true revolution. Truly revolutionary movements only occurred in the West.* The founding of the United States of America was based on a political revolution. With the success of the political revolution came tremendous social and economic changes. The establishment of Protestantism was based on a religious revolution. With the establishment of the first Protestant church came a multitude of other denominations, many of which are native to the New World.

The reformatory and revolutionary way of thinking is as central to the American way of life as it is contrary to the Chinese and even Hindu way of life. On the higher level it expresses itself as creativity. This concept is so glorified in American society that being considered creative is the highest form of praise while being called noncreative is the worst kind of condemnation. More generally it expresses itself as change. Change itself becomes good. It is on this basis that manufactured products have to change from year to year whether or not there is improvement, that the current year's edition of a book is better than the last year's, and the younger generation is somehow more efficacious and desirable than the older generation.†

We have in the United States of America a society which is truly exuberant with internal impetuses for change, not only in mores, fashions, and material standards of living, but also in fundamental institutions such as the family, the school, the church, the law and its operation, and the economy. This struggle for change inevitably threatens those whose best interests lie in the status quo. It tends also to arouse others who were once revolutionary in outlook but who have become so identified with their once-revolutionary position that they are fearful of any change. Finally those who desire change are also divided as to the kind of change they deem will save the country or mankind as a whole. Some outstanding expressions of these forces spread over a wide continuum (represented in Diagram IV as O_{1a}, O_{1b}, O_{1c}, O_{1d}, and O_{1e}). At both ends of the continuum are action groups which sometimes resort to violence, while in the center are action groups which deliberately rely on peaceful means such as propaganda, pressure, education, and so on. The objectives of these groups range from those aimed at restoring the conditions of a bygone area or some imagined greatness (O_{1a} in Diagram IV) to those desirous of drastic and basic or at least far-reaching changes in the status quo (O_{1e} in Diagram IV). Examples of the former extreme are the Ku Klux Klan, White Citizens' Council, and the American

* In popular thought, reform is more acceptable than revolution because it is less fearful. But in fact their differences are only a matter of degree. Reform is a milder change than revolution but both share the characteristic of wanting to replace that which has been in existence with something that is totally new, whether this replacement is to occur in social, economic, religious, or political areas of life.

† This desire for change is differentiated from the fear of an unfavorable attitude toward deviation. Changes which are desirable are regarded as acts of creativity while changes which are undesirable are relegated to acts of deviation.

Nazi Party, while those of the latter extreme are the Communist Party and other such radical groups. Closer to the center are the D.A.R., Veterans of Foreign Wars, and the American Legion (O_{1b} in Diagram IV) on one side, which generally desire the maintenance of the status quo, and the Civil Liberties Union, N.A.A.C.P., and the League of Women Voters (O_{1d} in Diagram IV) on the other side, which as a rule work for some graduated changes from the status quo. In the center are various missionary groups such as Salvation Army, W.C.T.U., and the Moral Rearmament Movement (O_{1c} in Diagram IV), which aim generally at individual conversion rather than social change.*

The other main expression of American resentment against conformity—namely, individual escapes or cathexes—can be entirely personal matters such as a house in the woods or hobbies like butterfly collecting, or organized group affairs such as dance or art clubs, bird watchers or girl watchers societies, Zen Buddhist gatherings, or spirit writing associations. The list is enormously long and anyone can think of a dozen or more after a moment's reflection.

It should be made clear at once that, in referring to these and other activities as "escapes" or "cathexes" we do not mean that all or most individuals who are involved in them consciously employ them as such and have, therefore, no other interest in what they are doing. On the contrary, many of what I designate as individual escapes or cathexes are reformist (such as antivivisection and prevention of cruelty to animals) or altruistic endeavors (such as many church and other related charities). Furthermore, many of these activities have obvious physical benefits to the individual (such as Vic Tanny's gyms and dance studios). What is suggested here is that, whatever other meanings these and other activities have for the individuals involved, most of them also serve, consciously or unconsciously, the function of psychological escape.

Three reasons seem to support this view. First, the same factors that encourage widespread ambition in American society are likely to generate more rebellion against conformity than can readily be channeled into reform and revolutionary movements. Second, avenues of individual cathexes have flowered in America to an extent unknown in China or India. Individual cathexes are few in the Hindu system, for the devotees of individual cathexes look for the same ultimate objective for salvation. The American cathexes are far greater in number because the devotees of them tend consciously to seek objectives that are different. Third, Hindu devotees of individual

* Religious denominations in modern times as a whole belong to the category at the center of this scheme (O_{1e}), though some churches or sects are more oriented toward social reforms than others. The examples used here are racial, religious, or political in nature but the forces described may find expression in numerous other avenues of human endeavor including the economic and the charitable.

cathexes concern themselves mostly with their place on the spiritual hierarchy, while American devotees concern themselves with personal happiness. Many clinicians and psychologists frankly speak of the therapeutic value of many of these activities.

As already noted, some individual cathexes find their way into groups. Not only do some who share the same cathexis tend to come together for sociability or security but others will consciously promote the popularity of certain forms of cathexes as a means of raising or achieving status. In this connection Hindus of the same interest are most likely to seek dependence upon a man who has obtained "powers" through skill, knowledge of scriptures, pilgrimage, or sadhuism. This man may become the founder of a new sect, which in time will turn into a new caste in the old hierarchy. Americans of the same interest are more likely than the Hindu to organize themselves into clubs. The self-reliant man likes to do it himself, or to try his hand at leading others, without waiting for a word or guidance from some holy man or man with special "powers." Individual cathexes will, therefore, be productive of a far larger number of clubs in the American system than castes in the Hindu system. Add to these the interest or hobby groups (from fan clubs devoted to comic strip characters to philatelists' societies) which entrepreneurs of many hues promote and help to materialize, we can then expect even more American clubs built on individual cathexes (M_5 in Diagram IV).

Both the reform and revolutionary movements and the individual escapes or cathexes lead to the fission of existing groupings or more often the formation of new ones. In the Hindu situation, the fission and formation of new groupings tend to proceed relatively slowly; in the American, fission and formation of such groupings tend to occur more swiftly. Furthermore, while the fissioned and newly formed castes in the Hindu situation have no other destination than the same structural fold, the fissioned and newly formed American clubs tend to have irreconcilable objectives and therefore will either threaten each other or in time drift farther and farther away from each other. The latter is perfectly in line with a tendency we have already mentioned as typical of the self-reliant man: dichotomization of the world into extremes based on the immutable distinction between self (and that with which the self is identified) and nonself (and that in which the self has no investment).

Not all the groupings which develop in the American system as a result of these processes are, of course, so clearly separable under the different categories presented in this analysis. Clubs founded on individual escapes M_5 in Diagram IV) are often exploited as big businesses (M_2 in Diagram IV). Clubs with reformatory or revolutionary objectives (M_4 in Diagram IV) can become a haven for many who seek individual escapes

(M_5 in Diagram IV). The line between fair means (M_2 in Diagram IV) in competition and unfair means (M_3 in Diagram IV) is sometimes blurred. Many competitive activities are carried on by individual efforts and remain outside any club. This applies not only to individual cathexes (M_5 in Diagram IV) but also may apply to reformist as well as conforming tendencies. Finally, even many clubs founded on the central purpose of pure intellectual exchange and stimulation among their members (such as learned societies) cannot escape some of the characteristics examined here: competition, intensified conformity (bigness through enlargement of membership, expansion of influence over government and public through propaganda, and so on), reformist movements which aim at changes from the status quo or return to the past, and fission or duplication in organization.

In contrast to the two Asian societies, the dynamism of the American society is particularly aided by its ideal of complete freedom of the individual. The Chinese ideal of complete harmony among men supports the forces of conformity and nothing else. The Hindu ideal of complete union with the Ultimate Reality supports both the forces of complete conformity and of resentment against conformity. The American ideal of the freedom of the individual supports resentment against conformity but does not support conformity. Through this resentment the American social organization increases its internal complexity and its dynamic, expansive power not only because of competition, conformity, and anticonformity on the group level, but also because of differences in conscience, disagreements, and quarrels, or simply the individual's desire to go into business for himself. This desire to be different and to be one's own boss is even operative among those ambitious individuals who intensify conformity as a means of competition. Even while they are conforming to the hilt they often have to pay lip service to the fight against conformity and to the need of being rugged individualists. The American society is one where orthodoxy is constantly being affirmed and constantly being challenged, where new orthodoxy is constantly being formed and constantly being challenged.

CLAN, CASTE, AND CLUB

In our analysis clan, caste, and club are each taken as the outward manifestation of a basic formula in which the individual finds his *modus vivendi* among his social relations, his cultural ideal, and his personal needs. The predominantly situation-centered Chinese family fosters in the individual a centripetal outlook. The basic expression of this outlook in interpersonal relations is mutual dependence. This outlook enables the Chinese individual to satisfy his need for sociability, security, and status with little difficulty in the framework of the cohesive Chinese clan and the Chinese ideal of complete harmony among men. Clan is but an extension of the family. Both are the same expression of the kinship principle. Membership in the clan is automatic and permanent. There is therefore little incentive for the individual to disengage himself from his permanent moorings in search of entanglements in the wider society and world. Between the Chinese Imperial Government and the clan there was a scarcity of intermediate groupings that were not based on territory or occupation. For two milleniums the only two well-known types of nonoccupational and nonterritorial association in this vaste middle region were "societies for saving papers with written characters on" and "societies for giving away free coffins." Even these and the craft guilds were all localized. The result is a remarkably tenacious but static society and culture. Self-advancement and advancement of one's family and clan tended to be identified with each other, for such advancement could only be achieved outside the kinship framework or without reference to it.

The predominantly supernatural-centered Hindu family fosters in the individual a centrifugal outlook. The basic expression of this outlook as applied to interpersonal relations is unilateral dependence. This centrifugal outlook tends to propel the Hindu individual away from his moorings in his family and forces him to venture into the unknown. Hence clan is hard to develop and solidify. Yet the Hindu, like all human beings, needs close psychosocial ties with fellow human beings for sociability, security, and status. Caste and subcaste, with their cohesive and yet fissiparous characteristics, are at once the Indian solution to this contradiction and an expression of it. Everywhere in India, caste is primarily a localized group in which the individual can interact with his fellow human beings and satisfy his social needs. However, underlying Hindu caste is the principle of hierarchy. This principle governs not only intercaste relations in India but all human relations, for its essence is unilateral dependence. The principle of hierarchy and the psychology of unilateral dependence are conducive to discontent with the status quo among the entire spectrum of the society. At the lower levels this discontent expresses itself when the illiterate common people rely upon a multiplicity of rituals for supernatural favors of every variety. At the higher levels it expresses itself when the learned pandits resort to concentration and other forms of mysticism or knowledge of the sacred books for approaching the Atma. Among both the high and the low the dependence upon holy men is widespread. Hierarchy means that man at every level is concerned with his relative position on a ladder, that there is the possibility of rise as well as fall. Unilateral dependence means that man at every level can ask for favors and that he does not have to concern himself with returning them. The ideal of union with the Ultimate Reality sets the final goal so high that man at every level (including the highest) is still led to look to something higher. The fact that man's dealing with the supernatural depends upon no measurable criteria and leads to no concrete results except in the fleeting experiences of individual mystics or in rare superhuman feats and personal miracles enables man at every level eternally to argue, to wonder, to dispute, and to hope.

The Hindu's search for the "great beyond," therefore, provides him with a widespread internal impetus for change. Yet since this search is not a means for individual independence but for *reliance* upon the unknown, this impetus for change can hardly enable the individual to break away from his tradition. Lacking any supernatural criteria for achievement, all the various concrete measures of greatness from erudition in ancient texts, personal miracles, individual abstentions, even to life as *samnyasi* and *samadhi* inevitably bring him back and confine him to the theory if not the reality of caste.

The result is a society and a culture remarkably dynamic in appearance but which in the long run undergoes little real change. Castes and subcastes will divide and redivide. Schisms and protestant movements will always mark the religious scene. But none of them will be a decisive and permanent break with the traditional context and framework. Those who have led the fissiparous movements will at some later date desire to come back. The mother body which has suffered from this defection will at some later date be equally happy to effect a compromise with the returned prodigal sons. Yet the resulting accommodation is never one of general unification into one group, with no internal lines of demarcation, but invariably one of a hierarchic structure with higher and lower groups on the same totem pole. Self-advancement is usually tied to advancement of one's caste or subcaste, but since caste distinction is based on arbitrary foundations such as marital practices or the privilege of wearing red slippers or facial ornaments, there is no limit to the number of caste groups into which the Hindu society can be divided.

The individual-centered American family fosters in the individual an intense concern with the self. In one respect it is similar to that of the Hindus. The American and Hindu outlooks are both centrifugal and therefore divisive and dynamic as contrasted to the Chinese outlook, which is centripetal and therefore inclusive and static. The American family orientation is, however, drastically different from its two Asian counterparts in that it glorifies self-reliance.* In neither the Hindu nor the Chinese situation does the individual stand or fall alone. If the Hindu advances, the gods have been good to him. If the Chinese does well, his ancestors must have been virtuous. The difference between the Hindu and the Chinese is that, while the Hindu is not sure which gods are good to him and even whether

---

* The self-reliant man who has failed may resort to dependence of some sort as defense but he is likely to regard that state as temporary rather than permanent.

or not the gods he depends on are well disposed toward him, the Chinese, by and large, has little doubt about his permanent place in the great continuum and about the intentions of the dead and the yet-unborn.

The American's uncertainty is far greater than the Hindu's. There is no human or god on whom he can depend without hurting his self-respect. Success is his own triumph and defeat his own burden. He can call in the world to celebrate his happiness, but he cannot share his misery even with his family and best friends. In the face of such self-reliance, and the ideal of freedom of the individual, the American solution to the problem of social needs is the formation of groupings among peers who enter into relationships with each other predominantly as equal, contractual partners. Membership in these clubs is nearly identical with membership in the American society. At any rate membership in them possesses an extraordinary importance in the total life of the United States. The constant process of emergence, division, merging, and multiplication of these clubs for achieving the most diverse objectives known to mankind is the secret of the dynamism of the American world.

The Chinese clan is cohesive to a high degree, without any significant desire to exclude. Since the cohesion is not based on abstract or idealistic aims but on birth and marriage, it is not hampered much by divisions due to fights over status or other issues, and its scope will always be determined by human fertility. Since everyone in the long run will achieve more or less just as honorable a place as everyone else, through age and seniority in generation, the forces making for competitive explosion are small.

Hindu caste is more divisive than cohesive. It is beset with quarrels over status. Its cohesion within a small group is inevitably accompanied by demonstrative signs of exclusiveness toward others. But since the overall orientation is a search for supernatural objects or objects of reliance, and since there are no visible criteria for achievement in that search, there are many relatively easy avenues for individual escape from the onus of low caste status through supernaturalism and caste and subcaste disputes or others. Supernatural disputes will never be decisive as long as the criteria for such disputes remain truly supernatural. Caste and subcaste disputes will never lead to irreconcilable showdowns as long as the end results are ultimately mutable, because they are embraced within the same ideological framework.

The American club is as cohesive as it is divisive. Its capacity for united action, over a given issue and during a particular period of time, is great, but its potentiality for internal rifts, which will pull the whole organization apart in short order, is also great. Since no person has an inalienable place in the scheme of things, and since everyone has to be continually vigilant to defend his self-reliance by achieving greater successes, those who are in high places are beset with anxieties that they must climb even higher or with fears that someone will encroach on their position from below. As to those who are on lower rungs of the social ladder, they will have equal or greater anxieties in their efforts to advance, and equal or greater fears of being hampered by those who are less fortunate. To the self-reliant person, the stake is great and the question of advancement or regression critical. For, if he does not advance, he will regress.

However, though the problems of the American individual are individualistic in nature, that is, each must struggle to rise or fall alone, he must combine with other equally individualistically oriented individuals to solve them. He forms and joins clubs to compete with other clubs. Without a kinship organization in which he can find permanence, propelled by a dichotomized world in which the difference between self and nonself is immutable, a self-reliant man must form or find groups till he and all that he represents or stands for has prevailed or become demonstrably superior over others. Hence the issues which divide or unite Americans are numerous as well as diverse: abstract and idealistic, concrete and mercenary, historical or local, extreme right or extreme left, or, in fact, purely emotional, personal, or even contrived. In an immutably dichotomized world Americans may come to regard any of these issues, whether substantial or not, as irreconcilable with others.

It is generally assumed that the struggle among big corporations or industrial magnates is economic. This view neglects the fact that the millionaire who must top last year's earnings is not so much after a steady livelihood as he is after status. It is similarly wide of the mark to assume that the struggle among the different churches and missions is religious. This view fails to see that the causes for denominational separation and conflict in the West increasingly have little to do with man's belief in the supernatural. In fact, I find the word "supernatural" gradually going out of circulation in American churches and that, when used, it is often identified with some sort of superstition. The more likely causes of the struggle among the different churches and missions tend to revolve around the earthly glamour and prestige derivable from size, power, and popularity of particular churches or missionary organizations. Being self-reliant, Americans find it difficult to conceive of the supernatural except in terms of one omnipotent and omnipresent God. Since Americans shun dependence, they will in fact be ashamed of the notion that the worshiper should depend upon his God even though "In God We Trust" is still a recurrent theme of sermons. This is not only expressed by proverbs such as "Pray to God and keep your powder dry" or "God helps those who help themselves" but is also shown by the American attitude that church attendance should not be accompanied by specific requests to God for personal favors. Even when the desire for such favors is most urgent, the self-reliant man is only supposed to ask God in general terms for strength so that he can go out and do it himself. The result is that God is identified, for all practical purposes, with "I" or "me." The American who goes to church to ask for specific favors will certainly feel defensive about it. This psychology is especially true of the Protestants but is showing signs of increase among the Catholics.[24]

The greatest fear of the self-reliant man is failure. In his scheme of things failure means the loss of avenues for the satisfaction of his needs of sociability, security, and status. For while there are many groups ready to welcome him when he succeeds, there is hardly any group on which he can fall back as a natural matter of course when he fails. Issues, therefore, become irreconcilable because the self-reliant man has no retreat. Issues will multiply because each self-reliant man must advance as a separate individual. Yet, whether in advancement or in retreat, the self-reliant man must still join forces with other self-reliant men, or hold on to them, for longer or shorter periods of time, with a determination not exhibited by his Chinese or Hindu brethren.

NOTES FOR CHAPTER IX

1. Paul C. Glick, *American Families* (New York: John Wiley and Sons, 1957), pp. 135–136. This may partially be due to the fact that those who have been married once tend most actively to seek remarriage. But this does not alter our argument here.

2. Kurt Lewin, *Resolving Social Conflicts: Selected Papers on Group Dynamics* (New York: Harper and Brothers, 1948), pp. 10–11 and p. 13.

3. *Ibid.*, pp. 18–23.

4. *Ibid.*, p. 20. We may find further confirmation of the American psychology in a later work by Alex Inkeles, Eugenia Hanfmann, and Helen Beier reporting part of the findings by the Harvard Project on the Soviet Social System. "The Russians think of people and evaluate them for what they are rather than in terms of how they evaluate ego, the latter being a more typically American approach"— "Modal Personality and Adjustment to the Soviet Socio-Political System," in Bert Kaplan (ed.), *Studying Personality Cross-Culturally* (Evanston: Row, Peterson, 1961), p. 210. Further on the authors state: ". . . our Russian subjects seemed to have a characteristically sturdy ego. They were rather secure in their self-estimation and unafraid to face up to their own motivation and that of others. . . . Compared to the Americans . . . they seemed relatively lacking in well developed and stabilized defenses with which to counteract and modify threatening impulses and feelings. The organization of their personality depend for its coherence much more heavily on their intimate relatedness to those around them, their capacity to use others' support and to share with them their emotions"—*Ibid.*, p. 212.

5. Francis L. K. Hsu, "An Anthropologist's View of the Future of Personality Studies," *Psychiatric Research Reports 2* (American Psychiatric Association, December 1955).

6. Edward S. Suchman, "The Values of American College Students," in *Long Range Planning for Education* (Washington, D.C.: American Council on Education, 1958), pp. 119–120.

7. The fact that there is no separation between the adult world and that of the children in India, and the fact that the Indian children are not encouraged to be independent of their parents are noted both by Mrs. Lois B. Murphy and by G. Morris Carstairs—Lois B. Murphy, "Indian Child Development," in Gardner Murphy, *In the Minds of Men* (New York: Basic Books, 1953), pp. 46–58; and G. Morris Carstairs, *The Twice Born* (London: The Hogarth Press, 1957). Carstairs, in addition, notes the fact that the presence of grandparents in the joint household greatly modifies the behavior of the child's own parents in that it causes the parents to be more aloof toward their own child. What these students have not had occasion to make clear is the fact that these are characteristics which Hindu India shares with traditional China although they are in sharp contrast to the characteristics of the West. Consequently, Mrs. Murphy errs greatly when she attempts to relate the relatively smooth transition between childhood and maturity with unstructured aggression in later years. For if these particular patterns of Hindu child-rearing practices are at the root of the communal riots which Dr. and Mrs. Murphy went to India to investigate, we should reasonably expect similar riots in China. The fact is riots are as prevalent in India in modern times as they are untypical of China at all times. In my view what distinguishes India from China is the former's supernatural-centered orientation of life, which leads to a divisive outlook and a diffused approach to life's problems on the part of the individual in India. In a separate paper I shall deal with differing ways in which basic emotions are controlled, channelized, and expressed in China, India, and the United States, and how the Indian way may be considered to provide more ammunition for riots than the ways of either China or the United States. ("Suppression, Repression and Effusion: A Limited Psychological Interpretation of Three Cultures," in preparation.)

8. Shepard B. Clough, *Basic Values of Western Civilization* (New York: Columbia University Press, 1960), p. ix.

9. *Ibid.*, pp. 53–54.

10. R. H. Lowie, *Primitive Society* (New York: Boni and Liveright, 1920), p. 257.

11. W. Lloyd Warner, *American Life, Dream and Reality* (Chicago: University of Chicago Press, 1953), p. 191.

12. David Riesman, "The Found Generation," *The American Scholar*, XXV, No. 4 (1956), pp. 430–431.

13. W. Lloyd Warner, *op. cit.*, pp. 192–193. The facts and statements on associational life which follow are all taken from the same source except as specifically noted.

14. Robert S. and Helen M. Lynd, *Middletown* (New York: Harcourt Brace, 1929), pp. 285–86.

15. Robert S. and Helen M. Lynd, *Middletown in Transition* (New York: Harcourt Brace, 1937), p. 280 and pp. 281–294.

16. W. Lloyd Warner, *Democracy in Jonesville* (New York: Harper & Bros., 1949), pp. 117–18.

17. W. Lloyd Warner, *op. cit.* (1953), pp. 193–94.

18. W. Lloyd Warner, Marcia Meeker, and Kenneth Fells, *Social Class in America* (Chicago: Science Research Associates, 1949), pp. 21–23.

19. David Riesman, *The Lonely Crowd* (New Haven: Yale University Press, 1950), pp. 11–26.

20. For example, see Henry Steele Commager, *The American Mind* (New Haven: Yale University Press, 1950), pp. 406–443, especially Section 5; Robin M. Williams, *American Society: A Sociological Interpretation* (New York: Alfred A. Knopf, 1951), pp. 387–388; and Harold J. Laski, *The American Democracy* (New York: Viking Press, 1948), p. 738.

21. William H. Whyte, Jr., *The Organization Man* (New York: Simon and Schuster, 1956).

22. S. Milgram, "Nationality and Conformity," *Scientific American* (December 1961), pp. 45–51.

23. Francis L. K. Hsu, "American Core Value and National Character," in Francis L. K. Hsu (ed.), *Psychological Anthropology: Aspects of Culture and Personality* (Homewood: Dorsey Press, 1961), VII, 223.

24. For a detailed analysis of American religious behavior as contrasted with Chinese religious behavior see Francis L. K. Hsu: *Americans and Chinese: Two Ways of Life* (New York: Abelard-Schuman, 1953), pp. 217–277.

Chapter X

CULTURE PATTERN AND
HUMAN GROUPING

To MAKE ORDER out of social chaos and to understand at least part of the diverse forces that shape human behavior, it is necessary to examine the complicated facts from a particular standpoint and to assume, implicitly or explicitly, that "other things are equal." That other things are never equal in human situations is *also* easy to see. But the alternatives are to undertake the impossible task of covering all variables or to give up the quest utterly.

In the foregoing chapters we looked at the most important modes of human grouping in premodern China, Hindu India, and the United States of America and at how these modes are related to the respective patterns of culture in the societies concerned. We organized our facts with the aid of several basic ideas. Foremost among them is the basic idea that all human beings, in order to carry on their ways of life, must live in *groups* composed of large or small numbers of other human beings. The first group in all three societies is the family.

The second idea we utilized is that of social needs, as distinguished from biological needs; in this context we used the term *need* as defined by Henry A. Murray—as a construct, or a hypothetical concept, which "stands for a force (the physico-chemical nature of which is unknown) in the brain region, a force which organizes perception, apperception, intellection, conation and action in such a way as to transform in a certain direction existing, unsatisfying situations."[1] In our scheme the three needs of sociability, security, and status are the "élan vital," the prime mover of behavior principally peculiar to human beings. Our assumption is that individuals remain in a group, seek group affiliation, conform to group norms, and even submit to the tyranny of the group because they find in the group individual satisfaction of the social needs which they fail to find elsewhere.[2]

The third idea we resorted to is *culture*, which is governed by a particular orientation. The first group with which every individual, in the normal course

232

of events, is affiliated is the family; but differing patterns of cultures will define for the individual whether he will find the satisfaction of his three social needs in this first primary group, or whether he will have to seek it elsewhere. The long conditioning process that goes on within the framework of the family would seem, from the known facts of psychology, to insure the tendency on the part of the individual to remain with the familiar. But many men have shown remarkable proclivities to reject their families and to explore or settle in far-off corners of the earth, and this has prompted sociologists such as W. I. Thomas to include the "wish for new experience" as one of the basic wishes of man,[3] and psychologists such as A. H. Maslow to postulate "self-actualization" as the highest need in the hierarchy of human motives.[4] Other formulations, such as those of Kurt Goldstein that the prime motivation of the human organism is "to realize its capacities," and that of Carl Rogers that behavior moves in the direction of "greater independence or self-responsibility,"[5] are variations on the same theme, mainly a Western one. What we have seen in the foregoing chapters is that, from the cross-cultural point of view, the postulate that the human organism universally moves in the direction of new experience or independence seems unfounded. The central orientation of each culture nurtures a particular psychological climate which fosters the individuals brought up in it to seek independence or be content with the status quo.

The fourth and last idea we resorted to is that each society rests on a certain framework, which is the *structure* of the social organization. The family in every society has the same basic kinship relationships, but particular kinship relationships may dominate over all others and be correlated with the kinship *content* which feeds the cultural orientation from generation to generation.

THE HYPOTHESIS AND ITS APPLICATION

Our hypothesis begins with a threefold observation: (1) the Chinese social organization is dominated by the father-son relationship and attributes of this relationship which feed the situation-centered orientation of the Chinese culture, expressed in the form of mutual dependence; (2) the Hindu social organization is dominated by the attributes of the mother-son relationship which feed the supernatural-centered orientation of the Hindu culture, expressed in the form of unilateral dependence; and (3) the American social organization is dominated by attributes of the husband-wife relationship, which feed the individual-centered orientation of the American culture, characterized by self-reliance. These varying patterns of psychocultural orientation affect the interpersonal relationships in the three societies so that the relationships between the individual and his family vary with them.

For the Chinese, his family and its direct and widest extension, the clan, are the beginning and end of his human universe. He can find in that kinship group all that is meaningful in his relationships with his fellowmen: his sociability, his security, and his status. Even if this typical Chinese has become a public hero in the wider society, he still usually returns to and retires in the village or town where his ancestral home, clan graveyard, and temple are located. He will attribute his success to what his parents did for him and repay his debts to them by honoring them and sharing with them all that success has meant to him. He and his wife will, in due course, be objects of similar benefits as their sons mature and rise. The cardinal measures of his worth as a human being are to be found in that group with which he is affiliated by birth.

If sometimes this Chinese person seeks entrance into nonkinship groups, it is usually and ultimately for the benefit of his kinship group. For he is convinced of the permanency of his place among his fellow human beings; for the overall ideological and theological foundation of his culture and the specific mechanisms of his social organization agree in assuring him of such a place. The outstanding characteristics of a society primarily held together by kinship principle, as contrasted to Hindu and American societies held together by other principles, is the centripetal outlook fostered among its members. Men belong to their deceased ancestors and to their unborn descendants. So strong is this centripetal orientation that women lose their own kinship affiliation and merge into their husbands' patrilineal family groups upon marriage, and belong to the deceased ancestors and the unborn descendants of their hubsands. The Chinese society can be described as one of *kinship solidarity* in the Durkheimian sense because kinship is its primary, and almost its sole, principle of organization. The principle has been of such great importance that even the loyalty and allegiance to the emperor on the part of his ministers and generals was subordinated to it.

For the Hindu, his family is but a relatively temporary point of reference in a vast unfathomable universe in which the supernatural, men, and all living things are at best expressions of differential achievements but more truly mere illusion. A man is born, matures, is duty-bound to marry and beget children, grows old, and then passes out of the world forever. His higher aspirations are his relationships with the unseen world of the spirits, which is another step toward the Great Ultimate. But though it is conceptually possible to find satisfaction of his social needs by communion with the supernatural, that relationship lacks definite points of reference or means of measuring failure or success. It is an extremely diffused and undefinable relationship except for the relative few who enjoy unusual powers of inner concentration and who do not need external stimuli. For a majority of Hindus *caste* is a refuge from the diffuseness generated by the supernatural orientation of the culture. The outstanding characteristics of Indian caste are principally negative and defensive in nature, being concerned with localized taboos and prohibitions which maintain the hierarchy among castes, and only secondarily positive and constructive in purpose, as with jajmani and when caste panchayatis, often indistinguishable from village panchayatis, take actions other than enforcement of caste customs. Yet the Hindu individual with his centrifugal outlook, linked to a supernatural cultural orientation and reinforced in each generation by the predominance of the mother-son relationship, cannot permanently be contained by caste walls. He will tend to seek greater things by spilling over these walls so as to achieve higher status through affiliation with and dependence upon higher powers. Since the basic mode of thought is dependence, this spilling over is never an individual process but one which involves the splitting of the group within the traditional ideological framework. The dominant approach is hierarchic. It is stated unmistakably in the scriptures that men are in different stages of propinquity to the Atma, though they may hope, in the unforeseeable future, for ultimate union with it. The result of this approach is horizontal: exclusiveness from others. But such horizontality is only superficial. For the first step toward improvement of one's status is to be insulated against those who are, or may be considered, or could be made to look, lower than oneself. This is the reason why, at any given point of time, the Hindu society presents the appearance of a multitude of self-enclosed groups contending for superiority and denying inferiority along the same supernaturally based social continuum. This caste society of Hindu India can be described as one of *hierarchic solidarity* in the Durkheimian sense because all these self-enclosed caste groups tend to be dependent upon some other castes higher or lower than they for services which they themselves, for ritual reasons, cannot perform or are prevented from performing.

For the American, his family is strictly a sort of nursery to prepare him for his future on his own. By express definition the family consists of a man, his wife, whom he finds on his own, and his unmarried children whom he and his wife plan to beget, often with an eye on their desired standard of living. His parents have no permanent hold on him. Even more tenuous are his relationships with his remoter relatives. His life's aspirations are his individual advancement and achievements, preferably as a completely free agent. He resents being dependent on anyone and is likely, in the final analysis, to be suspicious of anyone except of his wife and minor children, who are really dependent upon him.

The American's centrifugal outlook, linked to his individual-centered cultural orientation and reinforced each generation by a kinship organization dominated by the husband-wife relationship, thus compels him to seek his social needs outside the family. Yet, though trained to be independent of his parents, he nevertheless has to depend upon other fellow human beings not only for nourishment and for support of his ventures in success or failure, but also for their faith in him and even for trivial conversation. This poses for him some basic problems, which he tries to solve by developing elaborate usages, rules, and regulations governing interpersonal relationships of all kinds, whether these be social, economic, religious, or political. These usages, rules, and regulations are designed with two ends in view. On the one hand they must guarantee his individual privacy, his right to associate with those of his fellow human beings with whom he chooses to associate, and his right to do so only when such association is desired by him and to terminate such association when he no longer cares for it. On the other hand, they must assure him that such association is to the best of his interests, advances them, or at least continues them. Neither of these two ends is always attainable to the complete satisfaction of all concerned, for the privacy and best interests of one individual do not as a rule accord with those of others. Furthermore, as often as not, the individual objects to the bondage of prevailing customs, practices, or morality, and attempts to break out of it. It is the process of the eternal American conflicts which make American society so dynamic and exuberant. In this process men combine and split and recombine in free associations which we have designated, for purposes of this book, as *clubs*.

Though their centrifugal outlook is similar to that of the Hindus, the dominant American approach to life is profoundly different from its Hindu counterpart. The ideological foundation, the theological sinew, the thousand and one organizational details of the society, and the consciously repeated educational, economic, and political slogans in America all point to the horizontal emphasis on equality and freedom. Men are born equal and free. Such inequality and lack of freedom as exist at present are nothing but temporary imperfections to be swept away in time. And there is no question but that the political, religious, economic, and even social forces are shaping the society as a whole and, in spite of many signs to the contrary, moving in the direction of more freedom and greater equality for the underdogs. However, the result of this dominant equalitarian approach is often inevitably and unsuspectingly hierarchic. When the individual is propelled by his centrifugality out of his primary group, he has to seek some other group in its place. When his affiliation with a nonkinship group is loose because of equality and freedom, he must resort to more groups, bigger groups, or better groups in order to ensure his desired share of sociability, security, and status. The inevitable consequence is a perpetual competition among individuals and among groups for higher place, and realignment of individuals into new groups for the same purpose.

The basic similarity between the Hindu and the American situations is the individual's lack of permanent anchorage in the kinship organization and consequently his tendency to centrifugality in search of other groups for satisfaction of his social needs. Their basic differences are that the Hindu tendency to centrifugality is channeled within the same ideological framework, so that no matter into how many castes the Hindus are divided, the desired end results are similar or accommodative, while the American tendency flows into many directions, so that the diverse free associations or clubs which Americans form and join often are aimed at and lead to totally different objectives which have either no reference to each other or are entirely destructive of each other. If we resort to an analogy, we might say that the Hindu competition occurs on a single totem pole, so that no matter how many competitors there are, they are in front or behind each other in a single sequence, and they aim at the same top; but that the American competition is productive of many different totem poles, because many or most of the competitors would like to start their own totem poles so as to eliminate other totem poles or to reach a destination far away from those of the others.

The American type of society characterized by free associations can be described as one of *contractual solidarity* in the Durkheimian sense, since the fundamental social development is horizontal, toward more equalitarianism and more frontiers, with the central idea that individuals need not be bound to each other except when they choose to submit to such bondage.

"VARIETIES OF HUMAN VALUE"

There is unexpected support for our conclusions about the three ways of life from the philosopher Charles Morris's study of values through the questionnaire method summarized in his book entitled *Varieties of Human Value*.[6] His questionnaires were administered to students in ten societies (United States, China, India, Japan, Norway, Canada, Pakistan, England, New Zealand, and Italy) but "the best and most extensive samples" are from the first three, which happily coincide with the scope of our inquiry here. It is of great interest that some of Morris's results on conceived values or "beliefs concerning the good life" in general agree with ours, though some of his interpretations are not, from our point of view, entirely satisfactory. That is to say, a careful perusal of Morris's findings convinces us that they, too, show individual-centeredness, situation-centeredness, and supernatural-centeredness to be most important ingredients, respectively, in the American, Chinese, and Hindu worlds. Of the American students Morris says: "The factor scores give the impression that the United States students are activitistic and self-indulgent, less subject to restraint and less open to receptivity than any of the other four groups (India, Japan, China and Norway) and second lowest in inwardness."[7] What seems, however, confusing to Morris is the fact that the American students secondarily also stress a way which provides for "contemplation and enjoyment as well as for action," and that their written comments show that a number of persons, in "accepting" the latter way, also "wish to link with it the attitudes of social concern and responsibility."[8] The reader who has followed the extended analysis of the dynamics of American culture and personality given in the foregoing pages will find it easy enough to see the intrinsic connection between self-reliance and enjoyment on the one hand and contemplation, action, and social concern on the other. Morris sees them as incongruous because he has not taken into consideration the intricate relationship between individual needs, social norms, and cultural ideals. In this new perspective even the fact that "unlike students in the other three groups [China, India, and Norway], some of them [the United States students] suggest* that all the ways are unsatisfactory and that no attempt should be made to formulate an alternative lest life be restricted and forced into a mold"[9] becomes perfectly intelligible. This is one of the clearest expressions of resentment against conformity and a desire for complete freedom of the individual.

The responses from Indian students to Morris's questionnaires are also readily understandable. Here "the distinctive and controlling element" in the "value pattern is represented by tradition-oriented Way 1" which gives a "high place to inwardness though it has also made room for action and devotion."[10] Morris obviously regards "devotion" as being very different from "inwardness," though it would seem that they are intrinsically part and parcel of each other if the most important object of this devotion happens to be God or the Ultimate Reality or Atma. Church budgets, Sunday services, and social activities are so overwhelmingly identified with religion in America that it is perhaps hard even for a man of Dr. Morris's perspicacity to view "devotion" except in terms of external objects or persons.

The Indian students not only underscored the way just discussed but also other ways and factors indicating a desire for "enjoyment and progress in action" and for "integration of diversity," as well as for stoic "control of the self."[11] For Morris the Indian students emphasize these secondary choices because they are "under the pressure of urgent social problems (such as extreme and widespread poverty)," because they recognize "the need for social reconstruction" and that, therefore, they find "the reconciliation of tradition and reconstruction a pressing problem, and as a phase of this problem, the integration of inwardness and outer activity."[12] What the philosopher has neglected is the fact that the inwardness, which is one of the utmost expressions of supernatural devotion, has long been linked, in the Hindu scheme of things, through the concepts of *karma* (work) and espe-

* In addition to filling out the prepared questionnaires a "small percentage of the respondents" gave written suggestions concerning "a desirable mode of life" (Morris, p. 47).

cially *anasakti* (non attachment), with joy and action, so elegantly propounded in the *Bhagavad-Gita;* and the fact that "integration of diversity"
is the very essence of the centuries-old Hindu pantheistic thought which
links the most mundane practices with the purest spiritual aspirations.*

These links we have already seen in Chapter VIII of the present volume.
Morris is aware of the teachings of this most popular of Indian scriptures
but he only relates them to the few Indian students who endorse "control the
self stoically." There is no doubt about the prevalence of "urgent social
problems" in India but it seems unnecessary to resort to their pressure as an
explanation for the secondary Indian choices when there is ample evidence
that all of the incongruous elements in the responses are, in the Hindu world,
parts of the same traditional fabric. The fact that the Indian students volun-
teered "twice as many comments . . . as came from American students."[13] is
another indication of this. Indeed Morris himself touches on the all-inclusive
(or diffuse) tendencies in Indian culture, though he gives them only a minor
mention, when he observes that "the [Indian] comments show a great range
of diversity; all of the dimensions of value find a voice, as they have done
in the cultural tradition of India."[14]

This conclusion—that the Indian students' secondary choices may not be
so much prompted by pressure of urgent social problems of the present as
by their sacred and diffuse heritage from the past—finds further support in
the nature of Morris's Chinese responses. In 1948, when the Chinese responses were obtained, the Chinese students were in the midst of even
greater hardships and turmoil than their Indian counterparts. The year 1948
was the worst in post-World War II China. With the Formosan revolt and
massacre just over, it was a year of runaway inflation, rampant official cor-
ruption, frequent acts of police brutality, and rapidly advancing social dis-
order. In addition, the deteriorating military situation made the threat of
Communist conquest of the nation more real every day. But "there is," in
Morris's words, "considerable difference between the Chinese value patterns
and the Indian" and, in respect of their high score for "enjoyment and

* Mahatma Gandhi essentially gave this Indian tradition a new confirmation by way
of a fresh twist when he tried, or as he called it, "experimented" with everything he could
think of, from eating raw sprouted wheat as a means of avoiding cooking, sharing his
bed and even the cover with women as a means of ascertaining "if even the least trace of
sensual feeling had been evoked in himself or his companion," to conducting strikes as
an avenue of passive resistance, all this leading in the end to the conclusion that "there is
no other God than Truth" and that "the only means for the realization of Truth is Ahimsa
(non-killing)," M. K. Gandhi, *An Autobiography or The Story of My Experiments
with Truth* (Ahmedabad: Navajivan Publishing House, 1927), pp. 503–4; Nirma Kumar
Bose, *My Days with Gandhi* (Calcutta: Nishana, 1953), p. 174 and others; and Madeleine
Slade, *The Spirit's Pilgrimage,* "The autobiography of Madeleine Slade, an English
woman of privilege, who, as Mira Behn, renounced home and country to become an
intimate and trusted disciple of Mahatma Gandhi," (New York: Coward-McCann, Inc.,
1960).

progress in action" and low score for "withdrawal and self-sufficiency," "the China sample is like that of the United States but is even more extreme."[15]

Furthermore, in contrast to the Indian students, the "written comments and suggestions from the Chinese students were proportionately fewer than from any other sample."[16] The situation-centered Chinese tends in general to be sensitive to what his place is in the immediate scheme of things (e.g., the context in which he is given a specific set of questionnaires to answer) and acts accordingly rather than be venturesome toward actions outside the scope of the questions asked. From this angle no more revealing data can be found in support of the three ways of life outlined in the foregoing chapters than that the Indians volunteer more comments and suggestions than the Americans, endorsing all dimensions of values; that the Americans volunteer half as many comments and suggestions as the Indians, objecting to all definite formulations of ways of life; while the Chinese volunteer proportionately fewer comments and suggestions than any other group, emphasizing service to fellow men but also balance between one's "obligation" "to one's self and to others," with no concern for "integration of diversity" at all.

Finally Morris's concluding remarks about his Chinese sample are the best exposition of Chinese predilection for mutual dependence among men:

> In summary, the value pattern of the Chinese young people, as it appears in this study, is actively and socially oriented to an extreme degree and hence is antithetic to those modes of life directed primarily toward the self or toward nature. Yet the temper is not ascetic or grim but warmly human. While there is hardly a trace of a demanding possessive self, there is some evidence that the ancient Chinese stress on the cultivation of the self was still a living force.[17]

What Morris might have underlined is that the Chinese stress on "the cultivation of the self" is not centered merely in the self, but rather in the place of the self among fellow human beiengs.

THE DIFFERENCES BETWEEN CASTE IN THE UNITED STATES
AND CASTE IN INDIA

From our analysis it becomes clear that caste in India and caste in the United States are profoundly different. Many scholars, including Allison Davis, Kingsley Davis, John Dollard, Gunnar Myrdal, and Lloyd Warner have described the Negro-White relationship in the United States, and particularly in the southern United States, as one of caste. Though a few are critical of such usage, the reasons given to back up the criticisms are weak and not based on realistic assessment of the facts. So far as I know, Gerald D. Berreman's paper, based on his field work in a village in northern Uttar Pradesh, India, and read at the annual meeting of the 1959 American Anthropological Association and subsequently published in the *American*

Journal of Sociology, is to date the only careful comparison, using field data, between castes in the two societies.

Berreman has no trouble in showing the fallacies inherent in the arguments advanced by Charles S. Johnson, George E. Simpson, J. M. Yinger, and Oliver C. Cox in their efforts to distinguish between castes in India and in the United States. He observes:

> Central to these distinctions is that caste in India is passively accepted and endorsed by all on the basis of religio-philosophical explanations which are universally subscribed to, while Negro-White relations in America are characterized by dissent, resentment, guilt and conflict. But this contrast is invalid, resulting, as it does, from an idealized and unrealistic view of Indian caste contrasted with a more realistic, pragmatic view of American race relations.[18]

Berreman has little difficulty in demonstrating how inadequate these views are. And he proceeds to make a detailed comparison between the caste relations in Sirkanda, especially between the twice-born and untouchable castes, and race relations in the southern United States. Berreman defines caste as "hierarchically ranked endogamous divisions of society in which membership is hereditary and permanent" and shows how both situations fit it. He finds: (1) "rigid rules of avoidance between castes," with some types of contacts "defined as contaminating, while others are non-contaminating"; (2) the maintenance of the position of the high castes by "powerful sanctions" as well as rationalization of it by "elaborate philosophical, religious, psychological or genetic explanations"; (3) caste is determined by birth; (4) economic, sexual, and prestige gains on the part of the high castes at the expense of the low castes; (5) "enforced deference" from low castes to high castes; and (6) resentment on the part of the low castes against the high castes and devious attempts to raise one's status.[19] Besides what Berreman has given here there is the fact that, under both systems, the individual who has "passed" from a lower to a higher caste can never admit his low-caste origin without losing his new-found status.

Granted all these facts there are two fundamental differences which these facts do not negate. First, the overall ideological-theological precepts of India provide justification for the caste system while the overall ideological-theological framework of the United States refutes it. This point was noted by some of the sociologists Berreman criticizes, but Berreman excludes it from his analysis because it is a question of ideal views. But ideals as Great Traditions in Redfield's sense certainly interact with the Little Traditions embodied in diverse local realities. Furthermore there has been enough work done along this line by scholars such as McKim Marriott[20] to convince us that even the illiterate villagers in India would consider both traditions indigenous. In the racial picture of the United States today we are witnessing one of the best illustrations of how the Great Tradition of American democratic and liberal ideals gradually spreads itself through the federal courts, the major newspapers, schools, etc., to overshadow the Little Tradition embodied in southern parochial and segregationist worlds. From this standpoint it is obvious that to ignore the overall ideals will be as much a scientific fallacy as to ignore the local realities. In overall ideals the Hindu and American cultures are drastically different.

The second Hindu-American difference flows from the first. The Indian's reaction and the American's reaction to caste are characteristically dissimilar, and this difference is functionally related to their difference in ideals. Berreman's own report on Sirkanda is most revealing:

> Caste as such was not often seriously questioned in the village. Objections were characteristically directed not at "caste" but at "my position in the caste hierarchy." . . . In Sirkanda those low-caste people who spoke most piously against high-caste abuses were likely to be equally abusive to their low-caste inferiors. However, no low caste was encountered whose members did not seriously question its place in the hierarchy. A sizeable literature is accumulating concerning castes which have attempted to alter their status. Such attempts were made in Sirkanda.[21]

What Berreman describes here applies, so far as I can see, with great accuracy to every part of India. But it is not in the main true to the Negro-White situation in the United States. At one place or another it is not uncommon to find some well-situated Negroes assuming attitudes toward not-so-well-situated Negroes approximating those which they resent on the part of the whites. Individual "passing" is a well-known phenomenon. But the characteristic attack as embodied in the overall social, political, religious, and economic movements in America is against any caste idea or system itself, not against any mistaken placement of any individual or group on any hierarchic ladder.

Caste in India is therefore primarily a shield behind which the dependency-inclined individual, high and low, can entrench himself against diffuseness of the social organization and assure for himself a satisfactory place in it, without calling the caste system itself and the philosophy and theology behind it into question. Caste in the United States, on the other hand, is primarily an active weapon by means of which the self-reliant man can expand the sphere of his superiority (not just keep it), or a temporary evil to be swept away in the long run. The most important expression of the former is Nazi Germany's ghastly "final solution to the Jewish problem." The most important expression of the latter is exemplified in the American Civil War, the Supreme Court decisions on desegregation, the N.A.A.C.P. fights, union improvements, and the like. Though seemingly contradictory to each other, the Nazi totalitarian view and the Anglo-American liberal view agree on the same point: to neither is the caste system tolerable and both battle for its complete liquidation, not mere change of the position of any individual in the caste hierarchy.

There are, of course, many Americans who resort to caste as a shield in the Hindu sense and who want no change in the system which gives them so many more privileges than their inferiors. There are also some Hindus who, even before the impact of the West, initiated movements against the caste system and ideology as such. Jainism, Buddhism, and the Lingayat sect are each a concrete expression of their founders' desire to eliminate the caste system. But the Westerners who entrench themselves behind their racial caste walls are fighting a losing battle. This is why even ardent segregationists in the southern United States are compelled to defend their position by pleading the "unreadiness" of the Negro. The overall ideological background of the United States makes it necessary for even these people to designate caste as an expediency. Conversely the Hindu movements which aimed at abolition of the caste system ended up either having no place in India (Buddhism) or becoming caste groups themselves, or differentiating castes among themselves within the same caste system that they set out to abolish (Jainism, the Lingayat sect, and many others).

With the impact of the West and national independence coming to India on Western terms, Western equalitarian ideology rooted in Western culture has entered the Indian scene as a new force. However, the significance of this new force to the future of the Indian social fabric remains to be seen.

Looking back at the psychocultural forces operating in the three societies, it becomes understandable that the Chinese, though they have had slavery during many periods of their long history, did not develop a caste system. In their social organization they have never left the kinship principle because they did not need to resort to other principles of human grouping to any significant extent. The ethical dominance of the father-son relationship assures them of the permanency of the primary constellation of human beings among whom each individual finds his inalienable place. For the Chinese, the boundary of this circle of human relationships divides his more immutable inner world from his more mutable outer world (see Diagram V-*a*). Into this inner world there can be few intrusions and from it there are still fewer defections. For his relationship with the outer world is likely to be measured against the requirements of that with his inner world. He is not likely to become too excited over men, events, or abstract principles except when these have direct bearing on that inner world.

In the Hindu social organization the kinship principle is of far less importance than it is in its Chinese counterpart. The dominant mother-son relationship is conducive to diffused unilateral dependence. It fits in well with a cultural tradition in which nearness to and reliance on the unseen powers

DIAGRAM V

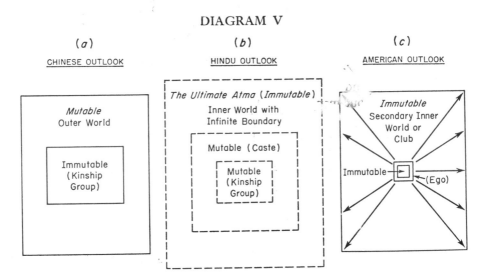

CHINESE OUTLOOK

(b)

HINDU OUTLOOK

(c)

AMERICAN OUTLOOK

CHINESE OUTLOOK. Self is hammered in and regulated by kinship organization which is vertically oriented; but it is assured of a place in that organization. It has no desire to leave that organization and expand into the outer world. The different inner worlds (clans) have no great cause for conflict with each other (except in practical matters such as water rights), since their boundaries are expandable only by birth and marriage.

HINDU OUTLOOK. The diffused orientation of the self is combined with the high goal of complete dependence upon, and union with, the Ultimate Atma. That dependence and union are inevitable even if the self acts in contradictory ways. For the Ultimate Atma, which is the inner world, is so wide as to embrace anything and everything. All men, things, and gods are intrinsically part and parcel of that same great inner world. Consequently, the different castes, being only parts of the all-embracing inner world (Atma), have no irreconcilable conflicts with each other. They merely struggle for a higher place on the same ladder within the same inner world. Since the inner world is infinite, everything in the universe is in effect mutable; the line of immutability, which in other cultures is more or less well defined, is really unknown in the Hindu culture.

AMERICAN OUTLOOK. The horizontal orientation of the self coincides with a desire to break through all barriers and be independent. In doing so it must seek and establish its own destiny, by expanding itself to conquer more of the external world and incorporate it into its own small inner world. In order to do so the individual not only has to deal with other expanding inner worlds within his own secondary inner world (club) but usually comes into irreconcilable conflict with other expanding inner worlds (clubs) outside his own.

are the most desired objectives of life. Since the Atma *is* all, the all-embracing mother-son relationship prepares the individual for a high expectation of mutability among all phenomenon. The boundary of the Hindu's inner world is therefore as extensive as that governed by the limitless Atma (see Diagram V-*b*). This inner world embraces all men, things, and gods. Within it all men, things, and gods are more or less mutable. The Hindu can therefore be zealous about many objectives but often has little difficulty in giving up one for another. The Hindu will also open his personal life, his intimate problems, and even his secrets to other human beings more readily than his Chinese and American brethren. The diffuseness of this conception of life is compensated by the hierarchic principle of caste to make group living possible for the individual. But the diffuseness of this conception of life together with the hierarchic principle can never limit the aspirations of the individual and holds him within the caste regulations and barriers. Hence the Hindus have had many caste-eliminating protestant movements which ended in becoming separate castes within the same all-embracing system.

In the American social organization the kinship principle is even less important than in the Hindu situation. The dominant husband-wife relationship leads to impermanence of the kinship system and compels the individual to search for self-fulfillment among his peers. The keynote of his psychology is marked by insistence on his independence and freedom. To live like a human being he is obliged to combine with other individuals, but such a combination is tolerated only upon the mutual agreement (the contractual principle) that characterizes the free association or club. His true inner world, in the final analysis, consists of his own private self and, secondarily and as extensions of that self, those humans, things, gods, and principles in which the self has invested and with which it has identified (see Diagram V-*c*). For the American this large or small unit is the immutable inner world, as contrasted to the mutable outer world. Americans are great champions of causes, whether these be supernatural, moral, political, or humanitarian, and America is a land of extreme specialization, whether it is in craftsmanship, sex appeal, intellect, or charity. In varying degrees of vehemence each champion of a cause looks at the external world in terms of those who are with him and therefore seeing things his way, and those who are not with him, and therefore hostile to him. What he hopes for most is the conversion and incorporation of more and more of that mutable outer world into his larger and larger immutable inner world.

The dynamism of the American society is founded on two fundamental problems confronting the self-reliant man. On the one hand he must, in combining with others, defend his own immutable inner world while relating it to the equally immutable inner worlds of other self-reliant men with the objective of expanding their respective and separate immutable inner worlds. On the other hand, each group of self-reliant men, being members of the same secondary inner world, must develop more and more effective means of competing with or eliminating other groups of self-reliant men similarly combined, especially those directly in the path of its expansion.

Of the three types of societies, that which is based on the kinship principle is the least dynamic. For the individual in this type of social system, membership in his clan is his first and last station. There is no place else for him to go that is equally attractive. But the societies organized on the hierarchic and contractual principles are far more dynamic. For the individuals in these social systems not only must find satisfaction for their social needs outside of the kinship grouping, but their respective present conditions outside it are still temporary. Both look for some ultimate destination that is far beyond the present. Here we come upon the most crucial difference between the Hindu and American situations. In the American club the self-reliant man looks forward to the ultimate triumph of his club with its particular cause (including support for or opposition to caste-slavery) over most or all other clubs with their causes. But in the Hindu caste the dependency-inclined man looks forward to his eventual ascension through the caste ladder and union with the Ultimate Soul. Consequently drastic changes can come about within relatively short periods of time in the American caste situation, but such cannot be expected in the Hindu caste situation except under Western and external impact.

WIDER IMPLICATIONS

We have analyzed in our present book the three ways of life and their attributes and have seen how they are connected with the respective patterns of family, of clan and caste when present, and of free association in the three societies. We do not know how these particular ways of life originated in the beginning. Archaeological researches, geographical inferences, and historical inquiries may throw some partial light on this point, but it will be only partial. The quest for historical origins is decidedly not a problem that the student of anthropology profitably tackles. But the anthropologist can say that, in each generation, the historically given institutions, usages, ideas, and even accidents shape the psychosocial aspirations of the individual while the psychosocial aspirations of the individual also act and react in turn to reshape the historically given institutions, usages, ideas, and accidents for the benefit of future generations.

A way of life, however, which is at the very root of such fundamental human groupings as family, clan, and caste, cannot but have implications which go far beyond them. A detailed examination of how the three different ways of life express themselves in religion, politics, economy, science and technology, philosophy and art, music and literature will be the task of a later publication, a companion to this volume. But a brief excursus can be made here.

The Chinese and the Hindus share many characteristics in religion. They both believe in many many gods—benevolent ones, fierce ones, evil ones, ambivalent ones as well as indifferent ones. Neither has a state church nor an overall priestly hierarchy which exercises administrative control over the secular government or even attempts to interfere with it. Neither the Hindus nor the Chinese have any compunction about going to different temples or appealing to diverse deities for the same concrete request, be it for sons, prosperity, or recovery from illness. Both believe in reincarnation—a belief that an individual's condition of life is determined by his merit or demerit in his previous existence, just as his present conduct will determine his comfort or misery in his next. These by no means exhaust the similarities between Chinese and Hindu ways in religion. In all of these and other characteristics the two Asian societies are in sharp contrast to their American counterpart.

But the differences between them are tremendous in quantity and quality. Their differences can be understood if we look at the Chinese as tending to have positive relations with men but negative attitudes towards the gods, while the reverse is true of the Hindus, since they seek positive relations with gods but entertain negative attitudes towards men, except holy men. The Chinese will go to gods almost wholly because they have requests to make, but the Hindus will worship the supernatural as a matter of daily devotion. The Chinese will make pilgrimages primarily when in need, but the Hindus consider them as important at all times. The Chinese treat the question of the origin of existence or its ultimate destiny as either irrelevant or obvious. The Hindus emphasize the oneness of gods and all creatures and have produced diverse theological thoughts and, with their diffused outlook, have had numerous revivalist and protestant movements; as time goes on there will be more of the latter, not fewer. For the Chinese, man's dependence upon his fellow men is primary, and gods exist to strengthen human bonds and assure human prosperity. For the Hindu, man's dependence upon his fellow men and prosperity is illusory, and man lives almost entirely for the purpose of service and devotion to gods. Hence the most important classics in China preach a system of ethics on man's relationship with fellow men, while most Hindu classics have to do with the adoration and ways of the gods.

There are other far-reaching differences. The numerous Chinese gods are essentially like the Hindu gods in that they may be both strong and weak, good or evil. But the Chinese have far fewer tales and myths than the Hindus describing the exploits of their gods for the simple reason that they are far less interested than the Hindus in supernatural matters. For the Chinese, gods and spirits exist, now or forever, for his harm or protection, but he does not seek them. Confucius' answer to one of his disciples summarizes the Chinese attitude well: "Respect gods and spirits but keep them at a distance." For the Hindus the ultimate aim of life is man's striving to achieve oneness with the supernatural. Not satisfied that he can invoke some gods and spirits for protection and keep others from harming him, he must actively seek them. This is why there exists a striking contrast between Chinese and Hindu representations of gods and spirits. The Chinese supernatural representations are, as a whole, restful, nearly static in sitting or standing positions; the Hindus representations must, as a whole, be characterized as greatly active and dynamic, in warlike attitudes, inspirational gestures, or sexual congress.[22]

Finally, because of their differing concerns, Western impact has produced in Chinese and Hindu two divergent lines of religious evolution. Since their primary concern is with human relationships, the products of the modern Chinese school system are as a whole irreligious except perhaps for the few converted to Christianity. All of them tend to neglect indigenous Chinese forms of worship except as a concession to the feelings of their parents. No modern Chinese school even touches on traditional worship in its curriculum, except in unfavorable terms. This occurred long before the arrival of the Communists and is obvious among the Chinese in Hawaii and elsewhere. With their overwhelmingly supernatural-centered tradition, the products of the modern Indian school system tend to be as religious as their forefathers. There are of course some students who claim to be agnostic or indifferent or spiteful toward traditional Hindu practices. But I have met more who participate in rituals, pray at temples, worship sadhus, or make pilgrimages in earnest. As early as the 1930's, it was very difficult to find modern trained Chinese intellectuals who took indigenous Chinese religious beliefs seriously, while even today in the 1960's it is extremely common to see Western-trained Hindu intellectuals who remain faithful, theoretically and in practice, to Indian sacred tradition. As in China, Christianity has made but a small dent in the total Indian population (though its Indian dent is larger than its Chinese one), but in contrast to the situation in China, Western impact has seen a most exuberant revival of Hinduism, not only in the form of streamlined protestant missions like that of Ramakrishna (also known as the Vedanta Society) but also in plain traditional personal cults centered in one or another holy man or sadhu. One of the newest Indian universities, the Benares Hindu University, has a magnificent chapel with an enormous Siva lingam, which was still under construction when I last visited there in 1957.

Americans, in contrast to both the Chinese and the Hindus, tend to seek positive relations with men as well as with the supernatural. The Hindus, in sharp contrast to the Chinese, tend to maintain the closest contact with their gods, but they do not make the kind of personal and immediate identification with the supernatural that Americans do. The inner world of the Hindus, as we have seen, is infinite and limitless. The elements in such an inner world do not have to be closely integrated or even integrated at all. Consequently, between a Hindu and his god or gods there is much room for maneuver; imperfections and even contradictions can flourish side by side with the neatest and most immaculate theological and ideological formulation without posing significant psychological problems for him. At any rate, his ultimate union with the Atma is in the infinitely remote future. This is the chief reason why the Hindu gods possess not only supernatural powers and wisdom but also diverse human frailties and trickery; not only spouses, but also illicit lovers. Having a far smaller and certainly more definite inner world, Americans do not have the same latitude for tolerating inconsistencies and contradictions as the Hindus. Their theoretical view of the future may include a world in which all are equal and happy: a universalistic type of thinking just like the Hindu's conception of the Atma, but for one basic difference. In the Hindu scheme the angel and the devil, the holy and the profane, action and inaction, indulgence and abstention are all intrinsic and necessary elements of its fabric, since these opposites are mutable; but the American scheme is, in the usual "people's theology," an all-or-none proposition: either the good has triumphed over the bad or the bad has done so over the good, since these opposites are immutable.* It is a world which, for practical purposes, is all white or all black, and in which the winner takes all and the loser loses all. It is probable that, conceptually, the American's inner world is usually smaller than the Hindu's except for the extremely ambitious when they are at their theoretical broadest. As for the actuality, the individuals who are ambitious go about expanding themselves by incorporating, on their own terms, the mutable external world into their own immutable inner worlds, while those who are less ambitious go about living their normal lives by insulating their own immutable inner worlds against invasion by other immutable inner worlds.

The bearing of this psychological pattern on the Western conception of the supernatural is obvious. That conception has gone through three significant transformations. First, in spite of a long history of polytheism in the West, monotheism prevailed with Judaism and especially Christianity. This monotheism has sometimes been confused with the concept of the supreme deity found in many diverse societies. What Western monotheism claims is that only one God is true and all others are false. Furthermore, the coming of Protestantism heralded the modern era in which each little group,

---

* Some modern theologians have tended to speak of evil *and* good, but how far they are willing to depart from the all-or-none proposition is not yet clear.

and even each individual, has its and his own private version of the absolutely true God.

Second, Westerners probably attribute to God only that which is good, pure, and exalted, relegating the evils of the world to the work of the Devil. In Christian theology, God not only has no mate, but even when He sends His only son to save man, the Saviour must come by way of a virgin. Both absolute monotheism and the purist view of God fit in well with our analysis of the American's immutable inner world as distinguished from the mutable external world, and his tendency to conquer and incorporate more and more of the latter into the former. Given this dichotomy, it is natural that each self-reliant man, together with those who see things his way, must have an inner world that is all true, pure, and good. These give them the fire and the justification for expanding their inner world at the expense of the external world.

The third transformation in the Western conception of the supernatural follows almost inevitably from the first two. This is that God is humanized and personalized. For many Protestant Americans there was something wrong, or at least unreal, when President Kennedy mentioned angels in his inaugural address. In a majority of Protestant churches the "other world" is no longer discussed and it is rare to find a college student who thinks that other worldly spirits have anything to do with his church. There are many scholarly attempts to define religion while excluding the concept of the supernatural. This is most characteristic of the approach of John Dewey, father of modern American education, who objects to the concept of the Unseen and for whom religion is identified with pursuit of values or ideals.[23] A. Eustace Hayden, after examining the transformation of the Christian God from theistic to nontheistic forms, concludes that "a host of shadowy figures who bear the name of God are all that remains for thinkers of the once robust Christian deity, Sovereign Lord of heaven and earth."[24] He then enumerates twenty-two definitions of God by philosophers and theologians from Samuel Butler and August Comte to E. S. Brightman and John Dewey. These definitions range from elaborate tongue-twisters such as "a conscious person of perfect good will limited by the free choices of other persons and by restrictions within his own nature" (E. S. Brightman) to simple substitutions such as "a Cosmic Mathematician" (Sir James Jeans); from early theistic ones such as "a Christlike God" (Bishop F. J. McConnell) to totally nontheistic ones such as "the Imagined Synthesis of Ideal Ends" (John Dewey).[25]

If we characterize religion among the Chinese as a system in which man's relationship with the supernatural is limited because of his relationship with other men, and religion among the Hindus as a system in which human relationship is determined by man's relationship with the supernatural, then we must characterize religion among the Americans as a system in which man's relationship with the supernatural is subordinated to man's expansion of his own self and to everything that such expansion requires, from material goods to naked power.

The Chinese and Hindu approaches to the supernatural are similar in that they both seek dependence upon such unseen powers, as distinguished from the American approach which, though protesting dependence upon the unseen powers, seeks actively to control them. But since the Chinese dependence is marked by mutuality while Hindu dependence is characterized by unilaterality, the Chinese will feel more constrained in their demands on the gods while the Hindu will ask for everything. Consequently the Hindus, the Chinese, and the Americans tend to form a continuum in their activities connected with ritual elaboration. The Hindus, with their insatiable unilateral demands on the gods, will add ritual after ritual and idol after idol. There is no doubt that the Hindus have the largest number of "living" gods and the greatest accumulation of active rituals in the world. The Chinese demands on the gods are limited by their sense of mutuality. They talk about "reasonableness," and their "reasonableness" is naturally measured in terms of their pattern of kinship. "You can't ask the gods to give you what your forebears have withheld from you" would express the Chinese sentiment. They have many rituals and many gods, but these do not multiply as do their Indian counterparts. The Americans talk about "In God we trust," but they really mean that "God only helps him who helps himself." Consequently the Americans have not only made monotheism more militant by increased schism, but are also reducing ritualism to an almost nonexistent point as well as eradicating, regardless of sect, all non-English (i.e., unintelligible) words in it.

The differing approaches to the supernatural analyzed here tend to lead to significantly different attitudes on the part of the individual towards his fellow men concerning religion. The Chinese attitude is likely to be: "I may be asking this god for a favor by offerings and sacrifices, but you don't have to do so if you don't care to"; the Hindu attitude is likely to be: "The different deities we worship are only one God in diverse forms, for we are all part of the same Universal Soul, and whether you like it or not, you cannot really escape it"; while the American attitude is likely to be: "I believe in this God, outside of whom there is no other God; you should and had better worship him too." To Hindus and Americans the Chinese approach seems too opportunistic and too irreligious; in the eyes of Chinese and Hindus the American approach results in too many schisms among people who have no reason to be schismatic and puts too much emphasis on sizes of churches and on turning churches into social clubs.[26] To Americans and Chinese the Hindu approach seems replete with glaring opposites and too full of absurd rituals and often blatantly sexual representations.

This is why I believe that only in the Western way of life can we find and expect serious rivalry between religion and science, or church and government. The Chinese are too much tied up in their human relations to care about the supernatural enough to enter into real fights between the sacred and the profane. The Hindus tend to have no reason for such fights since everything belongs to religion, and since man tends truly to leave everything to God. It is only when man wishes to master the universe as a justification for his own existence that there will be sustained struggles not only between the supernatural and man, but between those who identify themselves with the power of the supernatural and those who identify themselves with the power of man. Attempts to reconcile religion and science are also likely to appear again and again in the latter type of social system, to the dissatisfaction of all concerned in the long run.

In the area of politics and leadership, the basic similarities between the Chinese and the Hindus are three: neither people originated ideas of democracy, political freedom, human rights, or equality as militant ideals; both peoples have had *de facto* democracy of a sort at the village level; and neither the Chinese nor the Hindus have had objection to despots provided they were benevolent. On these points the Chinese and Hindus are both basically different from the Americans; this point we shall deal with shortly. But two outstanding *differences* in political behavior between the Chinese and the Hindus can be understood at once in terms of our hypothesis and do not require extensive explanation. As we noted in Chapter IV, the Chinese have had a more unified and more continuous series of centralized dynastic governments than the Hindus have ever had. Many of the Indian dynasties, by Chinese standards, were extremely small. The very small ones did not rule more than a few hundred square miles or so, and even the largest never encompassed the whole country, *all* of India. Furthermore, local leaders tended to claim raja-ship. One of the outstanding things which strikes the Chinese in India is how indiscriminately the title *king* is claimed by so many. In extreme cases, such as the Pramalai Kallar of Madras, as we have already pointed out, the tendency is to apply the title of the king or chief (*devar*) to all males.

Superficially, the greater centralization and continuity of the Chinese political organization would seem to be contradictory to the Chinese centripetal outlook resulting from cohesion within their kinship groups. For, as commonly observed during the last hundred years of Western impact, the Chinese were prevented from national cohesion by too much loyalty to family and clan. What this superficial view has failed to take into consideration is that there are basic differences between the modern Western states founded on nationalism and traditional Chinese states rooted in familism. In the former the people are attracted to allegiance to or support of the wider political framework and its leaders, but in the latter most of the people merely acquiesce in the autocratic rule of their emperors and officials. The Chinese central empires were each able to encompass the enormous territory of China not so much because the Chinese actively lent them support as because the various contenders for the throne gave up relatively easily. In Chinese political history there has been the recurrent fact that once the different factions saw the rise of a probable victor, they tended to make peace with him and to seek a subordinate place in the sun; in this way they thought to ensure the integrity and continuity of their immutable inner world, the kinship group. The Hindus, whose inner world is the infinite Atma, have, however, difficulty in determining a clear boundary of their defendable realm. Since this realm embraces everything, and since all things within it are mutable, the victor is not sure about the finality of his victory and the vanquished need never concede the totality of the defeat. The result is a never-ending strife for supremacy. Add to this the lack of permanence of the kinship group, which makes it necessary for the individual to seek anchorage elsewhere, as well as the tendency of the Hindu to make unilateral demands on those in superior or inferior positions, and we have the psychological material for the lack of political unity in Indian history as a whole.

Other Chinese-Hindu differences in politics and leadership are no less far-reaching but only one of them can be discussed here. This is the fact that Chinese rulers had little to do with religion. Once a year the ruling emperor in China performed sacrifices at the Temple of Heaven, not as head of a state church (this did not exist) but as head of the nation; the sacrifices were performed in the interest of peace and prosperity within the ruler's domain. But Chinese emperors who involved themselves personally in supernatural matters, usually for individual immortality, were by and large the weak rulers; and even among the weak ones, they were the exception and not the rule. Not once did a priest wield any great authority or become the right-hand man of a successful ruling emperor. The emperorship was based on secular power and with this secular power the emperor could consecrate gods and spirits and promote, demote, or condemn them. Even local officials, being the representatives of the emperor, could do the same; some of them exercised the right. This pattern did not change with Western impact. When Generalissimo Chiang Kai-shek was converted to Methodism in the early 1930's, Westerners who hoped for Christianization of China were at first elated, but soon they were disappointed. For Chiang's conversion made no impression one way or the other on the Chinese common man. As far as the common man was concerned, it would have made no difference if Chiang had been converted to Zoroastrianism, Islam, or stark animism, so long as he remained Chiang Kai-shek. If the Chinese emperors and their officials had what Max Weber calls charisma, their charisma was vastly different in substance from that of their Hindu counterparts.

The Hindu rulers have much to do with religion. The normal Indian ruler would be as devoted to ritual offerings to the supernatural as he would be to secular affairs. Daily devotion is the rule rather than the exception. No ruler of India ever thought he was more powerful than God. Even the Mogul emperor Akbar, who was antagonistic to Islam and at one time arrogated to himself the power of final authority in theological matters, was still interested in pooling the best of all religions to form one sect. One or more Brahmans served as honored assistants to practically every ruler. Few rulers made important moves without priestly consultation. In a few instances at least, Brahmans became rulers. As we noted in Chapter III, quite a few Hindu kings and princes retired and took up the life of a sadhu. Some Hindu rulers who were converted to Jainism starved themselves to death in accordance with the Jain idea of salvation.

Most important of all is the fact that, from the point of view of the people, some Hindu rulers were God reincarnate and were worshiped as such. In premodern times the inhabitants of some Chinese localities would build a temple dedicated to a departing official who was particularly benevolent and wise; some wealthy individuals would worship their deceased parents in a similarly exaggerated fashion. They might even believe that the benevolent official was the reincarnation of a certain famous official in the court of an ancient emperor, or even the reincarnation of a god. But these sentiments were generated by the benevolence and wisdom of the officials and were not often so concretely expressed. The unimportance of this attitude in Chinese society is shown by the fact that none of the modern leaders of China has ever been so treated. The Chinese notion was that an official, like the emperor, was someone whom the common man should keep at a distance. But the Hindu attitude toward rulers remains different even today. The result is that the popular Hindu leaders tend to be saintly as well as politically wise. In this regard we do not even have to refer to the all-too-familiar case of Mahatma Gandhi, but can point to a number of other examples without difficulty. The fact is that even though individual leaders do not care about the supernatural and tend frankly to be nonreligious, the followers will impute to them supernatural qualities and look upon them as supernatural. Prime Minister Nehru is one illustrious example of this. Both in his writings and his speeches he seems to be as far away from Hinduism as any Chinese. It is doubtful if he believes in any supernatural power at all. This does not, however, prevent some of his people from coming to his presence for darshan or from worshiping him as a god. In fact recently a temple was built for him in Bombay Province (now divided into Mahagujarati and Maharashtra) and the claim was made that he was the reincarnation of the Lord Vishnu, all of which brought on Nehru's express indignation.

At a local level the existence of this Hindu attitude is equally prevalent. In early 1955, the deputy commissioner in charge of the Bankura District, West Bengal, noticed that he had a constant silent visitor who squatted outside. When the deputy commissioner entered or left the office, the visitor would stand up and come close as though to speak about something, but he would not break his silence. At first the official thought this was one of the villagers wanting to see him with a complaint or request and paid him no particular attention since such visitors were many on every working day. After a period of time the man was finally asked about his purpose. The man told his story as follows:

> He was a resident of a village about fifty miles away in Bihar. He used to suffer from terrible stomach pains. He had tried all sorts of medication and performed pujas (worships) without getting relief. He had finally gone to the local Siva temple and prostrated before the god and prayed that he be made well. He would prostrate himself thus, he told the god, and never get up again, unless he was made well. After a day he felt better. So he went home. That night he had a dream in which the god appeared and told him that he would be made well provided he did as instructed. The god told the patient that the reason for his stomach trouble was that he had offended his deceased father. His father's spirit was the cause of it. His father's spirit had now reincarnated into the person of Mr. X, the deputy commissioner of the Bankura District at that time. For the patient to become completely well it was necessary for him to get the darshan (spiritual radiation) of his father's incarnation from time to time. Hence the man's silent presence at the deputy commissioner's place day after day.

After a few days the man left, only to appear again about three months later. He said he was getting better all the time, but he wanted to make sure. The deputy commissioner assured him that he did not have to come all the way to the office from his home village each time he wanted darshan, but that he could send a post card and would get a reply with the official darshan. Shortly after that the deputy commissioner was transferred to a district in the northern part of West Bengal and did not see the man again.

I discovered incidents of the same sort at least three times in western Uttar Pradesh and in Mysore. And when I related them to a number of Indian students, businessmen, and officials, they told me that such cases were not unusual. The case not only shows how the relationship between the Hindu and his official is different from its counterpart in China, but also illustrates well a point we made in Chapter III, namely the precarious relationship between the Hindu and the spirits of his deceased ancestors.

The American approach to politics and leadership is greatly different from that of the Chinese and the Hindus. We have already noted, in a previous connection, the basic differences in organizing principles. The American society, being a direct descendant of the English, was founded explicitly on the ideas of democracy, political freedom, human rights, and equality. Even though no democracy is perfect, America has known more of democracy than either of her Asian sisters. The one fundamental psychological difference between the individual in the United States and that in Hindu India or China is that the former will consciously seek independence and try to make his own decisions, while the latter will seek, or at least acquiesce in, dependence and having decisions made for him. Hindus entertain higher dependency expectations than the Chinese *vis-à-vis* their governments and leaders, for two reasons. On the one hand, the wider political organization is within the Hindu's infinite inner world but outside the more limited inner world of the Chinese. On the other hand, the Hindu tendency to *unilateral* dependence feeds a desire for a much higher level of demands than the Chinese tendency, which is to *mutual* dependence and in which return in measure is implied in every demand. As long as the wider government can succor him in his efforts to buttress his inner world, however, or at least does not interfere with them, the Chinese is pleased to receive all the aid that it can offer. But he is not likely to seek any personal or spiritual identification with his leaders as would the Hindu.

The Americans tend to be opposed to open despotism, even of the benevolent type. The individual-centered and self-reliant Americans must see their leaders in some way as not only representing their own aspirations but also as reflections of their own attributes. They must feel that their leaders are under their control, however small or symbolic that control may be. Consequently, though the leaders must wield power, they must, by and large, wield it in a manner at least suggestive of public consent. The leaders must show external signs of equality with all. In fact, American leaders tend to have far less private life than their Chinese or Hindu counterparts. The rocking chair that the President uses or the gowns worn by the First Lady are both cause for public concern in America, while such matters would stir no discussion at all in the Asian societies.* The authority and stability of the American government are dependent upon its general economic prosperity, as well as on its immediate ability to "deliver the goods." This is the case to a much greater extent in the United States than in China and India, in spite, indeed probably because, of the fact that the Asian attitude in general is more dependent than independent.

China and India also each have a number of their own differences from

---

* On the other hand, spectacular extravagance in high places may cause anger among any people if the majority is poor. The recent stir in Ghana due to the purchase of a gold bed by a cabinet minister's wife may be a case in point.

America. The American proverb, "from log cabin to White House," is reminiscent of the Hindu's liberal application of the term *king* to men who have no reason to claim it. However, not being supernatural-centered, Americans tend to have a much more realistic assessment of the political climate than do the Hindus. In fact, they often tend to be too realistic, since they shun possible losers. In every American election there is a motley conglomeration of dark-horse candidates whose chances of success are very small indeed. Such candidates have practically no following, and are literally regarded as crackpots by most. Modern India is beset by a proliferation of political leaders whose qualities are diverse in the extreme and whose chances of success are also about as remote. The difference is in the astonishing number of Indians who are willing to follow such leaders. The result is that, despite their dependent personal outlook and long experience under autocratic governments, Hindus have profound difficulties in achieving political unity, because of this very proliferation of claims to leadership.[27] Selig S. Harrison in an extremely penetrating recent book concludes that the future of the political unity of India is by no means certain and that the greatest challenge to it comes from linguistic divisions of the country.[28] In this he echoes the sentiment of the famous Indian sociologist G. S. Ghurye.[29] In the light of our present hypothesis, it is at least a strong possibility that the linguistic multiplicity of India is more the *result* of Hindu psychological centrifugality, analyzed in the foregoing pages of this book, than the *cause* of such centrifugality. For in language, ancient China was also divided into many regions. But instead of accentuating their regional linguistic differences, the Chinese achieved a remarkable linguistic unity not only in the written but also in the spoken language. Written Chinese is one throughout China. But even China's dialect differences have been very much misunderstood. There are about eight dialects, in addition to the Mandarin, which are largely unintelligible to each other and to the Mandarin.* But all eight are distributed along a thin coastal belt in Southeast China between Shanghai and Canton. The rest of the country, from the great northwest and the mountainous southwest to Manchuria, speaks slightly varied forms of the Mandarin. The centrifugal psychological orientation of the Hindus and the centripetal psychological orientation of the Chinese may at least have

---

* The exact extent of their mutual unintelligibility is not scientifically reported. With a little effort it is not hard for a Mandarin speaker to make himself understood in Shanghai, or for a Swatow speaker in Canton. All these speeches share the same grammar. Some Western linguists may say that these Chinese speeches are different languages, not dialects, though they do not yet have universally accepted criteria for such a distinction. (For a discussion of the criteria and their application see S. A. Würm and D. C. Laycock, "The Question of Language and Dialect in New Guinea," *Oceania*, XXXII, No. 2 (December, 1961), 128–143). But Chinese linguists have so far regarded them as dialects and not languages.

something to do with the drastically differing linguistic conditions of the two subcontinents.*

On the other hand, in spite of the self-reliant personal outlook and individualism, the American government has achieved a remarkable degree of political stability and the two major American parties have no competitors. A usual explanation for this contrast in political behavior between India and America would probably be that Americans have had much longer experience in governing themselves whereas the Indians are newcomers to political democracy. My view is that the differences in psychological orientation, which lead to proliferation of leaders in one culture and a desire to back the realistic winners in the other, constitute also a most crucial ingredient in the situation.

The case of China provides us with a partial proof for the contention. The Chinese also have not had experience with democracy, as the West understands the term. But Chinese government under the Nationalists before the recent change of regime, and their government under the Communists now, have both had a remarkable degree of stability and unity. The Nationalists under Chiang Kai-shek labored under tremendous difficulties. Since 1842, all the major Western powers have enjoyed special privileges in China and exercised severe political and economic controls over the country. Between 1911 when the Manchu dynasty fell and 1928 when Chiang Kai-shek's forces politically and militarily brought China under one government, the country was a chaotic land of war lords most of whom were under the thumb or influence of one or another foreign power. Even after Chiang unified China, Japan was engaged in direct military aggression against her territorial integrity, leaving a trail of murder, rape, and arson, and none of the Western powers except Russia, Germany, and Austria even relinquished its special privileges in China. In spite of these disabilities, Chiang's regime was remarkably stable between 1928 and 1937. Even in the blackest days of the Japanese occupation of China, when the cause for China's independence looked hopeless, when no Western powers offered a helping hand except Russia, Chiang was able to prevent any internal defection in favor of collaboration with the Japanese. The establishment of the Communist regime in China since 1949 and its stability and solidarity have given further support to our thesis, even though the time is still too short for a political change involving so vast a country to reveal its full stature and impact.

The fact that the Communist ideology is so drastically different from the

* The fact that the Chinese written language is ideographic while the written languages in India are based on systems of alphabets may have helped the separation of Indian languages. But the fissiparous tendency in the larger aspects of Indian society and culture is so obvious that it is doubtful that the use of alphabets could have created it.

indigenous psychocultural orientation has led some observers to suspect that the Communist regime in China could not possibly succeed, and has led others to an opposite course in the search for indigenous elements in Chinese culture and history which favor Communism. Both positions are unsound. What is to be realized is that there is a basic distinction between the Communist regime as a political administration and the Communist regime as the expression of an ideology. The thesis of this book is that, while seeking fulfillment of needs as individuals, human beings in every society are conditioned by the ideas embodied in their culture which express themselves, on the one hand, as ideals which guide or inspire them in action and, on the other, in the basic principle or principles which govern the many ways they relate to each other. In this process they are also inevitably limited by the functional prerequisites common to all societies mentioned in the introductory chapter of this book. The public pronouncements of policy of every political regime tend to be colored by its ideals while its actual performances must be severely limited by the expediencies and practical requirements essential for its existence and continuation and the existence and continuation of the society as a whole with reference to its own peculiar geographical, historical, and ecological conditions. Consequently, we should not be surprised when Chinese leaders, whoever they are and however extreme their outlook, speak in terms of Confucian precepts such as "cultivation of the self"[30] while enforcing ruthless measures which allow no privacy or time to the individual himself at all; the Hindu leaders emphasize nonviolence and spirituality but resort to arms to liquidate the colonial remnants on its soil; and the United States leaders reiterate freedom, equality, and Christian love and yet support dictators whose jails are full and who have no compunction in shooting down any opposition. In all cases the practical is not the ideal, for they are dictated by different considerations.

The Communist regime as the expression of a militant and missionizing ideology is an altogether different proposition. The Chinese centripetal outlook fostered in their family and clan life has never given them an incentive for missionary zeal or work or for wider human groupings and movements. This was why the Chinese as a whole were never enthusiastic about Christianity; when and if converted, they were more likely to be frankly opportunistic about it than otherwise. Practically all the missionaries in the world are Westerners in spite of the fact that the Chinese population is several times the size of its European counterpart at any point of history. The missionizing aspect of any ideology, whether religious, social, or political, finds its ablest and most ardent agents among Westerners but never among the Chinese. The plain fact is that Communism went to China from the West, with Western or Western-trained and -inspired leadership, exactly as did Christianity, capitalism, democracy, modern science and technology.

All of these Western-originated social, political, economic, and religious movements, as our analysis in the foregoing pages has demonstrated, spring from the Western way of life of which that of the United States is a variant and in which contract, not kinship, is the basic principle of social grouping. The chances of any long term success of Communism as an ideology are similar to those of the other Western ideologies, which depend upon how quickly and to what extent the kinship principle of social grouping can be replaced by some wider principle closer to contract. All the aforementioned Western ideologies and movements have aimed at reducing the importance of the kinship principle in China during the last hundred years, and they have certainly succeeded in undermining it to a degree. Communism as the latest major Western ideology has not only benefited from the process already started by its predecessors but also has greatly broadened and accelerated it. In this context, the Communist attempt to communize China becomes understandable. It is simply the most extreme means to disengage the Chinese, once and for all, from their age-old centripetal attitude toward the primary groups, so that they may be more easily propelled into identification with and involvement in issues, personalities, and movements in the politically dictated wider arena.*

In totalitarianism no less than in democracy the first and foremost prerequisite is that the individual be freed from the attachments, rewards, and obligations in a network of mutual dependence according to the kinship principle in order that he may transfer his attachments, duties, and obligations elsewhere. In this regard the basic problem of political development in India, in spite of her psychocultural peculiarities, is similar to that of China, namely, how to free the individual from the attachments, rewards, and obligations in a network of unilateral dependence according to the hierarchical principle in order that he may transfer the same to a wider grouping or groupings built on the contract principle and all that the latter entails.

The shape of things to come after that can differ greatly, while the basic process remains the same. In totalitarianism the ensuing wider groupings will be primarily state-dictated and state-regulated, with occasional concessions to the individual's desires. In democracy the ensuing wider groupings will be largely privately organized and privately maintained, with grudging allowances to state interference. The trend toward either is at the expense of the Chinese or the Hindu way of life.

---

* The present (1960, 1961, and 1962) food difficulties in mainland China are most probably the direct result of the Communist government's attempt to push too fast a program of transformation which is too extreme. How far the new regime and its non-Chinese ideology will eventually succeed in China depends upon many factors, one of which is whether the powerful elements in China are capable of learning from their mistakes.

NOTES FOR CHAPTER X

1. Henry A. Murray et al., Explorations in Personality (New York: Oxford University Press, 1938), pp. 123–124.

2. We also postulated close interrelationship among the three social needs, as well as variation in social needs from individual to individual and from society to society. But these postulates are not crucial to the present analysis and are therefore left out of it.

3. W. I. Thomas and F. Znaniecki, The Polish Peasant in Europe and America (New York: Alfred A. Knopf, 1927), Vol. I, pp. 72–73.

4. A. H. Maslow, Motivation and Personality (New York: Harper and Brothers, 1954), p. 15.

5. Kurt Goldstein, "Organismic Approach to the Problem of Motivation," Transactions (New York Academy of Sciences, 1947), Vol. IX, 218–230; and Carl R. Rogers, Client-Centered Therapy: Its Current Practice, Implications and Theory (Boston: Houghton Mifflin, 1951).

6. Charles Morris, Varieties of Human Value (Chicago: University of Chicago Press, 1956).

7. Morris, ibid., p. 48.

8. Morris, ibid., p. 48.

9. Morris, ibid., p. 47.

10. Morris, ibid., p. 54.

11. Morris, ibid., p. 54.

12. Morris, ibid., p. 54.

13. Morris, ibid., p. 53.

14. Morris, ibid., p. 53.

15. Morris, ibid., p. 58.

16. Morris, ibid., p. 59.

17. Morris, ibid., p. 59.

18. Gerald D. Berreman, "Caste in India and the United States," American Journal of Sociology, LXVI, No. 2 (1960), 121.

19. Ibid., pp. 122–123.

20. McKim Marriott, "Little Communities in an Indigenous Civilization," in McKim Marriott (ed.), Village India (Chicago: University of Chicago Press, 1955), pp. 171–222.

21. Berreman, op. cit., p. 125. In the published version of Berreman's paper the following paragraph was added to the version orally presented at the American Anthropological Association 1959 Convention: "There are, of course, Negroes and organized groups of Negroes, such as the black supremacist 'Muslims' recently in the news in the United States, who want to invert the caste hierarchy; conversely, there are low-caste people in India who want to abolish the entire system. But these seem to be atypical viewpoints. The anti-caste religions and reform movements which have from time to time appealed with some success to lower castes in India, for example, Buddhism, Islam, Christianity, Sikhism, have been unable, in practice, to remain casteless. This seems to be a point of real difference between Indian and American low-caste attitudes, for in America objection is more characteristically directed toward the system as such" (p. 125). However, Berreman added in a footnote: "Whether this difference in attitude is widely correlated with multiple, as compared to dual, caste systems, or is attributable to other dif-

ferences in the Indian and American situations, can be established only by further comparative work" (p. 125, Note 19). The first paragraph quoted here seems to indicate that Berreman agrees with our views expressed in this chapter, but his footnote to it indicates that he regards the multiple-caste situation in India, as contrasted to the two-caste situation in the United States, as being a possible cause for the fundamental difference in attitudes which he acknowledges. My view is that the multiplicity of castes in India and the two-caste situation in the United States are results or expressions of the basic difference in attitudes rather than its causes. Castes mushroom in India precisely because there is little indigenous attack against the caste system as such in that society. Castes do not mushroom in the United States because the overall philosophical-theological framework is antithetic to it there.

22. Three present-day interpretations of the Siva linga worshiped in many Hindu temples are known to me. (1) It is simply a symbol of God; (2) it is a symbol of interaction between the male and female principles of the world; and (3) it represents the sexual act.

23. John Dewey, *A Common Faith* (New Haven: Yale University Press, 1934).

24. A. Eustace Hayden, *Biography of the Gods* (New York: Macmillan, 1941), pp. 276–283.

25. *Ibid.*, p. 282.

26. Some readers, because they believe divisiveness to be evil, will see in this analysis a derogatory slur on church life in America. I have no such meaning in mind at all. In the first place, divisiveness and cohesiveness are used merely descriptively. In the second place, those who attach an undesirable meaning to divisiveness should reflect on the fact that, but for Western divisiveness, Protestantism in Christianity would never have been born. In social life no less than in physical life, dynamism leads to divisiveness.

27. An excellent description and analysis of the wide variety of Indian political leaders and the diverse natures of their leadership are offered in a recent publication, Richard L. Park and Irene Tinker (eds.), *Leadership and Political Institutions in India* (Princeton: Princeton University Press, 1959).

28. Selig S. Harrison, *India, the Most Dangerous Years: Can the Nation Hold Together?* (Princeton: Princeton University Press, 1960).

29. G. S. Ghurye, "Indian Unity—Retrospect and Prospect," *Group Prejudices in India* (Bombay: Vora, 1951), p. 120.

30. Herlee G. Creel, *Chinese Thought: From Confucius to Mao Tse-Tung* (Chicago: University of Chicago Press, 1953), pp. 254–257.

Annex

A THEMATIC APPERCEPTION TEST STUDY OF CHINESE, HINDU, AND AMERICAN COLLEGE STUDENTS*

THIS STUDY is something of an experiment along an unbeaten path which must be considered separately from the body of the book. Though it may provide some evidence relevant to, or supportive of, some parts of the book, the facts, arguments and conclusions given in the foregoing pages must stand or fall on their own. The study is an exploratory move taken in the hope of finding a scientifically feasible way of utilizing some form of projective test on a considerable scale cross-culturally, as an aid to certain forms of anthropological field work.

I. DATA AND APPROACH

The roughly 600 Thematic Apperception Test stories on which this study is based were collected in the autumn and winter of 1961 from about 300 college students† in the social sciences‡ by Hsu. They were first subjected

* By Blanche G. Watrous and Francis L. K. Hsu. Mrs. Watrous received her Ph.D. in Anthropology from Northwestern University in 1949. Her dissertation on *A Personality Study of Ojibwa Children* was written under the supervision of A. I. Hallowell and M. J. Herskovits, and was based on her field work among the Lac de Flambeau Indians in Wisconsin. Dr. Watrous is currently Professor of Anthropology, East Carolina College, Greenville, North Carolina.

† The following sets of responses were excluded from consideration: two from the Indo-American Society because the subjects were Chinese; two from the Lady Irwin College because the subjects were Ceylonese; and one from Northwestern University because the subject was South African.

‡ Except for those in the Indo-American Society. The Indo-American Society is organized under the sponsorship and financial support of the USIS to which all interested college or senior high school students are welcome.

263

to blind analysis* and interpretation by Watrous. Her analysis and interpretation form Sections II and III of this Appendix. These are followed by
Hsu's comments and interpretation in the light of Watrous's conclusions,
which form Section IV. Section V contains joint remarks in conclusion by
both authors. Hsu obtained the Taiwan, Hong Kong, and Hindu fantasies in
the course of a field trip to Taiwan, Hong Kong, and India in the winter of
1961. The American students were enrolled in one of his anthropology
courses at Northwestern University in the fall of 1961. A few basic points
pertaining to the subjects appear in Table A-1.

Table A-1. DISTRIBUTION OF THE SUBJECTS

| | | SEX | | AGE | | |
LOCATION	NO.	M	F	FREQUENCY	GROUP	EDUCATION
U.S.A.:	38	14	24	19–24	Northwestern University	Social sciences
CHINA:						
Hong Kong	50	18	32	19–22	Hong Kong University	Social sciences
Taiwan	40	20	20	19–22	Taiwan University	Social sciences
INDIA:						
Calcutta	58	58	0	17–20[a]	Vidyasagar College	Social sciences
Calcutta	52	0	52	18–19	Asutosh College	Social sciences
New Delhi	39	0	39	16–18	Lady Irwin College	Education
Calcutta	26	23	3	15–17	Indo-American Society	Various subjects

a. A few students in the Far Eastern universities omitted their ages.

The average age of the Northwestern students is a few years older than
the Hindu students, while the Chinese students fall between the two estimated means. The Indo-American Society students are the youngest in
chronological age, the majority being 15 and 16. In certain colleges, from one
to three students are considerably older. For example, one Northwestern
graduate student lists his age as 40, three Vidyasagar males give the age of
30, and three Taiwan students list their ages as 28.

To secure a relatively large number of responses from the three cultures
it was necessary to shorten the test material. Only Card 1 and Card 12BG
in Murray's TAT were used: Card 1 because of its stimulus value in evok-
ing a variety of interpersonal interactions; Card 12BG because of its nonhuman content and its potential for eliciting associations to the natural en-

* "Blind" analysis in the present instance means that Watrous did not see a copy of
Hsu's manuscript but does not mean that the interpreter of the test results knows nothing
about the three ways of life seen by the collector of the tests. When Oberholzer analyzed
the 37 Rorschach test protocols collected by Cora Du Bois, he knew nothing about the
Alorese way of life because no writing on it existed before the publication of Du Bois'
The People of Alor (Minnesota University Press, 1944). Watrous, on the other hand, besides being an American, had certainly read a number of publications on India, China and
the United States before she was confronted with these TAT responses. The seven
groups of responses were given to Watrous in separate envelopes each bearing the
identity of a particular group of responses.

vironment. An additional factor in this selection relates to the contrasting appraisal of the two pictures by clinicians in the United States. Card 1 is generally considered "the single most valuable picture in the TAT" if attempts were to be made "to make statements about the total personality."[1] Conversely, Card 12BG is not considered "too useful in any specific case except in suicidal or very depressed subjects."[2] The possibility that students in other cultures might not react to the stimulus value of these pictures in a manner similar to that of subjects in the United States seemed to merit exploration.

All these tests were administered by Hsu personally in a classroom situation. Except for his own class at Northwestern University, Hsu was in each case introduced by the instructor of the class as a Professor of Anthropology from Northwestern University, U.S.A., who was administering the same psychological test among college students in several parts of the world. The administrator gave the standard instruction provided in Form A of Henry A. Murray's *Thematic Apperception Test Manual*.[3]

After the introduction each subject was given a Thermofax reproduction of Card 1. All were requested to write down their stories on sheets of paper which they had ready. Each student was asked to write on his response sheets his name, age, sex, place of birth, religion, academic status, and in India, his caste. In addition, each student was asked to take from five to ten minutes for each card, to write more than one story for each picture if desired, and to write in any language that he or she felt most comfortable with. He was told that the pictures were not photographs but were simply created by an artist. Some subjects did give more than one story to one card. In the analysis below, varying projections to the same card by one subject are treated as one single story. The last item of instruction was prompted by Hsu's experiences in Taiwan where a few students made the inquiry as to whether they were photographs, and in India where some students asked him, after the testing session was over, what "really" was in the pictures and what he (Hsu) thought was in the pictures. One copy of Card 1 from the Harvard University Press edition of the TAT was put on the blackboard in each session to show the students the original from which the Thermofax versions were reproduced.

In Hong Kong and Taiwan instructions were given in Chinese, the responses were written in Chinese or English and the Chinese responses were translated into English by Hsu. In India instructions were given in English to the Indo-American Society and Lady Irwin College students. In Asutosh and Vidyasagar Colleges instructions were given in English first and then in Bengali (in each case by the instructor of the class). A total of 52 stories were written in Bengali by 23 Asutosh and 6 Vidyasagar students and translated into English by Dr. Moni Nag and Mrs. Uma Guha of the Anthropological Survey of India, Calcutta. But all of the students tested have studied English for at least five years and can speak and read it with varying degrees of proficiency.

After collecting the responses to Card 1, Thermofax reproductions of Card 12BG were then distributed, and responses to them were collected later, with no additional instructions.

The Thematic Apperception Test is assumed to yield data on interpersonal relationships and internalized goals and values, together with attitudes related to self-acceptance or self-awareness. It seems to us possible that, administered to subjects with varying cultural traditions, it might elicit some clues related to modal personalities of the different groups both in their original environment and, in the case of the Far Eastern subjects, under the impact of Western contact.

In general, the contents of the fantasies are analyzed with minimal emphasis on depth interpretation. The interpretation follows well-established lines of reasoning. For example, the introduction of additional figures such as parents, a teacher, or peers into Card 1, which contains only a boy sitting at a table looking at a violin, suggests heightened awareness of the human environment, and a greater need for emotional involvement with other people. Conversely, those subjects who concentrate solely on the character in the picture may be considered less spontaneous, more inhibited in their relationships to other people. Card 12BG is a landscape scene of a rowboat drawn up on the bank of a woodland stream. In the analysis of this picture special attention is focused on the extent to which the subjects are sensitive to the nonhuman environment, and the extent to which they relax with nature. Those who are apparently not threatened by solitude are interpreted as showing attitudes of self-acceptance.

The first category of the projective materials analyzed in both cards is Interpersonal Relationships. With reference to Card 1, this category is then divided into subcategories: Father, Mother, Other Individuals, No Individuals, Dependency, and Resistance (see Table A-2). If a parent or other individual is projected as having died, this person is also scored in the subcategory of appropriate relationship. If "parents" or "family" are seen in the picture, both Father and Mother are scored. The category Dependency is scored only when this behavior is explicitly verbalized; for example, "The boy wanted a violin of his own but his parents were too poor to buy one for him." The category of Resistance includes projection of overt rebellion against parental authority and passive aggressive resistance. As an example of the latter, the boy breaks the violin or notes that the strings are broken.

In terms of plot the manifest content of Card 1 frequently elicits stories of achievement. This category presents scoring difficulties; few subjects in this sample project the degree of positive achievement so readily apparent in

Table A-2. RESPONSES TO TAT CARD 1

SUBJECT	VIDYASAGAR		ASUTOSH		LADY IRWIN		INDO-AMERICAN		TAIWAN		HONG KONG		EVANSTON	
Number	58	(100%)	52	(100%)	39	(100%)	26	(100%)	40	(100%)	50	(100%)	38	(100%)
Interpersonal Relationships														
Father	3	(6%)	11	(21%)	20	(51%)	9	(35%)	17	(42%)	15	(30%)	19	(50%)
Mother	1	(2%)	10	(19%)	18	(46%)	8	(30%)	12	(30%)	14	(28%)	20	(53%)
Other Persons	13	(24%)	10	(19%)	20	(51%)	18	(69%)	17	(42%)	12	(24%)	29	(76%)
No other human beings	44	(76%)	27	(52%)	10	(26%)	3	(11%)	11	(27%)	27	(54%)	3	(8%)
Dependence	4	(8%)	1	(2%)	7	(18%)	4	(15%)	4	(10%)	4	(8%)	1	(3%)
Resistance	11	(19%)	2	(4%)	10	(26%)	7	(27%)	15	(37%)	15	(30%)	26	(68%)
Fantasy														
Achievement Imagery	14	(24%)	17	(33%)	21	(54%)	22	(85%)	16	(40%)	20	(40%)	20	(53%)
Reverie	44	(76%)	35	(67%)	18	(46%)	4	(15%)	24	(60%)	30	(60%)	18	(47%)
Death	2	(3%)	5	(9%)	7	(18%)	1	(4%)	5	(13%)	1	(2%)	4	(10%)
Blindness	7	(11%)	6	(11%)	7	(18%)	1	(4%)	0	—	1	(2%)	0	—
Brokenness	7	(12%)	1	(2%)	7	(18%)	4	(16%)	3	(8%)	2	(4%)	2	(5%)
Mutability	1	(2%)	7	(13%)	2	(5%)	2	(8%)	0	—	0	—	0	—

the examples of Issei and Nisei stories reported by Caudill and De Vos.[4] In their study "positive achievement" includes clear-cut motivation: "(a) the boy wanted to be a violinist . . . and succeeds by working hard; (b) he is puzzled how to solve the task but keeps working at it; (c) his parents want him to become a violinist and he does so successfully."[5] In our present study the category Achievement Imagery follows McClelland *et al.* Our Achievement Imagery includes their subcategories "Competition with a Standard of Excellence," "Unique Accomplishment," "Long-Term Achievement," "Long-Term Involvement." Stories fulfilling at least one of McClelland's criteria are scored A.I. Stories which project McClelland's "Doubtful Achievement Imagery" (e.g., a person engaged in a commonplace task) or "Unrelated Imagery" (no reference to accomplishment) are scored as Reverie.[6]

In Card 12BG, Interpersonal Relationships include the subcategories of One Individual, Two Individuals, Two-plus Individuals (any number greater than two) and No Individual (see Table A-3). If the subject projects himself, i.e., the first person singular, verbalizing his affective reaction to the natural environment or solitude, One Individual is scored. One Individual is also scored if the fantasy projects a human character formerly at the scene. (For example, "The fisherman who once owned this boat has moved away.") "People at a picnic," "a party in the wood," "the entire family on an outing" are scored Two-plus Individuals.

The second major category, Sensitivity to the Physical Environment (i.e., nonhuman) is based on numerical count of descriptive adjectives or nouns elaborating the landscape scene. The scale is arbitrarily decided upon as follows: Vivid Sensitivity when seven or more adjectives are used; Average Sensitivity includes at least three descriptive adjectives; No Sensitivity is scored for subjects who exclude any reference to natural scenery description (for example, boys who go on an outing and become involved with robbers, murderers, etc.).

The reaction of the students to Card 12BG (Table A-3) frequently conformed to one of two distinct patterns: either they reacted to the manifest content of the picture stimulus with Reverie-type associations; or apparently threatened by solitude, they produced imaginative plots related to romance or adventure; hence, the categories Reverie and Plot.

The number and kind of picture stimuli used necessarily limited the scope of the blind analysis. As noted above, neither card includes parental figures. When parental figures were "introduced" in the absence of such manifest stimulus, the assumption was made, following Henry, that they may normally be thought of as representing "the subject's need to complete the picture stimulus with figures whom he considers an integral part of the plot as suggested by the actual stimulus picture."[7] Many subjects, however,

Table A-3. RESPONSES TO T A T CARD 12BG

RESPONSE	VIDYASAGAR	ASUTOSH	LADY IRWIN	INDO-AMERICAN	TAIWAN	HONG KONG	EVANSTON
Number	56 (100%)	50 (100%)	39 (100%)	23 (100%)	40 (100%)	50 (100%)	38 (100%)
Interpersonal Relationships, %							
One individual projected	26	24	15	26	28	29	16
Two individuals projected	4	6	15	4	25	13	34
Two or more individuals projected	42	36	59	67	28	33	34
No human beings projected	27	34	8	0	15	26	10
Sensitivity to Physical Environment, %							
Vivid sensitivity to physical environment	13	26	28	8	13	52	29
Average sensitivity to physical environment	81	54	61	16	55	46	32
No sensitivity to physical environment	5	20	10	67	38	2	39
Plot	13	15	59	74	25	15	32
Reverie	87	84	41	26	75	85	68
Death	11	15	30	17	23	8	10
Mutability	6	20	20	8	0	0	0

failed to associate to parental figures, thereby leaving notable lacunae in possible interpretation not only of affective relationships with parents, including patterns of dependency and resistance, but also of possible parental stimulation for achievement. Likewise, without the use of cards which normally elicit heterosexual involvement, sibling rivalry or aggression, interpretation of such behavior is not possible. This analysis is, therefore, not comparable to the intensive studies of modal personality made by such scientists as Wallace,[8] Kaplan,[9] or Gladwin and Sarason,[10] or even the more limited study of Mulligen on Maori adolescents.[11] The limited number of norms available for TAT analysis and current uncertainty as to the meaning of such norms used in cross-cultural studies also preclude subjecting these data to refined statistical methods.[12] No effort is made here to interpret basic personality structure or total personality. It is possible, on the other hand, to observe how certain reactions occurred in integrated clusters, suggesting varying patterns of cultural behavior in response to the same picture stimuli.

A final category concerns fantasies among the Hindus but rare among the Americans or Chinese. This category contains projective materials in which the subjects anthropomorphize fauna, flora, and inanimate things and seem to fail to make absolute distinctions between subject and object. Hsu suggests the category Mutability to describe this behavior, which is used in the analysis of responses to both Cards 1 and 12BG.

II. ANALYSIS OF GROUPS (WATROUS)

American (Northwestern University Students)

The American students show two distinct trends in their fantasy projections: either they tell one integrated story of approximately 200 words in length, or they project from one to five brief, alternative themes. The two trends are almost equally represented in number with little distinction between the sexes. In general, these young people appear spontaneous, gregarious, energetic, and imaginative, showing strong need for peer acceptance and pronounced rebellion against parental authority. There is little evidence of constraint or caution in a new situation, but at the same time there is fairly striking conflict with respect to feelings and ultimate goals. There is a marked difference between their response to the external environment of people and the external environment of nature (nonhuman); for example, the Americans show limited sensitivity to nature in the manner of Wordsworth or Keats and little of the *Weltschmerz* reaction frequently associated with college students of late adolescent or young adult age. Their perceptual accuracy is sharp, with a need to distinguish between subject and object. They are oriented to action although they do not necessarily project goals related to hard work or sustained effort. Fantasying action is a stronger need than projecting mood. There is little indication from the reactions to the two cards that these young people have been concerned with poverty, illness, and accident or that religious or spiritual feeling is integrated into their personality. For the most part they appear threatened by solitude and show little empathy for reflection and contemplation.

Spontaneity, energy, and ambition are suggested both by the well-integrated stories and by the number of alternative projections. The need to be gregarious and that for peer acceptance are indicated by the fact that 76% of students introduce Others in Card 1 and 68% of them introduce two or more individuals in Card 12BG. In the former group, one-half project fantasies with overt reference to peers. These students are immediately aware of interpersonal relationships with their parents, with one-half of them associating to parents in Card 1. Reactions to parental control are coupled with strong resistance to authority, 68% of them projecting resistance, and at the same time with minimal overt dependency (only 3%). The maternal figure is more often singled out as the object of resistance: "Oh, mother, I've practiced one hour already. Can't I go out and play baseball?" On the other hand, many of the Americans are ambivalent about their resistance: alternative themes are frequently of a reverie type in which the boy "dreams of becoming a great violinist." This readily available defense through fantasy seems to meet two needs of almost equal prominence: for slightly more than one-half the group (53%) fantasy relates in Card 1 to Achievement Imagery; in the remainder fantasy serves as an escape from such projections as in the following: "He is gripping his day dreams as a means of keeping from the act of starting his practicing." Playing the violin, as Henry has observed, is a current middle-class American value which has become a frequent source of conflict between parents and children, especially male children;[13] violin playing by boys is interpreted as a "sissy" activity.

Oral needs with overt associations to food are frequently noted. In particular, family picnics are a common theme in response to Card 12BG. The major emphasis, however, is concerned with interpersonal relationships, in particular resistance to parental authority and involvement with the peer group.

Chinese: University of Hong Kong Students

The Hong Kong students as contrasted with American students project on the whole shorter stories without alternative plots. They also appear more cautious, more restrained, less spontaneous, and more accepting of self. They are less egocentric, less aggressive, less resistant to authority. Where

American students show eagerness to be involved with other people, the Chinese students frequently show lack of intensity in interpersonal relationships. At the same time the Chinese are more sensitive to the external environment of nature, reacting with sensuous imagery to landscape stimuli.

Caution, restraint, and less spontaneity in a new environment are suggested by shorter stories without alternative plots in Card 1. Where 68% of the stories given by American students show resistance to authority, only 30% of the stories given by the Hong Kong students are resistive. The lesser involvement of the Hong Kong students with other people is apparent in the fact that 54% of the Hong Kong stories include no other individual in Card 1 as contrasted with only 8% of the Americans; and 26% of the Hong Kong stories introduce no people to Card 12BG, as contrasted with only 10% of the American stories. The Hong Kong students show minimal interest in peer competition and minimal need for peer acceptance. The outstanding behavior of the Hong Kong students lies in their sensuous, effortless response to the boat scene of Card 12BG: 52% project vivid imagery; 46% show limited responsivity and only 2% are totally indifferent to it. None of the other groups tested reflect this behavior pattern to a comparable degree.

The imagery projected is analogous to the response of the Chinese Hawaiian adolescents to bright color in the Rorschach test, as noted by Hsu, Watrous, and Lord,[14] where such responses were interpreted as showing more mature emotionality than white Americans of comparable age on the mainland of the United States. With the same comparison in mind, the Hong Kong group's reluctance to project alternative plots, their less vivid imagination suggest that the Hong Kong students, like the Hawaiian Chinese, are less inclined to exploit fantasy defenses in problem-solving than the Americans. Some similarity between the American and Hong Kong students is evident in a limited number of fantasies which are indistinguishable from one group to another on blind analysis. Specifically, sometimes a Hong Kong story in Card 1 involves resistance to parental authority and (more infrequently) a need for peer involvement. Conversely, a relatively small number of American fantasies to Card 12BG include vivid, sensual imagery to the landscape. Achievement Imagery of the Hong Kong students is slightly less prominent (40% of these Chinese as compared with 53% of the Americans project clear-cut motivation in this direction). More significant, however, is the fact that the American students react to Card 1 as if a choice of behavior were possible to them: a choice between practicing and not practicing, a choice between working or engaging in peer-group activity; while the Chinese students are less inclined to show concern with choice, at the same time appearing more thoughtful and meditative.

Chinese: Taiwan University Students

"Robert who has no sunshine," the only Taiwan story with a title, seems to project the prevailing mood of youth in that island at this time. This symbolic vein is echoed in the 12BG story featuring "a couple who took their children into the forest to get cool," but who "forgot a child in the forest." Dysphoric effect with a sense of defeatism and vague, nebulous irritability is fairly characteristic. For example, Resistance in Card 1 is indicated by projecting the boy as being "tired" or "having a headache"; or that "he feels unpleasant," "the teacher scolds," etc. Achievement Imagery is tinged with lack of confidence. "Other people can play; why can't I?" "I cannot learn very well; the only thing I can do is study the construction in order to mitigate my sorrow." "Why is my sound so ugly?" "The sound is not the kind of sound that will correspond to the strings in my heart. I feel very, very sad." Projections of Death are not infrequent—a parent in Card 1, a child or a lover in 12BG. These young people seem lacking in optimism, uncertain as to ultimate goal, with the "broken string" of the violin speculatively symbolizing their reaction to the future rather than resistance at the moment.

Except for the dysphoria noted above, the Taiwan stories are difficult to classify in terms of a distinct mode. No facet of Taiwan behavior as interpreted from the TAT responses is strikingly different from those of American and Hong Kong youth. For example, like the young people in Hong Kong, the Formosa group are more likely to project meditation than to fantasy action. But like those of the American students the Taiwan stories contain considerably less vivid sensitivity to the natural environment: 13% of the Taiwan stories show vivid sensitivity while 38% show total indifference to this stimulus. (The Hong Kong projections to Card 12BG are 52% vivid imagery, 46% limited sensitivity, and only 2% total indifference.)

The Taiwan projections to Card 1 suggest approximately equal involvement with parents and with other individuals. Resistiveness is fairly prominent although apathetic (37%). In Achievement Imagery and Reverie they have given an identical number of projections with their Hong Kong compatriots. For the most part strong motivation for success is lacking and Achievement Imagery is expressed without much zest or enthusiasm for goal attainment. Many of the projections to Card 1 suggest a feeling only of a task to be performed as summarily as possible.

Projections to Card 12BG are in the main brief, 4 to 6 lines. Of the 25% of Taiwan subjects who project two individuals in this card, 23% perceive them as lovers. The stories lack intensity of emotional involvement. Could it be inferred that neither interpersonal relationships nor the natural environment gratify the emotional needs of these young people? Or could it be said that these students have perhaps lost some of the sense of security provided by the traditional Chinese family constellation and are, consequently, resistive to authority in a passive manner? Or could it be that the current cultural rewards on Taiwan stimulate neither individual initiative nor creative energy in problem-solving?

Hindu: Vidyasagar College Students

The picture stimulus of the boy with the violin elicits from 54 of the 56 Vidyasagar students an identical association—that of "thinking": "A good boy . . . thinks how to play"; "a boy thinks about his future life"; "the boy is thinking about his duty"; "the boy is deeply thinking about some tunes to be composed." (Interestingly, of the two young men who do not project "thinking," one perceives the boy as a "European"!) The empathy of these males for reflection in lieu of action or interaction in response to a new situation may also be inferred from their reluctance to associate to other individuals or to project achievement imagery: 73% related only to the boy, with no other individuals; and 69% projected reverie without achievement need. These are the highest percentages in these categories of the seven groups tested. Consistent with the emphasis on "no other individuals," the Vidyasagar males almost completely ignore parental figures, with only one student (2%) associating to the mother and three students (6%) projecting a father figure. Thus, the resistance noted in 19% of the stories is inferred for the most part from the broken strings of the violin and not directly from external authority figures.

The majority of the Card 1 fantasies are brief: four or five lines, with apparent limitations in vocabulary and difficulty with English grammatical constructions. Yet though the administrator of the test (Hsu) specifically asked the students to use their mother tongue if they felt so disposed, only three students elected to do so. This fact, together with the fact that the Card 12BG stories are longer and more spontaneous, suggests that the limiting factor of language difficulty should not be exaggerated. Forty-two percent of the students project two or more individuals to the landscape scene of Card 12BG. As in Card 1, the mental activity is of a musing type, 87% projecting reverie with plot. The small number of students who show no sensitivity to the external environment (5%) is comparable to the Hong Kong group (2%).

The stereotyped fantasies on the whole project minimal influence of Western society and only limited references to Hindu culture. The Hindu reference is apparent in occasional associations to Indian place names and Indian individuals, with the tiger most frequent among animals. The influence of traditional patterns must thus be inferred from the intellectual approach to problem-solving, in particular the emphasis upon thought rather than action, a feeling of reverence when occasional religious associations occur, and, in contrast with the Americans especially, complete unconcern with peer acceptance and approval of others. Marked emotional inhibition is suggested by their fantasies to the two cards. It could be speculated that these students, when contrasted with their exuberant counterparts in the Indo-American Society, whose stories are examined below, are lacking in urbanity and intellectual sophistication. One might surmise that they come quite possibly from a socio-economic status different from that of the members of the Indo-American Society.

To the Western psychologist, their preoccupation with thinking suggests a lack of commitment to action or feeling. One also wonders if the tentative approach of these Vidyasagar students to the test environment is not consistent with their tentative approach to other cultural patterns of the West. They may conform superficially to this alien way of life. Emotionally and intellectually, however, the Vidyasagar are Hindu.

An instructor in an American college, on reading the Vidyasagar fantasies, would assume some collaboration among the students. This impression is based on the fact that two stories are identical and that the projections show a remarkable degree of uniformity (e.g., no plot is found in a majority of the stories; 73% of the projections to Card 1 introduce no other human beings; 54 out of 56 students are preoccupied with thinking). This uniformity is striking even when compared with the other three Indian groups. On the other hand, the projections to Card 12BG show less uniformity and much more spontaneity, 42% of the students introducing two or more individuals to the boat scene. Either the emotional threat of a new situation, i.e., the beginning of a test environment, evokes inhibition as a prevailing personality pattern or the Vidyasagar students are more at ease with a relatively unstructured situation where no definite action involving other human beings is demanded of them.

Hindu: Asutosh College Students

The emotional and intellectual affinity of the Vidyasagar College students with traditional Hindu culture is implicit and only inferred. With Asutosh College students (all girls) this affinity is explicit and verbalized. The command of English in the 29 stories written in the alien language is superior to that of Vidyasagar males. With the greater linguistic fluency, Hindu patterns of thinking and feeling become vibrant and distinctive. The boy perceived by the Asutosh females is the "thinking" boy of the Vidyasagar males, but the Asutosh females project with fluidity of style and traditional

Hindu color and intensity of feeling. Thus, the Asutosh boy tries to understand "the essence of the instrument," "to solve by his perception," "to know what the actual thing is," and he "minutely observes the structure." As with Lady Irwin students, to be discussed below, the violin is "the only friend (of the orphan boy), a faithful friend of his life"; "Don't forget me and I shall help you as long as I can." Again contrasted with Vidyasagar, the greater range of English vocabulary of Asutosh girls is matched by their wider range of imagination. Some of the Asutosh fantasies are similar in culture-hero projection to the stories from the Indo-American Society; others to those from Lady Irwin College. It is doubtful if any of these stories, on blind analysis, would be interpreted as American.

The Hong Kong students react to the external environment with descriptive adjectives. The Asutosh college students, more than any other group, project human emotions into the fauna, the flora, the boat, as if the fauna, the flora, and the boat were integral parts of the society of man and as if the distinction between subject and object were of little moment. "The same pain which is in the mother's breast has also arisen in the mind of the tree by seeing the motherless child"; "but the blossoms of those trees make the small birds happy" (examples of fantasy response to 12BG). Emphasis on trees could be related to current Hindu religious rites. Like Lady Irwin students, the Asutosh girls seem well acquainted with Hindu poverty and death. They are more often dysphoric than consciously optimistic. The dysphoria is, however, accepted as apparently all life experiences of the Asutosh group are accepted—without resistance—and without a seeming awareness of choice in life decisions. With preponderance of reverie over verbalized achievement need (67% as contrasted with 33%) as well as over plot (84% to 16% in 12BG), these young women are less inhibited in self-expression, more congruent with the totality of environmental factors, and more overtly responsive to religious and philosophical stimuli than any of the seven groups in our study. These students react to environmental stress with emotional sensitivity and vivid poetic imagery, with passive acceptance of that which cannot be changed.

The Asutosh students are more similar to the Vidyasagar than to the other groups in their reluctance to introduce additional individuals in their fantasies. For example, 21% associated to a parental figure in Card 1, while 52% introduced no other person. As contrasted with the Americans, no student expressed resistance to parental authority, and as contrasted with 18% of Lady Irwin students, only 2% projected dependency. In the absence of picture stimuli with parental figures, it can only be conjectured that the Asutosh girls accept their parents passively, uncritically, possibly sublimating meaningful interpersonal relationships in their deep involvement with religion.

Hindu: Lady Irwin College Students

Lady Irwin is a female teacher's college. The subjects' interest in the emotional and intellectual welfare of young students is readily apparent in their projections to Card 1. In certain respects the projections of these young ladies appear similar to those of the Americans (for example, 54% A.I. as compared with the Americans' 53%), and their educational philosophy of "understanding the child" is consistent with that taught in American college departments of education. Their environmental settings and place names are, however, frequently British. These students, like the Americans and the Indo-American Society students to be discussed below, tell relatively long stories with rich plots, suggesting vivid fantasy life. Compared with the Indo-American Society students, Lady Irwin girls project slightly higher dependency (18% as compared with 15% of Indo-American Society males), but an almost identical degree of resistance to authority (26% as compared with 27% of the Indo-American males). These projections suggest a greater degree of ambivalence toward patterns of independence and dependence in these two groups, possibly a function of their noticeable westernization. In certain respects, however, striking differences set Lady Irwin students apart from both Americans and Chinese in fantasy projection. These are (a) concern with Hindu poverty (30% of Lady Irwin subjects describe this condition in Card 1 as compared with minimal or no concern with it among the non-Indian groups), and (b) concern with death or other physical misfortune (18% project death in Card 1 and 25% associate to death in Card 12BG, while 18% project the boy in Card 1 as blind). The latter percentage contrasts sharply with no projection of blindness by United States or Taiwan students, 2% by Hong Kong students. In death projection, the Lady Irwin girls exceed all other Indian and non-Indian groups, though the four Indian groups stand out as a whole noticeably different from the other groups, especially from the Hong Kong Chinese and Americans in response to Card 12BG. In blindness projection to Card 1, not only do the Lady Irwin girls exceed all other groups but the four Indian groups (13%, 11%, 18% and 4%) stand out in conspicuous contrast to the non-Indian groups (2% for Hong Kong students and none for either American or Taiwan students). However, it is probably reasonable to assume that such relatively frequent projections of poverty, death, and blindness reflect at least in part current conditions with which these subjects are acquainted. Misidentification of the violin occurs (projected by 15% of these students as "toy," "book," or "train"), and just as for the Asutosh College group, the violin is projected as having human attributes, for example, as a "friend," by 5% of the group. More frequently (20%) these subjects give human attributes to phenomena of nature: "The leaves of all that tree covered his body and the birds sing a prayer for him." Consistent with this feeling tone, Lady Irwin students verbalize their deep reverence of God: "These forests are God created"; "the father looked around and thanked God for the close of another day." This preponderantly Hindu phenomenon suggests a structuring of reality with different dimensions from that of the Americans and Chinese, a world in which everyday life situations are permeated by intensity of religious feeling.

Hindu: Indo-American Society Students

In sharp contrast with Taiwan youths, the Indo-American Society students (a majority of whom are males) are intensely involved with their fantasy projections, determinedly ambitious, and significantly competitive. Where the Taiwan youths appear defeatist, the Indo-American Society boys are optimistic. In chronological age this group is younger on the average than the other groups tested, and the immature affect of adolescence is occasionally reflected in these students' concern with adventure. Intellectually, however, they appear disciplined, combining their optimism ("dreaming of a bright future"; "though he was young, he was very keen") with realistic formulations of goal attainment ("one had to put forward his best in such cases and go up against any obstacle in the path"; a boy "greatly interested in music and wanted to know everything possible about it"). The goals of these youths suggest both British and traditional Hindu influences: Sir Isaac Newton, James Watt, Krishnon (sic), Chander (great writer in Urdu), and Rabindra Nath Tagore are culture heroes.

Many of these boys have recently passed their matriculation examinations —an event which is overtly reflected in their stories projecting competitive situations. In general, these boys are zestful, spontaneous, and spiritually inclined; unlike the American and Taiwan students, religious imagery is frequently projected. In contrast to the Hong Kong youth, the Indo-American Society boys show almost no sensitivity to the natural environment, only 8% projecting vivid sensual responses, 16% average sensitivity, and 67% a total absence of this behavior. The spontaneity of these boys is indicated by their involvement with other individuals and in a concern with their own goals. For example, all of the Indo-American Society boys project people to Card 12BG while 85% show Achievement Imagery in Card 1— the highest percentages obtained in all the categories among all the groups tested. Achievement Imagery is not, however, consistently related to musical proficiency; many of the boys associate to the violin in Card 1 only peripherally, concentrating rather on mechanical ingenuity and scientific goals. These rather long stories with well-organized plots project the buoyancy, resiliency, and intelligence of emotionally healthy students who seem to have integrated into their personality many of the "ideal" patterns of both Western European culture and the traditional culture of India. These young males are highly motivated to achieve and appear to have the energy and drive traditionally associated with the West. Unlike the Americans, however, need for peer acceptance is not significant. Just as for the Americans, success may be for these youths a mark of masculinity—as exemplified in one of the many projections involving examinations: "[he] should not accept defeat as he was a boy and tried again." It might be speculated that a successful engineer represents optimum achievement for the Indo-American Society males. Conflict of interest seems to be a contributing factor in resistance to parental authority. It occurs with drive for success. In these fantasies resistance is related to the varying goals of child and parent. However, the prevailing Hindu pattern of a thoughtful, contemplative approach to problem-solving is also apparent. For example: "One day James Watt . . . began to think and discovered the truth of the steam engine." The distinction between subject and object, while less nebulous than that of the Lady Irwin and Asutosh College students, is not always clear. This fact can be interpreted from folklore references (the "helpful animal" theme), from anthropomorphizing astronomical bodies ("He, the Sun") and inanimate objects (". . . waiting for the violin to begin playing by itself") and from such religious projections as "she by the grace of the Almighty changed herself into an old woman and began to preach truth and piety."

III. GROUP TRENDS (WATROUS)

In evaluating the test results the interpreter lacked the advantage of generally accepted norms for any of the categories used, for the TAT is not usually analyzed in this way. What has been done here is an attempt to analyze the materials in an unconventional manner in order to reveal group trends, if any, without, however, claiming too much for the product.

Despite the internal variations within each of the seven groups analyzed and, despite the differences observed between the two Chinese groups and among the four Indian groups, certain trends may be noted which distinguish, as a whole, the American, Chinese, and Hindu fantasies. The American students as a group focus in their fantasies on resistance to authority, on need for peer acceptance and personal independence, and on the assumption that a choice of decisions in life experiences are available to them. They are spontaneous and imaginative. Their main approach to problem-solving is through action. They seem to entertain some uncertainty in their attitudes about the self.

The Chinese fantasies convey less spontaneity, less gregariousness and less concern with peer acceptance than do the American responses. They are also generally more thoughtful. The Hong Kong Chinese, of all the groups, appear more relaxed than other groups in attitudes toward the self, whereas the Taiwan Chinese seem to lack direction and optimism.

The Indian fantasies vary most from the other two cultures in a number of ways: in their fuzziness of boundaries between animate and inanimate, and between subject and object, their religious bent, and their tendency to resort to meditation rather than action for problem-solving. Certain basic characteristics seem to separate the Vidyasagar males and the Asutosh College females on the one hand and Lady Irwin College females and Indo-American Society students (mostly males) on the other. The fantasies from the former two groups seem more distinctly Hindu intellectually and emotionally while those from the latter two groups seem to reflect patterns of interpersonal relationships and achievement imageries more in accord with Western personality than the other Indian groups. However, fantasies from all four Indian groups are characterized by meditative trends. Furthermore, the fantasies of Indian females as a whole (the traditional Asutosh girls and the more Western-oriented Lady Irwin girls) are similar in their contrast to those of Indian males. Indian female fantasies convey more passivity and spontaneous projection relating to harmony with the universe as well as more verbalization of traditional Hindu religious stimuli than those of Indian males.

Finally, the same picture stimulus certainly failed to elicit comparable reactions among the different groups. For example, the "middle-class" implications of the boy with the violin in Card 1, so well-known in American responses, are not found in responses by the non-American groups.[15] These groups are simply not sensitive to such implications and they perceive Card 1 without connecting it with "sissy" behavior—an apparent emotional threat to Americans. They also respond to Card 12BG, which is seldom used by American clinicians, with considerable fluidity and without the usual connotation of depression or suicidal feelings.

IV. COMMENTS AND INTERPRETATION (HSU)

A

While we began our work on these TAT responses with no idea of relating this Annex to the theme of the book, one cannot but note that the results turn out to be more supportive of its main hypotheses and analytic results than otherwise. The resistance by the Americans to parents and authority, their need for peer group acceptance and hence conformity to its demands, and their approach to problem-solving in terms of action rather than thought or contemplation—these traits apparent in the TAT responses have all been discussed in the book. Their high score in ambition well befits their love of equality, and their spontaneity and desire for choices or al-

ternatives express, on the conscious level, their emphasis on individual freedom. More deeply, the latter may be related to their doubt about self as
well as their ambivalence about dependence and independence. Such doubts,
in turn, are not unconnected with the need for peer acceptance and conformity noted before.

Watrous is of the opinion that the Chinese responses from Hong Kong
are dissimilar from those from Taiwan except that they both are, compared
with the American responses, less concerned with peer acceptance and
more thoughtful. She is struck by the discordant and aimless note which
seems to overshadow the Taiwan responses but which are absent in the
Hong Kong responses. This discordant note is indeed noticeable in the outlook of a majority of youths as well as adults to many visitors to Taiwan
today and it undoubtedly is related to the difficulties inherent in the political
and economic facts of Taiwan today. Apart from the larger picture, individual frustrations are evident. High school graduates find it difficult to
enter colleges and universities; college and university graduates find it difficult to seek graduate education or work. The present institutions of higher
learning in Taiwan turn out at least 20,000 college graduates every year. Of
this total, not many can achieve employment commensurate with their education and only a fraction of those who apply succeed in entering the United
States for advanced training. In a certain sense students in crowded Hong
Kong share some of these same frustrations but they do not live in a heavily
political atmosphere originating from a governmental objective so difficult
of attainment; they are free to leave and return to the Colony if they wish;
their aspirations are more commensurate with their possible achievements;
and above all, more of them are not separated from their families and are
not suffering from total lack of contact with their families on the mainland. From this point of view Taiwan students are less "natural" or "ideal"
subjects for our TAT study than their Hong Kong counterparts.

Even so, what leads Watrous to see the Taiwan fantasies as being different from the Hong Kong ones is not really so prominently found in her
analytic categories as in the feeling tones of the responses. When we ignore
the feeling tones of the fantasies we shall note that the two groups of Chinese
responses are not only identical in Achievement Imagery and Reverie with reference to Card 1 but also similar in Interpersonal Relationships. In response
to Card 1 the fantasies from both Chinese groups show almost equal involvement with parents and with others* (in contrast to American fantasies
in which involvement with others is greater than involvement with parents);
and similar ratios between Dependence and Resistance (about 1:3 in contrast to American fantasies in which the ratio is about 1:20). All of these are

* In the case of Hong Kong the involvement with parents is somewhat greater than
with others.

in keeping with the Chinese situation-centered way of life in which even the adolescent individual does not have great need for resisting parents; for although the father-son relationship is the center of Chinese social organization, its inclusive and continuous nature enables the individual to involve himself in other relationships without first having to shed his parents. A similar picture obtains in their responses to Card 12BG. In these fantasies the Americans appear to be much more gregarious than both groups of Chinese. The only striking difference between Hong Kong and Taiwan fantasies is that many more of the former than the latter involve no human beings (54% versus 27% in Card 1 and 26% versus 15% in Card 12BG). Even here the two Chinese groups differ from each other far less than they differ as a whole from the Americans (54% and 27% among the two Chinese groups versus 8% among the Americans in Card 1; 26% and 15% versus 10% in Card 12BG). Being usually much more enmeshed in a network of automatic human relationships than the Americans, the Chinese do not have as much need as the Americans to work for such relationships. This is, I think, also why, as Watrous observed in her intepretation, the Chinese tend to be more self-accepting than the Americans.

B

To probe into the matter further, I reclassified all the responses into certain broad categories quite different from those employed by Watrous. Some of the conclusions derived from this new classification will be touched upon throughout the rest of my comments but one new category is particularly relevant to the point made here, namely, the Chinese have less need than the Americans to seek human relations and therefore seem more self-accepting. This new category is Enjoyment in Card 12BG defined in terms of expressions of happiness, beauty, excitement, or contentment. The response of each subject is considered as a whole and it is classified only once (or according to the first response in case of alternatives) under the category of Enjoyment if it contains any of the expressions just given but no expression in the opposite direction. When this is done the results obtain that are shown in Table A-4. What we see here are at once the remarkable similarity between the two Chinese groups on the one hand and the remarkable difference between the two Chinese groups and the American group on the other. Though far less concerned with personal enjoyment than the Americans, Chinese can enjoy themselves alone as well as with others; the Americans show a much stronger urge to seek the company of others for the same purpose.

Another kind of response which may be regarded as supportive of the observation that the Chinese are more self-accepting than the Americans is to

Table A-4. PERCENTAGES OF CHINESE AND AMERICAN SUBJECTS
WHOSE RESPONSES TO 12BG ARE JUDGED "ENJOYMENT"[a]

NATURE OF RESPONSE	PERCENTAGE OF TOTAL NUMBER OF SUBJECTS OF RESPONSES		
	TAIWAN	HONG KONG	EVANSTON
Enjoyment	17 (43%)	25 (50%)	32 (87%)
NO. OF PERSONS INVOLVED	PERCENTAGE OF ABOVE		
Alone	47%	47%	28%
Two or more persons	53%	53%	72%[a]

a. The response of each subject is counted only once according to the prevailing theme. In case a subject gives two or more alternative responses only the theme of the first response is used here and in subsequent tabulations, except where noted. But if all the alternative responses are separately added to the total of each group, these figures for Evanston become even larger, while the Hong Kong figures remain about the same. Taiwan gives no alternative responses to Card 12BG.

be found in a category of responses to Card 12BG which I have designated as Noncommittal Description, which is employed for responses lacking any expression of emotional or aesthetic involvement or even curiosity. The percentages of responses fitting this category among the three groups are as follows: Taiwan, 20%; Hong Kong, 30%; and Evanston, 8%. The Americans are simply more desirous of external involvement than the Chinese. This conclusion is further augmented by the fact that all Noncommittal responses by the Americans are alternative ones, while the Chinese Noncommittal responses are sole ones.

The similar extent to which the two Chinese groups associate Card 12BG with enjoyment raises the question whether Watrous's observation that the Taiwan group is dysphoric is more apparent than real. My feeling is that it is not, and that one solid piece of evidence for this dysphoria in Taiwan responses is found in the much greater frequency of Death themes among them than among Hong Kong responses to both cards (see tables A-2 and A-3). Take the Death associations to Card 12BG, for example. Here the percentages for the two Chinese groups and one American group are as follows: Taiwan, 23%; Hong Kong, 8%; and Evanston, 10%. In the case of Taiwan, all Death associations constitute the sole responses, while in the case of Hong Kong three of the four responses making up the 8% total are alternative responses and are, therefore, presumably of lesser importance. Furthermore, the qualities of the Taiwan and Hong Kong Death associations are markedly different. All four Death responses from Hong Kong involve violence. Three of them involve each a murder which is given as an alternative response to another one involving two lovers having a good time. For two subjects the *murder* and the *love* responses are unrelated. But the murder association of one of these subjects involves a man killing an invited "friend" or "a girl or his wife," whom he strangles and whose body he sinks into the bottom of the river by tying a stone to it, while the third subject adds the following line in parentheses after giving one response with two lovers on a picnic and a second with a murderer digging a hole to bury the body: "Hope the lovers would not discover the body!" These and the fact that the remaining one Death response from Hong Kong involves "a young man and his sweetheart" drowned in a storm while rowing in a boat suggest a linkage between romantic rendezvous and sudden violent death in the minds of the Hong Kong youths. But the substances of the Death responses from Taiwan are quite of another hue. To begin with, all except one of the responses associating to death have nothing to do with murder. The characters die of illness, old age, accident, or suicide. The single response involving murder is committed by a man and woman who have to abandon their illegitimate child because the society is against their marriage. In the four romantic responses one involves double suicide because the parents of the couple are against their marriage, a second involves a count who commits suicide because his wife died of illness, and a third involves a pair of sweethearts who grow up together, but unfortunately one dies of an incurable disease, leaving the man broken-hearted and in despair when he surveys the scene. The fourth romantic response goes as follows:*

> This is a spot deep in the mountains and thick forest. It is very far from human habitation. Many years ago a pair of lovers came as a result of their rebellion against evil forces of society. They wanted to preserve their pure hearts and sacred love. The two of them discarded their family and society and left in a boat to escape from a sinful city to look for an oasis (t'ao yuan) outside of the human habitation. After many sufferings (of course in their hearts they are extremely blessed) they came to this spot. This was a place of their ideal habitat. Here they have only lovely trees and flowers. The world was theirs. Many years have passed. They have passed away. This morning the first rays of the sun are praying for the events that passed and blessing them.

In comparing the Hong Kong and Taiwan responses associating to Death one is struck by an insistent and insidious pathetic undertone in the latter which is absent in the former. The Hong Kong characters seem to be lively and in full control of their destiny till some unexpected violence extraneous to them stops their lives. The Taiwan characters, on the other hand, are forced to die by society, by natural forces, by sentiment. They are gradually worn down. Their death seems to be an integral part of the life of the victims; it merely, and perhaps unavoidably, unfolds itself at some stage of the human

---

* Unusual grammatical constructions, peculiar uses of words, or errors in spelling, if any, in all fantasies are reproduced in this Annex as they are given by the subjects.

drama. I think it is this contrast which leads Watrous to note the dysphoria in the Taiwan responses.

While this greater prominence of Death associations in Taiwan than in Hong Kong responses may, as Watrous noted, have something to do with the present peculiar circumstances of that island stronghold, we cannot but wonder also about the reason for the intimate linkage between romance and violent death in the Hong Kong but not in the Taiwan responses. I suggest that this difference is at least in part reflective of the fact that the Chinese society in Taiwan shows less Western impact than its counterpart in Hong Kong. Table A-5 presents the picture with some clarity. In Taiwan the traditional Chinese customs are still obvious and strong, though romancing between the sexes does occur among some. If the romance does not meet with

Table A-5. RESPONSES TO 12BG INVOLVING "LOVERS" AND "DEATH" FROM TAIWAN, HONG KONG, AND EVANSTON

BEHAVIOR OR RESULT	TAIWAN	HONG KONG	EVANSTON
Two lovers enjoying themselves	4 (10%)	2 (4%)	11 (30%)
Two lovers escaping or escaped from society or pursuers (forbidden love)	1 (2.5%)	2 (4%)	None
Love and Death			
Natural death (forbidden love)	1	None	None
Double suicide (forbidden love)	1	None	None
Infanticide (forbidden love)	1	None	None
Illness	1	None	None
Suicide due to love	1	None	None
Murder	None	4 (8%)	None
Total	10 (25%)	8 (16%)	11 (30%)
Death not associated with lovers	4 (10%), 2 due to accidents	None	4 (10%), 2 due to accidents and 2 due to senseless murder
Total number of responses or subjects (1 response = 1 subject)	40	50	37

the approval of parents and society, not only escape but also drastic measures such as double suicide or infanticide may become necessary. The fact that two of the ten responses connected with love are associated with illness or suicide strengthens this observation. Under the Chinese emphasis on the father-son axis, romantic expressions even between a man and his wife are discouraged rather than encouraged. In Hong Kong, by comparison, Western romancing between boys and girls is probably a somewhat more common occurrence. Though restrictions are still evident, they are far from as severe as the Taiwan subjects see them. Of the two Hong Kong responses in which love is linked with escape, one (subject a male) involves a man and a woman who are eloping because "their family (*sic*) prevented them from getting married," while the other (subject a female) ends in a harmless and even frivolous note. It goes as follows:

> It was a Spring morning. The trees were white with blossoms. There was a gentle mist veiling the woods and the lake. Jonathan and I had a walk in the woods. We just strolled round, silently, breathing in the freshness of the flowers. After half an hour or so, Jonathan suggested that we rented a boat and rowed round the lake. It was not a bad idea and I thought, "How romantic it is to be in a small boat with your beloved on a Spring morning."
>
> We were just about to board on the boat when I caught sight of my stern parents among the blossoming trees. Immediately I pulled Jonathan away and ran in the opposite direction as my parents. Jonathan was greatly puzzled. We went back to the boat-renting service and paid for our one hour "tour" in the boat. That is why you see the boat empty on the bank of the lake. Do you spy my parents, reader?

However, though Love is not clearly linked with Death due to parental or societal opposition, its direct association with Murder in one response and indirect association with Murder in three responses suggests that romance is dangerous. It is as though the Hong Kong youngsters, having been educated in English style schools, consciously consider romance as more or less the acceptable custom but unconsciously they hear a danger note from sanctions rooted in the Chinese traditional way of life. In other words, the father-son axis and its basic attributes, such as opposition to romantic love and suppression of erotic expression between men and women in public, remain strong psychological forces in these students. The only minor point of evidence seemingly contrary to this interpretation is that Taiwan subjects have given more responses containing "two lovers enjoying themselves" than have our Hong Kong subjects. My conjecture is that romancing between two lovers is probably more academic for Taiwan students than for Hong Kong students. It represents something that they would like to do but that most of them have found it impractical to do. This is shown by the fact that of the four Taiwan responses in this category, three are extremely brief and almost noncommittal. The following one is typical:

This is the season when the flowers are in full bloom. The still surface of the lake reflects the blue sky. A pair of lovers row a boat to the edge of the lake. For certain reasons they both went ashore to take a walk. That is why the boat is left there by itself.

The only one in this group which is longer is a highly impersonal projection. It goes as follows:

It has been raining for several months. There is no place on earth which is free from water. Everywhere you look you find extensive white water.

Adam and Eve are riding the ark. They floated everywhere. Weather later on became cleared up. The two of them floated with the ark which stranded on land. Not long after thick bushes and fruit trees grow up in the place where the boat is stranded. This is the Garden of Eden. They are living together happily.

The two Hong Kong responses in this category are by way of contrast much more detailed and intimate. One subject uses the first person singular in her narrative, ending with the sentence: "There, my love and I will spend many an enchanted afternoon, just relaxing and receiving the blessings of Nature, forgetting all the miseries and troubles of the world." The other subject describes two lovers having a "launch (*sic*) picnic down the small stream," "lying on the grass," "playing hide-and-siik (*sic*)," etc.

However, in spite of these differences, the Hong Kong associations to romance still have much in common with their Taiwan counterparts. For example, the Hong Kong association to elopement (12BG) is not a simple elopement as Americans would see it:

Two people had just left this same boat few minutes ago. They are young man and young woman. They had left their home during the night. They were eloping. They were lovers. Their family prevented them from getting married. Now they running to a place where they could find freedom, then they could do what they wanted. But where was this 'place.' They were not certain. They only ran ahead, until they reached their destination.

American elopers will certainly have more definite ideas as to the location of this "place" where they can "find freedom" and "do what they wanted." The sense of lack of clear destination in this Hong Kong response is another indication of the reality of a norm against romantic love which still prevails generally in the culture. Its prevalence makes the lovers realize that loving each other and running away by themselves are not enough. There are literally forces bigger than both of them. On the other hand the sentiment expressed in this very Hong Kong response may also be connected with the external political and military reality under which the Colony exists today. In this regard another category of responses peculiar to Hong Kong and Taiwan (but absent in those of all other groups tested) seems to provide us with additional support. This consists of responses which have to do with Escape themes—4 (10%) among Taiwan responses* and 7 (15%) among Hong Kong responses. One response in each of the two groups refers to some ancient event, the Taiwan subject mourning about ancient wars and devastation of human life, while the Hong Kong subject is reminded of a Utopia described by the ancient Chinese scholar T'ao Yuan-ming. The rest of the responses in both groups deal with the flight from danger, hiding from discovery, or avoidance of crowds. This is a theme that is uniformly absent in any other group tested. It certainly is not inappropriate to the psychology of inhabitants on crowded islands with economic uncertainty as well as political and military clouds hanging over them.

However, when the two groups of Chinese responses are compared with the Evanston responses, the contrast is startling. Another look at Table A-5 will show that for the Evanston students "two lovers enjoying themselves" not only forms 30% of the total responses but there is no danger of any sort entailed. There is neither parental opposition nor any question of social disapproval. The American associations to Death simply have nothing to do with romance. Furthermore, the American lovers regard their actions together with a lightheartedness unknown to their Eastern counterparts. To the Hong Kong or Taiwan students, romancing is an extremely serious life-and-death matter. For Evanston students, on the other hand, it may lead to relatively permanent bonds, but frequently it is merely a passing, though enriching, experience as the following Evanston response shows:

> The small boat remained where the two had left it months before. Neither of them would ever forget that lovely early Summer afternoon. They had met quite accidentally. He had just graduated from undergraduate technilogical school and was pondering his future in the quite isolated solace of the country. He wondered if he would be successful and happy; he wondered if he would really accomplish something or just be another expendable cog in a gigantic masterwork. He was completely absorbed in his own thoughts of himself when he practically stumbled over a young girl, quite attractive, who was obviously upset over something. She too had just finished another year at college and now she was being sent to Europe with her aunt to "broaden her culturally," and the very thought of it brought her near to the point of tears. She desperately wanted to stay near her home, her family and her friends, if only for the short span of the summer months. She was broken hearted and this was the situation when they met, two very unhappy people all wrapped up in themselves. After the awkward embarrassment of this unexpected discovery on the part of each had subsided, they began to walk, quickly at first, hesitantly, two strangers in a world of quiet and beauty, and for the time being anyway, theirs. And then more and more honestly, it is easier sometimes to be honest with a stranger to a degree that would be impossible with your closest friend, they revealed themselves to each other. They talked. They laughed. They walked. They even found an old boat and they drifted down the creek together to the accompaniment of their secret desires. It was a won-

* In addition, one Escape response is found in the Taiwan group as an Alternative.

derfully sweet outlook. The afternoon seemed to pass so quickly. They pulled the little boat up on the bank and exchanged farewells. They will probably never meet again. It was a rewarding experience that neither will ever forget.

An examination of the Death associations not connected with love among the three groups is interesting. The Taiwan students obviously have a greater preoccupation with death than the other two groups, but their Death is either caused by love or social pressure or accident—not by murder.* The Hong Kong students' Death is all by murder, linked directly or indirectly with romantic love, but not by any other cause. The Evanston students have the least desire to associate to Death. Their Death not only has no connection with romantic love but also tends to be without causation. Two of their four Death responses are attributed to accidents; the other two are un-caused. In one of the latter, the subject says that this picture (12BG) "was taken a few minutes before somebody was murdered." She then goes on to describe how the young victim, a male, was waylaid by a murderer be-hind the tree, strangled to death after he screamed, thrashed, and struggled. The murderer then buried his victim "in a shallow grave under the rowboat and slipped away, his footprints muffled by the grass." The subject then concludes her story thus:

> It looks like there is a lion or some other member of the cat family to the left and behind the tree which is crouching in the bushes. There are insects around which will dig underneath the ground and devour the body under-neath the rowboat.

The other Death response from the Evanston group is a most ingenious construction of a senseless murder:

> The tree in the picture is not an ordinary one; the sap that coarsing through its limps has a strange poisen in its content. It also emits a wonderful smell, fragrant, wonderful, irressatible. people are drawn to this strange tree. In summer one always notices a picnic spread beneath its branches, a person reading, meditating. They come by foot from the neighboring town or by boat up the stream. However, the poisen in the bark will react only with a specific combination, the true at heart need never fear, even the weak and cowardly are safe, murderers have slept beneath its branches, sucked the fragrant twigs and roots without perishing. The mystery of the tree is a wonder to all, striking at seemingly good people, pillars of their local villages. Last year a handsome young fellow came with his book, rowed upstream in a old row boat, never was seen again alive. Several strollers noticed him earlier that day munching his lunch and engrossed in his book. His disappearance was connected with tree. In his hand was one of the roots of the fragrant tree. The area was shocked, he was such a well-liked fellow. Alas, why was he taken, what is the secret.

* A single Taiwan response involving killing of an illegitimate child by two lovers "because they cannot marry" is considered capitulation to social pressure.

In other words, among the three groups, our Evanston students see the least connection between death and life's activities. In terms of the projected data as a whole and in terms of what we have seen of the Chinese and American ways of life presented in the main body of this book, I believe it is an inescapable conclusion that the Taiwan responses are commensurate with the Chinese culture and psychology and the Evanston responses with the American culture and psychology, while the Hong Kong responses represent some sort of intermediary state, a Chinese base with Western incursions.

C

In contrast to the Chinese and American groups, the four Indian groups present certain uniformities not touched upon in Watrous's analysis. Table A-6 shows the percentages of Indian subjects whose responses to 12BG are

Table A-6. PERCENTAGES OF INDIAN SUBJECTS WHOSE RESPONSES TO 12BG ARE JUDGED "ENJOYMENT"

NATURE OF RESPONSE	VIDYASAGAR	ASUTOSH	LADY IRWIN	INDO-AMERICAN
Enjoyment	17 (26%)	11 (23%)	7 (21%)	6 (26%)
No. of persons involved:		PERCENTAGES OF ABOVE		
Alone	47%	64%	30%	50%
Two or more persons	30%	27%	57%	33%
Impersonal enjoyment	23%	9%	14%	17%

judged Enjoyment. The figures in it are examined to best advantage if compared with those in Table A-4. One glance will show that the percentage of Indian responses in the Enjoyment category is far smaller than that of either the Chinese or the American fantasies. The percentage is lowest in the Lady Irwin responses and highest in the Indo-American responses; but even the Indo-American responses in this category are only about half of the Chinese and about one quarter of the American responses.

In contrast to both the American and the Chinese, three out of four of the Hindu groups associate to Enjoyment Alone more than they do with Two or More Persons. In addition, as Table A-6 shows, there is a kind of Enjoyment response which is highly impersonal that the Indians give but that the Chinese and Americans do not give. Although according to one of Mrs. Watrous's tables (Table A-3), 26% of the Hong Kong and 15% of the Taiwan responses to Card 12BG contain no specific individuals, her basis consists of responses mostly found in my Noncommittal Description category. Some of the Taiwan and Hong Kong Enjoyment responses are also seemingly impersonal, but on closer examination they invariably turn out to have some reference to the person or persons in contrast to their Indian counterparts (four responses from the Vidyasagar group and one response each from the other three Indian groups). The following two examples will convey my meaning:

> (1) *Response by Vidyasagar Male:* It is a lovely garden and the scenery of the garden is very charming. Snow falling on the trees and grasses. A boat laying under a tree. The snow on the trees and the grasses means that the flowers blooms in beautifully manner and it also seen that snow falls from the trees on the grasses and boat.
>
> (2) *Response by Taiwan Male:* This is a beautiful place where hundreds of flowers bloom and cattle drop like snow flurries. A strem runs through the forest. The beautiful scenery is a sight that many people come to enjoy. There is a boat under the tree. To view the scenery from the boat by rowing the boat is a most delightful thing for the heart and the spirit.

Furthermore if we examine all of the Enjoyment responses of the Indian subjects we shall find that at least half of them have an impersonal quality that is absent in the Chinese Enjoyment responses. The following is one from a Vidyasagar male in poetic form which is found in the Two or More Person category in Table A-6.

> There was a forest on the bank of a river.
> The natural beauty of the forest looks how charming.
> If when we go to the forest our mind will also fills up with the beauty of the forest.
> And if we has a boat on the particular forest then we could able to fill the beauty of the forest and also we could think about how the natural beauty are!
> By the boat we could able to see the hole of the forest and from the boat we could find how river and the forest are!
> So the natural beauty are of undescrible.
> If among us any one may be poet then his mind will fills up with the beauty of the nature.
> The beauty is the undescrible.
> Many part of our country describe about the Nature.
> An English poet says that we could understand how the natural beauty are when we are in the forest means; returing from the forest we can distinguise the nature from unnatural things.

The Evanston responses contain no impersonal sentiment and only three of them fit the Noncommittal Description category. Two of these are second responses and only one is a first response among three alternatives.

A second peculiarity of the Indian responses to 12BG is the expression of Fear, Danger or Dysphoria in General, although the percentages of Indian responses in this category are not overwhelming. The Indian responses tend toward the fear or danger, whereas the few Chinese cases tend toward milder dysphoria. For example, of the two Asutosh responses in this category, one centers upon ferocious animals ready to kill "any man" who "comes to such a place like this," while the other centers upon a girl thinking and being very sad to the point of "dropping tears" about how "she and Dick used to go out on their secret cruise in that boat." The second fantasy ends with the following sentence: " 'The fate of life' she thinks to herself and sighs." One of the three Lady Irwin responses in this category ends with the following sentiment: "The physical appearance is not charming but it looks dull. This photograph shows [as] if no one used to come to this place. It looks very lonely and dangerous as it shows." In contrast the two responses from Taiwan in this category are quite mild. In one the female subject, after describing the scene in noncommital fashion, concludes thus: "It seems that this little boat was used by someone and then discarded." The other subject speaks of 12BG as a forest after rain in one autumn day and ends with the following comment:

> This is really a spot of a public park which is not usually discovered by
> · most people. The pond is used for throwing fruit peels by the people who
> frequent the park, but this spot looks very dirty. It seems that it hasn't been
> swept for many months.

There are two other responses that border on Dysphoria but not impersonal in the Taiwan group. One concerns a man who rowed a boat which was blown by sudden wind and rain into "this wild island." He is poor and has gone to collect some firewood "so that he can get a fire to warm himself." The other one goes as follows:

> Once I went to the uninhabited place to hunt. I went past many high
> mountains and rivers. After walking a long way I discovered a small wooden
> boat in a swamp. I believe that someone had been there before. Probably he
> also liked the natural life of the primitive times. But I did not find him this
> time. I feel disappointed.

It is somewhat difficult to put these last two responses in the general Dysphoria category. The single response from the Hong Kong group which expresses general Dysphoria is one which describes the boat as belonging "to the villagers." "They have no pier to tie their boat to and they have to pull it on shore when it is not in use. The picture seems very lonely and deserted."

One of the most unusual themes in the Indian responses is Abandonment. In Table A-7 the designation of this category is Abandonment or Loss of Way. All the Indian responses in this category refer to Abandonment and one case each from Taiwan and Hong Kong refers to Loss of Way. The Taiwan response describes parents going to the woods with their children to escape the heat "during the hottest summer." But when they returned home they "forgot a child in the forest." "The child spent the night in the forest all by himself" is the ending of this response. The response from

Table A-7. OTHER RESPONSES OF INDIAN, CHINESE AND AMERICAN SUBJECTS TO 12BG, AS PERCENTAGES OF TOTAL NUMBER OF SUBJECTS OR RESPONSES

NATURE OF RESPONSE	VIDYASAGAR	ASUTOSH	LADY IRWIN	INDO-AMERICAN	TAIWAN	HONG KONG	EVANSTON
Fear, Danger or Dysphoria in General	11%	4%	9%	None	5%	2%	None
Abandonment or Loss of Way	15%	11%	6%	4%	2.5%	2%	None
Noncommittal Description	21%	17%	12%	None	13%	20%	None[a]
Death	11%	15%	30%	17%	23%	8%	10%
Lovers	1.5%	4%	9%	None	25%	10%	30%
Alternatives	1.5%	None	None	None	2.5%	8%	29%

a. Evanston students give three such responses, but all of them are alternative responses and therefore not represented here.

Hong Kong describes a boy of thirteen and his sister of eleven approaching "the densely forested area" in a boat "without their parents' notice." The boy, "in spite of his sister's opposition," took her into the forest to catch butterflies. The story ends thus:

> At the sight of the butterflies, the girl forgot all about her previous opposition and jumped with delight to help his brother to catch the butterflies. On and on they went, and until evening they were confronted with the problem "which is the way to go back?" With fear they did not know how to get out of the maze. The boat was there quietly and their parents were eager to have their children back.

It should be noted that in the Hong Kong response the children are at fault while the parents eagerly seek their return, but even in the Taiwan case the parents presumably also want their lost child back. In other words, what is involved in these responses is Loss of Way or separation due to the *accidental* factor but not deliberate or purposeful abandonment. There are a total of seventeen Abandonment or Loss of Way responses from the four Indian groups, with Vidyasagar leading way ahead (10 responses), Asutosh (5 responses) second, Lady Irwin (2 responses) third, and Indo-American Society (1 response) fourth. Fourteen of these are clearly Abandonment while only four are Loss of Way or separation. Three of the latter four end with the return of the lost individual to the group from which he or she was separated earlier, but none of the Abandonment responses develops in this direction. A typical short response in this category is one from a Vidyasagar male, as follows:

> The picture, it appears that it is a garden with a big tree and its side a boat. In the boat a baby is sleeping. The parents of the baby left him in the garden. But the big tree saves the child from the sun rays and rain. The parents of the child had no sympathy and kindness to the child.

A typical longer response is from an Asutosh female, as follows:

> There stands a very large tree. Throughout the ages he has faced events of various kinds, today he is old. He is the protector of all men, animals, birds. The traveller tired of the sun comes and takes rest under his shade. The birds have made their nests in his leaves. They consider that tree as safe shelter. A mother has left her child in that pan. The wailing of the child is piercing his [her] breast. It appears to him that the child's mother has left the child perhaps in great sorrow, great suffering. The same pain which is in mother's breast has also arisen in the mind of the tree by seeing the motherless child.

The expressions "the tree saves the child from the sun rays and rain" and "the same pain which is in mother's breast has also arisen in the mind of the tree by seeing the motherless child" are what Watrous scores as Mutability in her part of the interpretation. They occur often throughout the

Indian responses classified under diverse categories but are especially common here. The causes of Abandonment range from unknown ones (as in the second response just given), lack of parental sympathy (as in the first response just given), to fate. A good example of fate as cause for Abandonment is the following given by an Indo-American Society male:

> This picture reminds me of the birth of a very famous poet of Tamil land, namely OVVAIYAR. She was the daughter of a famous sage, and her mother gave birth to her, while she and her husband were travelling through a dense forest. The mother, with her feminine mind, naturally wanted to take the child home. But the sage, who foresaw things, did not approve to it. He said that, the child was going to become a famous poet and moral instructor in the future, and in spite of the wishes of the mother, left the child in an open basket in the dense forest. It is further said that a flood caused the basket to float away and reach the hands of a Brahman, who had no child. That Brahman found much spiritual awe in the baby and nursed her. When she became mature, she was forced to marry, but she did not. She, by the grace of the Almighty changed herself to an old woman and began to preach truth and piety. She, however, did not find any new religion.

This power of fate is also apparent in an Asutosh female's response in which a "young couple" was advised by "a Prophet" that "they would have a child which would turn out to be a thief . . ." After the birth of their son "one night they took him in a box and left the child in a forest like place." The child was cared for by some woodcutters and became a big man. But "it so happened that as one day he was going to cut wood he lost his way and he met a gang of robbers who forced him to join their group. Thus he became one of them." Our subject then goes on in the rest of the response to expound on how we have to "bow down to fate."

More than half of the responses in this category from Vidyasagar have adults (or at least grown youngsters) as the abandoned or separated. The following is a good example.

> These is a Tale of a Fisherman.
> Once some fisherman went out for catch fish in a river. They were full of instrument for catch fish. But one of them separate from their companions. He is very thinking. He reach alone in a lonely place of the forest. But he also find that a small river flows behind the dark lonely forest. And he sees a boat beside the jungle. He glad or cheerful to see boat also. But he is unable to go to the boat. He is something fears also.

One of the two responses from Lady Irwin classified in this category might not have been so classified but for the presence in Indian responses of the theme of Abandonment and for the frequency with which plants and other inanimate things are given human or animate attributes. This is a fantasy to 12BG about Abandonment of things:

Once upon a time the boat which was like a gift to the family who stayed near the forest is now a rotting boat. This is the way one's life is in this world. The things that are near and dear to you vanishes as the days pass by.

Once upon a time the family was living happily near a forest by the river side. They earned their living by rowing the boat from one side to another or by joy rides. The days past by. They earned quite a lot of money and decided to settle elsewhere. Thus they migrated leaving most of their belongings like the boat and a few extra things. They went with an idea that they would manage with the money they had. They little knew what was in store for them. Time went by. They little realized that the little things they left behind would give them all that they wanted. The boat was let loose. This boat with no direction found its way into a marshy place where trees and plants were. Thus a thing which was useful has been wasted.

On the other hand the family realised the financial problems and learnt that with little things what people could do.

The gloomy and tragic nature of this fantasy has an obvious affinity with the following response from a Vidyasagar male showing distinct ambivalence toward the scenery in 12BG.

In the deep forest the trees are full of froots and flowers. There is a lake and on the lake there is a boat. But in this deep forest there are no living person. Then I reached at this place and I found the picture. It is so silent that I can not explane. When I reached there I get fear because I am the person who live in the localaty. Although I am afraid but the picture is so beautiful to me that I can not forget it. When a poet sees it once then he must not forget it. I am not a poet minded but I can not forget the seenery.

The importance of responses indicating Abandonment or Loss of Way from the Indian groups is reinforced by the fantasies dealing with Death. Quantitatively all of the Indian groups associate to Death more frequently than do the Hong Kong and Evanston groups. The Lady Irwin group exceeds even Taiwan in this respect. But it is the qualitative picture which truly distinguishes the Indian responses from the non-Indian responses. Table A-8 demonstrates this very well. Of a total of 28 associations to Death only one is caused by "murder" (Indo-American) and one by "suicide" (Lady Irwin). The outstanding cause of Death among the Indian responses is Loss of Way in jungle and/or Eaten by Wild Animals, or Shipwreck and/or Eaten by Wild Animals. Six out of seven Vidyasagar responses, five out of seven among the Asutosh responses, five out of ten among the Lady Irwin responses and three out of four among the Indo-American responses belong to these categories. Loss of Way, Eaten by Wild Animals, and Shipwreck are grouped together and considered of similar psychological significance because they all express a highly fluid relationship between the individual (or a group of individuals) and his (or their) unknown and unfamiliar environment which is full of threat, uncertainty, and death. Furthermore even

the only Hindu association to Suicide, as we shall see below, signifies the
same thing. For this reason the following War association from an Indo-
American male is included in this group:

> It was so quiet in the meadow. That was what struck the man first—the
> silence. After the thunder of the guns and the screams of the dying men and
> horses the meadow seemed a veritable haven of silence. True, a bird carolled
> from the large tree standing in the meadow and the stream chuckled its way
> past, but what did this matter, it was peace. It was peace to the man lying at
> the foot of the tree with his hands clasped tightly over his body.
>
> The old boat which nudged the bank of the stream gently brought back
> memories to the man. Memories of a childhood spent running barefoot
> through the woods, of fishing in the stream near his home. Memories of him
> growing up, going through school and then the most searing memory of all
> when his father and mother died a result of an enemy shell fired early in this
> war—this senseless war. He had entered the army for a good reason—revenge.
> He lay on the turf for a good reason—he was sorely wounded—dying.
>
> But as he lay there he felt no fear and no anger in fact no pain. The peace
> of the scene had entered into his very soul and when the soul is at peace so is
> the body. He looked up through the interlaced branches of the tree at the
> blue sky, he looked down at the stream wending its never ending way and at
> the trees, at the grass, at everything around it. He heard faintly what sounded
> like singing—it was a bird chirping in the tree. He felt at peace with the
> world. He knew that he was dying but there was no regret only a great sense
> of joy, that he could leave the world at such a beautiful place. And then he
> was at peace at last.

The similarity between the psychological elements in this battlefield and
those inherent in Loss of Way or Shipwreck is obvious. In both, danger and
threat are part of an external environment in which the only certainty is
that of death.

Among Indian Death associations Unknown Causes are also considerable.
Among the non-Indian groups only one Taiwan response fails to give the
cause of death, but among the Indian groups four fall into this pattern. Unknown Causes may signify the desire to be noncommittal, but in view of
the dominance of Abandonment, Loss of Way, Shipwreck, and Being Eaten
by Wild Animals in Indian fantasies, it seems at least arguable that Unknown
Causes, too, may be related to the Hindu's diffused outlook and human relationships in which uncertainty outweighs certainty.

The types of activities involved in the Indian associations to Death, as
compared with their Chinese and American counterparts, also bear out this
conclusion. Of a total of 28 Indian Death associations, only two involve a
romantic relationship; two, friendship among men (in one, the friends are
a band of robbers); one, love of a boy for his dog, and three, family relationships, making a total of eight. The remaining eighteen involve all sorts of
casual relationships from "attachment to boat" and "roaming alone," to

Table A-8. ACTIVITIES AND CAUSES IN "DEATH" ASSOCIATIONS TO 12BG AMONG HINDUS, CHINESE AND AMERICANS

DEATH ASSOCIATIONS	VIDYASAGAR	ASUTOSH	LADY IRWIN	INDO-AMERICAN	TAIWAN	HONG KONG	EVANSTON
Activities Connected with Death							
Unspecified	2	3[a]	1		2		
Attachment to boat			1				
Love of dog			1				
Attempt to be like nature			1				
Work to support self		1	1				
Adventure (hunting, butterfly catching, exploring, fishing, enjoying self, hunting treasure, etc.)	1	2		1	2		3
Play (children)	1						1
Robber gang	1						
Friendship			1				
Love		1	1		5	4	
Support for family			1				
Bringing aid to mother			1				
Revenge for parents				1			

			1[b]				
Roaming alone	1						
Traveling (also sailor on tour)	1			1			
Summer resort				1			
Causes of Death							
Loss of way		1	5	1	1		
Eaten by wild animals	2	2					
Loss of way and eaten by wild animals	3						
Shipwreck	1						
Shipwreck and eaten by wild animals		1		1			
War				1			
Illness			1		1		
Accident			1		2		2
Murder				1		4	2
Infanticide					1		
Old age		1			1		
Suicide			1		2		
Unknown	1		2		1		

a. One response involves a family lost together.

b. "The family members of him were come to search him they found him died over there and they make his grave over there and come back."

"traveling" and various kinds of specified or unspecified adventures. Several points are immediately clear. First, Chinese fantasies of Death are most closely associated with love between a man and a woman; American fantasies of Death are most closely associated with play or adventure activities; and Hindu fantasies of Death are associated with a wide range of activities. If we take Death fantasies as signifying some severe problem and an extreme mode of its solution, then we must see that for the Chinese love of a man and woman is the central problem here, for the Americans individual enjoyments are the central problem here, while for the Hindus many different activities constitute the problem here and therefore the problem is diffused. These differences are of particular interest in connection with Card 12BG which provides stimuli primarily from "nature" and only secondarily "human." It is probable that "nature" evokes in the Hindu minds more human problems of a severe kind than it does either in Chinese or American minds. The Americans do associate Death to nature, but their associations have to do with light-hearted and playful self-enjoyment; and the Chinese also associate Death to nature but their associations are concentrated in close human bondage inherent in love between the sexes and social pressure against deviation. Only the Hindus seem to see a deep intermingling between, or make constant attempts to integrate, eternity and nature and human beings, thus reducing the importance of ties among men. Even the two Indian responses involving "love" between a man and a woman illustrate this observation well. In both of them death comes to the lovers without any reason whatever. It just comes. In one response (from an Asutosh girl) the two lovers, after sitting "in the boat and boating" every evening being happy and full of songs, with "animals like deer and birds coming to them, simply did not return one night." The subject goes on as follows:

> But, what happen then? One day, deer was waiting to hear the song. Birds were ready to fly, but no song was heard. They waited till night, but no sign of their coming. Boat was also there waiting for their arrival but they did not arrive. They all waited for two days and they found them there but dead and they were buried there. How can birds enjoy now? How can deer stay in that place where he was always getting enjoyment? They went away from there. Trees could not do anything but shade away their leaves. Oh! That boat! It was still waiting there. Nature a while is sad and will never be happy anywhere. Nature shows its sign of sorrow and regret for two young lovers.

The response describes how the lovers feel as much as it deals with how the animals and the plants and the boat feel. In the other response (from a Lady Irwin girl) the fantasy begins with Snow White who lives in a "little, cosy village." She is all alone and hates the arrival of Spring every year. She goes out for a change after her work. She is sad when she sees her little boat on the river all empty, "specially when the trees were full of blossoms and water was shining and how nice the body looked if only she had someone to go boating." The subject's fantasy develops as follows:

> Well, all days are not the same. Snow White would also meet someone young and handsome to add joy to her life. One day she did. As she was rowing the boat a stranger asked her to carry him to the other side. This happened every day and they could not stay without each other any more. She came and waited near the boat every day for him and he did always come. But one day he did not. No one knew where he had disappeared to. She cried for him but it was all in vain. But one day a light approached her. She found a young man who asked her to accompany him. He took her to heaven where they both stayed happily. The Spring came every year and found the village very quite without Snow White. The boat still lay there empty. All the charms had left with Snow White.

The final sentences of this response essentially express the same sentiments as does the last half of the first response except that the interrupted love continues in the world of the gods.

By way of contrast, the Chinese responses linking love and death are preoccupied with the lovers' attachment to each other or other people's reaction to them, no human sentiments being attributed to the natural surroundings at all. Even when supernatural overtones are injected into the response, as they are by one Hong Kong female, she dwells on the fears of the living for the "ghosts" of the dead lovers, "since people who meet a violent death haunt the place where they had died."

The widest spread of activities associated with Death is given by the Lady Irwin girls. From this group we have two strongly family-connected responses and one weakly family-connected response, to one from the Indo-American group and none from the other two Indian groups, in addition to one "love" response already discussed above. The two strongly family-connected responses are (1) a girl goes into the woods with a lamp to bring her mother back but she falls into the river and dies, and (2) a poor man, already overburdened with work in support of his family of wife and two little children, injures himself in a flooded river and cannot find his boat in the dark and therefore is drowned. The one weakly family-connected response from a Lady Irwin subject mentions "family members" who bury him in the jungle where he lost his way and died.*

However, the Lady Irwin group balances itself at the other end of the Hindu scale by non-family-connected activities in association with death. One of these concerns a boy's love of a dog and a second concerns a man who works to support himself. But a third one deals with a girl named Petty.

---

* The only other references to the family in Death responses are one from the Asutosh group in which "some family" loses its way and dies of starvation and thirst, and one from the Indo-American group in which a son joins the war to revenge the death of his parents in the hands of the enemy.

The response begins by stating that "she lived in a hut with her mother near a forest." According to this statement this response should have been classified as one involving family life but as it develops, the family element is completely taken out of the picture by the subject. The response continues with . . . "Petty was a very brave girl and used to go into the forest every day." The rest of the fantasy follows.

> One day as she was wandering about she came to a place where the scenery was very beautiful. She discovered a small lake with a small wooden boat in it. She was very happy to find it and danced out of joy. She wondered how that boat came there. She thought the fairies might have left it for her, as she was so fond of all these things.
> Petty used to go there every day and enjoy the fun. One day she fell ill and dreamt that the fairies were carrying her to the fairyland, there she saw many beautiful things, but she cried bitterly, because she could not find her boat there. The fairies said that if she would remember that boat, they will never send her to land. So nobody saw that little girl again in the forest. But voices seemed to be coming from that boat—"Petty, Petty, where are you?"

The response which wrestles hardest with the totality of the problem of integrating man and nature begins by extolling the beauty and wonder of nature and then speaks of a man named Gopal "who was born in the surrounding of nature that is in Kashmir . . . in Kashmir he saw the beauty of nature and became interested in that only." Then:

> During early childhood he appreciated the nature but as he started doing advanced studies he became more and more confused, because it is very difficult to study the complexity of nature.
> Natural beauty can be seen and appreciated but can not be studied. Same proved true in his life also. He became so interested in colourful things that he forgot to see the realities in human life. He be imaginary. A man can never live in the world of dreams. He wanted to create something like nature but failed.
> As he grew older responsibilities of life also came with existence, but he never developed the power of realistic thinking so he tried to get out of that but it was difficult. He was depressed because of nature and ultimately he committed suicide by sailing a boat and while his boat was in the middle, he jumped into the valley and finished his life in nature only.

The rarity of Love in association with Death in Indian responses (as contrasted to its frequency in Chinese responses) seems to suggest that Love in Indian fantasies has a significance similar to that it has in American fantasies, namely, it is of great importance but divorced from Death associations. Actually this is far from being the case. A brief look at Table A-7 shows that, in general, the Hindus associate to Love far less than do the Chinese and the Americans. Only one Vidyasagar response to 12BG concerns Love, which turns out to be a sort of retelling of the famous Indian story of Sakuntala. There are two responses concerning Love in the Asutosh group and three in the Lady Irwin group but none in the Indo-American group. The inescapable conclusion seems to be that the Indians associate to Love least and almost casually, that the Chinese associate to Love considerably more but with trepidation, whereas the Americans associate to Love most and with a sense of boundless enjoyment. The extent and the pattern of association to Love among the three peoples fit well with our data presented in the last column of Table A-7. This column shows the percentages of subjects giving alternative responses to 12BG with reference to the total number of subjects in each of our seven student groups. The Indian subjects give practically no alternative fantasies to 12BG. The more westernized Hong Kong subjects have produced more alternatives than the less westernized Taiwan subjects. The Evanston subjects lead the field, leaving the others far behind. If love between a man and a woman carries the meaning of spontaneity and choice on the part of the individual, then it has very little room in the Hindu world as it is embodied in the Hindu social organization and the Hindu ideal. Alternatives are rare because all existences are preordained by a power that is higher than all and from which there is no escape. Love between a man and a woman as well as the spontaneity and choice which go with it are also out of line with the Chinese way of life as embodied in the Chinese social organization and Chinese ideal. But since their obstacles are human beings who occupy positions of authority within the well-defined limits of the kinship group, there is some room for maneuver. However, being firmly rooted in that group, the Chinese will find attempts to alter the *status quo* painful all around, for their conflict cannot easily be solved by emergence from, or rejection of, the elders. The Chinese world has nurtured in them a continuity and inclusiveness of outlook so that they are likely to be too involved in their elders to relish clear-cut victories over them. This is why the Chinese associations to Love are so intimately connected with their associations to Death. Love between a man and a woman as well as the spontaneity and choice which go with it are for the Americans nearly the be-all and the end-all for the solution of all problems of man, nature and God. This is why Love associations are all Enjoyment and no Death. It is interesting that the only two Evanston responses which mention God are both Love fantasies.

D

Some general statements about the responses to 12BG are in order. First, it is obvious that the Evanston students react to 12BG with an overwhelming feeling of Enjoyment in company of other individuals, especially persons of the opposite sex or peers. The Indians on the other hand react to the same stimulus with the least feeling of Enjoyment, tending heavily to be alone and especially to assume the impersonal point of view. The Chinese fall between the two extremes, both with reference to Enjoyment and with reference to the ratio between Enjoyment by Self to Enjoyment with Two or More Others.

Second, the Hindus as a whole react to 12BG with more negative feelings such as Fear, Abandonment, or Death than do both the Chinese and especially the Americans. The high Taiwan association to Death (which may be related to the peculiar political and military environment of that island) is balanced by the very low Hong Kong association to Death. The importance of Dysphoria, Abandonment and Death in the Hindu responses is further augmented by the fact that an overwhelming majority of the causes of death in Indian Death associations are found in the general category of Loss of Way, Shipwreck and Being Eaten by Wild Animals, responses which indicate highly uncertain or hostile relationships with the external environment.

Third, the Indian responses to 12BG as a whole suggest the extreme insignificance of the individual vis-à-vis the forces inhabiting the external world. This contrasts sharply with the American responses in which the individual's wishes are paramount. The Chinese responses again fall in between these two extremes. This gradation is particularly evidenced by the insignificance of Love responses among the Indians, the greater importance of Love responses among the Chinese and the even more pronounced importance of such responses among the Americans.

Watrous proposes in her interpretation (Section III) that the Chinese are more self-accepting than the Americans. This view is largely based on the fact that the Chinese more than the Americans can enjoy themselves without involving peer groups. The reader may receive the impression that the Indians are even more self-accepting than the Chinese since they seem to have even less need for peer involvement. This is not, however, a correct inference. A clearer view of this point will emerge if we turn now briefly to the responses of all three cultural groups to TAT Card 1.

All three conclusions which emerge from the responses to Card 12BG find support through a preliminary examination of the reactions of our subjects to Card 1. A more detailed analysis of these responses will be included in a later publication, so this Annex may not be too bulky and become the tail that wags the dog. But some impressions can be reported here. Among the responses to Card 1, the Evanston students see in the picture principally a problem of resisting parents (with the accent on resisting rather than not resisting) and finding the self through hard work and peer activities; the Hong Kong and Taiwan students see in it principally a matter of following the wishes of the father or mother or both or an older sibling (with resistance to them in a minority of instances) and finding success in hard work and in assistance from persons of superior accomplishments or wisdom; while the Indian students see in it principally meditation by the self, sometimes fantasying success (with least involvement with family members either as particular objects of resistance or of compliance) and of more sadness than enjoyment.

Most of these points can be gleaned from Table A-2 above, in Watrous's section of the analysis. According to that table the fantasies of the two least westernized Indian groups (Vidyasagar and Asutosh) show higher percentages of Reverie and lower percentages of Achievement Imagery than any other group; the Americans show higher percentages of Achievement Imagery and lower percentages of Reverie than all except the two westernized Indian groups (Lady Irwin and Indo-American); while the Hong Kong and Taiwan Chinese fall near the center of the spectrum. With reference to Resistance, the picture is perfectly clear, the Americans falling at one extreme and the Indians at the other extreme, with the Chinese in the middle.

However, two relatively more westernized Indian groups (Lady Irwin and Indo-American) do present us with some seeming difficulties. Contrary to the general observations just made, the Lady Irwin and Indo-American fantasies are higher in Achievement Imagery and lower in Reverie than all other groups of Indian and non-Indian fantasies. Then, in spite of the fact that, according to Table A-2, all Indian responses to Card 1 are lower in Resistance, the Lady Irwin and Indo-American groups come very close to the Chinese groups (26% and 27% versus 37% for Taiwan and 30% for Hong Kong). Even the very traditional Vidyasagar students register numerous Resistance responses (19%). Is there an explanation?

I suggest that there is, and that to find this explanation we must analyze the contents of the Resistance responses. The lower percentage of Resistance responses among all the non-American groups than among the American group may partly be due to the fact that the non-Americans do not happen to share what Henry regards as "a current middle-class American value which has become a frequent source of conflict between parents and children"[16] (as Watrous noted in her interpretation). But an analysis of the contents of all responses classified in Table A-2 in the Resistance category shows that the psychocultural differences run far deeper. The Evanston Resistance responses are true to our understood American form, namely, plain conflict between specific parental pressure or injunction and rebellion on the part of the child against it. To be sure, there are a number of Resistance responses from the Chinese groups and at least two from the Indian groups which would be difficult to separate from typical American responses. But many of the Chinese and most of the Indian Resistance responses deviate from this form. A majority of the Chinese Resistance responses from Hong Kong conceive the child's problem as due to conflict with his father or mother (often both) in the American form, but a majority from Taiwan see the problem of the child in terms of the adverse circumstances of the family group as a whole. The following two examples illustrate the two Chinese forms:

> (1) A boy about 10 is forced by his mother to learn the playing of violin. Everytime when he practises, he shows great reluctance. One day, being alone in the room, he is tired of the practice. Having laid the violin on the table, the boy sits down in front of the instrument, looking at it, with his chin in his hands and fingers pressing his temples. There he is thinking about the past famous violin players—why they could play so beautifully and were applaused by generations and their work was thought to be ever-lasting? Why now he has to be scolded and forced to do the same thing. Is it so important to him as to the other musicians? He thinks how delightful he will be if he can have games in the open air with their joyful friends. (Hong Kong.)
>
> (2) In a certain place there is a child. He has shown a great inclination toward music ever since he was very little. Especially he is interested in the violin. but his family is very poor. It has no ability to support him to learn the violin. In fact the family cannot even have money enough to buy him a violin. That is why the child feels extremely sad, but Heaven never disappoints a man who is really determined. That is why one day there was a wealthy man who gave him a violin. He feels very happy, but he at the same time is faced with another big problem. He realizes that his talents are limited. At the same time there was no one to instruct him in the art. That is why he is very sad, but eventually he still becomes a very famous violinist. (Taiwan.)

The Hong Kong pattern reminds us, of course, of what was observed earlier: that our Hong Kong students appear to have been more westernized than our Taiwan subjects; but the Taiwan pattern is understandable in a way of life where the kinship principle of social organization predominates over others. There the ties of birth and marriage are expected to continue indefinitely. In such a culture the individual tends to see his problems as problems of his family group rather than of his own, and their solution cannot, therefore, be his emergence from that group. In other words he is likely to identify his own problems with problems of his family or some extended group.

A majority of the Indian Resistance responses share one characteristic: the boy's problem is that he wants to play the musical instrument (or do something else if the violin is ignored by the subject), but his father or mother (or both or some other family member) do not allow him to do it. This is especially true of Lady Irwin and Indo-American responses among which Resistance, as we noted earlier, is high. The following example is typical of Lady Irwin Resistance responses:

> There was a small boy who loved to play on violin, but his parents did not like this thing so every time he would start to play on it, the mother would come and say stop this nonsense. The father used to say—that this boy is good for nothing. He not at all interested in his studies. What is use of becoming a violinist.

But it was rather difficult to change the boy. Every time he learnt a new tune, or heard a new song, he would practice it on his violin. So one day the father got very angry and turned the boy out of the house. The boy took his violin with him. He was not anxious to meet new adventures in his life. On his way he had many difficulties, roaming here and there. But he did not care for hail or storm—the boy had one aim—he wanted to learn to play more efficiently on violin. Finally on his way he met a group of musicians. They were enjoying a picnic. The boy sat nearby and started playing on his violin. The leader of the group was impressed by his skill. He took the boy with him. There for several years he learnt his skill, and finally became a famous violinist.

Indo-American's Resistance responses are somewhat more varied in content but the Lady Irwin type of response does occur and the father or mother is nevertheless the impediment, as the following response shows:

There are times in life when every person, of every age, whether man, woman or child, comes across moments of conflict, especially when some decision has to be made. This was one such moment for Thomas. He was ten years old, and the time had come for him to decide what he would do. He was to chose between becoming a violinist, what his father, a celebrated violinist wanted him to become, or start learning the trumpet, an instrument for which he had a certain fascination. But, there was just one hitch, and that was, that his father, though a celebrated violinist was not so successful in keeping the coffers full, a financial flop, he was unable to pay for the course his son wanted to take, but would easily be able to teach him the violin himself.

Tom sat there looking at the violin. It was an old one of his father's. He picked it up and ran his fingers over the strings, yet undecided because he could not understand why his father was unable to pay for his trumpet lessons.

At last he got up, dusk had fallen long since and as he passed his window, he could see the stars winking at him from there. That did it. He ran out of his room and down the stairs. The stars were twinkling now and would so henceforth too and he would grow up and learn to play the trumpet when he can earn for himself.

Only two responses in the Vidyasagar group are judged Resistant in nature. One of them is given below:

Here is a boy looking over a violine. The violine is an instrument of music but the boy does not know how to handle it. He is thinking, that from such a few strings, how it is possible to got a beautiful harmonic sound. His mind want to know that, who invented this music. Suddenly an idea comes to his mind. He thinks perhaps his father can help him. He wants to learn it clearly. But his father is now at office. He wants to know, what are the things inside it. But his eagerness will come to light, when father will return from house.

My view is that there is a basic difference between seeing the parent as the stipulator of a positive norm (such as studying the violin) and seeing the elder merely as an impediment to a positive goal desired by the child. In the individual's process of growing up, his first experiences with parents are as agents of negative restraints and only later as sources of positive norms. The former are therefore, more primitive and generalized because they come earlier and they are less specific than the latter.

My major conclusion concerning the Hindu world throughout the book is built on the looseness of the kinship bond, the diluted condition of all human relationships (necessitating caste as a compensatory device against this uncertainty among men) and a diffused world orientation on the part of the individual regulated more by impediment than by suppression or repression. I further postulated that this particular type of orientation is introduced and reinforced in each generation through the greater predominance of the mother-son axis in the nuclear family over the father-son and husband-wife axes. The Indian responses provide us with no specific corroboration of the role of the mother-son axis (though Chinese and American responses are indicative, as we saw above, of the respective importance of the father-son axis in one way of life and husband-wife axis in the other). They do, however, by the fact that the parent figure is fantasied in Card 1 as restraining the child from specific goals rather than pressuring him toward them, strongly suggest relatively diffused interpersonal relationships more characteristic of that between mothers and their children which come earlier to the individual, than of that between fathers and their children, which usually come later. The mother-child relationship is more diffused than the father-child relationship not only because it tends to be established earlier, when the infant is less capable of motivating itself to specific goals, but also the very nature of the mother-child relationship is, as pointed out in Chapter III of the book, more diffused than other relationships.

This diffused outlook is probably at the root of why the Indo-American and Lady Irwin fantasies are so high in Achievement Imagery, not only in sharp contrast to those of the other two Indian groups but also exceeding all non-Indian groups. The characteristic of a diffused outlook is that it is more fluid and therefore more liable to extremes, than one which is channelized in specific directions. The extreme opposites exhibited in the fantasies of Hindu students may not be unrelated to the fact that Lady Irwin and Indo-American students have been subjected to more Western influences. But such extreme opposites are far from rare in Hindu life; her extremely diverse schools of philosophy and widely contradictory religious beliefs and practices are but two pronounced examples.

From the same standpoint we can also better understand why Resistance responses in the Vidyasagar group (Table A-2) are so high (19%). The Vidyasagar responses that Watrous has classified under the category of Resistance would have been resistive in the context of the American culture but not in that of the Hindu world. The fact is that most of the Vidyasagar responses classified under Resistance are ones in which the boy is seen as being alone and sad vis-à-vis the instrument, either because it is broken or because of other difficulties. In the American cultural context where the nuclear family is close-knit and where, for the child, the hands of his parents are strong and ubiquitous such responses can indeed be legitimately regarded as indicative of Resistance. But in the Hindu cultural context, where neither the nuclear family nor the hands of the parents have comparable importance, such responses are not as reflective of Resistance as they are of the Aloneness. This observation is additionally corroborated (1) by the small number of Enjoyment responses and the preponderance of responses indicating Aloneness, Dysphoria, Abandonment and Loss of Way, etc., to Card 12BG (Tables A-6 and A-7); and (2) by the fact that extraordinarily few Vidyasagar responses to Card 1, in contrast to those of other Indian groups, contain any reference to interpersonal relationships at all (see Table A-2).

V. CONCLUDING OBSERVATIONS

In reviewing our separate analyses and interpretations contained in Sections III and IV of this Annex, we have been surprised at the extent to which the projective materials stimulated by two TAT cards turn out to be related to and corroborative of Hsu's hypothesis on the differences between the three worlds. And our surprise is all the greater in view of observations made by several students, among others Kaplan and Wallace, that the intragroup variability in personality seems to be very great and that intergroup differences tend to be much smaller, leading "to the conclusion that there is less variability among cultures than was expected."[17] We believe that projective studies using the complete Rorschach or full complement of TAT cards may be an impediment rather than an advantage to our understanding of intergroup differences. These tests in full are designed to probe deeply into the psychic structure and content of single individuals which are much less shared by others than those day-to-day levels of personality, necessitated by the identity and role of individuals as participating members of a particular society, in conformity to the normative components of its culture.* Our suggestion is, tentative though it must remain, that the use of a few cards, such as TAT 1 and 12BG, may very well prove to be a much better aid to the student of man for understanding personality in its group perspective than its individual perspective. Besides the economy of time and energy, we suggest that this is a technique and approach well worth our consideration and experimentation on purely scientific grounds. We had a glimpse of the rich potentialities of this approach when we compared the

---

* After completing this writing, we find that a point similar to this has been made by Goldschmidt and Edgerton ("A Picture Technique for the Study of Values," *American Anthropologist*, Vol. 63 No. 1 (February 1961), pp. 28–29). However, Goldschmidt and Edgerton's remedies are very different from the procedure proposed here.

findings of the present volume with those of Charles Morris on value through the use of questionnaires.

Finally, it seems that the numerical count of categories selected for analysis may be considered a reliable index of personality differences only where striking variations in emotional approach occur, for example, the spontaneity of the Americans as contrasted with the diffidence of the Indians of Vidyasagar College in response to Card 1; or the impressive resistance of the Northwestern students as contrasted with the low incidence of such projections among the Asutosh group. The feeling tone, which is necessarily subjective in interpretation, is frequently more revealing of at least the emotional trends in the fantasies than the quantitative data. The broader question here is the degree to which quantitative data can validly describe an entity as complex as the human personality. Possibly the answer lies in a more sensitive blending of the objective and the subjective in the interpretation of projective tests as an adjunct to studies in Psychological Anthropology.

NOTES FOR THE ANNEX

1. Leopold Bellak, *The Thematic Apperception Test and the Children's Apperception Test in Clinical Use* (New York: Grune and Stratton, 1954), p. 101.

2. Lawrence Abt and Leopold Bellak, *Projective Psychology* (New York: Alfred A. Knopf, 1950), p. 211.

3. Henry A. Murray, *Thematic Apperception Test Manual* (Cambridge, Mass.: Harvard University Press, 1943), p. 3.

4. William Caudill and George De Vos, "Achievement, Culture and Personality: The Case of the Japanese Americans," *American Anthropologist*, LIII (1956), pp. 1102–1127.

5. *Ibid.*, p. 1108.

6. David C. McClelland, J. W. Atkinson, R. A. Clark, and E. L. Lowell, *The Achievement Motive* (New York: Appleton-Century-Crofts, 1953).

7. William E. Henry, *The Analysis of Fantasy* (New York: John Wiley and Sons, Inc., 1956), pp. 86–87.

8. A. F. C. Wallace, "The Modal Personality Structure of the Tuscarora Indians as Revealed by the Rorschach Test," *Bull., B.A.E.,* 150 (1952).

9. Bert Kaplan, "A Study of Rorschach Responses in Four Cultures," *Papers of the Peabody Museum of American Archaeology and Ethnology, Harvard University,* 42, No. 2 (1954).

10. Thomas Gladwin and S. B. Sarason, *Truk: Man in Paradise* (New York: Viking Fund Publications in Anthropology No. 20, 1953).

11. G. D. Mulligen, *Maori Adolescents in Rakan, a TAT Study,* Publications in Psychology No. 9, Monographs on Maori Social Life and Personality No. 2 (Wellington, New Zealand: Victoria University College, 1957).

12. William Henry, "Projective Tests in Cross-Cultural Research" in Bert Kaplan (ed.), *Studying Personality Cross-Culturally* (Evanston: Row, Peterson and Company, 1961), p. 593.

13. William Henry, "The Analysis of Fantasy," *loc. cit.*, p. 147.

14. Francis L. K. Hsu, Blanche G. Watrous, and Edith M. Lord, "Culture Pattern and Adolescent Behavior," *International Journal of Social Psychiatry*, VII, No. 1 (1961), pp. 33–53.

15. According to William E. Henry, Card 1 is generally considered "a middle-class picture in that it presents an issue more appropriate to the social definition made by that large group. The struggle with the conflict of free choice and an imposed task is thus one of the basic common themes to this picture. The aura of ambition is, of course, the second, most generally symbolised by stories of the virtuosity of the boy and the potential future musical success." (William E. Henry, "The Analysis of Fantasy," *loc. cit.*, p. 147.)

16. William E. Henry, *ibid.*

17. Bert Kaplan, "Cross-Cultural Use of Projective Techniques," Chapter 8, in F. L. K. Hsu (ed.), *Psychological Anthropology* (Homewood, Ill.: Dorsey Press, 1961), p. 241.

BIBLIOGRAPHY

Aberle, D. F.; Cohen, A. K.; Davis, A. K.; Levy, M. J., Jr.; and Sutton, F. X. "The Functional Prerequisites of Society," *Ethics,* LX, No. 2 (January 1950), 104–111.

Abt, Lawrence, and Bellak, Leopold. *Projective Psychology.* New York: Alfred A. Knopf, 1950.

Arens, Richard, and Lasswell, Harold. In *Defense of Public Order.* New York: Columbia University Press, 1961.

Bailey, F. G. *Caste and the Economic Frontier.* Manchester: Manchester University Press, 1957.

Basham, A. L. *The Wonder That Was India.* London: Sidgwick and Jackson, 1956.

Bellak, Leopold. *The Thematic Apperception Test and the Children's Apperception Test in Clinical Use.* New York: Grune and Stratton, 1954.

Berreman, Gerald D. "Caste in India and the United States," *American Journal of Sociology,* LXVI, No. 2 (September 1960), 120–127.

The Bhagavadgita. Translated by S. Radhakrishnan. London: George Allen and Unwin, 1948.

Bierstedt, Robert. "Sociology and Human Learning," Presidential address read at the annual meeting of the Eastern Sociological Society, April, 1959, *American Sociological Review,* XXV (1960), 3–9.

Blunt, E. A. H. *The Caste System of Northern India.* London: Humphrey Milford, Oxford University Press, 1931.

Bohannan, Paul J. "Conscience and Collective and Culture," in Kurt Woolf (ed.), *Emil Durkheim (1860–1918).* Columbus, Ohio: Ohio State University Press, 1961.

———— "Kinship and Social Organization," in preparation.

Bose, Nirma Kumar. "Caste in India," *Man in India,* XXXI, Nos. 3 and 4 (1951), 115–116.

———— "Some Aspects of Caste in Bengal," in Milton Singer, "Traditional India: Structure and Change," *Journal of American Folklore,* LXXI, No. 281 (July 1958), 397–412.

Bouglé, C. *Essais sur le régime des castes.* Travaux de l'Année Sociologique. Paris: F. Alcan, 1908.

Brahmavaivarta, Ganapatikhanda, Chap. XL, according to Vasishtha, quoted in *The Cultural Heritage of India,* Vol. III, Sri Ramakrishna Centenary Memorial. 3 vols. Belur Math, Calcutta: Sri Ramakrishna Centenary Committee, 1936[?].

Carstairs, G. Morris *The Twice Born.* London: The Hogarth Press, 1957.

Cattell, Raymond B. *Personality and Motivation, Structure and Measurement.* Yonkers-on-Hudson, N.Y.: World Book Company, 1957.

Caudill, William, and DeVos, George. "Achievement, Culture and Personality: The Case of the Japanese Americans," *American Anthropologist,* LIII (1956), 1102–1127.

Chakladar, Haran Chandra. "Social Life in Ancient India," in *The Cultural Heritage of India*, Vol. III. Sri Ramakrishna Centenary Memorial. 3 vols. Belur Math, Calcutta: Sri Ramakrishna Centenary Committee, 1936[?].

Chapple, E. D., and Coon, C. S. *Principles of Anthropology*. New York: Henry Holt, 1942.

Clough, Shepard B. *Basic Values of Western Civilization*. New York: Columbia University Press, 1960.

Codere, Helen. "A Genealogical Study of Kinship in The United States," *Psychiatry*, XVIII, No. 1 (Feb. 1955), 65–793.

Cohn, Bernard S. "The Changing Status of a Depressed Caste," in McKim Marriott (ed.), *Village India*. Chicago: University of Chicago Press, 1955.

—— "The Pasts of an Indian Village," *Comparative Studies in Society and History*. (The Hague: Mouton & Co.), III, No. 3 (1961), 241–249.

—— "Some Notes on Law and Social Change in North India," *Economic Development and Cultural Change* (Chicago: University of Chicago), IX (1959), 79–93.

Commager, Henry Steele. *The American Mind*. New Haven: Yale University Press, 1950.

Coon, Carleton (ed.). *A Reader in General Anthropology*. New York: Henry Holt, 1948.

Cotu, Walter. *Emergent Human Nature*. New York: Alfred A. Knopf, 1949.

The Cultural Heritage of India. Sri Ramakrishna Centenary Memorial. 3 vols. Belur Math, Calcutta: Sri Ramakrishna Centenary Committee, 1936[?].

"Deficiency Motivation and Growth Motivation," in M. R. Jones (ed.), *Nebraska Symposium on Motivation*. Lincoln: University of Nebraska Press, 1955.

Desai, I., and Damle, Y. B. "A Note on the Change in the Caste," in K. M. Kapadia (ed.), *Professor Ghurye Felicitation Volume*. Bombay: Ghurye 60th Birthday Celebration Committee, 1954.

Dewey, John. *A Common Faith*. New Haven: Yale University Press, 1934.

Dhillon, Harwant Singh. *Leadership and Groups in a South Indian Village*. New Delhi: Planning Commission, Program and Evaluation Organization, Government of India, 1955.

Doré, Henri. *Researches into Chinese Superstitions*. Translated by M. Kennelly. 13 vols. Shanghai: T'usewei Printing Press, 1914–1938.

Dube, S. C. *Indian Village*. Ithaca, N.Y.: Cornell University Press, 1955.

Dumezil, G. *Mitra-Varuna*. Paris: Payot, 1948.

Dumont, Louis. *Une sous-caste de l'Inde du Sud*. Paris: Mouton et Cie, 1957.

—— and Pocock, D. *Contributions to Indian Sociology* (Paris and The Hague: Mouton & Co.), No. 2 (April 1958), an irregular publication.

Durkheim, Emile. *De la division du travail social*. Translated by George Simpson under the English title, *The Division of Labor in Society*. Glencoe, Ill.: Free Press, 1947.

The Early History of India. (4th ed.) Oxford: Oxford University Press, 1957.

Emerson, Ralph Waldo. "Self-reliance" in Norman Foerster (ed.), *American Poetry and Prose*. Boston: Houghton Mifflin, 1934.

Fei, H. T. *Peasant Life in China: A Field Study of Country Life in the Yangtze Valley*. London: Routledge and Kegan Paul, 1939.

Firth, Raymond. *We, the Tikopia*. New York: American Book Company, 1936. (Quoted in Homans, *The Human Group*.)

Foerster, Norman (ed.). *American Poetry and Prose*. Boston: Houghton Mifflin, 1934.

Foster, George M. "What Is Fold Culture?" *American Anthropologist*, LV (1953), 159–173.

Freedman, Maurice. *Lineage Organization in Southeastern China*. London: The Athlone Press, 1958.

Fuchs, Stephen. *The Children of Hari: A Study of the Balahis in the Central Provinces*. New York: Frederick A. Praeger, 1951.

Gamble, S. D. *Ting Hsien, A North China Rural Community*. New York: International Secretariat, Institute of Pacific Relations, 1954.

Garuda Purana. Translated by Ernest Wood and S. V. Subrahminyam, with an introduction by Sri Chandra Vasu. (The Sacred Books of the Hindus series, ed. Major B. D. Basu, retired.) Bhuvaneswari Asrama, Selahabad: Sudbindra Natha Vasu, Panini Offices, 1911.

Ghurye, G. S. *Caste and Class in India*. (2nd ed.) Bombay: The Popular Book Depot, 1959.

———— "Indian Unity—Retrospect and Prospect," *Group Prejudices in India*. Bombay: Vora, 1951.

Giles, Herbert A. *A Chinese-English Dictionary*. 2 vols. (2nd ed.) Shanghai: Kelly and Walsh, 1912.

Gladwin, Thomas, and Sarason, S. B. *Truk: Man in Paradise*. New York: Viking Fund Publications in Anthropology No. 20, 1953.

Glick, Paul C. *American Families*. New York: John Wiley and Sons, 1957.

Goldschmidt, Walter R. *Man's Way: A Preface to the Understanding of Human Society*. New York: Henry Holt and Company, 1959.

———— and Edgerton, Robert B. "A Picture Technique for the Study of Values," *American Anthropologist*, Vol. 63, No. 1 (February 1961), 28–29.

Goldstein, Kurt. "Organismic Approach to the Problem of Motivation," *Transactions*, IX. New York Academy of Sciences, 1947.

Gough, Kathleen. "Caste in a Tanjore Village," in E. R. Leach (ed.), *Aspects of Caste in South India, Ceylon and North-West Pakistan*. (Cambridge Papers in Social Anthropology, No. 2.) London: Cambridge University Press, 1960.

———— "Cults of the Dead among the Nayars," in Milton Singer (ed.), *Traditional India: Structure and Change. Journal of American Folklore*, LXXI, No. 281 (July 1958), 446–478.

———— "The Social Structure of a Tanjore Village," in McKim Marriott (ed.), *Village India*. (Memoir No. 83.) Washington, D.C.: American Anthropological Association, June 1955.

Harrison, Selig S. *India, the Most Dangerous Years: Can the Nation Hold Together?* Princeton, N.J.: Princeton University Press, 1960.

Hayden, Eustace A. *Biography of the Gods*. New York: Macmillan, 1941.

Henry, William E. "Projective Tests in Cross-Cultural Research," in Bert Kaplan (ed.), *Studying Personality Cross-Culturally*. Evanston: Row, Peterson and Company, 1961.

———— *The Analysis of Fantasy*. New York: John Wiley and Sons, Inc., 1956.

Hocart, A. C. *Caste, A Comparative Study*. London: Methuen, 1950.

Homans, George C. *The Human Group*. New York: Harcourt, Brace, 1950.

Hsu, Francis L. K. *Americans and Chinese: Two Ways of Life*. New York: Abelard-Schuman, 1953.

———— "American Core Value and National Character," in *Psychological Anthro-*

pology: Aspects of Culture and Personality. Homewood, Ill.: Dorsey Press, 1961.

────── "An Anthropologist's View of the Future of Personality Studies," *Psychiatric Research Reports 2.* American Psychiatric Association, December 1955.

────── "A Closer View of China's Problems," *The Far Eastern Quarterly,* (November 1946), 50–64.

────── "On Behalf of Comparative Civilizations through Interdisciplinary Cooperation," in Ainslee Embree (ed.), *Approaches to Asian Civilization.* New York: Atherton Press, 1963.

────── "Incentives to Work in Primitive Communities," *American Sociological Review,* VIII, No. 6 (December 1943), 638–642.

────── "Kinship, Ancestor Worship and Kingship," in preparation.

────── "Kinship and Ways of Life: An Exploration," in F. L. K. Hsu (ed.), *Psychological Anthropology: Approaches to Culture and Personality.* Homewood, Ill.: Dorsey Press, 1961.

────── "People of Gods," in preparation.

────── (ed.). *Psychological Anthropology: Approaches to Culture and Personality.* Homewood, Ill.: Dorsey Press, 1961.

────── *Religion, Science and Human Crises.* London: Routledge and Kegan Paul, 1952.

────── "Structure, Function, Content and Process," *American Anthropologist,* LXI, No. 5, Pt. 1 (October 1959), 790–805.

────── "Suppression, Repression and Effusion: A Limited Psychological Interpretation of Three Cultures," in preparation.

────── "Suppression, Versus Repression, A Limited Psychological Interpretation of Four Cultures," *Psychiatry,* XII, No. 3 (August 1949), 223–242.

────── *Under the Ancestors' Shadow.* New York: Columbia University Press, 1948.

Hsu, Francis L. K.; Watrous, Blanche G.; and Lord, Edith M. "Culture Pattern and Adolescent Behavior," *International Journal of Social Psychiatry,* VII, No. 1 (1961), 33–53.

Hu, Hsien Chin. *The Common Descent Group in China and Its Functions.* (Viking Fund Publication in Anthropology, No. 10.) New York: Wenner-Gren Foundation for Anthropological Research, 1948.

Hutton, J. H. *Caste in India.* London: Oxford University Press, 1951.

India's Villages. West Bengal, India: Development Department, West Bengal Government Press, 1955.

Inkeles, Alex; Hanfmann, Eugenia; and Beier, Helen. "Modal Personality and Adjustment to the Soviet-Socio-Political System," in *Studying Personality Cross-Culturally,* ed. Bert Kaplan. Evanston: Row, Peterson, 1961.

Kapadia, K. M. *Hindu Kinship.* Bombay: 1947.

────── (ed.). *Professor Ghurye Felicitation Volume.* Bombay: Ghurye 60th Birthday Celebration Committee, 1954.

Kaplan, Bert (ed.). *Studying Personality Cross-Culturally.* Evanston, Ill.: Row, Peterson, 1961.

──────"Cross-Cultural Use of Projective Techniques," Chapter 8, in F. L. K. Hsu (ed.), *Psychological Anthropology.* Homewood, Ill.: Dorsey Press, 1961, 241.

────── "A Study of Rorschach Responses in Four Cultures," *Papers of the Peabody Museum of American Archaeology and Ethnology, Harvard University,* 42, No. 2 (1954).

Karve, Irawati. *Hindu Social Organization*. Bombay: 1958.

——— *Hindu Society—an Interpretation*. Poona, India: Deccan College, 1961.

——— *Kinship Organization in India*. (Deccan College Monograph Series,) Poona, India: 1953.

Klineberg, Otto. *Social Psychology*. (2nd ed.) New York: Henry Holt, 1954.

Kluckhohn, Clyde. "Theoretical Bases for an Empirical Method of Studying the Acquisition of Culture by Individual," *Man*. (London: Royal Anthropological Institute), XXXIX.

Jones, M. R. (ed.). *Nebraska Symposium on Motivation*. Lincoln, Neb.: University of Nebraska Press, 1955.

Laski, Harold J. *The American Democracy*. New York: Viking Press, 1948.

The Laws of Manu. Translated by G. Buhler. Vol. XXV in *The Sacred Books of the East*, ed. F. Max Muller. Oxford: Clarendon Press, 1886.

Leach, E. R. (ed.). "Introduction" in *Aspects of Caste in South India, Ceylon and Northwest Pakistan*. (Cambridge Papers in Social Anthropology, No. 2.) Cambridge: Cambridge University Press, 1960.

Levine, Seymour. "Stimulation in Infancy," *Scientific American* (May 1960), 81–86.

Lew, Ling. *The Chinese in North America*. Los Angeles: East-West Culture Publishing Association, 1949.

Lewin, Kurt. *Resolving Social Conflicts: Selected Papers on Group Dynamics*. New York: Harper and Brothers, 1948.

Lewis, Oscar. *Village Life in Northern India*. Urbana: University of Illinois Press, 1958.

Lindesmith, Alfred R. and Strauss, Anselm L. *Social Psychology*. (Rev. ed.) New York: The Dryden Press, 1956.

Linton, Ralph. *The Cultural Background of Personality*. New York: Appleton-Century-Crofts, 1945.

——— *The Study of Man*. New York: Appleton-Century, 1936.

Long-Range Planning for Education. Washington, D.C.: American Council on Education, 1958.

Lowie, R. H. *An Introduction to Cultural Anthropology*. New York: Farrar and Rinehart, 1940.

——— *Primitive Society*. New York: Boni and Liveright, 1920.

Lynd, Robert S., and Helen M. *Middletown*. New York: Harcourt, Brace & Co., 1929.

——— *Middletown in Transition*. New York: Harcourt, Brace and Co., 1937.

McClelland, David C. *The Achieving Society*. Princeton, N.J.: Van Nostrand, 1961.

McClelland, David; Atkinson, John W.; Clark, Russell A.; and Lowell, E. L. *The Achievement Motive*. New York: Appleton-Century-Crofts, 1953.

MacIver, R. M. *Social Causation*. New York: Ginn, 1942.

Madan, T. N. "Is the Brahmanic *Gotra* a Grouping of Kin?" *Southwestern Journal of Anthropology*, XVIII, No. 1 (Spring 1962), 59–77.

Mahabharata, quoted by Haran Chandra Chakladar, "Social Life in Ancient India," in *The Cultural Heritage of India*, Sri Ramakrishna Centenary Memorial, Vol. III. 3 vols. Belur Math, Calcutta: Sri Ramakrishna Centenary Committee, 1936[?].

Majumder, R. C. *The History and Culture of the Indian People*. 5 vols. London: George Allen and Unwin, 1957.

Majumder, R. C.; Raychandhuri, H. C.; and Dalta, K. C. *An Advanced History of India.* London: Macmillan & Co., 1948.

Mandelbaum, David. "The Family in India," *Southwestern Journal of Anthropology,* IV, No. 2 (Summer, 1948), 123–139.

———— "Social Groupings," in H. L. Shapiro (ed.), *Man, Culture and Society.* New York: Oxford University Press, 1956.

———— "The World and the World View of the Kota," in McKim Marriott (ed.), *Village India.* (Memoir No. 83.) Washington, D.C.: American Anthropological Association, June 1955.

Marriott, McKim. "Interactional and Attributional Theories of Caste Ranking," *Man in India,* XXXIX, No. 2 (April–June 1959), 92–107.

———— "Little Communities in an Indigenous Civilization," in McKim Marriott (ed.), *Village India.* (Memoir No. 83.) Washington, D.C.: American Anthropological Association, June 1955.

———— "Structure and Change in a U. P. Village," in *India's Villages.* West Bengal, India: Development Department, West Bengal Government Press, 1955.

———— "A Technique for the Study of Caste Ranking in South Asia," paper read at American Anthropological Association meetings, 1957, Chicago.

———— (ed.). *Village India.* (Memoir No. 83.) Washington, D.C.: American Anthropological Association, June 1955. Also Chicago: University of Chicago Press.

Maslow, A. H. *Motivation and Personality.* New York: Harper, 1954.

Mayer, Adrian C. *Land and Society in Malabar.* Oxford: Oxford University Press, 1952.

Mead, M. *Coming of Age in Samoa.* New York: W. Morrow, 1928.

Milgram, S. "Nationality and Conformity," *Scientific American* (December 1961), 45–51.

Morris, Charles W. *Varieties of Human Value.* Chicago: University of Chicago Press, 1956.

Muller, F. Max. *Ramakrishna, His Life and Sayings.* London: 1938.

Mulligen, G. D. *Maori Adolescents in Rakan, a TAT Study,* Publications in Psychology No. 9, Monographs on Maori Social Life and Personality No. 2. Wellington, New Zealand: Victoria University College, 1957.

Murdock, George P. *Social Structure.* New York: Macmillan Co., 1949.

Murphy, Gardner (ed.). *In the Minds of Men.* New York: Basic Books, Inc., 1953.

Murphy, Lois B. "Indian Child Development," in Gardner Murphy (ed.), *In the Minds of Men.* New York: Basic Books, Inc., 1953.

———— "Roots of Tolerance and Tensions in Child Development," in Gardner Murphy (ed.), *In the Minds of Men.* New York: Basic Books, Inc., 1953.

Murray, Henry A. *Thematic Apperception Test Manual.* Cambridge, Mass.: Harvard University Press, 1943.

Murray, Henry A. et al. *Explorations in Personality.* New York: Oxford University Press, 1938.

Nair, Mrs. Kusum. *Blossoms in the Dust.* London: Duckworth, 1961.

Naroll, Raoul. *Data Quality Control, a New Research Technique.* New York: The Free Press of Glencoe, 1962.

Newell, W. H. "Goshen, a Gaddi Village in the Himalayas," in *India's Villages,* West Bengal, India: Development Department, West Bengal Government Press, 1955.

Sister Nivedita (Miss M. E. Noble). *The Web of Indian Life*. London and Bombay: Longmans, Green, 1904.

Northrop, F. S. C. *The Meeting of East and West*. New York: Macmillan, 1946.

Opler, Morris E. "Factors of Tradition and Change in a Local Election in Rural India," in Richard L. Park and Irene Tinker (eds.), *Leadership and Political Institutions in India*. Princeton: Princeton University Press, 1959.

―――― "The Place of Religion in a North Indian Village," *Southwestern Journal of Anthropology*, XV, No. 3 (1959), 219–226.

―――― and Singh, Rudra Datt. "The Division of Labor in an Indian Village," in Carleton S. Coon (ed.), *A Reader in General Anthropology*. New York: Henry Holt, 1948.

―――――――― "Economic, Political and Social Change in a Village of North Central India," *Human Organization*, II (1952), 5–12.

Park, Richard L., and Tinker, Irene (eds.). *Leadership and Political Institutions in India*. Princeton, N.J.: Princeton University Press, 1959.

Parsons, Talcott. *The Social System*. Glencoe, Ill.: Free Press, 1951.

Piers, G., and Singer, Milton B. *Shame and Guilt: A Psychoanalytic and a Cultural Study*. Springfield, Ill.: Charles C Thomas, 1953.

Pocock, David F. " 'Difference' in East Africa: A Study of Caste and Religion in Modern Indian Society," *Southwestern Journal of Anthropology*, XIII, No. 4 (Winter, 1957), 289–300.

―――― "Inclusion and Exclusion: A Process in the Caste System of Gujarat," *Southwestern Journal of Anthropology*, XIII, No. 1 (Spring 1957), 19–31.

Pradhu, Pandharinath. *Hindu Social Organization*. (3rd ed.) Bombay: The Popular Book Depot, 1958.

Radhakrishnan, S. "Introductory Essay," *The Bhagvadgita*. London: George Allen and Unwin, 1948.

Redfield, Robert. *Peasant Society and Culture*. Chicago: University of Chicago Press, 1955.

―――― and Singer, Milton. "The Cultural Role of Cities," *Economic Development and Cultural Change*. (Chicago: University of Chicago), III (1952), 53–73.

Riesman, David. "The Found Generation," *The American Scholar*, XXV, No. 4 (Fall 1956), 421–436.

―――― *The Lonely Crowd*. New Haven: Yale University Press, 1950.

Rogers, Carl R. *Client-Centered Therapy; Its Current Practice, Implications and Theory*. Boston: Houghton Mifflin, 1951.

Schutz, William C. *FIRO*. New York: Rinehart, 1958.

Shah, A. M. and Shroff, R. G. "The Vahīrancā Bārots of Gujarat: A Caste of Genealogists and Mythographers," in Milton Singer (ed.), *Traditional India: Structure and Change. Journal of American Folklore*, LXXI, No. 281 (July 1958), 248–276.

Shapiro, H. L. (ed.). *Man, Culture and Society*. New York: Oxford University Press, 1956.

Shastri, Nilakanta. *A History of South India*. Oxford: Oxford University Press, 1955.

Simmel, Georg. *The Sociology of Georg Simmel*. Translated, edited and with an Introduction by Kurt H. Wolff. Glencoe: The Free Press, 1950.

Singer, Milton. "The Cultural Pattern of Indian Civilization: A Preliminary Report of a Methodological Study," *Far Eastern Quarterly*, XV, No. 1 (November 1955), 34.

────── Personal communication.

────── (ed.). *Traditional India: Structure and Change*. Philadelphia: The American Folklore Society, 1959. Also *Journal of American Folklore* LXXI, No. 281 (July 1958).

Singh, Dudra Datt. "The Unity of an Indian Village," *Journal of Asian Studies*, XVI (November 1956), 10–19.

Smith, V. A. *Early History of India*. Oxford: Oxford University Press, 1957.

Spiro, Melford E. "An Overview and a Suggested Restoration." in *Psychological Anthropology*, ed. Francis L. K. Hsu. Homewood: Dorsey Press, 1961.

Srinivas, M. N. "Introduction," in *India's Villages*. West Bengal, India: Development Department, West Bengal Government, 1955.

────── *Marriage and Family in Mysore*. Bombay: New Book Company, 1942.

────── *Religion and Society among the Coorgs of South India*. Oxford: Oxford University Press, 1952.

────── "Varna and Caste," in S. Radhakrishnan *et al.* (eds.), *Essays in Philosophy*. Baroda: The University of Baroda, 1954. (Republished in *Introduction to the Civilization of India*. Chicago: Syllabus Division, University of Chicago Press, 1957.)

Steed, Gitel P. "Life History Documents, I (Indrasingh)" (hectographed). New York: Columbia University Research in Contemporary India Project, 1950.

────── "Personality Formation in a Hindu Village in Gujarat," in McKim Marriott (ed.), *Village India*. (Memoir No. 83.) Washington, D.C.: American Anthropological Association, June 1955.

Stevenson, H. N. C. "Caste (Indian)," *Encyclopædia Britannica* (1957 ed.), Vol. 4, p. 982.

────── "Status Evaluation in the Hindu Caste System," *Journal of the Royal Anthropological Institute*, LXXXIV, Pts. 1 and 2 (1954), 45–65.

Steward, Julian. *A Theory of Cultural Change*. Urbana: University of Illinois Press, 1960.

Suchman, Edward S. "The Values of American College Students," in *Long Range Planning for Education*. Washington, D.C.: American Council on Education, 1958.

Sumner, William, and Keller, A. G. *Science of Society*, Vol. I. 4 vols. New Haven: Yale University Press, 1927.

Thomas, P. *Hindu Religion, Customs and Manners*. (2nd ed.) Bombay: D. P. Taraporevala Sons and Co., undated.

Thomas, William I. *Social Behavior and Personality*. New York: Social Science Research Council, 1951.

Thomas, D. I. and Znaniecki, F. *The Polish Peasant in Europe and America*. New York: Alfred A. Knopf, 1927.

Thurston, Edgar. *Castes and Tribes of Southern India*. 7 vols. Madras: Unwin, 1909.

Varma, V. P. *Studies in Hindu Political Thought and Its Metaphysical Foundations*. Banares, 1954.

Wallace, A. F. C., "The Modal Personality Structure of the Tuscarora Indians as Revealed by the Rorschach Test," *Bull., B.A.E.*, 150 (1952).

Warner, W. Lloyd. *American Life, Dream and Reality*. Chicago: University of Chicago Press, 1953.

────── *Democracy in Jonesville*. New York: Harper & Bros., 1949.

————, Meeker, Marchia, and Fells, Kenneth. *Social Class in America*. Chicago: Science Research Associates, 1949.

Watson, Robert I. *Psychology of the Child*. New York: John Wiley & Sons, 1959.

Weber, Max. *The Religion of India or The Sociology of Hinduism and Buddhism*. Translated by Hans H. Gerth and Don Martindale. Glencoe: Free Press, 1958.

Whyte, William H., Jr. *The Organization Man*. New York: Simon and Schuster, 1956.

Williams, Robin M. *American Society: A Sociological Interpretation*. New York: Alfred A. Knopf, 1951.

Wolff, Kurt (ed.). *Emil Durkheim (1860–1918)*. Columbus, Ohio: Ohio State University Press, 1961.

Würm, S. A., and Laycock, D. C. "The Question of Language and Dialect in New Guinea," *Oceania*, XXXII, No. 2 (December 1961), 128–143.

Young, Kimball, and Mack, Raymond W. *Sociology and Social Life*. New York: American Book Company, 1959.

Young, Paul T. *Motivation and Emotion*. New York: John Wiley & Sons, 1961.

Yuan, Yeh-Yu. *Chung Kuo Ku Tai Hsing Shih Ti Yien Chiu* or *A Study of the System of Surnames in Ancient China*. Shanghai: Commercial Press, 1936.

INDEX OF AUTHORS

Aberle, D. F., 9, 11
Abt, Lawrence, 310
Arens, Richard, 153, 161
Atkinson, John W., 160, 310

Bailey, F. G., 119
Basham, A. L., 80, 176, 191
Beier, Helen, 229
Bellak, Leopold, 310
Benedict, Ruth, 18, 167
Berreman, Gerald D., 240–242, 261
Bierstedt, Robert, 22
Blunt, E. A. H., 134, 137
Bohannan, Paul J., 8, 11
Bose, Nirma Kumar, 36, 58, 115, 119, 239
Bouglé, C., 14, 128–131, 134, 137
Brightman, E. S., 250
Butler, Samuel, 250

Carstairs, G. Morris, 49–50, 59. 106, 120, 230
Cattell, Raymond B., 153, 161
Caudill, William, 268, 310
Chakladar, Haran Chandra, 55
Chapple, E. D., 147, 159
Chiao, Cheng, 136
Clark, Russell A., 160, 310
Clough, Shepard B., 204, 230
Codere, Helen, 195–196
Cohen, A. K., 9, 11
Cohn, Bernard S., 20–21, 26, 68, 113
Commager, Henry Steele, 231
Comte, Auguste, 250
Coon, Carleton S., 26, 122, 147, 159
Cotu, Walter, 155, 160–161
Cox, Oliver C., 241
Creel, Herlee G., 262

Damle, Y. B., 191
Datta, K., 79

Davis, A. K., 9, 11
Davis, Allison, 240
Davis, Kingsley, 240
Desai, I., 191
De Vos, George, 268, 310
Dewey, John, 250
Dhillon, Harwant Singh, 110, 120
Dollard, John, 240
Doré, Henry, 174
Dube, S. C., 43, 50, 59, 80, 107–109, 118, 120
Dubois, Cora, 21, 264
Dumezil, G., 129, 137
Dumont, Louis, 14, 25, 40, 59, 110–112, 120, 128–134, 136
Durkheim, Emile, 8, 11, 24, 101, 111, 234–235, 237

Edgerton, Robert B., 309
Embree, Ainslie T., 26
Emerson, Ralph Waldo, 3, 10
Erickson, Erik, 197

Fei, H. T., 79
Fells, Kenneth, 230
Firth, Raymond, 140, 158
Foster, George M., 25
Freedman, Maurice, 65–67, 79, 101, 111, 119, 136
Fuchs, Stephen, 43, 58–59, 79, 119, 121

Gamble, S. D., 136
Gandhi, M. K., 239
Gesell, Arnold, 196
Ghurye, G. S., 96, 102, 118–119, 124–136, 188, 257
Giles, Herbert A., 136
Gladwin, Thomas, 270, 310
Glick, Paul C., 229
Goldschmidt, Walter R., 164, 309
Goldstein, Kurt, 233, 261

Gough, E. Kathleen, 44–45, 58, 107, 119–120

Hanfmann, Eugenia, 229
Harrison, Selig S., 257
Hayden, A. Eustace, 250
Henry, William E., 268, 271, 310
Hocart, A. M., 14, 129–134, 137
Homans, George C., 138–159, 169
Honigmann, John, 21
Hsu, Francis L. K., 26, 54–55, 59, 78–79, 135, 158–159, 191, 229–231, 272, 311
Hu, Hsien Chin, 72, 79, 92, 136
Hu Shan, 82
Hutton, J. H., 124, 134, 136–137

Inkeles, Alex, 229

Jeans, Sir James, 250
Johnson, Charles S., 241

Kapadia, K. M., 59, 81–82
Kaplan, Bert, 229, 270, 309–310
Karve, Irawati, 25, 55, 62, 78–82, 119
Keller, A. G., 153, 161
Klineberg, Otto, 153
Kluckhohn, Clyde, 26

Laski, Harold J., 231
Lasswell, Harold, 153, 161
Laycock, D. C., 257
Leach, E. R., 113, 121
Lederer, William J., 216
Levine, Seymour, 160
Levy, M. J., Jr., 9, 11
Lew, Ling, 136
Lewin, Kurt, 197, 229
Lewis, Oscar, 19–20, 22, 26, 82, 106, 109–110, 120
Li, Chi, 136
Lindesmith, Alfred R., 151, 160
Linton, Ralph, 78, 153, 161
Lord, Edith M., 272
Lowell, Edgar L., 160–161, 310
Lowie, R. H., 73, 79, 207, 230
Lynd, Robert S. and Helen M., 210–212, 230

MacIver, Robert M., 24, 26

Mack, Raymond W., 9, 11
Madan, T. N., 69
Majumder, R. C., 79
Malinowski, B., 149
Mandelbaum, David, 78, 96, 118
Marriott, McKim, 16, 26, 39, 43, 58, 68, 80, 106, 115, 118, 133–134, 137, 241, 261
Maslow, A. H., 153, 161, 233, 261
Mayer, Adrian C., 119
McClelland, David C., 153, 160, 268, 310
McConnell, Bishop F. J., 250
Mead, Margaret, 78, 167
Meeker, Marcia, 230
Milgram, Stanley, 216, 231
Miller, Robert J., 108, 114
Mitra, Priti, 115
Morris, Charles, 158, 164, 237–240, 261
Muller, F. Max, 59
Mulligen, G. D., 270, 310
Murdock, George P., 61, 78
Murphy, Gardner, 59, 191
Murphy, Lois B. (Mrs. Gardner), 49, 59, 78, 178, 191, 196, 230
Murray, Henry A., 149, 160, 232, 261, 264–265, 310
Myrdal, Gunnar, 240

Nair, Mrs. Kusum, 121
Naroll, Raoul, 26
Newell, W. H., 79
Nivedita, Sister (Miss M. E. Noble), 53, 59
Northrop, F. S. C., 1, 10

Oberholzer, Emil, 264
Opler, Morris Edward, 19–20, 26, 121, 136

Park, Richard L., 26, 262
Parsons, Talcott, 150–151, 160
Piaget, Jean, 196
Piers, G., 191
Pocock, David F., 14, 25, 119, 128–134, 136
Prabhu, Pandharinath, 58, 78, 81, 118

Radhakrishnan, S., 4, 11, 118, 171, 173–174, 181, 191
Ramakrishna, Swami, 53

Ravchaudhuri, H. C., 79
Redfield, Robert, 16, 23–25, 241
Riesman, David, 209, 216–217, 230–231
Rogers, Carl R., 233, 261
Rousseau, J. J., 204

Sarason, S. B., 270, 310
Schutz, William C., 153, 161
Shah, A. M., 58
Shapiro, H. L., 78
Shastri, Nilakanta, 73, 79, 80
Shroff, R. G., 58
Simmel, Georg, 154
Simpson, George E., 241
Singer, Milton, 16–17, 23–26, 58, 79, 191
Singh, Rudra Datt, 20, 26, 121, 136
Slade, Madeleine, 239
Smith, V. A., 74, 79
Spiro, Melford E., 156, 161
Spitz, R., 196
Srinivas, M. N., 16, 26, 28, 43, 54–55, 58–59, 95–97, 99–100, 102–105, 107, 114, 116–119, 129, 132
Steed, Gitel P., 32, 35, 47–48, 50, 58–59, 80
Stevenson, H. N. C., 119, 129, 131, 137, 191
Steward, Julian, 159
Strauss, Anselm L., 151, 160

Suchman, Edward S., 202, 230
Sumner, William, 153, 161
Sutton, F. X., 9, 11

Tao, Yuan-Ming, 164
Thomas, P., 191
Thomas, William I., 153–154, 161, 233, 261
Thurston, Edgar, 82
Tinker, Irene, 26, 262
Tiruvalluvar, Saint, 32

Varma, Viswanath Prasad, 129

Wallace, A. F. C., 270, 309–310
Warner, W. Lloyd, 142, 209–212, 215, 230, 240
Watrous, Blanche G., 263–280, 309–311
Watson, Robert I., 52, 59, 160
Weber, Max, 1, 10, 254
Whyte, William H., Jr., 216, 220, 231
Williams, Robin M., 231
Würm, S. A., 257

Yinger, J. M., 241
Young, Kimball, 9, 11
Young, Paul T., 160
Yuan, Yeh-Yu, 136

Znaniecki, F., 261

SUBJECT INDEX

Absolutist thinking, 3
Acintya, 4
Action groups in U.S., 221–22
Adolescence, juvenile delinquency during, 203; cultural differences in, 201–202; pressures in America, 201–204
Adoption, 166
Adult world and children's world, separation in different cultures, 230
Agastya, 62
Alores, 21
Altruism in human action, 141
Ambedkar, Dr. (late leader of untouchables), 196
Ambition, limitations in different cultures, 214–15; role in Chinese society, 167; unlimited nature in America, 215, 222
Anāsakti (asakti), 239. See also Nonattachment.
Ancestors, 29, 31, 37–39, 40–41, 42 ff., 54, 55, 69–71, 78, 79, 98–99, 127; attitude of modern Chinese toward, 37, 41, 45, 71, 100; benevolence of Chinese, 45–46; glory of as means of individual status, 100; living up to the status of, 166; manes, 55; precarious relationship of Hindu to, 46; reunion with the dead, 42–43, sharing punishment or honor with, 44, 71–72; spirits, 45, 46; annual worship in India, 43–44; picnic with, 71; reliability of in China, 225; temples to, 65–66, 69, 70–71, 82–92
Ancestor worship, among Chinese in Formosa, 79; centralized government and, 143; Chinese belief in, 41, 143, 159; exceptions in India, 39–40
Anthropological Survey of India, 13
Anukul Thakur, 187
Apollonian Zuni, 167

Arapesh, 167
Aryan, 68, 94
Asākti, 239
Ascetics, 50, 58
Ashramas, 29, 34–35, 48, 55, 58
Ashta gramis, 99
Association, see Club
Atma, see Universal soul
Attachment and life, 178–79
Aum, see Universal soul
Authority, hostility toward among Americans, 146
Avatara, see Reincarnation

Baganda, 21
Ballalasena, Bengal king, 58
Begging, in India, 182
Behavior, multiple standards of Chinese, 2
Bhadralsali, 44
Bhagavad Gita, see Hindu scriptures
Bhagavadi, 44
Bhaktism, 186
Bible, 15
Bimbisara, 35
Biological needs, 149–150
Brahmacharya, 34, 48
Brahman-Pandit, 68
Buddha, 35, 188
Buddhism, 67, 125, 243; as a protestant movement in Hinduism, 184, 186–88
Burial grounds, as public shrines, 41–42; Hindu fear of pollution by, 41

Capitalism, 142
Caste, ancient principle, 94; as expression of conflict, 188; characteristics, 94–98, 179, 227, 235; cohesive grouping in India, 93, contradictory attributes, 170–71; cooperation between higher and lower, 130; dietary rules,

131–32; differences between India and the U.S., 240 ff.; discrimination of higher toward lower but not vice-versa, 130; divisive process of, 189; economic privileges and, 113–116; endogamy, 99; factions within, 106–107, 110; fear of encroachment and loss of, 127, 133; fear of pollution of higher by lower, 38; fissionary tendencies of, 98, 104–105, 107, 114, 124 ff., 184; Desba vs. Nadu, 104; hierarchy, 111, 115, 128–29; importance to Hindu, 6; imitation of higher by lower, 130–31; ideal, importance of, 242; interactional theory, 133–135; Japanese and, 132–33; kinship ties and, 103; leadership, lack of in, 110–111; modern conditions and, 190; number in India, 124, occupations and, 102–103, 121, 189–90; one-colorness vs. others, 104; opposition between, 130; as shield for personal inferiority, 242–43; proliferation due to desire to raise status, 184–185; pure and impure in, 129, 132–33; caste-raising efforts, 97, 106, 114–15, 124; caste-rank, giving and receiving food as symbols of, 133–34, 189; caste-ranking, impossibility of, 96–98, 118; repulsion in, 128–30; revolt against higher, 113; right-hand vs. left-hand divisions in, 104; rules, 241; rules affecting relationship between, 130; sharp contrasts, 185; solidarity, 102–108; specialization in hereditary occupations, 128–29; superiority of higher over lower, 170–71; territorial groupings and, 108

Caste council (*panchayat*), function of according to Srinivas, 105; nature of according to Dube, 107–108; no distinction between village council and, 101–102, 109, 119

Castes: Ashrafin, 96; Balahi, 38–39, 43, 62, 68, 98; Banya (or Baniya), 39, 98; Beda, 97; Bhadralak, 96; Brahman: 4, 16, 19, 38–39, 47, 49, 63, 68–69, 94–99, 101, 107, 110, 115, 129, 131–35, 171, 181–82, 185, 190, 254; Agradani

Brahman, 95; Barendra Brahman, 95; Bhonga Brahman, 95; Chkatri Brahman, 95; Kulin Brahman, 95; Nambudiri Brahman, 108; Rarhi Brahman, 95; Saraswat Brahman, 95; Shrotrya Brahman, 95; symbiosis with Kshatriya, 129–130; Tiwari Brahman, 95; Upadhaya Brahman, 95; Valmiki Brahman, 97; Chamar, 21; Chandala, 94; Coorgs, 33, 39, 40–43, 45, 68, 97, 102–103; Amma Coorgs, 97; Devadasi, 19; Gaddi, 68; Gujarati, 14; Jain, 58, 125; Jats, 19, 109; Kallar, 40; Ambalakkarar Kallar, 111; Pramalai Kallar, 40, 110, 113, 252; Kayastha, 38, 63, 97, 99, 115, 132; Koli, 39; Kshatriya: 14, 26, 39, 47, 68, 94–95, 97, 127, 131–132, 135, 183, 190; Marwari, 40, 41; Mehtar, 98; Namasudra, 97; Mayar, 39, 40, 42–45, 108; Nonia, 121; Panchama, 94; Pandhar-Pese, 96; Parayer or Pariah, 101; Patidar, 39, 132; Pedaekar, 96; Potters, 104; Rajput, 28, 39, 62, 68–69, 98–101, 131; Reddy, 95, 97; Sashlikar, 96; Shenvi, 96; Sikhs, 188; Sudra, 16, 94, 97, 101, 130; Thakur, 21, 121; Untouchables, 14, 16, 39, 97–98, 110, 129, 189; Vahivanca, 38–39, 68; Vaidya, 38, 115; Vaishnavat, 39; Vaishya, 94–95, 97, 131; Yogi, 97

Cathexes, 170; *see also* Individual cathexes

Catholics and Protestants, differences in America, 228–29

Center for the Study of Leisure, study on college graduates' aspirations by, 209

Chandragupta (Maurya), 35, 73

Change, Chinese lack of internal impetus to, 2; external impetus to in America, 221–22; fear of in America, 221; forces for in Hindu society, 189; Hindu dynamism without real, 5; in human society, 180; internal impetus for in America, 221; internal impetus for in India, 226

Charisma in different cultures, 254

Chatterjee, Prof. Suniti Kumar, 174

Chiang Kai-shek, Generalissimo, 71, 253–54, 258

Child-rearing, differences in practices of, in three cultures, 78; Hindu patterns of, and riot, 230; human relations and, in China, 181; love and, 160; status and, in India, 181

Children, glorification of in U.S., 195

Chinese, in South Seas, 159; in U.S., 159

Chinese family, its lasting protection of the individual, 165

Choudhury, Nirendra C., 74

Christianity, 15, 20, 173, 186, 188, 248, 249, 250, 259

Chu, 64

Chu Ke Liang, 170

Churches, fading of the concept of supernatural in American, 228–229

Clan (clans), alliances of for survival in China, 100; characteristics of Chinese, 72, 227; Chinese, contrasted to Hindu caste, 125–27; criteria for, 60–61; elders, lack of in Hindu, 69, 101; endogamous circles of, 99–100, 130–31; enlargement efforts in China, 168; and family in China, 127; feuds between Chinese, 125–26; fissiparous tendency, lack of in Chinese, 125 ff.; geographical variations in, 71; government and its relation to, 73–78; importance of Chinese, over subdivisions, 65; importance to Chinese, 6–7; intermarriage, 99; joint responsibility and glory of, 71–72; loyalty to, 169; meaning of term, in India, 67–68; names of Chinese, in China and overseas, 123–126; negative aspects of, in India, 69; organization, lack of, in India, 68; resolution of tension in, 82–92; security of Chinese, 169; similarity of Hindu clan to caste, 116; social class and, 70–71; tension in Chinese, 66–67, 69–70; unimportance of, in Hindu society, 69–72, 77–78; *see also Gotra;* Lineage; *Tsu*

Club (clubs), American youth and, 209–10; as solution to problem of lack of close human relationships, 207; class and, 211–13; cliques in, 215; defined, 6, 207–208, 227–28; extent of in America, 210–11; activities in, 211–12; importance of, in America, 6, 204, 208–209, 236; voluntary and involuntary, distinguished, 207

Communism, 142; as political administration and expression of ideology differentiated, 259–260; in China, 239, 260

Comparative method, importance of, 14, 24–25

Compartmentalized thinking, 2

Competition, conformity and, 168, 218–19; extent of, in different cultures, 215; in Chinese society, 167–68

Concepts, as tools for building theories, 152; importance of, 151; improper use of, 151–52

Concubinage, prohibition of, 58

Conflict, among self-reliant men, 245–46; between kinship loyalty and formation of state, 252–53

Conformity, absence of resentment against, among Chinese, 170, 220; by fair means, 219–20; conflict in American society due to, 3; factors making for, in America, 216 ff.; in Chinese society, 167–68; intensified by unfair means, 219; lack of inner conflict among Chinese due to, 2; prejudice and, 218; protest against in America, 217–18; rebellion against, and individual cathexes in America, 222–23; resentment against in America, 220; resentment against ritual and caste, in India, 183 ff.; self-reliance and its direct link with, 217

Confucius, precepts of, 15, 29, 67, 164, 174, 248

Conspicuous consumption, 148

Content, 47–48, 67, 233; concept of, in social organization, 27; of the American family, 194–95

Contract principle, attributes of, 207–209

Contractual solidarity, 237

Contradictions: between the extreme abstract and the extreme concrete in Hindu society, 185; caste system as expression of, in Hindu society, 190; in individual-centered orientation,

207; in supernatural-centered orientation, 189

Creativity, importance in America, 221

Cultivation of the self in China, 240

Cultural ideal, as sanction and inspiration for behavior, 165–68; relationship with values, 164

Cultural orientation, question of two centuries of, in Hindu India, 68

Cultural shock, 17

Culture, attitude toward small town and, 145–46; culture core, 1–2; effects upon leadership of, 143–44; ideology as part of, 142; importance in human group, 141 ff., 232–33; neglect by Homans, 141 ff., superior and inferior relationship affected by, 143; supernatural as part of, 142

Darshan, 254–55

Dasa, 94

Data, sources of, in this book, 12–13, 25; sources of, in TAT, 263–64

Dead, Chinese and Hindu attitudes toward, 36 ff.; differential relationships with the, 45–47; Indian fear of pollution by, 38; rejection of the, 42–43; shrines and graveyards as attitudes toward the, 39–41

Declaration of Independence, 49

Dependence, mutual, 1–2, 3, 7, 9; rejection of, 7, 195, 196, 200–202; unilateral, 4, 7, 9, 52–53

devar, 252

dhar, 109

dharma, 4, 5, 179, 182, 215

Diffuseness of Indian world, 176, 239

Divisiveness and dynamism, 252

diwali, 43

Durkheim, 8, 101, 111

Dynamism of society, American society and, 245–46; contrast of in America, China, and India, 224–46; role of culture and, 157–58; sources of, 154

Dynasties, comparative duration in China and India, 73–77; dependence on vigorous rulers in India, 75–76; misunderstandings concerning Chinese, 77–78; foreign invaders and Chinese, 76

Early experiences, importance of, 155; of the American child, 194 ff.; of the Chinese child, 168; of the Hindu child, 48–49, 178–79

Ecological factor and man, 147–48

Educational system in U.S., 197

Eisenhower administration, 219

Endogamy, 95, 130, 193; clans or gotras forming circle of, 99–101; subcaste, 99, 102, 104; *see also* Caste

Environment, elements of according to Homans, 139 ff.; imperfect adjustment of man to his physical, 148, importance of human, 148–49

Epics, Indian, 14, 15, 38, 55, 175

Equality, compared to Hindu nonattachment, 207; problems of relating with fellow human beings due to, 207

Ethics, core of Chinese, 2; *see also* Conformity; Equality; Freedom; Nonattachment

Ethnocentrism, anthropological variety of, 23

Exogamy, clan, 61–62, 68, 72; village, 99, 109

External system of a group, according to Homans, 139

Family, 55, 60, 168–69; and clan, loyalty to, 169; centrifugal tendencies in, 60, 72–73, 123; centripetal tendencies in, 60, 72–73, 123; characteristics of American, 193 ff.; comparison of American, Chinese, and Hindu, 234–35; content of Chinese, 47; differences between Chinese and Hindu, 29–46; differences in role in three societies, 6; in different societies, 60, 78; problems of the individual in Hindu, 170–71; relationships according to Manu, 29–31, 55–58; renunciation of, 34–36; separation of generations in American, 196; similarities between Chinese and Hindu, 28–29; *see also* Marriage; Parent-child relationship; Primary group

Family counsellor, role in America, 193

Family names, number of Chinese, 123

Fang, 63–66

Father-daughter relationship, 28

Father-son relationship, 48–49, 162; attributes of, 50–53, 56–57, 60–61, 165

Fear of failure, in America, 229; in China, 168

Fear of inferiority, in America, factors fostering it, 214–15, 218; in China and India, 217

Filial piety, 2, 29–30

Food, giving and receiving as symbols of caste rank, 133–34

Freedom, absence of the concept in China, 206; as ideal life of American, 204; joint declaration of Roosevelt and Churchill on, 205–206

Freud, Sigmund, 200

Friendship, 141

Funerals, 37–38

Gadi, 104

Gandhi, Mahatma, 50, 176, 188, 239, 254

Garuda Purana, 42–43

Genealogy, as caste-raising technique in India, 68–69, 98–99; contrast between Chinese and Hindu attitudes toward, 38–39, 100; records, 78, 100; tracing bureau, 168; variations in records of, 71

Generations, separation between the, 200–201

Genesis, 53

German and American personalities contrasted, 197

God, American definitions of, 249–50; Hindu conception of, 171; Western conception of, 174–75

Gods, clean and unclean, 117–18; differences in representations between Chinese and Hindu, 248; Hindu relationship with, 5, 7, 44, 47, 185–86; man's relationship with in China and India, 247; officials treated as, 254–55; reliability of Hindu, 226–27; techniques for dealing with, 54

Gotra (gotram): 6, 61 ff.; and marriage, 62–63, 99; castelike nature of, 124; different appelations of, 62, 80–82; uncertainty of meaning, 67–69, 72

Government, authoritarian vs. despotic or autocratic, 77; centralization in China, 75–77; difference between state and society, 77; lack of centralization in India, 73–75

Graham, Billy, 34

Grandparents, role of, 198–99

Great Tradition, 16, 18, 23–24, 241–42

Grihapati, 31

Grihastha, 31, 34, 48

Guda, 107–108

Guha, Mrs. Uma, 265

Guilt and repression, 177–78

Guru, see Teacher

Hermits, 50; Chinese style, 170

Hierarchic solidarity, 235

Hierarchy, as basic principle of Hindu social organization, 180; Hindu vs. American, 111–112; in other societies, 182; its link with unilateral dependence, 181; symbols of differentiation of, 190–91

Himalaya, 50

Hindu religious practices, 173

Hindu scriptures, 13–15, 29–30; Bhagavad Gita 175 ff.; Upanishads, 13, 171

Hinduism, Protestant movements in, 125, 186

Historical background of China and India, 73–78

History, use in social analysis, 14–15

Holy man, 5, 42, 188; see also Priest; Sadhu

Household, ancestral, 43; taravad, 43–44

Human groups, cohesiveness and divisiveness in relation to, 73, 124–25; culture and, 141 ff.; development of, 5; family as basic to, 5–6; growth of society dependent on increase of, 5; implications of three different, 246–47; importance in human existence, 232; individual and, according to Homans, 138; internal solidarity and hatred of outsiders in, 145–46; normal dynamism of, 125, 127; Puritan reaction to, 147; self-interest and, 141; tendency to return to place of origin and, 145–46; theory of, 138 ff.

Humanist religion, 142

Human nature, 158

Human relations: reciprocity in, 54; importance in Chinese society, 164–

65; in China and India contrasted, 247; *see also* Permanent human relationships

Husband-wife relationship, in American family, 193-95, 245; in Chinese marriage, 28; in Hindu marriage, 31; reference to in Laws of Manu, 58, tension in, 66

Hu Shih, Dr., 69

Hypergamy, 78, 99–101, 130–31

Identity, 160–61

Ideology, as part of culture, 142

Immutability, and dominance of husband-wife relationship, 196; of all men and self-reliance, 196; of self from others, 206; problem of complete, 180

Impediment and effusion, 177–78

Imperial examination, Chinese, 93, 100

Individual cathexes, 222; and big business, 223; and castes, 223; and clubs, 222–23; as sanctioned by ideal of Atma, 185; leading to religious movements in India, 186; resulting from American resentment against conformity, 220, 222

Individual-centered orientation, characteristics of, 1–3, 226–227

Indra, 58

Inheritance, in Bengal, 55; in India and China, 28; in Malabar Coast, 55; in U.S., 193; matrilineal, 55; recent legislation affecting, 55

Inner world vs. outer world, 243 ff.

Internal system of a group, according to Homans, 139

Inwardness and outward action, in Hindu thought, 238–39

Jainism, 184, 186, 243, 254

Jajmani, 179

Japanese, and intermarriage, 145; Benedict on, 18; caste among, 132–133; suppression, 177

Jati, 95, 129; *see also* Caste; Subcaste

Jesus, 173–74

Jhan, Sri Benodananda, 187

Judaism, 186, 249

Juvenile delinquency, cultural forces for, 203–4

Karanavan, 43, 45

Karma, 238

Kaska Indians, 21–22

Kathaks, 15

Kennedy administration, 219, 250

Kinship, attributes of, 164; basis of, 2; Hindu and Western compared, 175; lack of affiliation with in U.S., 204; solidarity in Chinese culture, 168–69, 234; in India, 181

Kulapanjika, 38

Lao Tze, 173–74

Latin America, 27–28

Leadership, as affected by culture, 143–44, 252 ff.

Li, 90

Lien-tsung, 62

Lineage, 44; and clan, 61

Lingayat, a protestant sect in Hinduism, 186, 188, 243

Linguistic diversity, in China and India, 256–58; as result, not cause of psychological centrifugality, 257–58

Little Tradition, 16, 18, 23–34, 241–42

Louis XVI, 15

Magna Carta, 15

Mahabharata, 14, 15, 38, 55, 175

Mahalaya, 43

Maharashtrian (Maharshtran), 28, 99

Manes, 55; *see also* Ancestors

Mantra, 33

Manu, Laws of, criteria for, 55–56; family relationships according to, 29–33, 56 ff.; female's relationship with relatives, 29–30, 57 ff.; male's relationship with relatives, 29–30, 57 ff.; teacher-pupil relationships according to, 29–30, 57 ff.

Marriage, ceremony in China and India, 31, 36, 186; Chinese clan position no bar to, 100; concubinage and, 32, 50; contrast between Romantic Love and arranged, 196; Hindu clan restrictions on, 99–100; of Gods, 185–86; preferential, 28, 193; in the United

States, 193; widowhood, 32–33, 46; widow remarriage, 55, 132
Māyā, 4, 182
Meiji Restoration, 15
Methodology, critique of assorted techniques, 19–25; explanation of, 13–19, 27, 263–265
Migrations, 123
Militarism, 142
Missionary zeal, lack of in China, 259–60
Monks, see Priests
Monotheism, 143, 185, 249–50
Morality, absolutist, 3; multiple standards of, 4
Moslem, 95
Mother-son relationship, 28–29, 48–49; attributes of, 50–54, 56, 60–61, 244–46
Mutability, and mother-dependence, 196; and the Hindu, 175; problem of the individual due to, 175 ff.; vs. immutability, 52–53
Mutual dependence, 12, 48, 51, 54, 127, 162 ff., 175

Nad, 108–109
Nag, Dr. Moni, 265
Narasimha, 58
National independence impact of and Western culture, in India, 243
Need, dynamic and nondynamic meaning of, 160; felt, imputed, disputed, 160; need orientations, 151
Nehru, Prime Minister Jawaharlal, 254
Nepotism, foundation of in Chinese society, 167–168
New experience, a culture-bound concept of need, 153–54
Nirguna, 4
Nonattachment, and concept of equality compared, 207; as a solution to the Hindu problem of lack of closeness among men, 175; impracticality of in life, 176–79; relation to joy and action, 239
Nonkinship groups in China, 234
Norms, 142; and religion, 142, 144–45

Okka, 41
Okkaliga, 104; see also Caste Council

Old age, care of, 35–37, 46–47
Opium-smoking, 50
Organization man, 216–17
Oriental vs. occidental, 1
Origin of the universe, lack of interest among the Chinese in, 174
Other-directed man, see Conformity

Paglababa, a holy man, 187
Panchayat, see Caste council
Pandit, 19; see also Teacher
Pantheism, 143, 239, 247–48
Parental barrier to independence in America, 201–202
Parental influence in U.S., China, and India compared, 198–200
Parent-child relationship, 2–3, 29–30, 56, 230; contrasted in three cultures, 198 ff.
Parochialization, 16
Passivity and mass violence, link between, 178
Paths of life, according to Charles Morris, 237 ff.
Peer group, cultural difference in the importance of, 202–203
Permanent human relationships, in China, 168–69; lack of in America, 206–207, 227; uncertainty of in India, 173–77
Persecution, and insecurity, 218; of scientists by religionists, 142; see also Prejudice
Personality, American and German contrasted, 197; American and Russian contrasted, 229
Petramasa, 43
Phulmel, 99
Pilgrimage, 47, 49, 50
Pirs, 42; see also Holy man
Plotinus, 173
Political development, in India and China contrasted, 73–77
Political stability, in China and U.S., 258
Political system, U.S. and Latin America contrasted, 27–28
Political unity in different cultures, 252–54

Politics and leadership, China and West contrasted, 252–53; China and India contrasted, 252–56; India and United States contrasted, 256–57; proliferation of political candidates in America and India, 257–58
Politics and religion, in India, 254–55; in China, 253–54
Polygyny: 28; serial, in U.S., 194
Polytheism, 143, 247, 249
Potlatch, 148
Pravara, 44, 81
Prejudice, kinds, 218–19; related to conformity, 219–20
Priests, 5, 34, 36, 47, 170, 174
Primary group, 3, 5–6, 7, 8, 10, 34, 47; movement of the individual from into secondary groups, 156–58
Privacy, effect on interpersonal relations in America, 200–201
Protestantism, 249–51
Pseudo-kinship, 167
Psychologists, different from anthropologists and sociologists, 140
Puritan ethics, 159

Ramakrishna, 53, 188, 248; Mission, 186
Ramayana, 38
Reform movements, absence of in China, 220–21; in American life, 222–24; in India, 220–21, 245, 249–51
Reincarnation, 4, 174
Religion, according to Homans, 142; attitude toward, in India and U.S., 248–49; coexistence of Hindu beliefs in, 5; contrast between American, Chinese, and Hindu, 250–51; contrasts in Hindu attitudes toward, 185; cosmology as part of, 142; devotee, in China and India, contrasted, 186–87; theory vs. practice in, 186; humanism in, 142; proliferation of idols in Indian, reasons for, 251; protestant movements in Indian, 186; psychological conflict in, 249; schism, absence of in Chinese culture, 67; schism in American and Indian cultures, 249–51; science rivalry in Western society but absence in

Eastern societies, 252; sects become castes in Indian, 187
Renunciation of family, 34–36
Repression, suppression, and effusion, 176–78
Retarded growth of infants, due to lack of human care, 160; evidence from experimental psychology, 160
Revolution, American, 16; fed by inner conflicts, 3; French, 15; Industrial, 15
Reward and obligation, as gift-making, 166; in Chinese society, 54, 165–67, 182; in Hindu world, 7, 54, 173, 182; ratios in different social systems, 167; scrupulous equivalence in America, 213–14
Rishis, 62; *see also* Teacher
Ritual, and caste, 189; cleanliness, 38, 49; in Hindu weddings, 186; purity of the Brahman, 129 ff.
Rockefeller Foundation, 25
Role, 8, 160–61
Romantic love, and immutability, 196–97; as element of kinship content, 194; not basic to marriage in China and India, 28
Rorschach, 21–22, 272
Russian personality, contrasted to American, 229

Sacred thread, 121, 131–132
Sadhu: 19, 187–188, 248, 254
Sadhuhood, reasons for choosing, 188
Sages, 19
Saints, 29, 31, 32
Samnyasa, 34–37, 48, 50, 188
Samoa, 60, 78
Sanskritization, 16, 39, 97
Sati, 41, 58
Saudi Arabia, 27
Science and religion, 142–143
Scientific method, 151; relation of details to whole, 18–19, 22–24
Scientific theory and incompatible facts, 20–21
Scientism, pitfalls in, 19–23
Secondary groupings, 5, 8
Security, concept of, 152–153; in Chinese system, 2, 50–51, 72, 168

Segregation of male and female in Hindu household, 48–49

Self and non-self, 196–97, 243–246; see also Mutability vs. immutability

Self-interest and human group, 141, 157–58

Self-realization, a culture-bound concept, 153–54

Self-reliance, and God, 54; and immutability, 196; defined, 195; evidence for among college students in U.S., 195–96; individual-centered world characterized by, 2–3, 7; influence on interpersonal relations, 206–207; teaching of weakens bonds between American parents and children, 201

Sentiments: according to Homans, 140–141; as expressions of three social needs, 153–156

Sexual act as an inferred behavior, 159

Shame and suppression, 177–78

Shastras, 13, 174

Shivananda, Swami, 187

Situational determinism, 164–65

Situation-centered orientation, characteristics of, 1–2, 48, 224–25; conduct and, 165, 240; mutual dependence and, 162

Siva, 185, 248

Siyaka II, King who became an ascetic, 58

Small town, differential tendencies to flee from, 144–46

Sociability, concept of, 152–53

Social distance in the U.S. and Germany, 197

Social grouping, centrifugal and centripetal tendencies of, 7–8; principles of, 8

Socialization, 9, 47–54, 193–200

Social mobility, vertical and horizontal, 216

Social needs, 7, 10, 149–50; attachment and, 178–79; culture-bound, 153; defined, 149; fear of not receiving, 166–67; Hindu problems involved in satisfying, 170, 180; Homans' sentiments and, 140, 150; importance among human beings, 154–55, 232; mechanisms

for achieving, 160–61; Parsons' orientation of the actor and, 150; promotion of particular kind in some cultures, 153, 160–61; sociability, security, and status defined, 153

Social organization, comparison of Chinese and Hindu, 47–48, 77; comparison of Chinese, Hindu, and American, 233 ff.; structure and content of, differentiated, 27–28; see also Family

Social problems, pressure of on Indian students, 239

Society, dominant ideas of, 9–10; dynamics of American, 213; functional prerequisites of, 1, 9; growth or stagnation of, 5; pressures of, on the American adolescent, 202–203

Soldiery in China, 170

Solidarity, of village and caste, according to Srinivas, 102–104; as psychic or behavioral cohesion, 8, 111–13; as relationship, 8, 101; Bohannan's definitions of, 8; horizontal vs. vertical, 101; indication of lack of, in India, 104–109, 114–115

Sororities and fraternities, multiplicity of, 208; variation of their exclusive nature in different areas, 208–209

Spanish settlers, role in Mexican independence, 159

Sradh (srada, sraddha), 47, 55, 95

Stages of life, 29, 34–35, 48, 55, 58

Standards of conduct, multiple, 2, 165

Status, concept of, 152–153; differences between Chinese and Hindu attitudes toward, 4, 180, 182–83; raising of, 21, 28–29, 97 ff., 115, 190; ritual and secular, 131, 132; symbols of, 133, 214–15

Structurist, 67

Struggles among Americans, bases for, 228

Subcaste, 96, 98–99, 101–102, 124; basis for distinction of, 102; factions in, 104 ff.; solidarity, 102–104, 112; see also Jati

Success, American definition of, 210; measures of in China and America, 214–15, 227; success-seeking, 211

Success or failure, lack of concrete means of measuring, according to Hindu ideal, 234–35.

Superior and inferior, in caste system, 170–71; interaction between, 146; lack of resentment toward superior among the Chinese, 126, 146–47; relationship affected by culture, 143

Supernatural, and Hindu ideal, 173; as part of culture, 142; gradual disappearance of the concept in American churches, 228–29; reliance of Hindu on, 5; transformations in Western conceptions of, 249–50

Supernatural-centered orientation, characteristics of, 3–5, 48, 53–54, 225–26; contradictions in, 189

Suppression, 176–78

Tao, 173

Taoism, 36, 67, 173; popular, 173–74

Tao Te Ching, 173–75

Taravad, 43–44

Tata of Gujara Dynasty, 35

Teacher (guru, pandit, upadhyaya), 19, 29, 33–34, 44, 46, 48, 225; teacher-pupil relationship according to Manu, 57

Tevar, 110

Thakur, Anukul, a holy man, 187

Thematic Apperception Test, Abandonment and Loss of Way responses to, among Indians, 292–96, related to Death responses, 296–97; Achievement Imagery in, 272–73, and Reverie, differences among four Indian groups in responses, 305; Action in, 279; anthropomorphization of nonhuman beings and things in, 270, 276; as method in group studies, 309–10; attitude about self in, 279; blind analysis, limitations of, 269–70; categories in classifying responses, 266–68; content differences among different cultures, 305–307; cultural differences in responses of Taiwan and Hong Kong, 286–88; Death, and love, 284–85; Death related to casual and nonhuman reasons among Indians, 297–303; Death related to unknown causes among Indians, 297; themes, 283–90; Death, differences between Taiwan and Hong Kong, 283; Death, differences between Chinese and Americans, 283–84; Death unrelated to love among Americans, 288–90; differences between Americans and both Chinese groups, 281–82; differences between Hong Kong and Taiwan responses; Dysphoria, among Indian, 276, 304; Dysphoria, among Taiwan students, 273–74, Dysphoria, relation to death due to hostility from or uncertainty in external environment, 304; Enjoyment, alone and impersonally among Indians, 303; Enjoyment among Indians contrasted with other two groups, 290–92; Enjoyment by self or with others among Chinese and Americans, 282–90; Enjoyment with others among Americans, 303; Fantasy, contents of, 266 ff., Fantasy, involvement with, among Hindus, 278; Fear responses among Indians, 291–93; feeling tone, importance of in interpretation of group results, 310; Frustrations of school and college graduates in Taiwan, 281; impersonal nature of Indian responses, 290–91; interpersonal involvement, 272, 276; interpersonal relationships in different cultures as revealed by, 266–67; interpretation difficulties due to lack of existing cross-cultural norms, 279–80; Mutability in, 280; Peer acceptance, 275; Peer competition, 272; Personal independence, 279; place of the individual vis-à-vis the external environment, 304; positive injunction vs. negative impediment, 307–308; Religious associations, 275; Resistance to authority, 272–73, Resistance, differences among four Indian groups in responses, 305, 308–309; Reverie, 281; Romantic Love, views of in three cultures, 302–303; sensitivity to physical environment as shown by, 268–70; shorter version of, reasons for use, 264–65, 309–310; similarities

between Hong Kong and Taiwan responses, 281–82; Spontaneity, 278; tentative approach to environment by descriptive adjectives, 276; Thinking and contemplation, 274, 275–76
Theory, relation to facts, 67
Time lag, in cultural transformation, 21
"TINSIT," "tendencies-in-situation" according to Cotu, 155
Tirukural, 32
Traditionalization, 21
Tsing Ming, 71
Tsu, 61 ff.; characteristics of, 72; cleavage in, 65–67; tension in, 66, 69–71, 82–92; unitary tendencies of, 66; variation of strength, 71, 79–80
Tsung, 62
Tze, 63

Ultimate reality, see Universal Soul
Unilateral dependence, defined, 4, 52, 54, 175; begging as expression of, 182; relationship of caste to, 179
Universalism, 3
Universalization, 16
Universal self, see Universal Soul
Universal soul, 4, 170–71, 173, 174–75, 181–82, 184, 192, 215, 224–25, 234, 244–45, 251–52; apex of all statuses, 180–81; as ideal goal of Hindus, 44, 179–81, 183, 187, 249; its role in justifying everything, 184–85
Untouchable Uplifting Movement, 106
Upadhyaya, see Teacher
Upanishads, 13, 171

Values, 142, 164, 237–40; conceived, 142, 237; object, 142; operative, 142

Vanaprastha, 34, 48
Variation, among human beings, 9
Varna, as distinct from jati, 96 ff.; defined, 94–95; interdependence with jati, 129; see also Caste
Vedanta movement, 53, 186, 248; see also Ramakrishna Mission
Vedas, 13, 15, 29–30, 55, 174
Vegetarianism, 131–32, 190
Vigrahapala, king turned ascetic, 58
Village unity, according to Gough, 107, due to emergencies, 116–18, 169
Vivekenanda, Swami, 187

Watrous, Dr. Blanche, 14, 263
Ways of life, evidence from test situation, 240; hypothesis on the basic nature of Hindu, Chinese, and American, 1–5; origin not an anthropologist's problem, 246
Wenner-Gren Foundation for Anthropological Research, 25
Western impact, attitudes toward traditional religion in China and India under, 248; differential results in China and India, 248
Widowhood, in India and China, 28, 32–33, 55; position in old age, 34; prohibition against widow remarriage as tool for caste rank, 97
Will, freedom to make or rules governing, 193
"With one colorness," 104
Worship of the young, 194–95
Wu fu, relationship, 63–64, 66

Yoruba, 21